"*The Spiritual in the Secular* offers a series of compelling studies documenting the scholarly work that missionaries did. . . . Reopens a closed chapter in the history of science."

— Derek Peterson
University of Michigan

"This book deals with contributions to social policy, social amelioration, and the advancement of knowledge, made in the course of mission by an extraordinary gallery of different kinds of people, Africans very much included. . . . The lingering ghosts of misapprehension are served notice by a band of sober scholars, and we see emerging the lineaments of complicated truths."

— David Martin
London School of Economics

"At a time when the historical and contemporary boundaries between the sacred and the secular in the social sciences are under intense examination, *The Spiritual in the Secular* will resonate well beyond the particular historical situations its contributors so compellingly illuminate."

— Joel Robbins
University of California, San Diego

STUDIES IN THE HISTORY
OF CHRISTIAN MISSIONS

R. E. Frykenberg
Brian Stanley
General Editors

STUDIES IN THE HISTORY OF CHRISTIAN MISSIONS

Alvyn Austin
China's Millions: The China Inland Mission and Late Qing Society, 1832-1905

Chad M. Bauman
Christian Identity and Dalit Religion in Hindu India, 1868-1947

Michael Bergunder
The South Indian Pentecostal Movement in the Twentieth Century

Judith M. Brown and Robert Eric Frykenberg, *Editors*
Christians, Cultural Interactions, and India's Religious Traditions

Robert Eric Frykenberg
*Christians and Missionaries in India:
Cross-Cultural Communication Since 1500*

Susan Billington Harper
*In the Shadow of the Mahatma: Bishop V. S. Azariah
and the Travails of Christianity in British India*

Patrick Harries and David Maxwell, *Editors*
The Spiritual in the Secular: Missionaries and Knowledge about Africa

D. Dennis Hudson
Protestant Origins in India: Tamil Evangelical Christians, 1706-1835

Ogbu U. Kalu, *Editor,* and Alaine M. Low, *Associate Editor*
*Interpreting Contemporary Christianity:
Global Processes and Local Identities*

Donald M. Lewis, *Editor*
*Christianity Reborn: The Global Expansion of Evangelicalism
in the Twentieth Century*

Jessie G. Lutz
Opening China: Karl F. A. Gützlaff and Sino-Western Relations, 1827-1852

Jon Miller
*Missionary Zeal and Institutional Control: Organizational Contradictions
in the Basel Mission on the Gold Coast, 1828-1917*

Andrew Porter, *Editor*
The Imperial Horizons of British Protestant Missions, 1880-1914

Dana L. Robert, *Editor*
Converting Colonialism: Visions and Realities in Mission History, 1709-1914

Wilbert R. Shenk, *Editor*
North American Foreign Missions, 1810-1914: Theology, Theory, and Policy

Brian Stanley
The World Missionary Conference: Edinburgh 1910

Brian Stanley, *Editor*
Christian Missions and the Enlightenment

Brian Stanley, *Editor*
Missions, Nationalism, and the End of Empire

John Stuart
*British Missionaries and the End of Empire:
East, Central, and Southern Africa, 1939-64*

T. Jack Thompson
*Light on Darkness? Missionary Photography of Africa
in the Nineteenth and Early Twentieth Centuries*

Kevin Ward and Brian Stanley, *Editors*
The Church Mission Society and World Christianity, 1799-1999

Richard Fox Young, *Editor*
*India and the Indianness of Christianity: Essays on Understanding—Historical,
Theological, and Bibliographical—in Honor of Robert Eric Frykenberg*

The Spiritual in the Secular

Missionaries and Knowledge about Africa

Edited by

Patrick Harries & David Maxwell

WILLIAM B. EERDMANS PUBLISHING COMPANY
GRAND RAPIDS, MICHIGAN / CAMBRIDGE, U.K.

© 2012 Wm. B. Eerdmans Publishing Co.
All rights reserved

Published 2012 by
Wm. B. Eerdmans Publishing Co.
2140 Oak Industrial Drive N.E., Grand Rapids, Michigan 49505 /
P.O. Box 163, Cambridge CB3 9PU U.K.

Library of Congress Cataloging-in-Publication Data

The spiritual in the secular: missionaries and knowledge about Africa /
edited by Patrick Harries & David Maxwell.
    p.   cm. — (Studies in the history of Christian missions)
Includes bibliographical references and index.
ISBN 978-0-8028-6634-9 (pbk.: alk. paper)
1. Missions — Africa.   I. Harries, Patrick.   II. Maxwell, David, 1963-

BV3500.S64   2012
266.0096 — dc23

2012004738

www.eerdmans.com

Contents

CONTRIBUTORS	xi
ACKNOWLEDGMENTS	xiv
ABBREVIATIONS	xv

Introduction: The Spiritual in the Secular 1
Patrick Harries and David Maxwell

1. Natural Science and *Naturvölker*:
   Missionary Entomology and Botany 30
   Patrick Harries

2. Missionary Linguistics on the Gold Coast:
   Wrestling with Language 72
   Erika Eichholzer

3. Of Fetishism and Totemism: Missionary Ethnology and
   Academic Social Science in Early-Twentieth-Century Gabon 100
   John Cinnamon

4. Missionary Ethnographers and the History of Anthropology:
   The Case of G. T. Basden 135
   Dmitri van den Bersselaar

CONTENTS

5. From Iconoclasm to Preservation: W. F. P. Burton,
   Missionary Ethnography, and Belgian Colonial Science ... 155
   David Maxwell

6. Dora Earthy's Mozambique Research and the Early Years
   of Professional Anthropology in South Africa ... 187
   Deborah Gaitskell

7. Ideology in Missionary Scholarly Knowledge in Belgian Congo:
   Aequatoria, Centre de recherches africanistes; The Mission
   Station of Bamanya (RDC), 1937-2007 ... 221
   Honoré Vinck

8. Christian Medical Discourse and Praxis on the Imperial
   Frontier: Explaining the Popularity of Missionary Medicine
   in Mwinilunga District, Zambia, 1906-1935 ... 245
   Walima T. Kalusa

9. Strange Bedfellows: The International Missionary Council,
   the International African Institute, and Research into
   African Marriage and Family ... 267
   Natasha Erlank

10. Dorothea Lehmann and John V. Taylor:
    Researching Church and Society in Late Colonial Africa ... 293
    John Stuart

11. Mission, Clinic, and Laboratory:
    Curing Leprosy in Nigeria, 1945-67 ... 313
    John Manton

    INDEX ... 335

Contributors

JOHN CINNAMON is an associate professor of anthropology and an affiliate of Black World Studies at Miami University (Ohio, USA). He teaches courses on cultural anthropology, African oral traditions, and religions of Africa. He has published in the *Journal of Colonialism and Colonial History, History in Africa,* and *Social Sciences and Missions,* and has edited volumes on equatorial African landscapes and the historical imagination, the anthropological contributions of missionary ethnographers, and the relation between religion and politics in late colonial and postcolonial Gabon. He spent 2008 in Gabon on a Fulbright-Hays Faculty Research Abroad Fellowship studying the history of the "Mademoiselle" spirit movement and Gabonese healers and healing practices.

ERIKA EICHHOLZER studied general linguistics and Africanistics in Zurich, Cologne, and Legon (Ghana). Currently she is finishing her Ph.D. thesis on the development discourse in the Akan language. Her main research interests are the Akan languages in Ghana and Côte d'Ivoire, Ghanaian migration, and mission history in West Africa.

NATASHA ERLANK is currently the head of department at Historical Studies, University of Johannesburg. She has published widely on Scottish missions and African Christians in South Africa, including on the gendered aspects of missions. She is busy with a book on the history of black mainstream/historic Christianity in South Africa in the early twentieth century, as well as a coedited volume on the centenary of the African National Congress. She has published in the *South African Historical Journal, African Studies, Journal of Southern African Studies,* and *Gender and History.*

CONTRIBUTORS

DEBORAH GAITSKELL is a research associate of the History Department at the School of Oriental and African Studies, where she previously taught for some years. She has also lectured at London University's Goldsmith's and Birkbeck Colleges and at the Institute of Education. Her range of published articles and book chapters covers women and mission Christianity in South Africa, female education and domesticity, and churchwomen's groups. A former editor of the *Journal of Southern African Studies*, she has assembled special journal issues on "Women and Missions," *LFM Le Fait Missionnaire* 16 (July 2005) and (with Wendy Urban-Mead) "Transnational Biblewomen: Asian and African Women in Christian Mission," *Women's History Review* 17, no. 4 (September 2008).

PATRICK HARRIES is professor of African history at the University of Basel. He is the author of *Butterflies and Barbarians: Swiss Missionaries and Systems of Knowledge in Southeast Africa* (2007) and *Work, Culture, and Identity: Migrant Laborers in Mozambique and South Africa, c. 1860-1910* (1994). He is presently writing a book on the "Mozbieker" community of freed slaves and contracted workers at the Cape.

WALIMA T. KALUSA is a lecturer at the University of Swaziland, where he teaches African history. Between 2007 and 2009 he was a research associate at Cambridge University, working on the project "History of Death in Africa." He has published articles and book reviews in both Zambian and international journals. He is author of *Kalonga Gawa Undi X: A Biography of an African Chief and Nationalist* (2010).

JOHN MANTON is a research fellow in the history and anthropology of African biosciences at the London School of Hygiene and Tropical Medicine. His research deals with the interactions between medical research, clinical practice, and welfare and development in Africa, and he has written on the relations between missionary and state leprosy control services in colonial Nigeria, and on global developments in the treatment of leprosy in the mid–twentieth century.

DAVID MAXWELL is Dixie Professor of Ecclesiastical History at Cambridge University and Fellow of Emmanuel College. He is author of *Christians and Chiefs in Zimbabwe: A Social History of the Hwesa People, c. 1870s-1990s* (1999) and *African Gifts of the Spirit: Pentecostalism and the Rise of a Zimbabwean Transnational Religious Movement* (2006). He was longtime editor of the *Journal of Religion in Africa*. He is currently writing a book about missionaries and African agents in the creation of colonial knowledge in the Belgian Congo.

Contributors

JOHN STUART teaches history at Kingston University, London. His research focuses mainly on British Protestant missionaries in eastern, central, and southern Africa during the twentieth century. He is completing a book on missionaries and the "end of empire" in those regions, encompassing the period 1939-65.

DMITRI VAN DEN BERSSELAAR is senior lecturer in African history at the University of Liverpool. His work on knowledge production in the context of colonialism emerged from his interest in missionaries and ethnicity in Nigeria. Recent publications include (with Zachary Kingdon) "Collecting Empire? African Objects, West African Trade and a Liverpool Museum," in *The Empire in One City?* edited by Haggerty, Webster, and White (2008), and the book *The King of Drinks: Schnapps Gin from Modernity to Tradition* (2007) on the cultural meanings given to imported gin in West Africa. His current research focuses on the careers of Ghanaian and Nigerian employees working with a major European business during the colonial and postcolonial eras.

HONORÉ VINCK lived and worked in the Democratic Republic of the Congo between 1972 and 1999 as a Catholic missionary and as director of the Æquatoria Research Center in Bamanya, near the town of Mbandaka. He is presently a member of the Belgian Royal Academy of Overseas Sciences and of the Centrum voor Historische Pedagogiek at the Katholieke Universiteit Leuven, Belgium. He is the editor in chief of *Annales Aequatoria*. His research and publications focus on land tenure in colonial Africa, African colonial schoolbooks, and the history of school education in the former Belgian Congo, and include "The Influence of Colonial Ideology on School Books in the Belgian Congo," *Paedagogica Historica* (1995).

Acknowledgments

This collection emerged out of a workshop entitled "The Secular and the Spiritual: Missionaries and Knowledge about Africa" convened in Basel by Patrick Harries and David Maxwell from 30 November to 1 December 2007. Numerous institutions and individuals helped make the event a success and this subsequent volume possible.

Luccio Schlettwein and Dag Henrichsen of the Basler Afrika Bibliographien generously hosted the workshop and provided funding through the Carl Schlettwein Stiftung. Other sources of funding were the Reisefonds der Universität Basel, Freiwillige Akademische Gesellschaft (Basel), Kommission für Forschungspartnerschaften mit Entwicklungsländern (Switzerland), the Sokrates-Programm (European Community), and the British Social and Economic Research Council, grant no. RES-000-23-1535.

Vital assistance in the planning and administration of the workshop came from Franziska Rüedi, Jacqueline Rodel, and Anna Vögeli of the Historische Seminar, Basel, backed up by Veit Arlt in the Basel Centre for African Studies. Marcel Dreier did a sterling job as coordinator, ensuring that the conference was both a convivial event and run on schedule.

Other colleagues made a significant contribution to the discussion and debate that shaped this volume. These were Veit Arlt, Gregor Dobler, Marcel Dreier, Paul Jenkins, Sara Pugach, Ulrike Sill, and Guy Thomas.

Finally, we are grateful to Derek Peterson for his comments on the first draft of the manuscript and to Eerdmans Series Editors Robert Frykenberg and Brian Stanley for their support in seeing this collection through to publication.

Abbreviations

AAB	Archives Africaines: Ministère des Affaires Etrangères, Bruxelles
AEG	Africa Education Group, IMC, Edinburgh House
AMEC	African Methodist Episcopal Church
AMU	African Mineworkers' Union
BELRA	British Empire Leprosy Relief Association
BJI	*Bulletin des juridictions indigènes et du droit coutumier Congolais*
BMA	Basel Mission Archives
BMS	Berlin Missionary Society
BSAC	British South Africa Company
CAM	Central African Missions
CBMS	Conference of British Missionary Societies
CCAR	Church of Central Africa Rhodesia
CEM	Congo Evangelistic Mission
CEMR	*Congo Evangelistic Mission Report*
CMML	Christian Missions in Many Lands
CMS	Church Missionary Society
CMSA	Church Missionary Society Archives
CSSRC	Colonial Social Science Research Council
CWM	Council for World Mission
CWW	Committee for Women's Work
DRC	Democratic Republic of the Congo
FMCNA	Foreign Missions Committee of North America
HCB	Huileries du Congo belge
IAI	International African Institute
ICCLA	International Committee on Christian Literature in Africa

ABBREVIATIONS

IIALC	International Institute of African Languages and Cultures
IMC	International Missionary Council
INEAC	Institut pour l'étude agronomique du Congo
IRM	*International Review of Missions*
ISRAC	Institute of Scientific Research in Central Africa
LMS	London Missionary Society
MMM Ogoja	Medical Missionaries of Mary Ogoja Convent
MRAC	Musée royal de l'Afrique Centrale
MRCI	Medical Research Council of Ireland
MSC	Congregation of the Missionaries of the Sacred Heart
NAE	Nigerian National Archives, Enugu
NAI	Nigerian National Archive, Ibadan branch
NAZ	National Archives of Zambia
NLS	National Library of Scotland
PTS	Propaganda-Treatment-Survey
RAC	Royal Africa Company
RDC	La République Démocratique du Congo (Democratic Republic of the Congo)
RGS	Royal Geographic Society
SAAAS	South African Association for the Advancement of Science
SAB	Société anonyme belge
SAJS	*South African Journal of Science*
SOAS	School of Oriental and African Studies, University of London
SPCK	Society for Promoting Christian Knowledge
SPG	Society for the Propagation of the Gospel in Foreign Parts
SWA	South-West Africa
UCCAR	United Church of Central Africa, Rhodesia
UMCA	Universities' Mission to Central Africa
UMCB	United Missions in the Copperbelt
UNICEF	United Nations Children's Emergency Fund
USPG	United Society for the Propagation of the Gospel
UWAG	University of Witwatersrand Art Galleries
VOC	Dutch East India Company
WCC	World Council of Churches
WHO	World Health Organization
WHS	Women's Help Society
Wits	Witwatersrand University
WMA	Women's Missionary Association (SPG)

INTRODUCTION

The Spiritual in the Secular

PATRICK HARRIES AND DAVID MAXWELL

Missionaries as Scholarly and Literary Tropes

In England, at the beginning of the nineteenth century, the missionary was seen as a kind of tinker who, in the opinion of the Reverend Sydney Smith, could not look a gentleman in the face. This view was echoed by a traveler who said that no great insight was necessary to understand that English missionaries to Tahiti were "selected from the dregs of the people."[1] By the mid–nineteenth century the social position of Protestant missionaries had been transformed. They were no longer regarded as religious eccentrics but as representatives of Victorian values. Many missionary societies had emerged out of new prominent groups in urban industrial society described by Chris Bayly as the "middling sort."[2] Their new prominence can be seen as a manifestation of the self-confidence and respectability of these aspiring classes: "The new missions, then," wrote Richard Gray, "depended not on the governing elite, on the establishment, but on the literate, earnest, prospering middle classes and skilled artisans, who made missionary periodicals the most widely circulated literature of the Victorian era."[3]

Nevertheless, in spite of missionaries' increased social standing, there remained a good deal of public skepticism about them. This stretched from the

---

1. Niel Gunson, *Messengers of Grace: Evangelical Missionaries in the South Seas, 1797-1860* (Oxford, 1978), p. 31.
2. Chris Bayly, *The Birth of the Modern World, 1780-1914* (Oxford, 2005), chapter 9.
3. Richard Gray, *Black Christians and White Missionaries* (New Haven, 1990). This was most clearly the case in the established Anglican Church that drew its missionaries from Germany, Switzerland, and the African continent for much of the nineteenth century.

caricatures of Dickens in *Bleak House* to the popular representation of missionaries in film in the twentieth century when, as John Mackenzie notes, they were usually depicted either "as figures of fun or people with high ambitions who are frustrated by the overwhelming forces they take on, not least the power of human nature itself." The widespread music hall and cartoon representation of the culinary encounter between missionary and cannibal requires little comment, but these representations are striking because they amount to the precise opposite of missionaries' own self-image as "a people who controlled their own natural and human environments with the help of their technology, science, and Western medicine, as well as through their moral aura, their moral force and state of grace."[4] In the late nineteenth century when amateur science was viewed as an educational and recreational activity at almost all levels of society, missionaries also viewed themselves as both students and bearers of Western science of every sort. Yet this aspect of their enterprise, including its early modern precursors and developments in the twentieth century, has been much neglected.

Until recently, the figure of the missionary did not fare well in Africanist historiography. From the 1960s to the late 1980s it was unfashionable to make missionaries the explicit object of study. Nationalist, Marxist, and Africanist historiography cast them as cultural imperialists: the heroes of a discredited colonial historiography one root of which lay in the missionary societies' hagiographical volumes. Scholars argued that missionaries had disparaged and undermined indigenous cultures in ways that made them complicit in colonial domination. While these assertions bore some truth, they were often sweeping, overgeneralized, and improperly interrogated. Instead scholars chose to write about a different type of Christianity. Africanist historians were in search of the resilient African initiative that had produced new and vibrant forms of Christianity or that, in association with missionaries, had created successful peasants, entrepreneurs, and political leaders. In their search for a usable past, scholars wrote increasingly about African independent churches — the Zionist, Aladura, and Apostolic Churches led by great African prophets such as Shembe, Harris, and Masowe who could be turned into protonationalists and resistance figures. In the 1960s and 1970s, it looked as if the future of African Christianity lay with these movements, and so it made sense to research them.[5] But the passage of time showed that most Afri-

---

4. John Mackenzie, "Missionaries, Science and the Environment in Nineteenth-Century Africa," in *The Imperial Horizons of British Protestant Missions, 1880-1914*, ed. Andrew Porter (Grand Rapids, 2003), p. 128.

5. For surveys of this vast literature see Terence Ranger, "Religious Movements and Politics in Sub-Saharan Africa," *African Studies Review* 29, no. 2 (1986); Norman

can Christians continued to adhere to the historic mission churches, and scholars returned to them. By reading between the lines of missionary sources in combination with oral history, historians and anthropologists came to grasp that the real agents of Africa's Christianization were Africans themselves: evangelists, catechists, native agents, teachers, and Bible women. To these need be added freed slaves in many parts of Africa; labor migrants moving into southern Africa in search of work and returning home with a new religion; and movements of evictees — Christian peasant farmers moved to make way for white settlers. In his classic 1994 study *The Church in Africa, 1450-1950*, Adrian Hastings concluded: "The Christian advance was a black advance or it was nothing. It was one in which ever so many more people were involved but very few of whom we can ever name . . . in general the black advance was far more low-key and often entirely unplanned or haphazard."[6] There were never enough missionaries or mission stations to account for the remarkable expansion of Christianity in twentieth-century Africa. "The most important mental transformations occurred far from missionary eyes."[7]

Anthropologists had long been critical of missionaries. Edward Tylor thought missionaries were "so occupied in hating and despising the beliefs of the heathen, that they always misinterpreted native life."[8] When they eventually examined the history of mission churches, anthropologists' innovative studies retained traces of an earlier, functionalist approach. This portrayed Christianity as a force responsible for the destruction of indigenous worldviews and downplayed the African initiative behind the composition, spread, and indigenization of mission churches.[9] Other recent scholarship, influenced by postcolonial theory, has analyzed missionaries as agents in the making of colonial and metropolitan identities.[10] Following Edward Said's

---

Etherington, "Recent Trends in the Historiography of Christianity in Southern Africa," *Journal of Southern African Studies* 22, no. 2 (1996); Adrian Hastings, "African Christian Studies, 1967-1999: Reflections of an Editor," *Journal of Religion in Africa* 30, no. 1 (2000); David Maxwell, "Writing the History of African Christianity," *Journal of Religion in Africa* 36, no. 4 (2006): 20.

6. Adrian Hastings, *The Church in Africa, 1450-1950* (Oxford, 1994), pp. 437-38; Patrick Harries, *Work, Culture, and Identity: Migrant Laborers in Mozambique and South Africa, c. 1860-1910* (Portsmouth, N.H., 1994), pp. 76-77, 105-6, 177, 213-20.

7. Etherington, "Recent Trends," p. 217.

8. Christopher Herbert, *Culture and Anomie: Ethnographic Imagination in the Nineteenth Century* (Chicago, 1991), p. 152.

9. Susan Thorne, "Imperial Pieties," *History Workshop Journal*, 2007, pp. 326-27; Jean Comaroff and John Comaroff, *Of Revelation and Revolution*, vol. 1, *Christianity, Colonialism, and Consciousness in South Africa* (Chicago, 1991).

10. Cf. Susan Thorne, "Religion and Empire at Home," in *At Home with the Empire:*

pathbreaking *Orientalism* (1978), and Valentin Mudimbe's idea of a "colonial library," they have read missionary publications for their imperialist discourses to show how Africa was used as a negative trope in the delineation of the colonial "other," a means of self-construction of European identities of race, class, and gender.[11] But while missionaries frequently used the tropes of darkness and savagery to elicit funding from their readers, they just as frequently stressed the picturesque and romantic sides of African life in their anthropological writings. At the same time, their publications also contained fascinating references to science as "ordered knowledge."[12] After reading Said and Mudimbe, it is easy to see this knowledge as a set of prejudices and presuppositions imposed on the imperial hinterland in ways that reinforced Europe's progress and confidence. And indeed, missionaries often arrived in Africa with ready-made understandings of the natural and human environment to which they had been brought by their vocation. But through their collaboration with native informants and assistants, and in conjunction with their intellectual peers in the colonies and at home, many missionaries developed new ways of understanding their situation, and in the process they brought African ways of ordering and understanding the human and natural environment to the attention of the world.[13] Living on the edge of empire, and beyond its confines, missionaries quickly became men-(and occasionally women)-on-the-spot who supplied scholars in the metropole with rare and exotic plant and animal specimens, objects of indigenous material culture, and information on a wide range of subjects. The essays in this volume attempt to recapture the contribution of these amateur intellectuals to zoology,

---

Metropolitan Culture and the Imperial World, ed. Catherine Hall and Sonya O. Rose (Cambridge, 2006); Patrick Harries, *Butterflies and Barbarians: Swiss Missionaries and Systems of Knowledge in South-East Africa* (Oxford, 2007), chapter 2; Anna Johnston, *Missionary Writing and Empire, 1800-1860* (Cambridge, 2003). Jean and John Comaroff were the first to draw our attention to the role of missions in the construction of alterity. See their *Of Revelation and Revolution*. For a discussion of their work and reference to the wider literature on alterity, see Elizabeth Elbourne, "The Word Made Flesh: Christianity, Modernity and Cultural Colonialism in the Work of Jean and John Comaroff," *American Historical Review*, April 2003, pp. 442-43.

11. Edward Said, *Orientalism* (New York, 1978); V. Y. Mudimbe, *The Idea of Africa* (Bloomington, Ind., 1994).

12. J. M. Mackenzie, ed., *Imperialism and the Natural World* (Manchester, 1990), p. 5.

13. Richard Price refers to the construction on the Eastern Cape frontier of a "colonial knowledge" that portrayed indigenous people as little more than stereotypes. This way of seeing was developed largely by missionaries whose ideas were reshaped by their experiences in the region during the tumultuous 1840s-1850s. Price, *Making Empire: Colonial Encounters and the Creation of Imperial Rule in Nineteenth-Century Africa* (Cambridge, 2008), pp. 154-56.

entomology and botany, medicine, and, particularly, linguistics and social anthropology. But missionaries were also deeply involved in other fields of measurement and delineation that can only be alluded to in this volume. These ranged from geography, cartography,[14] meteorology, and hydrography[15] to archeology and paleontology.[16] A missionary family could embrace several scientific disciplines. Frederic Ellenberger (1835-1919) produced the first history of the Basotho people in 1912, and his son Victor went on to pioneer the study of rock art in the Drakensberg. His eldest son, Henri, became a leading figure in the historiography of psychiatry, François a professor of geology at the Sorbonne, and missionary Paul (born 1919) a world authority on dinosaur footprints. Paul was one of the first scientists to recognize the relationship between birds and dinosaurs.[17]

Carl Ritter, the leading nineteenth-century geographer, declared that he could not have written his magnum opus, the *Erdkunde*, without the help of missionaries who furnished him with a mass of basically reliable empirical material.[18] Early anthropologists such as Johann Bachofen and James Frazer were similarly dependent on missionaries for information on which they built theories about the nature and evolution of humanity.[19] Even the founders of modern anthropology, from Durkheim and Mauss to Radcliffe-Brown, drew on missionary writings to locate and understand the "laws" regulating

---

14. P. Kokkenen, "Religious and Colonial Realities: Cartography of the Finnish Mission in Ovamboland, Namibia," *History in Africa* 20 (1993); R. Kark, "The Contribution of 19th Century Protestant Missionary Societies to the History of Cartography," *Imago Mundi* 45, no. 1 (1993).

15. Aylward Shorter notes that all missions in German East Africa became meteorological stations after 1908 when the colonial administration distributed pluviometers for measuring rainfall. See also his references to the White Fathers as explorers, cartographers, hydrographers, and archeologists. Shorter, *Cross and Flag in Africa: The "White Fathers" during the Colonial Scramble (1892-1914)* (New York, 2006), pp. 190-91, 193. See also G. H. Endfield and D. J. Nash, "Drought, Desiccation and Discourse: Missionary Correspondence and Nineteenth-Century Climate Change in Central Southern Africa," *Geographical Journal* 168, no. 1 (2002); Henry Drummond, *Tropical Africa* (London, 1889), pp. 196-98, chapter 8.

16. Perhaps imprudently, Cardinal Lavigerie encouraged White Fathers to explore the ruins of Carthage. Joann Freed, "Le Père Alfred-Louis Delattre (1850-1932) et les fouilles archéologiques de Carthage," *Histoire et Missions Chrétiennes* 8 (December 2008).

17. David Ambrose, *Palaeontology* (Rome and Lesotho, 2005), pp. 10-16.

18. Thomas Laurie, *The Ely Volume; or, The Contributions of Our Foreign Missions to Science and Human Well-Being* (Boston: American Board of Commissioners for Foreign Missions, 1885), p. 3.

19. J. W. Cell, ed., *By Kenya Possessed: The Correspondence of Norman Leys and J. H. Oldham, 1918-1926* (Chicago, 1976), p. 72.

social intercourse that, confined to the edges of their world, they considered "primitive."

When it comes to studies of individual missionaries, our impressions are somewhat skewed. We know a lot about the strategies of leading missionary thinkers such as Henry Venn and Rufus Anderson. We have biographies of nineteenth-century missionaries such as David Livingstone and Robert Laws who helped pioneer empire but usually failed in their endeavors at conversion. And we have studies of liberals or opposition figures such as John Philip, Bishop Colenso, or Joseph Booth who stood out as exceptional critics of colonial policy.[20] However, relatively little is known about twentieth-century missionaries whose work coincided with Africa's Christianization.[21]

The dearth of research on twentieth-century missionaries is also significant because in this period the nature of the missionary movement changed considerably from the preceding centuries in social sources, theology, and practice. Britain declined as a sending nation, and many of the historic missionary agencies suffered a crisis of confidence. But the missionary movement was supplemented by new types of missionaries who were from an evangelical, Pentecostal, and "faith mission" background, often North American in origin.[22] By the middle of the second decade of the twentieth century, the period of colonial occupation and culture-contact was over and missionaries were beginning to change their theology and practice. They slowly shed their ethnocentric self-confidence and accompanying belief that African cultures were diabolical and in need of erasure before Christianization could occur. African cultures increasingly became the object of legitimate scientific study, and some missionaries began to see within them traces of an original monotheism. Others warned of the dangers of destroying African beliefs and practices before understanding their purpose. This was the period in which missionaries turned to ethnography with gusto and when functionalist anthropology and indirect rule were born.

Here it is important to study scholarly conversations and conferences because they tell us much about changing missionary mentalities, about con-

---

20. This point is made by Etherington in his review "Recent Trends," pp. 208 and 211.

21. But cf. Peter G. Forster, *T. Cullen Young: Missionary and Anthropologist* (Hull, 1989), and W. John Young, *The Quiet Wise Spirit: Edwin W. Smith, 1876-1957, and Africa* (Peterborough, 2002). For statistics on the dramatic Christianization of Africa in the twentieth century, see Elizabeth Isichei, *A History of Christianity in Africa: From Antiquity to the Present* (London, 1995).

22. Andrew Walls, "The Old Age of the Missionary Movement," *International Review of Mission*, 1987, pp. 26-32; Brian Stanley, introduction to *Missions, Nationalism, and the End of Empire*, edited by Brian Stanley (Grand Rapids, 2003).

flicting opinions — and about the formation of the policies that shaped practice. The World Missionary Conference at Edinburgh in 1910 called for missionary societies to produce anthropological monographs on the people inhabiting their fields of operation. In many ways modeled on the meetings of the British Association for the Advancement of Science, the Edinburgh conference laid the pathway for another important meeting that pushed the ecumenical movement to draw support from the human sciences for the missionary movement. This took place at High Leigh in England in 1924 when Edwin Smith advocated the "sublimation," rather than "elimination," of African customs considered unacceptable to Christian morality. This new strain of missionary anthropology soon won the grudging support of leading professionals in the field.[23] At the same conference Diedrich Westermann, a former lay worker with the North German Missionary Society, stressed the need to preserve and study African languages that, he claimed, in a way that echoed Herder, reflected the "soul" and "genius" of the African people.[24] The High Leigh conference and its successor at Le Zoute in Belgium in 1926 witnessed a remarkable coming together of colonial policy makers, missionary statesmen, and a handful of leading African and black American Christians.[25] The synergy derived from these circles could produce surprising political results. The ideas of the pioneering missiologist Gustave Warneck on the need to preserve African languages and customs influenced Calvinist theologians in South Africa to develop a notion of "apartheid" in the late 1920s.[26] Warneck's son, Johannes, the missiologist and director of the Rhenish Mission, whose anthropological work influenced George Basden, died in a Nazi concentration camp in 1944 because of his outspoken criticism of the Third Reich.

By 1930 missionary ethnographers had been largely marginalized by professional anthropology, but their sturdy monographs had produced a tradi-

23. Cf. Radcliffe-Brown, introduction to *Among the Bantu Nomads,* by J. Tom Brown (Philadelphia, 1926), p. 11; Bronislaw Malinowski, cited in Hortense Powdermaker, *Stranger and Friend* (London, 1966), p. 43.

24. Cell, *By Kenya Possessed,* p. 73; Westermann, "The Value of the African's Past," *International Review of Missions (IRM)* 15 (1926): 429.

25. Amongst those who attended the High Leigh conference were Max Yergan, Edwin Smith, Diedrich Westermann, Lord Lugard, J. H. Oldham, J. K. Aggrey, and R. Baëta. Conference of British Missionary Societies, file, 253, "Africa Education," High Leigh Conference September 1924, School of Oriental and African Studies. Le Zoute attracted a similar gathering, including the chief magistrate of the Transkeian territories and the historian W. M. Macmillan; see E. W. Smith, ed., *The Christian Mission in Africa* (London, 1926).

26. Hermann Giliomee, "The Making of the Apartheid Plan, 1929-1943," *Journal of Southern African Studies* 29, no. 2 (2003): 381.

tion of writing that served as a baseline for much of the discipline.[27] Missionary activity continued into the era of decolonization and, of course, into the postcolonial era.[28] After 1945 the pace of industrialization and urbanization quickened, bringing new social problems and the challenge of African nationalism. There was also a growing tide of Christian independency, and missionaries began to speculate what decolonization would mean for the church.

Outline of the Chapters

The papers in this collection address some of these gaps in the historiography by focusing predominantly on twentieth-century developments and by considering some hitherto neglected careers of evangelicals and Pentecostals. The first two chapters, however, draw out the antecedents of missionary scientific endeavor. Harries' survey outlines the remarkable range of missionary scientific work from the early modern period of the Catholic encounter in central Africa to the modern era of the nineteenth- and twentieth-century missionary movement. Focusing on botany and entomology, he shows how both Protestant and Catholic missionaries were responsible for much of the knowledge produced about Africa prior to the establishment of university disciplines. He also notes that missionary science became more concerted during the time of occupation and formal empire: "the gratification of curiosity that had marked earlier works on nature was increasingly replaced by a more systematic approach to its study. A cocktail of concerns, stretching from scientific curiosity to moral reparation and commercial zeal, fired much of the exploration of Africa." He shows how the "methodological skills and narrative traditions" associated with the study of natural history influenced the genre of social anthropology, imbuing it with a scientific objectivity. As missionaries helped pioneer the natural sciences in empire, so they now helped lay the foundations of imperial social science. Noting the remarkable Kikongo catechism produced by the Portuguese Jesuit Father Gaspar de Conceição in 1550, Harries reminds us that linguistic work by missionaries had deep roots. Erica Eichholzer's chapter on the development of Twi grammars by Basel missionaries working in West Africa develops this important theme. A missionary passion for linguistics, whether springing from curios-

---

27. Patrick Harries, "Missions and Anthropology," in *Missions and Empire,* ed. Norman Etherington, Oxford History of the British Empire Companion Series (Oxford, 2005).

28. On missionaries in independent Africa, see David Maxwell, "Post-colonial Christianity in Africa," in *The Cambridge History of Christianity,* vol. 9, *World Christianity,* ed. Hugh McLeod (Cambridge, 2005).

ity, a desire to proselytize, or an effort to better understand African cosmologies, is evident in many of the subsequent case studies.

John Cinnamon shows that missionaries sometimes developed analytical concepts to explain the information they gathered in the field. His chapter assesses the contribution and impact of two missionary ethnographers who worked in west-central Africa in this period, particularly Gabon. The first was the American Presbyterian Robert Hamil Nassau, who worked as a missionary from 1861 to 1906 and wrote a good deal on "fetishism." The second was the French Spiritan (Holy Ghost Father) Henri Trilles, who had several periods of service between 1893 and 1907 and whose research focused on "totemism." A number of chapters span this period of occupation and culture contact and the following period of imperial consolidation and identity formation for Africans. Dmitri van den Bersselaar considers the career of George Thomas Basden, who worked for the Niger Mission of the Anglican Church Missionary Society from 1900 to 1935 and published extensively on Igbo culture. David Maxwell's chapter focuses on the Pentecostal and faith missionary William F. P. Burton, cofounder of the Congo Evangelistic Mission in South East Belgian Congo, where he worked from 1915 to 1960. Maxwell considers the motivations, institutions, and processes that shaped Burton's scientific work on the Luba Katanga in relation to the practices of Belgian colonial science and the emergent discipline of Anglo-Saxon anthropology. He foregrounds the ontological tensions between Burton's Pentecostal faith and his scientific research and shows how these change over time.

In a similar fashion, Deborah Gaitskell devotes her chapter to the career of the Anglican Dora Earthy, who worked for the Society for the Propagation of the Gospel in Mozambique from 1917 to 1930. She considers the local and institutional factors that shaped Earthy's formation as a missionary anthropologist. She also looks at the reception of her monograph *Valenge Women: The Social and Economic Life of the Valenge Women of Portuguese East Africa*, published in 1933. Walima Kalusa's chapter examines missionaries who came to value indigenous discourses as much as imported ones, a theme that emerges in a number of other contributions. Focusing on colonial Zambia from 1906 to 1935, he writes about the work of medical missionaries of Christian Missions in Many Lands (CMML), better known as the Plymouth Brethren. He shows how in an era when medical science was still somewhat hit or miss in efficacy, Dr. Walter Fisher came to reconfigure his therapeutic system in terms of local medical knowledge.

Honoré Vinck considers the enduring influence of the Catholic Aequatoria Centre. Founded in 1937 by priests in the Congregation of the Missionaries of the Sacred Heart (MSC), the center, situated in Bamanya, near Coquilhatville, became a site for the production of knowledge about the Mongo people. Its journal, also called *Aequatoria,* published material on the history and peoples across the Belgian Congo and was circulated far beyond that region. Much of the influence of the journal can be attributed to two of its remarkable missionary editors, Gustaaf Hulstaert and Edmond Boelaert, to whom Vinck devotes a considerable part of his chapter. Both men were moved by notions of pure, authentic African languages and cultures that sprang from their own Flemish cultural heritage. Vinck shows how these notions shaped their anticolonialism and their research on Mongo ethnicity.

John Stuart's essay discusses missionary concerns in the period of decolonization. He considers the research careers of the English Anglican priest (later bishop) John V. Taylor and the German linguist and worker with the Berlin Missionary Society, Dorothea Lehmann. While Stuart adds to our knowledge of Taylor, the well-known theologian, missiologist, and Christian statesman, he also brings to light the hitherto unexamined career of the equally gifted Lehmann. A particular focus of his chapter is the research project that resulted in Taylor and Lehmann's influential book *Christians in the Copper Belt* (1961). This work examined the effects of postwar industrialization and urbanization, and considered their social implications with particular reference to Christian belief and practice.

Taylor and Lehmann's research received sponsorship and direction from two significant organizations. The first was the International Missionary Council (IMC), founded in 1921 from the Continuation Committee of the 1910 Edinburgh Conference and which represented ecumenical Protestant thinking. An equally important "secular" organization within which missionaries played a considerable role was the International Institute for African Languages and Cultures (later the International Africa Institute), founded in 1926. Natasha Erlank considers the collaboration of these two bodies in research on African marriage and the family, an increasing concern for missionaries in the postwar era who continued to see the family as central to the propagation and maintenance of the Christian faith. As Stuart observes, in this period "missions and churches required 'experts' of their own to advise, from a professional as well as a Christian perspective, on the problems of contemporary Africa, rural and urban." This professionalization of mission work was nowhere more evident than in the domain of health care. John Manton's chapter on missionary medicine in Nigeria from 1945 to 1967 provides a stark contrast to the healing practice of Walter Fisher outlined in Walima Kalusa's chapter. Manton shows how the colonial development policy "transformed the missionary leprosy worker from charismatic carer and healer in the midst of spectacular suffering into a bureaucratic manager, technician, and scien-

Introduction

tist." In the post-Versailles age, epitomized by Lugard's *Dual Mandate* (1922) and the Phelps-Stokes Commissions on African education, missionaries helped provide a crucial legitimating ideology of development to the colonial states in return for much-needed subsidies. Manton's paper shows how this relationship intensified in the post-1945 era when leprosy work could command a significant amount of state expenditure and some missionaries became medical experts, managing large institutions of healing. While this type of mission work had little evangelistic effect, the increasing entanglement of missionaries with the developmental aims of colonial states served as an important factor in safeguarding the church's existence in the postcolonial era.[29]

Missionaries as Scientists

Together the chapters raise fascinating and important themes. Missionaries could be remarkable polymaths practicing not one but several scientific disciplines. One, William H. Sheppard, the celebrated black American missionary to the Congo, according to Pagan Kennedy, "treated the missionary job title as an umbrella under which he could pursue his multifarious ambitions. Explorer, big game hunter, celebrity speaker, fund-raiser, art-collector anthropologist."[30] Like Sheppard, a number of those considered in this volume were intellectually formed in an era when boundaries between different types of knowledge were more porous, and hence they felt at liberty to range across them. Basden, Burton, and Earthy researched natural history. Hulstaert published more than twenty articles on entomology in the Congo and sent specimens to botanical gardens and museums in Belgium. And Trilles collected plants and insects for French institutions, having several of his specimens named after him. Both Burton and Earthy continued the well-established missionary tradition, mentioned by Harries, of collecting material culture for European and South African museums. A good number of the missionaries discussed were gifted linguists.[31]

Many missionaries located themselves within the Livingstone tradition of the explorer-missionary intent on bringing about an African renaissance through the powers of Christianity, commerce, and science. Livingstone was iconic in a number of senses. When he published his *Missionary Travels and*

29. David Maxwell, "Decolonisation," in *Missions and Empire*.
30. Pagan Kennedy, *Black Livingstone: A True Adventure in Nineteenth-Century Congo* (New York, 2002), p. 81.
31. See also Rachel Gilmour, *Grammars of Colonialism: Representing Languages in Colonial South Africa* (Basingstoke, 2006).

Researches in South Africa in 1857, he intended his researches to mark him out as a scientist, as was illustrated by the figure of a tsetse fly on his title page. He corresponded with some of the most notable scientists of his age: the director of Kew, the president of the Royal Geographical Society, the director of the British Museum, and the astronomer royal at the Cape. When Livingstone was received with considerable acclaim in Cambridge in 1857, his visit was considered as much a scientific event as a religious one. The publication of his lectures the following year carried an appendix by Adam Sedgwick, professor of geology, in which he surveyed Livingstone's contribution to the scientific study of Africa in the areas of the vegetable kingdom, meteorology and climate, the animal kingdom, hydro-geography, physical geography, and geology, with a footnote on linguistics. *Missionary Travels* was a best seller. It inspired hunters, administrators, scientists, as well as missionaries who were associated with Africa for the next century.[32]

A good number of missionaries, particularly Nonconformists, differed little from Livingstone in their humble beginnings. But like him, they shared the rigorous urge for self-improvement and the drive to respectability fostered by evangelical Protestantism. The experience and connections gleaned from training and then from the mission field could be transforming, and many missionaries transcended their social origins.[33] Not all were as prolific as those considered here, but a good number wrote pieces for journals, whether in the area of native affairs, ethnography, missiology, natural history, or geography. Others took useful photographs or contributed to museum collections of material culture or natural history.

A prominent theme in these essays is the missionaries' contribution to the development of social anthropology. This was particularly the case once the frontier had closed and missionaries were transformed into experts with the power to influence state policies in the field of native affairs. Modern missionaries realized that an understanding of native life and custom could ameliorate the condition of their charges and increase their willingness to convert. The growing ecumenical movement saw anthropology, education, and medicine as crucial areas of investigation for missionaries and debated these issues extensively at Edinburgh in 1910. Missionaries dominated the anthropological section of the South African Association for the Advancement of Science from its beginning and provided it with leadership until 1921, when Radcliffe-Brown was elected leader.

---

32. Mackenzie, "Missionaries, Science," pp. 107-8; Felix Driver, *Geography Militant: Cultures of Exploration and Empire* (Oxford, 2001), chapters 2, 4.
33. Jean Comaroff and John Comaroff, *Of Revelation and Revolution*, 1:80-85.

Introduction

Missionaries were collectors of objects and information, but some, like Trilles and Nassau, also gave meaning to their observations by applying to them new, scientific ideas. For those who regarded Genesis as a handbook of geology, Livingstone's speculations on the ancient connection between South America, Australia, and South Africa, following his discovery of fossil araucarias in the rocks of the Zambezi Valley, must have come as a shock.[34] Twenty years later Henry Drummond found evidence of deep time in the remains of fossil fish near the Shire River and in the vestiges of glaciology in the Eastern Cape.[35] Other missionaries were intent on understanding how native peoples, as much as metropolitan intellectuals, ordered and explained knowledge. This brought influential figures like Drummond and Junod to see natural selection, as much as the hand of God, behind the evolution of nature.[36] It led them to adopt unorthodox views, such as the polygenic origins of religion, or a more liberal approach to polygamous marriages, just as it reinforced their membership in Kant's religion of reason. But the application of the human and natural sciences to religion by these men drained their Christianity of enchantment, subjected faith to a new skepticism, and blunted evangelical enthusiasms. This would lead Malinowski to believe that Junod (and Edwin Smith) were more interested in people than in converting them.[37] The mobilization of science in support of new ways of restructuring society was taken to an extreme in Moslem Algeria, where the French Third Republic dispensed with Christianity altogether and instead based its colonial mission on a faith in the powers of science.[38] In the twentieth century science proved to be of great utility to the smaller colonial powers who felt impelled to demonstrate their fitness to rule. In their chapters Maxwell and Vinck show how, following the debacle of the Congo Free State in 1908, the Belgians engaged in scientific endeavors as a means of imperial reparation. Portugal sought to prove her imperial credentials to Britain and France, post-1945, through new endeavors in geography and social anthropology.[39]

---

34. H. H. Johnston, "Livingstone as a Man of Science," *Nature* 27 (March 1913): 89-90.
35. H. Drummond, *Tropical Africa* (London, 1889), chapter 8.
36. Drummond, *Tropical Africa*, chapters 6–7; Harries, *Butterflies and Barbarians*, pp. 140-44.
37. Powdermaker, *Stranger and Friend*, p. 43.
38. Michael A. Osborne, *Nature, the Exotic, and the Science of French Colonialism* (Bloomington, Ind., 1994), p. xii.
39. Ana C. Roque and Lívia Ferrão, "A Glimpse over the Land and Peoples of Mozambique: The Collections Assembled during the Colonial Period and Their Importance for the Rebuilding of the History of Mozambique," *African Research and Documentation* 99 (2005): 27-36.

The growing belief in the powers of biomedicine also inspired an increasing number of "pious physicians" to serve as missionaries. In 1900, Herbert Lankester, secretary of the Medical Committee of the Church Missionary Society (CMS), London, described medical missions as "the heavy artillery of the missionary army." In the same year the Ecumenical Missionary Conference, held in New York, declared that no mission could "be considered fully equipped that has not its medical branch." With Roman Catholic missions bound by the decrees of the Fourth Lateran Council, Protestant medical missionaries initially made the running. Their numbers rose to a high point of about 5.6 percent of the total Protestant missionary force in 1923 to coincide with the post-Versailles age of trusteeship and colonial development. However, the Catholic position changed rapidly after 1925 with the founding in America of the Society of Catholic Medical Missionaries, and later with changes announced by the Vatican in 1936 regarding the study and practice of medicine by those who had taken holy orders.[40]

The Vatican was particularly vigilant about the uncontrolled influence of scientific ideas on the Christianity practiced in different parts of the world. As Harries shows in this collection, Catholic missionaries worked manfully with the institutions of the French Republic in the sphere of the natural sciences but contested, with equal zeal, their production of strictly secular notions of religion. Émile Durkheim, Marcel Mauss, Arnold van Gennep, and their colleagues viewed religion as a social and historical construction, and belief as a product of the imagination. These views were criticized by the French-speaking Swiss Protestant missionary Henri-Alexandre Junod, but they were anathema to Catholics who saw in them the imposition of the Republic's anticlerical views on the youth of France. Catholic leaders in the mission field were also unwilling to abandon their notion of anthropology's role in the struggle against dark, heathen practices; nor could they accept the "materialist" views of scholars who traced the institution of marriage to an early promiscuity or who found "animism" rather than traces of monotheism in the spiritual beliefs of primitive people.[41] While Protestant missionaries tried to yoke secular anthropology to their attempts to forge a mobile, "African" Christianity, often in churches under indigenous leadership, Catholics attempted to control the emerging discipline and confine its energies to the construction of a single, universal Catholic Church. For this reason the jour-

---

40. Christoffer H. Grundmann, "Mission and Healing in Historical Perspective," *International Bulletin of Missionary Research* 32, no. 4 (2008): 185-88.

41. Cf. Alexandre Le Roy, *La religion des primitifs* (Paris, 1909), pp. 64, 67-69, 94. On Junod's views, see Harries, *Butterflies and Barbarians*, p. 214.

nal *Anthropos,* founded in 1906 outside Vienna by Society of the Divine Word missionary Wilhelm Schmidt, led its first issue with an article on "the scientific role of missionaries." Written by Alexandre Le Roy, a former missionary in west-central and East Africa, professor of religious history at the Institut Catholique in Paris, and more recently superior of the Congregation of Holy Ghost Fathers, the article outlined the need for a strictly Catholic missionary anthropology. Over the next few years a deep rift developed between Catholic and secular anthropology in France as Le Roy and his colleagues traded brickbats with the Durkheimians in Paris.[42] The Congress of Malines in 1910 laid the basis for a modern, Catholic anthropology concerned with the accumulation of knowledge, and its practical benefit, rather than fashionable theories and expendable ideas.[43] This divide would widen as Catholic universities in Belgium, the Netherlands, and Switzerland, as well as in France (where legislation barred the Institut Catholique from holding the status of a university), established anthropology departments that subordinated the secular theories and practices of the discipline to the missionary concerns of their church.

Missionaries and the Academy

By 1930, Protestant missionary ethnographers were beginning to lose out to university-based academics intent on professionalizing their trade.[44] The essays presented here illustrate the complexity of the missionary role in the penumbral origins of anthropology, underlining the contribution of these amateurs to the establishment of the discipline as a professional "science." This collection indicates that professional anthropologists (like their colleagues in the natural sciences) found it inconvenient to acknowledge not only the contribution of African assistants to their fields of research, but also that of other amateurs, such as missionaries (or more obvious handmaidens of empire such as government officials and soldiers). The essays stress that there was no one missionary community and that missionaries debated and disagreed on a range of topics, within their societies and between them. They

---

42. Emmanuelle Sibeud, *Une science impériale pour l'Afrique? La construction des savoirs africanistes en France 1878-1930* (Paris, 2002), pp. 68-71, 117-20, 204-5; Sibeud, "The Elusive Bureau of Colonial Ethnography in France, 1907-1925," in *Ordering Africa: Anthropology, European Imperialism, and the Politics of Knowledge,* ed. H. Tilley, with R. Gordon (Manchester, 2007), pp. 60-62.

43. Marc Poncelet, *L'invention des sciences coloniales belges* (Paris, 2008), pp. 173-76, 201-3.

44. P. Harries, "Anthropology," in *Missions and Empire.*

also recognize that missionaries often changed their views as they encountered local ideas and metropolitan theories through a broad range of experiences. Although the book is concerned with the missionaries' contribution to the history of "science," it does touch on their associated role in the expansion of the imperial frontier and in the emergence of local expressions of Christianity. It provides, above all, a critical approach to the secular achievements of missionaries that was often absent from the in-house productions of their societies.

This new strain of missionary history depends on sources of evidence that are found less in the archives of the missionary societies than in the scientific institutions to which the missionaries sent information and objects gathered in the field. These ranged from botanical gardens and herbaria to museums of natural history and ethnography to geographical societies and art galleries. Missionaries wrote for ethnographic journals ranging from Lucy Lloyd's short-lived *Folk-lore Journal* (1879-81) and the Catholics' *Anthropos* to the *Journal of the Royal Anthropological Institute, Journal of the Royal African Society, Bantu Studies* (later *African Studies*), *Africa*, and the *Zeitschrift für Ethnologie*. But they just as readily published serious anthropological essays in missionary journals like the *International Review of Missions* (1912), *Missionary Intelligencer, Church Missionary Review, Missionary Herald, Neue Allgemeine Missionszeitschrift, Portugal em Africa: Revista de Cultura Missionária* (1894), *Revue des missions contemporaines,* and *Foi et Vie*. Geographical journals also appeared to be a prime choice, especially for those who, like Basden and Burton, fancied themselves explorers in the Livingstone tradition. At a time when museums often outshone universities as institutions of colonial knowledge formation, missionaries regularly wrote for their in-house scientific bulletins and publications. Conversely, missionaries often preferred to influence colonial policy, customary law, indirect rule, the woman question, or ethnic formation by writing for native affairs journals or regional reviews like the *Nyasaland Journal* or the *Notes and Records* of the Gold Coast or Tanganyika. Missionaries had multiple intentions, writing in very different genres of expression for periodicals that ranged from Sunday school magazines to scientific journals. Nassau's *Fang in West Africa* was given at best an ambivalent reception in early anthropological journals, but it received glowing reviews in high-profile popular publications such as the *New York Times* and *National Geographic*.

While Nassau and Trilles wanted to contribute to then-current debates surrounding two early concepts in the anthropology of religion, namely, fetishism and totemism, van den Bersselaar seeks to contextualize the work of missionaries such as Basden "not in the first place within the 'official history' of anthropology, but rather within the specific emerging local traditions of anthropological knowledge production." But both Burton and Basden were little concerned about whether their work was academically acceptable, and were far more concerned to influence the policies of missionary societies and colonial officials. That Basden was an evangelical and Burton a Pentecostal partly explains their distance from and distrust of the academy, where more liberally minded missionaries dominated. Inspirational tomes by missionaries shaped work on the ground as much as academic ones. Dan Crawford's *Thinking Black: 22 Years without a Break in the Long Grass of Central Africa* (1912), an invocation to study language, proverbs, and riddles in order to master local modes of thought, stimulated Burton's ethnographic practice as much as the texts by Belgian Museum curators and South African anthropologists. It also shaped the medical practice of Walter Fisher.

While science was inseparable from mission, shaping notions of the modern individual self that missionaries sought to instill into their converts, the likes of Drummond and Junod were exceptional in their devotion to scientific practice. The passions of most missionaries, particularly evangelicals and Catholics, remained first and foremost religious ones: preaching, teaching, and dispensing the sacraments. Science was instrumental in the work of conversion. Vinck observes that it was a means of improving "missionary praxis." Eichholzer's chapter shows that the discipline of linguistics in Africa was an unintended consequence of the need to communicate the gospel. Basel missionary Hans Nicolai Riis wrote in the preface of his Twi grammar that language was a "tool . . . needed to raise . . . people from the dire depths of their paganism." Nevertheless, a passion and curiosity for the seemingly exotic peoples and landscapes also fired their research. The unstinting description and classification in pocket notebooks of what they saw — be it human, animal, vegetable, or insect — provided an antidote to the boredom that many experienced on an isolated mission station.

Missionary science did however find its way into the academy, and this had much to do with patrons, institutions, and networks. A small band of figures appear as inspirations and helpers in a number of the case studies. J. Tom Brown and other missionaries played an active role in the public seminars organized at the University of Cape Town by A. Radcliffe-Brown. "By far the greater part of the information about native life in South Africa that we do possess," wrote the first professor of social anthropology in the British Empire in 1926, "has been collected by our missionaries." Radcliffe-Brown criticized missionaries who unthinkingly destroyed African customs or refused to grasp their "real meaning," through either unwillingness or inability. But he thought many "enlightened missionaries" studied "native life" in ways that would better the condition of the people to whom they "devoted their lives and energies."[45]

As director of the International African Institue (IAI), Diedrich Westermann was important to William Burton, Dora Earthy, and Dorothea Lehmann. Winifred Hoernlé, described in Gaitskell's chapter as the "Mother of Social Anthropology in South Africa" and "a brilliant, inspiring, and warm-hearted teacher," helped both Burton and Earthy, in spite of her strong disapproval of the missionary's role in cultural change. Of particular importance was the University of Witwatersrand where other influential figures worked alongside Hoernlé, such as Clement Doke, the son of a Baptist missionary in Northern Rhodesia and professor of African languages, and Isaac Schapera, professor of social anthropology. Schapera had even stronger misgivings about missionary research and practice than Hoernlé but, like Radcliffe-Brown, recognized the contribution that missionary ethnography, collecting, and photography could make to the material and empirical foundations of social anthropology. Notably, Schapera would go on to edit seven volumes of David Livingstone's letters and journals. The University of Witwatersrand and later the Rhodes-Livingstone Institute in Northern Rhodesia (founded in 1937) acted as catalysts for Anglo-Saxon research on the African continent. The Central Africa Museum in Tervuren, Belgium, was the engine of Belgian research. Once again, key individuals figure as patrons. Both Burton and Hulstaert drew support from the museum's director, Henri Schouteden, and Joseph Maes, curator of the ethnographic section. As Vinck reveals, much Belgian Catholic research was published in-house in *Aequatoria,* but the journal and its editors, Hulstaert and Boelaert, maintained such a profile that it was widely circulated and taken at the University of Witwatersrand. Museums of natural history, herbaria, and botanical gardens played similar roles for missionary naturalists; the scientists attached to these establishments actively encouraged the endeavors of missionary collectors in the field.

The International Missionary Council (IMC), under the leadership of John Merle Davis, a second-generation missionary raised in Japan, and the council's first director of economic and social research, was crucial in the development of Protestant social science. Working closely with the IAI, it brought together missionaries, colonial administrators, and academics with shared interests in linguistics, marriage, kinship, and social change. Edwin Smith, former Primitive Methodist missionary to central Africa and prolific scholar, played a major role in this group, eventually acting as edi-

---

45. Radcliffe-Brown, introduction to *Among the Bantu Nomads,* p. 9.

tor of the IAI's celebrated journal, *Africa.* J. H. Oldham, also enormously influential, straddled the IAI and the IMC as well as the Conference of British Missionary Societies (CBMS). Oldham was able to generate much needed funding for research. He also founded and edited the *International Review of Missions,* the preeminent journal of missionary thinking between the wars, which was attached to the IMC. Another important figure who helped set the postwar research agenda of the IMC was the Swedish Lutheran missionary Bengt Sundkler, who acted as the council's research secretary in 1948-49.

The essays suggest some of the reasons why missionary ethnographers eventually tended to be sidelined by professional anthropologists. Schapera traced one of the reasons why professional anthropologists abandoned the armchair and engaged in intensive fieldwork to the "inadequacy" of the studies of "primitive people" undertaken by missionaries and others.[46] First and foremost missionary work was often unfashionable. As Cinnamon shows in his work on Trilles, missionaries often remained loyal to ideas they had encountered just prior to setting out for the mission field, long after such ideas had passed out of fashion. Likewise, Nassau stayed a committed degenerationalist, unreconciled to the work of cultural evolutionists. And Basden was still citing Nassau as late as 1938. The notion of degeneration proved attractive to both Catholic and Protestant missionaries as it charged them with restoring an ancient and original monotheism. Others looked to the theory of evolution to explain the customs that defined African tribes and placed them on a ladder of development headed by Europeans. Partly for this reason, missionaries as varied as Junod, Basden, Earthy, and Burton produced a "salvage" or "reconstructive" anthropology that fixed African customs in a timeless era untroubled by contestation or change. This allowed them to search for the very origins of the family, language, or religious belief in the African continent. It also allowed them self-consciously to assemble and collate accounts of "authentic" African practices before they could be transformed by the church and its religion. By capturing a dying world on paper, these missionaries sought to record customs on which later generations could build a truly African Christianity, family, or language and, in the process, assure the contribution of Africans to the genius of humankind. But as Gaitskell observes, by the late 1920s a new breed of professional anthropologist was increasingly critical of an amateur scholarship unwilling to tackle the forces of change and confusion enveloping Africa. Part of the problem lay in the missionaries' re-

---

46. Schapera, "Should Anthropologists Be Historians?" *Journal of the Royal Anthropological Institute* 92, no. 2 (1962): 154.

fusal to confront the full extent of what many functionalist anthropologists saw as their role in the "destruction" of rural beliefs and practices. But missionaries of the older generation were seldom equipped with the theory needed to analyze new and disturbing situations of "culture contact" and "social change" and, by the mid-1930s, felt increasingly uneasy when attending international conferences with professional anthropologists.[47] Stung by the criticisms of these secular colleagues, missionaries turned increasingly to more practical disciplines such as linguistics, social work, and applied anthropology.

However, there are other explanations for missionaries' love of unfashionable ideas. Many were unsettled by the changes that accompanied labor migration, proletarianization, and the cash economy of the 1920s and 1930s. They sought to preserve what they imagined to be a conservative, tribally bound world because this best suited their programs of Christianization. Leonard Beecher, Church Missionary Society member and subsequently Anglican archbishop of central Africa, typified thinking in the mid-1930s when he said the social goal of the CMS in Kenya was to produce "a contented, educated Christian peasantry." His colleague John Comely in Ebbu had similar aims: "My policy is to make Christians of the natives, to encourage them to stay in reserves, to develop and uphold the Tribal system."[48] While this reasoning allowed an African-based decentralized despotism to emerge in those areas of tropical Africa subjected to indirect rule, it served to further the ends of segregation in southern Africa.

An unacknowledged competition existed between missionaries conversant with the local language, environment, and people and professional anthropologists who entered the field as foreign intruders. As Erlank observes, "The intermediaries of most ethnographic work were missionaries and mission societies, playing a rather differently conceptualised role as culture broker (not from Africa to Europe, but from Europe to Africa)." Mission stations were often the first port of call for new researchers, and the hospitality, introductions, and initial explanations of local culture offered by missionaries often proved indispensable to the success of a project. Indeed, to save time some pioneering anthropologists actively sought out "good missionaries" for opening introductions to their fieldwork site, acknowledging that missionary dictionaries, and grammars, as well as compilations of local folklore and cus-

---

47. Cf. the New Education Fellowship Conference held in July 1934 in Johannesburg and, in the same year, the International Congress of Anthropological and Ethnological Sciences in London.

48. Cited in Robert Strayer, *The Making of Mission Communities in East Africa: Anglicans and Africans in Colonial Kenya, 1895-1935* (London, 1978), p. 90.

toms provided a useful baseline upon which to build.[49] As is evident from many of the essays in this volume, missionaries possessed good linguistic skills and benefited from extensive periods (often decades) in the field, or on its edges. While some missionaries remained "on the veranda," others left the institutional settings of mission stations to engage actively with local peoples. Missionary ethnographers frequently asserted these skills in their monographs in ways that could appear unsettling to professional anthropologists.[50] They particularly built personal relations of trust with assistants (often Christian converts) whom they acknowledged in their published works for their skills in both gathering and explaining information. By contrast, professional ethnographers arrived in the field with a training that explicitly rejected native ways of understanding. While missionaries used their linguistic skills to accumulate ostensibly antiquarian lists of native terms, professional anthropologists searched for laws (of initiation, kinship, or chiefly power) that only they could explain. At the same time, the professionals' search for social change led them to pay little attention to the taxonomies of material culture or crop types, or to the value ascribed to these objects by their African informants.[51] These blind spots in the anthropology developed by the professionals led a sensitive fieldworker like Monica Hunter, the daughter of a missionary in the Eastern Cape of South Africa, to ignore her African assistants' knowledge of material culture and to leave unacknowledged their contribution to her written work.[52] As Harries points out in this volume, professional anthropologists' disdain for certain forms of local knowledge initially blunted, and then finally halted, missionary publications on indigenous ways of ordering and understanding the natural world.

49. John W. Burton with Orsolya Arva Burton, "Some Reflections on Anthropology's Missionary Positions," *Journal of the Royal Anthropological Institute*, 2007, p. 13.

50. The vexed relation between missionary ethnographers and social anthropologists who were often closer in aims and methods than the latter cared to acknowledge has been the subject of several studies. See Burton with Burton, "Some Reflections on Anthropology's Missionary Positions"; Claude Stipe, "Anthropologists versus Missionaries: The Influence of Presuppositions," *Current Anthropology* 21, no. 2 (1980); S. Van Der Geest and J. Kirby, "The Absence of the Missionary in African Ethnography," *African Studies Review* 35, no. 3 (1992); Olivier Servais and Gérard van't Spijker, eds., *Anthropologie et missiologie XIXe-XXe siècles. Entre connivance et rivalité* (Paris, 2004).

51. Radcliffe-Brown thought "the natives themselves, of course, cannot explain the real meaning of the customs they follow." See his introduction to *Among the Bantu Nomads*, p. 10.

52. Andrew Bank, "The 'Intimate Politics' of Fieldwork: Monica Hunter and Her African Assistants, Pondoland and Eastern Cape, 1931-1932," *Journal of Southern African Studies* 34, no. 4 (2008).

Perhaps most importantly, the new, professional anthropology rested on functionalist explanations that saw the missionary as a destabilizing, destructive force in African society. By challenging kinship laws, religious beliefs, or the power of pagan chiefs, missionaries destabilized the natural balance of small-scale African social groups. Missionaries who adopted this "scientific" anthropology, rooted in the secular universities, had to accept the need to retain African customs once abhorred by their missionary antecedents. Edwin Smith, Henri-Alexandre Junod, Donald Fraser, and some of their colleagues at High Leigh and Le Zoute could accept the need to build a local Christianity on the trunk of authentic, African beliefs. But, perhaps under the influence of functionalist anthropology, a missionary like George Basden would take a far more pessimistic view of the colonial encounter. He believed British colonialism had "seriously disturbed" the "balance of life" in southeastern Nigeria. It had delivered a "death blow" to native law and custom from which the local system of values might never recover. Christianity should fill this gap, but it was "worthless idealism" to think that Africans would accept European views of how their values and beliefs should be reshaped. They themselves would decide what elements of their culture should be retained, and these would frequently not be the aspects favored by missionaries or church elders, largely due to the moral void created by the destruction of indigenous institutions.[53] A decade later, Bengt Sundkler, in the first edition of *Bantu Prophets*, provided detailed justification for Basden's fears when he documented how Africans in the subcontinent fasned new forms of Christianity out of a bricolage of religious practices; and hiothat their separatist churches threatened to serve as "bridges back to paganism."[54] From this perspective, it seemed that missionary anthropology had little practical influence on the constitution of an African Christianity as had been first proposed at High Leigh and Le Zoute.

This turn of events pushed missionaries to choose welfare work over a functionalist anthropology that required not just professional distance from the subject of study but a respect for institutions and practices they considered morally repugnant.[55] This commitment to social activism had emerged in South Africa in the 1920s when missionaries in the cities were first confronted by the social problems caused by rapid urbanization. In 1925, when professional anthropology focused almost entirely on small-scale rural societies, the General Missionary Conference of South Africa published a hand-

---

53. G. T. Basden, *The Niger Ibos* (London, 1938), pp. xii-xxii.
54. Bengt Sundkler, *Bantu Prophets in South Africa,* 1st ed. (London, 1948), p. 297.
55. Lucy Mair, "Anthropologists and Colonial Policy," *African Affairs* 74 (1975): 192.

book filled with articles on the social consequences of proletarianization and urban poverty. The compendium drew on the writings of both white missionaries and black political leaders sympathetic to the missionary movement.[56] The *International Review of Missions* also reflected this growing concern with social activism and welfare work in the urban areas. Just as professional anthropologists became the experts on tribal Africans and how "social change" disrupted their rural lives, a group of American missionaries, less influenced by the notion of "trusteeship" than their British counterparts, turned to practical ways of solving the social problems produced by industrialization and urbanization. Influenced by the Social Gospel movement's call for indigenous people to take charge of their lives, these missionaries organized leisure-time activities for urban Africa in institutions such as the Bantu Men's Social Centre in Johannesburg, and they encouraged multiracial politics through the joint councils and the Institute of Race Relations. Their commitment to social reform (or social control in the eyes of later Marxist critics) created a new approach to the study of African life that would become particularly evident on the Copperbelt of central Africa in the 1930s-1950s where the work of missionaries and anthropologists frequently overlapped.[57] Winifred Hoernlé was a strong supporter of the social reform demanded by missionaries on the Witwatersrand and eventually abandoned professional anthropology to devote herself to this cause. These concerns, particularly the role to be played by missionaries in the leisure time of African miners, featured prominently in a seminal report sponsored by the IMC and drawn up by John Merle Davis.[58]

---

56. These included Selope Thema, "Social Conditions of Africans," and John Dube, "Native Policy and Industrial Organisations"; see also James Henderson, "The Problem of Native Poverty." All in J. Dexter Taylor, ed., *Christianity and the Natives of South Africa: A Yearbook of South African Missions* (Johannesburg, 1925).

57. F. B. Bridgman, "Social Conditions in Johannesburg," *International Review of Missions* 15 (1926); J. Dexter Taylor, "The Rand as a Mission Field," *International Review of Missions* 15 (1926). See also J. D. Rheinallt Jones, "Missionary Work among the Bantu in South Africa," *International Review of Missions* 17 (1928), and missionary Ray Phillips, *The Bantu in the City: A Study of Cultural Adjustment on the Witwatersrand* (Lovedale, 1938). See also his *Rising Tide of Native Crime* (Johannesburg, 1940); Paul Rich, "Albert Luthuli and the American Board Mission in South Africa," in *Missions and Christianity in South African History*, ed. H. Bredekamp and R. Ross (Johannesburg, 1995), pp. 192-93.

58. J. Merle Davis, ed., *Modern Industry and the African: An Enquiry into the Effects of the Copper Mines of Central Africa upon Native Society and the World of Christian Missions* (London, 1933; 2nd ed. 1967).

The Legacies of Missionary Science

However, the rise of Marxist/materialist anthropology after the Second World War and the declining interest of university-based scholars in religion gradually sealed the separation of missionaries and professional anthropologists.[59] But the marginalization of missionaries from the development of anthropological theory and practice was not the end of the story. Van den Bersselaar notes that missionary "research remains valuable to scholars because of the specific ethnographic detail they offer, or because their interpretations have been enthusiastically embraced in the localities they were documenting." Missionary texts provide some of the best sources for historians seeking to reconstruct the period of culture contact in the late nineteenth and early twentieth centuries. And missionaries' subsequent desire to describe and show how different functioning parts of so-called tribal societies related to each other produced a wealth of data on material culture, trade and industry, religion, politics and culture, for those seeking to reconstruct the interwar period. Cinnamon shows how Nassau's work helped introduce the notion of the fetish into popular African and academic discourse. Trilles's controversial theory of the "Egyptian origins" of the Fang totemic cult retains an "enduring popularity" amongst local Fang studies enthusiasts. Basden saw himself as a representative of the Igbo within Nigeria and a spokesperson to the outside world; his work, which generalized a local model of the Igbo over a larger area, had a significant effect on the imagining and experience of Igbo ethnicity. Burton's collecting, photography, and ethnography influenced notions of Luba identity in a number of ways. His collections of sculpture and stunning ethnographic photographs helped provide the basis for a number of influential exhibitions of Luba art. He joined with Belgian administrators and legal practitioners in evolving notions of customary law. Like Basden's work on the Igbo, Burton's enthusiastic promotion of "Lubaland" helped extend the notion of Luba from a smaller (though enormously significant) precolonial polity into a colonial and postcolonial ethnicity. Burton's ethnography was taken up by the Luba ethnic nationalist and product of American Methodism, Jason Sendwe.[60] Missionary preoccupations and methods were quickly picked up by the first generation of educated African Christians and put to their own uses. Vinck notes that the influential Rwandan priest and scholar Alexis Kagame developed his language, history, and culture under Hulstaert's tute-

---

59. Walter E. A. van Beek, "Anthropologie et missiologie ou la séparation graduelle des partenaires," in *Anthropologie et missiologie*, pp. 41-43.

60. Harold Womersley, *Legends of the Baluba*, ed. Tom Reefe (Los Angeles, 1984), x.

Introduction

lage, publishing his first scholarly article in *Aequatoria*. Eichholzer's essay shows similar processes at work on the Gold Coast (Ghana).

One reason why missionaries' scientific contributions remain so useful is their reliance on local assistants and informants. Although the African contribution to knowledge production is not an explicit theme in this volume, it surfaces in a number of the essays.[61] Junod learned a great deal from and gave full credence to the knowledge and skills of Thonga specialists in both the natural and human sciences. Burton's understanding of secret societies along with his evangelistic strategy was shaped by the young male Luba evangelists with whom he worked, and Fisher's medical practice shifted in response to pressures from below. In contrast to the "shallow" data he collected from the Copperbelt, John V. Taylor's more successful research in Uganda drew heavily on local contacts and on his own knowledge of the vernacular. Earthy's research gained a great deal from the mediating role played by three female assistants, Mara, Rhoda, and Nyankwavane, and from the knowledge of an unnamed African catechist. Some Africans were far more than mere assistants. In his long relationship with Basel missionary Johann Christaller, David Asante worked as a collaborator and ally in the struggle to gain recognition for linguistic studies.[62] In the Congo, Hulstaert and Boelaert worked closely with three Mongo intellectuals: Louis Bamala, Pierre Mune, and Paul Ngoi.

However, Africans were not always "coproducers" of knowledge — or often junior partners. Missionaries were heavily reliant on Africans as informants, collectors, and researchers, but they took the data they provided and reclassified it, placing it into their own categories, publishing it in their own texts, and giving it their own meanings. One of the objects of the volume is to trace the passage of knowledge from "the field" to its final resting place on the printed page, and in that process the African contribution was often concealed. There were of course some notable exceptions such as "culture brokers" Edward Blyden and Samuel Johnson, who emerged out of the long history of West African engagement with Europe; or Z. K. Mathews, a member of Radcliffe-Brown's summer schools in Cape Town.[63] Another prominent

---

61. For broader discussion see Lyn Schumaker, *Africanizing Anthropology: Fieldwork, Networks, and the Making of Cultural Knowledge in Central Africa* (Durham, N.C., 2001).

62. Sonia Abun-Nasr, *Afrikaner und Missionar: Die Lebensgeschichte von David Asante* (Basel, 2003).

63. See essays in P. F. Moraes Farias and Karen Barber, eds., *Self-Assertion and Brokerage: Early Cultural Nationalism in West Africa* (Birmingham, 1990), particularly Robin Law, "Constructing 'a Real National History': A Comparison of Edward Blyden and Samual Johnson"; Monica Wilson, ed., *Freedom for My People: The Autobiography of Z. K. Matthews* (London, 1981).

example of an African able to shape and disseminate his own data was Jomo Kenyatta, the London School of Economics–trained anthropologist who was to become the first Kenyan president. Yet even he adopted and exploited a functionalist version of anthropology made popular by Malinowski and his associates. African intellectuals who wrote and published on culture did not appear in great numbers until the late colonial era. Hence they appear in only a handful of our chapters. The African context was very different from that found in India where there was a well-established, literate, indigenous tradition of knowledge production. Fundamentally, the emphasis of this volume is on *missionaries* as creators of texts, images, exhibitions, and policies; and on the contexts and encounters that influenced their intellectual world.

Though missionaries increasingly parted ways with professional social anthropology, their influence on university disciplines did not cease. Maxwell raises the question of the origins of African philosophy and African religious studies in his chapter. He demonstrates how Placide Tempels's classic, *Bantu Philosophy* (1945), emerged from the rich vein of research on the Luba, and more broadly, how missionary concern with systematizing African ideas of God developed into African religious studies.[64] In the post-1945 era of rapid social change, missionaries and their organizations came under renewed pressure to develop what Erlank terms an interest in the "particular character of Christianity."[65] As Stuart observes, "the Christian church's encounter with non-Western faiths, with nationalism and secularism, and with itself" continued to inspire a concern with what it meant to be an African Christian. Missionaries were acutely aware of the growth of independency and wanted to hold on to the process of indigenization of Christianity in the name of orthodoxy. A new type of research was needed to address such issues, and Taylor's *Christians of the Copperbelt* (1961) built on earlier experiences on the Witwatersrand to create what Stuart describes as "a kind of hybrid, part history, part sociological and anthropological analysis and part theological exploration." Taylor and his missionary colleagues developed an approach to

---

64. However, the successful ways in which missionaries on the Copperbelt organized libraries and sporting activities for Africans, especially under the auspices of Thomas Cullen Young, did much to inspire a renewed interest in cultural anthropology and the benefits it could bring to their profession. This revival was a feature of the World Missionary Conference at Madras in 1938; see Hendrik Kraemer, *The Christian Message in a Non-Christian World* (Grand Rapids, 1956). On Cullen Young, see Peter G. Forster, *T. Cullen Young: Missionary and Anthropologist* (Hull, 1989).

65. This interest began at Edinburgh, High Leigh, and Le Zoute in the years 1910-1929 and continued in the Copperbelt in the 1930s under the influence of John Merle Davis and others.

Introduction

the study of society that blunted the ability of African prophets to seize Christianity from below and that, instead, encouraged a theologically staged dialogue with African culture, later termed "inculturation."

In reality, these dialogues were often no more than "top-down" programs of missionary social engineering, and in consequence they were often met with indifference by African Christians who preferred their own creations of popular Christianity.[66]

The prospect of syncretism and fragmentation was initially one of missionaries' greatest fears for the future of the African church. But as the study of Africa moved in new and dynamic directions as colonies became independent and university departments turned to the study of the continent, a scholar like Bengt Sundkler came to change his mind on this issue. In 1949 he was appointed chair of church history in Uppsala, and this move to academia freed him from the obligation of defending religious boundaries and asserting missionary definitions of orthodoxy. By 1976, when he published *Zulu Zion,* he no longer viewed "nativistic" Christian movements, the subject of his 1948 *Bantu Prophets,* as "a bridge" that led back to paganism.[67] Instead, they had become "a bridge to the future." But whatever the shortcomings of some of Sundkler's initial conclusions, his research on South African Christianity was enormously significant from the outset. What missionaries had previously dismissed as "sects" or "Native Separatist Churches," Sundkler rechristened African Independent Churches providing wonderfully detailed and evocative accounts of their innovative ideas and practices.[68] The force of his work lay in his intricate prose portraits of the movements' prophetic leaders: their hymns, testimonies, and prayers, their ecstatic practice and mountaintop experiences. Sundkler's *Bantu Prophets* became, as Stuart notes, "required reading for missionaries bound for Africa," but its influence extended far beyond that, attracting the attention of Max Gluckman, founder of the Manchester School of Anthropology, who gave it an enthusiastic review in

---

66. Richard Werbner, "The Suffering Body: Passion and Ritual Allegory in Christian Encounters," *Journal of Southern African Studies* 23, no. 2 (1997): 314; David Maxwell, introduction to *Christianity and the African Imagination: Essays in Honour of Adrian Hastings,* ed. David Maxwell, with Ingrid Lawrie (Leiden, 2002), pp. 10-11; David Maxwell, *Christians and Chiefs in Zimbabwe: A Social History of the Hwesa People* (Edinburgh, 1999), pp. 92-93.

67. Walter E. A. van Beek, "Anthropologie et missiologie ou la séparation graduelle des partenaires," in *Anthropologie et Missiologie,* p. 34.

68. Bengt Sundkler, *Zulu Zion and Some Swazi Zionists* (Oxford, 1976), p. 305. Sundkler's shift is evident in the 1961 edition of *Bantu Prophets.* On syncretism as a missionary defense of religious boundaries, see Rosalind Shaw and Charles Stewart, introduction to *Syncretism/Anti-Syncretism: The Politics of Religious Synthesis,* ed. Shaw and Stewart (London, 1994), pp. 1-26.

the influential journal *African Affairs*.[69] In Uppsala Sundkler continued his academic and practical commitment to Africa, making him the pioneer of what Adrian Hastings calls "African Christian Studies."[70]

Finally, it is within this milieu of postwar missionary thinkers that antecedents of the discipline of professional African history can also be found. Another important transitional figure was Edwin Smith. Smith's work was highly appreciated by the first generation of African theologians. His functionalist, organic model of African society resonated with the homogenizing aspirations of nationalist politicians, even though his highly systematized view of the African pantheon drew heavily from Judeo-Christian sources.[71] Smith served as the external examiner of Isaac Schapera's Ph.D. thesis at the London School of Economics and went on to review Roland Oliver's *Missionary Factor in East Africa* (1952) for *African Affairs,* bestowing upon it his imprimatur.[72] By that stage, Oliver was pioneering the embryonic discipline of African history at the School of Oriental and African Studies in London University. As Stuart notes, Oliver also worked with John V. Taylor, encouraging him to embark on a later sequence of work on Uganda. Taylor's East African research was picked up by a group of young historians in the emergent Dar es Salaam "school" of African history who searched for high-quality, sensitive research on the region. His booklet *Processes of Growth in an African Church* (1958) has had an impressive longevity, providing the interpretative model of Christianization for John Iliffe's *Making of Modern Tanganyika* and more recently for John Lonsdale's essay "Kikuyu Christianities." Terence Ranger's sympathies were also initially shaped by Taylor's *Primal Vision* (1963).[73] In a similar manner, the pioneering historian of central Africa, Jan Vansina, built upon the work of *Aequatoria*. These examples of Smith, Taylor, and Sundkler can be multiplied with the critical biographies of other missionaries. They serve to show how missionaries continued to shape knowledge about Africa into the recent past. Oliver did, albeit briefly, acknowledge the contribution

---

69. Max Gluckman, "Review of Bantu Prophets in South Africa," *African Affairs* 48 (1949): 191, 167-68.

70. Hastings, "African Christian Studies, 1967-1999."

71. John Mbiti, *African Religions and Philosophy* (London, 1969).

72. Edwin Smith, review of *The Missionary Factor in East Africa, African Affairs* 52, no. 207 (1953): 163-66.

73. John V. Taylor, *Processes of Growth in an African Church* (London, 1958); Taylor, *The Primal Vision: Christian Presence amid African Religion* (London, 1963); John Iliffe, *A Modern History of Tanganyika* (Cambridge, 1979); John Lonsdale, "Kikuyu Christianities: A History of Intimate Diversity," in *Christianity and the African Imagination;* Terence Ranger, "Concluding Summary," in *Religion, Development, and African Identity,* ed. K. Holst-Peterson (Uppsala, 1985).

Introduction

of missionaries to geography, philosophy, and linguistics in his *Missionary Factor in East Africa*.[74] His awareness of this dimension of their work doubtless sprang from his proximity to a number of dynamic missionary thinkers. It is intended that this series of essays will revive interest in the pioneering work undertaken by missionaries in various fields of knowledge and that it will add to our understanding of the history of both the human and natural sciences in Africa.

---

74. Roland Oliver, *The Missionary Factor in East Africa* (London, 1952), pp. 90-92.

CHAPTER 1

Natural Science and Naturvölker: *Missionary Entomology and Botany*

PATRICK HARRIES

The history of science has traditionally rested on the heroic narratives of discovery produced by great men in the field. Little has been written on the humdrum sailors, soldiers, doctors, and colonial officials who carried questions and instruments into the periphery of their world. Even less has been written about their informants and the ways in which their knowledge contributed to the construction of science as a universal concept and practice.[1] Until recently, when scholars mentioned the role of missionaries in the spread of science, they often portrayed these men of the cloth as obdurate cultural chauvinists who fueled late-nineteenth-century racism with their wholesale denunciation of the dark practices and irrational superstitions of native peoples.[2] More recently, scholars have written about the contribution made by many missionaries to knowledge in a range of secular fields in scattered parts of the world. This new literature situates the driving force behind the missionaries' scientific interest in a curiosity that was more theological and intellectual than economic or administrative. Missionaries were natural

1. For recent exceptions, cf. J. Delbourgo and N. Dew, eds., *Science and Empire in the Atlantic World* (New York, 2008); K. Raj, *Relocating Modern Science: Circulation and the Construction of Knowledge in South Asia and Europe, 1650-1900* (Houndsmill, 2007); W. Beinart, K. Brown, and D. Gilfoyle, "Experts and Expertise in Colonial Africa Reconsidered: Science and the Interpretation of Knowledge," *African Affairs* 108, no. 432 (2009); Janet Browne, "Biogeography and Empire," in *Cultures of Natural History,* ed. N. Jardine, J. A. Secord, and E. C. Spary (Cambridge, 1996).

2. Philip Curtin, *The Image of Africa* (Madison, Wis., 1973), 2:324-26; Janet Browne, *Charles Darwin: Voyaging* (London, 1995), p. 328.

fieldworkers, salaried individuals who belonged to institutions capable of supporting global networks of intellectual activity.[3]

In this chapter I want to follow the links between missionaries practicing entomology and noneconomic botany in Africa and the institutions in Europe that supported this work. Global religious institutions allowed missionaries to collect and compare specimens, and observe their behavior, from an early stage in a wide range of ecological areas. At the same time, missionaries were able to build correspondence networks and personal ties that linked them to an eminently global field of scholarship. Missionaries were called by their profession to specific regions for long periods, undertook extensive travels, and acquired a knowledge of local languages and customs. They were among the last of the amateur savants who, in an age before specialist knowledge separated the arts from the sciences, practiced a holistic approach to the interaction between humans, animals, and plants. They lived "in the field," traveled widely, and communicated with indigenous individuals and communities in intimate ways over lengthy periods. In the process, some missionaries acquired an understanding of the ways indigenous people ordered and explained nature. This encounter between imported and local systems of knowledge engendered a synthesis of skill and know-how that, particularly in the "late Renaissance," was not dominated by metropolitan institutions or their wealthy and powerful patrons. The first part of this chapter looks at Catholic missionaries in central and northeastern Africa during this period; it examines some of the ways they wrote about nature. In the second part I turn to Protestant interlopers in a Catholic world before examining the work of major missionary-naturalists in the first half of the nineteenth century. In the fourth and longest section I highlight the widespread nature of missionary work in the natural sciences from the mid–nineteenth century. I then look briefly at some of the uses to which missionaries put this knowledge before moving to investigate how they interacted with indigenous naturalists. Here I

---

3. David N. Livingstone, "Scientific Inquiry and the Missionary Enterprise," in *Participating in the Knowledge Society: Researchers beyond University Walls*, ed. Ruth Finnegan (Basingstoke, 2005); Sujit Sivasundaram, *Nature and the Godly Empire: Science and Evangelical Mission in the Pacific, 1795-1850* (Cambridge, 2005); J. M. MacKenzie, "Missionaries, Science and the Environment in Nineteenth-Century Africa," in *The Imperial Horizons of British Protestant Missions, 1880-1914*, ed. Andrew Porter (Grand Rapids, 2003); Sujit Sivasundaram, "Natural History Spiritualised," *History of Science* 32 (2001); Neil Gunson, "British Missionaries and Their Contribution to Science in the Pacific Islands," in *Darwin's Laboratory: Evolutionary Theory and Natural History in the Pacific*, ed. Roy MacLeod and Philip F. Rehbock (Honolulu, 1994). See also Mark W. Graham, "'The Enchanter's Wand': Charles Darwin, Foreign Missions, and the Voyage of H.M.S. Beagle," *Journal of Religious History* 31, no. 2 (2007): 133-34.

show that, even as they separated science from superstition, and magic from materialism, some missionaries continued to believe that Africans systematized knowledge, and explained and exploited nature, in ways that were "scientific."[4]

I note in this final section that the professionalization of entomology and botany pushed missionaries into the category of "amateurs," a role that sharply devalued their contribution to natural history, and even more so that of the indigenous experts with whom they exchanged information.[5] The unimpeded movement of scientists and their institutions from the metropole to the periphery, of which Basalla and Latour write, helped professionalize botany and entomology in Africa and created a certain national autonomy in these fields.[6] But as I point out at the end of this chapter, Western beliefs and practices also came to reshape the definition of "science" on the edge of a world increasingly dominated by Europe. This chapter focuses squarely on the work of missionary naturalists. But I hope it will also suggest ways in which their societies served to spread the results of Africans' observations and investigations of nature. Finally, I hope it will give some indication of the ways in which science came to be viewed as both a "Western" practice and a system of belief that could be carried from a benevolent metropole to an empty periphery.

Exploration and the Systematization of Knowledge

The first Europeans to explore the coast of Africa were driven by a desire to find new sources of gold and to discover a sea route to the east. But they were also driven by a deep curiosity about the world and its elements. The Vatican at first took little direct interest in this "new world" and entrusted the spread of Christianity in Africa to the Portuguese Crown. The Portuguese returned the compliment by sending an Indian elephant to the court of Pope Leo X in

---

4. On science as "organized knowledge," see J. M. Mackenzie, ed., *Imperialism and the Natural World* (Manchester, 1990), p. 5. Arthur Radcliffe-Brown thought science to be "knowledge systematised"; *Cape Times*, 9 January 1924. David N. Livingstone stresses that the meaning of science is not preordained. It is a human construction, persistently under negotiation. Livingstone, *Putting Science in Its Place: Geographies of Scientific Knowledge* (Chicago, 2003), p. 13.

5. Alix Cooper shows this process at work in Europe in *Inventing the Indigenous: Local Knowledge and Natural History in Early Modern Europe* (Cambridge, 2007).

6. George Basalla, "The Spread of Western Science," *Science* 156 (1967); Bruno Latour, *Science in Action* (Milton Keynes, 1987).

Natural Science and Naturvölker

1511, and a rhinoceros a few years later. Both animals achieved enduring fame: Benini commemorated the popular "Hanno" in an obelisk on the Piazza della Minerva and Dürer drew an image of the rhinoceros (exotically armored and furnished with a horn on its back) that would burn itself into the European imagination for the next 250 years. A decade later King Manuel informed Leo X of a Christian king in Ethiopia, Prester John, who was prepared to subject himself to the Roman Church and ally himself with the enemies of Islam. During these years, support for missionary activity waxed and waned according to the interest of the Portuguese king and the times in which he lived. During the sixteenth century Mozambique developed an unenviable reputation for its fevers and fierce warriors while the slave trade undermined the Christian allies of the Portuguese in the kingdom of Kongo. The spices of the East Indies and the sugar of Brazil consumed the attention of both the Portuguese king and the first Jesuits who arrived in Kongo in the mid-1540s and in Ethiopia and Mozambique a decade later.[7] The Vatican was equally fickle in its funding of the spiritual salvation of Africa, although a series of Renaissance popes did serve as patrons for the publication, display, and circulation of work treating the continent.[8]

The small groups of missionaries funded by the Portuguese initially paid more attention to the spiritual and ecclesiastical needs of Africa than to the geology, botany, and zoology of the continent. Perhaps most notably, Father Gaspar de Conceição produced a Kikongo catechism in the mid-1550s (the predecessor of a Kikongo grammar published in Rome a century later).[9] But their works sometimes included short descriptions of nature — such as the list of wild animals and birds included by the Portuguese priest Françisco Alvarez in his account of the embassy sent by his king to Ethiopia in the 1520s.[10]

The Catholic Church provided employment for adventurers like Jan

---

7. Dauril Alden, *The Making of an Enterprise: The Society of Jesus in Portugal, Its Empire and Beyond, 1540-1750* (Stanford, 1996), pp. 55-56, 75-76, 213-15.

8. Most notably that of Filippo Pigafetta, who met the adventurer Duarte Lopes in Rome and based his *Relatione del Reame di Congo* (1591) on his notes. For the contacts between the papal court and Africa in the early part of the century, see Natalie Zemon Davis, *Trickster Tales: In Search of Leo Africanus, a Sixteenth-Century Muslim between Worlds* (New York, 2006), pp. 66-68.

9. Georges Balandier, *Daily Life in the Kingdom of the Kongo: From the Sixteenth to the Eighteenth Century* (New York, 1968), p. 231. Adrian Hastings stresses the influence of the Kikongo catechism written in 1624 by the Jesuit Father Mateus Cardoso. Hastings, *The Church in Africa, 1450-1950* (Cambridge, 1994), p. 91.

10. Alvarez, *Narrative of the Portuguese Embassy to Abyssinia during the Years 1520-1527* (1540; London, 1864), pp. 406-7.

Huygen van Linschoten, who spent over five years in the service of the Portuguese archbishop of Goa (1583-89). On his return home to Enkhuizen, Linschoten found the town had joined the United Provinces and declared its independence of the Spanish king who at that time ruled Portugal. The information he brought home about the Indian Ocean encouraged Dutch merchants to send an exploratory expedition in 1595 into this world controlled by the Portuguese. In his *Itinerario,* or travel book, Linschoten provided accounts of the Portuguese trading stations on the Asian edge of the Indian Ocean and, particularly, on the natural environment and commercial products of the region. He supplied his readers with long accounts of exotic pineapples, mangoes, cashews, a large variety of spices and woods, and rare and precious stones (including bezoars, used to counteract poisons and various diseases, which sold for more than a unicorn's horn in Europe). Linschoten wrote his book with the help of Bernardus Paludanus, a naturalist in Enkhuizen whose collection included objects gathered in West Africa and other parts of the world. Paludanus had studied at the University of Padua, had traveled in Egypt and Syria, and was familiar with the emerging genre of writing on the natural history of newly discovered lands. He influenced the composition of Linschoten's *Itinerario* in such a way that it emerged as a work of annotated scholarship as much as a personal account of one man's travels. Importantly for this chapter, the book included a brief description of Mozambique, where Linschoten spent two weeks in August 1583, and of the gold, ambergris, ebony, ivory, and slaves found at the island and used in the trade with India. The work also provided a description of parts of West Africa and west-central Africa, taken from existing accounts, and diffused this information through translations into English, French, German, and Latin.[11]

By the start of the seventeenth century, Portuguese support for the activities of the church in Africa had grown sufficiently for Father João dos Santos to publish a monograph on the natural history of Mozambique. A Dominican missionary who spent the years 1586-97 in Sofala, Tête, the island capital of Mozambique, and the Querimba islands, dos Santos wrote extensively about the fauna and flora of the region in his *Ethiopia Oriental* (1609).[12] This work contained chapters on the fruits and cereals of Mozambique as well as

---

11. Jan Huygen van Linschoten, *Voyage to the East Indies* (1596; London, 1885), 1:33, 271; 2:142-45. The work on west-central Africa was drawn from Pigafetta's description of the Congo (see note 8 above) while that on the "Gold Coast" came from the pen of a Dutch sea captain, Barent Ericksz, who visited the area in 1593. Harold Cook, *Matters of Exchange: Commerce, Medicine, and Science in the Dutch Golden Age* (New Haven, 2007), pp. 121-28.

12. Joao dos Santos, *Ethiopia Oriental, e varia historia de cousas notaveis do Oriente* (Evora, 1609).

on ants, beetles, sharks, fish, turtles, whales, lizards, crocodiles, snakes, lions, leopards, wild dogs, monkeys, baboons, and other animals. But dos Santos did not just provide a detailed account of the natural world; he occasionally compared plant species (such as the pineapples of Mozambique with those of Brazil) and stressed their utility. This led him to describe some startling diseases — such as the *entaca* that caused women to dry up and die slowly after taking an herb designed to terminate an unwanted pregnancy. At the same time, he described a malady that brought on blindness between sunset and sunrise. Even more startling were the antidotes to these ailments — such as ingesting the juice of another herb within twenty-four hours of contracting the *entaca*, or sleeping with a man in such a way as to pass the disease to him. The night blindness could be cured by washing the affected eyes in the drinking water of pigeons, by roasting and eating the intestines of lampreys, or merely by quitting Mozambique. The skin of a *thinta* fish was likewise a powerful medicine against colic when toasted, crushed, and drunk in a wine glass.[13] Marvels also made their way into dos Santos's book. He had heard that elephants lived for over 300 years and could breed and produce young only after 100 years. He knew that the coastal waters provided a habitat for swordfish that were as large as the whales with which they engaged in battles off the coast. Mermaids frequented the same waters, and their long incisors could be fashioned into beads used to counteract hemorrhoids and to diminish menstruation pains. Although the bodies of these "women-fish," from the belly to the neck, were like those of men and women, they were in truth more akin to women, they did not sing (as was generally believed), and they were unable to live out of water. To the northeast of Tête, a saltwater fountain had the capacity to transform bits of wood, when hurled into its waters, into heavy blocks of stone.[14] But Father dos Santos was also skeptical of many of the tales he heard. He doubted that enormous eagles were capable of seizing elephants and dashing them on the ground, as Marco Polo had claimed occurred on an island south of Madagascar. And although he was frequently assured that a snakebite could be cured by biting the reptile, he thought this "to be a fiction."[15]

Only after 1622, when the Vatican established its missionary wing, Propagande Fide, did the Portuguese reluctantly open their seaborne empire to missionaries drawn from other Catholic countries. This opening widened considerably in the 1640s when the Dutch occupied parts of Angola, and the

---

13. Dos Santos, *Ethiopia Oriental*, book 1, chapter 26; book 2, chapter 12.
14. Dos Santos, *Ethiopia Oriental*, book 1, chapters 25, 27; book 2, chapters 7, 16.
15. Dos Santos, *Ethiopia Oriental*, book 1, chapters 23, 24.

Spanish king, hoping to pierce the monopoly held by the Portuguese, funded the establishment of a Capuchin mission in west-central Africa. In 1648 the Capuchins produced a brief account of the tribulations faced by their order in this region and appended to it a long description of the natural and human environment. This included the first account of manioc in west-central Africa, as well as descriptions of a range of local and imported fruits and vegetables. It also provided a picture of the animals living in the area, particularly its fearsome population of ants.[16] By the 1660s there were about seventy Spanish and Italian friars working in the Kongo and Angola who, together with Portuguese soldiers and administrators, started to disseminate knowledge about the natural history of the region.[17]

At this time the Italian Capuchin Antonio Cavazzi produced a major work on the kingdoms of the Congo, Angola, and Matamba.[18] Cavazzi's account of the fauna and flora of west-central Africa contained much of the enchantment found in other contemporary descriptions of Africa. He described flowers of such strong coloring that it was almost impossible to look at them for any length of time. His elephants were giants whose tusks could hardly be carried by two strong men, yet an ant could kill this pachyderm by climbing into its trunk and biting its brain. His foxes could smell the decomposition of a man's body before he had died. His blind serpent was equipped with heads at the two extremities of its body. In this world, knowledgeable individuals could extract powerful talismans from some of these animals: for the stones extracted from the stomachs of elephants and monkeys served as bezoars that provided an antidote to both paralysis and dizziness, while mermaids' ribs could be fashioned into beads that cleansed the air just as they assisted the circulation of the blood. The carbuncle on the forehead of a local species of wild boar was known to serve as an antidote to all poisons and fevers.[19]

Knowledgeable individuals attempted to put their learning to other local uses, wrote Cavazzi, when he reported on the exorcism used to rid a ship of a monster (worthy of Maurice Sendak) found clinging to its mast one hundred

---

16. Jean-François de Rome, *La foundation de la mission des Capucins au Royaume du Congo (1648)* (Rome, 1648; new ed., Louvanium, 1964), edited and translated from the Italian by F. Botinck, pp. 87-102.

17. Cf. António de Oliveira de Cardornega, *História Geral das Guerras Angolanas* (1681; Lisbon, 1972), II, part 4.

18. John K. Thornton, "New Light on Cavazzi's Seventeenth-Century Description of Kongo," *History in Africa* 6 (1979): 253.

19. Antonio Cavazzi, *Relation historique de l'Ethiopie Occidentale* (1687; French ed., Paris, 1732), pp. 151, 153, 156, 163-64, 175, 178, 186, 201.

Natural Science and Naturvölker

leagues from the African coast.[20] He interspersed his description of "prodigies" and "marvels" with accounts of snakes (fifteen feet long) and wild cats, as well as different species of monkeys and crocodiles. He expressed a particular fondness for ants that, in the Old Testament (Prov. 6:6), are touted as an exemplary role model for lazy and indigent humans. Huge numbers of large, black *inzeni* ants marched in "marvellous order" led by a "commandant" at the head of their column and another at the tail. If one of these leaders was killed, the ants first buried him and then searched out the "murderer" and put him to death. Another type of ant, called *salalé*, was red and white, quite round and small, but extraordinarily well organized and diligent. This made it extremely dangerous as the members of its species could ingest a twenty-foot cloth in one night and were known to have brought about the collapse of the Jesuit church in Luanda. Like their formidable white kinsmen in America, these "ants" built their underground habitations around a domed chamber housing the "King." Another species of small black ant was strong and able to defend itself by emitting a very disagreeable smell. Flying ants made up yet another species. Cavazzi wondered at their practice of discarding their old wings on leaving the nest to grow new ones as this brought them to the attention of the natives who devoured them (along with crickets and locusts). Another species of ant was capable of mounting highly coordinated attacks on man or beast; swarming over their prey, these ants could strip it to the bone in a short while. A final species, imbued with a strong smell and a very painful bite, made its home in the trees.[21]

A new modernity entered Cavazzi's work when he anthropomorphized animals and divided them into types that could be compared across continents. At the same time, he directly observed animals and their behavior, commented on plants (eight varieties of palm tree), and listened to locals' views on their utility. He also employed drawings to great effect to document and inform his textual observations. These included drawings of the African rhinoceros (based on Dürer's Indian model), a monstrous swordfish, the underside of a mermaid (or "woman-fish"), and an oil palm (with cannibals in the background). In this last case he combined his "scientific" view of Africa with a view of the dark practices of the continent's inhabitants — and in the process showed how "science" (the illustration of the palm tree) could not be separated from the "subjective" (his view of the locals' dark practices).

The same mixture of modernity and medievalism is evident in the writings of another Capuchin missionary in the Congo. Jean-François de Rome

20. Cavazzi, *Relation historique,* pp. 126-27.
21. Cavazzi, *Relation historique,* pp. 179-85.

was concerned to describe only those aspects of the kingdom that he had "observed as an eye witness." In his search for accuracy, he often used African terms to describe plants and animals. Yet at the same time he believed that people in the Congo lived for well over one hundred years.[22] Written in the third quarter of the seventeenth century, Jesuit Jerónimo Lobo's *Itinerário* was perhaps the first "scientific work" on Africa.[23] Samuel Johnson, the major figure in English life and letters, certainly believed this when he translated the book into English in 1735 (from an earlier French translation). It contained "no romantick absurdities or incredible fictions," wrote Dr. Johnson in the introduction:

> whatever he relates, whether true or not, is at least probable . . . he appears . . . to have described things as he saw them, to have copied nature from life, and to have consulted his senses, not his imagination. He meets with no basilisks that destroy with their eyes; his crocodiles devour their prey without tears. . . . The reader will here find no region cursed with irremediable barrenness, or blest with spontaneous fecundity; no perpetual gloom or unceasing sunshine; nor are the nations here described either devoid of all sense of humanity, or consummate in all private and social virtues; here are no Hottentots without religion, polity, or articulate language; no Chinese perfectly polite and completely skilled in all sciences.

And indeed, Jerónimo Lobo did dare to criticize Pliny the Elder's statement that elephants had no joints — and that they had to sleep standing up. He also criticized those who thought the hot sun responsible for the black color of the Ethiopians, and he was skeptical of the idea (found in the *Physiologus*) that ostriches ate red-hot, heated iron bars — though he accepted it as a possibility.[24] But he did report on the unicorn — which he described as "a beautiful horse of a chestnut colour with black mane and tail." He even described different species of unicorns — those in a neighboring province had short tails, while those living farther away "have long tails and manes that go down to the ground." At Mozambique Island, he reported, moonlight killed those who failed to wear hats outside in September; and straw had to be placed on

---

22. Jean-François de Rome, *La fondation de la mission* (1648; Paris and Louvanium, 1964), pp. 84, 103.

23. Jerónimo Lobo, *The Itinerário of Jerónimo Lobo*, trans. D. M. Lockhart from the Portuguese manuscript, n.d. [1660s-1670s?], ed. M. G. da Costa (London, 1984).

24. Lobo, *Itinerário*, pp. 97, 163, 166-67. Jean-François de Rome also criticized the idea that a tropical climate produced black skins; *Fondation de la mission*, p. 103.

Natural Science and Naturvölker

brass bells and cannon to protect them from the damaging moonlight. Elsewhere, he recounted that bodiless voices could be heard in one particularly dry place where people simply disappeared. Lobo also recycled descriptions of snakes that had in their heads a stone like a bezoar (the size of an egg) that had powers against poison. Smaller snakes had stones in their stomachs — but these were the size of a nut. He believed the bezoar and the unicorn's horn to be the most "effective antidotes" against snakebite — though when he fell ill with fever they did not seem to help him as much as goat urine, or bleeding by an Ethiopian villager using animal horns and a wad of paper (that perhaps acted as a spiritual defense).[25]

Lobo also saw the world as a Jesuit and so described a corposant (or Saint Elmo's fire) as a holy body that the sailors on his ship greeted with religious fervor. He believed God responsible for a terrible locust plague sent to punish the Ethiopians, and he wrote of a marvelous fountain that produced magic waters. This fountain had sprung up suddenly in 1541 when Christovão da Gama arrived in Ethiopia with 400 Portuguese soldiers to support the Christian king of the country against the Moslem jihad led by Ahmed Gran. But when da Gama was defeated and captured by Gran, he was decapitated — and where his head hit the ground the fountain "burst forth."[26] As Kaspar von Greyerz has shown, there was an easy compatibility and convergence in early modern Europe between ideas drawn from the Old Testament, the Greek and Roman classics, and the new discoveries. Well into the eighteenth century, leading scientists in Europe compiled their findings from a range of sources in which later generations would find fables and magic.[27]

What I have tried to show in this section is that the pre-Enlightenment sensibilities of Europeans and Africans were close to one another, and that locals reinforced missionaries' ideas, or provided them with useful knowledge. Indeed, the image of the double-headed snake or the elephant-slaying ant (or leech), the powers of a bezoar-like stone, and the individual's belief that he or she could pass on a malady by sleeping with an unsuspecting victim would remain common images in parts of Africa into the twentieth century. So would a belief in the bush spirits found in desolate places and the medical properties attributed to amulets and other protective talismans.[28] Perhaps

25. Lobo, *Itinerário*, pp. 41, 60, 137, 166. Jean-François de Rome also mentions cupping and bleeding; *Fondation de la mission*, pp. 120-21.

26. Lobo, *Itinerário*, pp. 12, 208, 214, 249.

27. Kaspar von Greyerz, ed., *Religion and Culture in Early Modern Europe, 1500-1800* (Oxford, 2008), pp. 18-23, 191.

28. Cf. in the Grassfields of Cameroon. Hastings, *The Church in Africa*, p. 75; Edwin

most importantly, local knowledge infused mermaids' ribs, bezoars, and carbuncles, as well as the missionaries' panoply of cures, with special use values crucial to global trade. The causes of disease were often local in nature, but the effectiveness of indigenous antidotes and remedies could appeal to a much wider, world market. In this sense collecting was not just about assembling objects; it was also about assembling the knowledge that gave those objects both intellectual meaning and commercial value.

The College Museum established in Rome by the Jesuit theologian and polymath Athanasius Kircher (1602-80) reflected the world discovered by missionaries and men of science, and featured particularly their maps of Africa.[29] But the Catholic Church's grip on knowledge would be increasingly challenged as Protestant nations from northern Europe first cracked and then broke the monopoly held by Portugal over the commerce of Africa. When the Dutch burst into the Indian Ocean at the beginning of the seventeenth century, they brought with them a new form of capitalism. But they also introduced new ways of looking at nature that were closely tied to their reformist, Christian beliefs.

Protestant Beginnings

The first Dutch fleet arrived along the coast of southeast Africa in 1602 — the year merchants in the Netherlands founded the Dutch East India Company (VOC). When attempts to seize the large Portuguese fortress on Mozambique Island failed, the Dutch turned to the Cape as a port of call on the way to the east. In 1624 a VOC fleet making its way to the East Indies stopped at Table Bay where the missionary Justus Heurnius collected plants, and made drawings and descriptions of ten species. It was one thing to accumulate this knowledge — and quite another thing to disseminate it. Justus did this by sending the drawings from the East Indies to his brother Otto in Leiden, who passed them to Johannes Bodaeus Stapelius, whose father Egbert printed them in *Theoprasti Eresii de Historia Plantarum* (Amsterdam, 1644).[30] Justus and Otto had graduated as doctors at the University of Leiden where their fa-

---

Smith and Andrew Dale, *The Ila-Speaking Peoples of Northern Rhodesia* (London, 1920), II, p. 224; H.-A. Junod, *The Life of a South African Tribe* (London, 1927), 1:393, 406; 2:339, 548.

29. Raymond Phineas Sterns, *Science in the British Colonies of America* (Urbana, Ill., 1970), pp. 35-43; Paula Findlen, *Possessing Nature: Museums, Collecting, and Scientific Culture in Early Modern Italy* (Berkeley and Los Angeles, 1994).

30. M. C. Karsten, "Heurnius and Hermann, the Earliest Known Plant Collectors at the Cape," *Journal of South African Botany* 29 (1963): 26.

ther was a professor of medicine. A deeply religious man, Justus decided to become a missionary instead and wrote a "Memorandum on the evangelical mission to be undertaken to the Indies" in which he called on the VOC to promote Christianity in its territories. However, the VOC, like its equivalent in the Atlantic, the Dutch West India Company, showed little inclination to bring the turbulence of religion to its economic activities. But some of its employees were missionaries or ministers of religion whose engagement with natural history was supported by a system of patronage and power that extended far beyond the companies for which they worked.

The VOC expanded rapidly in the eastern Indian Ocean, seizing Batavia in 1619, Colombo in 1656, and Macassar a decade later. While the Dutch West Indian Company consolidated its position in the south Atlantic by capturing Elmina in West Africa from the Portuguese in 1637, and briefly taking hold of parts of Brazil in the 1640s, the VOC established a refreshment station at the Cape in 1652. The sprawling Dutch seaborne empire turned Amsterdam and Leiden into centers for the collection of knowledge about the Americas, the Indies, and Africa. Several directors of the VOC served as patrons for the collection of the curiosities found in their trading settlements, and they supplied their king with a stream of *nouveautés* in the field of nature.[31]

The Cape was a halfway station for the Dutch fleets making their way to the east, and the missionaries who visited its shores inevitably aimed to establish themselves elsewhere. A French Jesuit on his way home from Siam, Guy de Tachard, stopped at the Cape in March 1686 and received from VOC naturalist Hendrik Claudius information on the human and animal inhabitants of the region. Governor Van der Stel regarded this as an illicit acquisition of knowledge that, when de Tachard's book appeared in print, resulted in Claudius's expulsion from the VOC settlement.[32] In 1706 the missionaries Bartholomäus Ziegenbalg and Heinrich Plütschau stopped at the Cape on their way to the Danish trading colony of Tranquebar on the Malabar coast of India. Employed by the Halle mission, both men wrote about the plants and animals they encountered at the VOC outpost near the tip of Africa, as well as

---

31. Especially the mayors of Amsterdam and Delft, Nicolas Witsen (1641-1717) and Hendrik d'Acquet. R. P. Brienen, "Nicolas Witsen and His Circle: Globalisation, Art Patronage, and Collecting in Amsterdam Circa 1700," in *Contingent Lives: Social Identity and Material Culture in the VOC World*, ed. Nigel Worden (Cape Town, 2007), pp. 446-47. The Dutch governor at the Cape, Simon van der Stel, established a small museum in the Gardens and, together with governors such as Joan Bax van Heerentals and Ryk Tulbach, sent large consignments of exotic plants, animals, and insects to Leiden.

32. L. C. Rookmaaker, *The Zoological Exploration of Southern Africa, 1650-1790* (Rotterdam, 1989), p. 18; Cook, *Matters of Exchange*, pp. 323-24.

about the flora and fauna of the East Indies.[33] When the VOC missionary François Valentijn returned home in 1714, he wrote a historical account and geographical description of all the VOC settlements in the East, including the Cape, where he had lived on four occasions.[34]

The Dutch established the first of the great global trading companies, but the English and French soon followed them. Jean-Baptiste Colbert, Louis XIV's finance minister, saw missionaries as men on the spot who could send home reports on the natural history of the areas of the world to which they were carried by their profession.[35] When the Royal Africa Company (RAC) fastened itself to the coast of West Africa in 1672, this British company quickly developed a trade in slaves as its principal economic activity. From the RAC headquarters at Cape Coast, the Reverend John Smyth sent the first plants from the Gold Coast to James Petiver at the Royal Society in London. Petiver took his knowledge to exclusive venues, like the Temple Coffee House, where he met with other collectors and wealthy patrons. In this environment he discussed the West African plants with Hans Sloane, and published a catalogue, with their names and properties, in the *Transactions* of the Royal Society (of which Sloane was at that stage the secretary).[36] Sloane later bought the contents of Petiver's "museum," and the plants duly entered his collection. He also bought numerous other collections, such as that of the Leiden botanist Paul Hermann, who had worked for the VOC at the Cape and elsewhere in the Indian Ocean.[37] The "curiosities" gathered by Sloane reflected the awe and wonder with which people gazed on the expanding natural world and heightened the urgency for it to be ordered and explained. Yet his collection, which formed the basis of the British Museum in 1759, also contained specimens that reflected older ways of seeing. In this way the fingers of Egyptian mummies (thought "proper for contusions" or bruises) were ranged alongside ground amethyst (an antidote for drunkenness), nephrite, and jade (be-

33. O. H. Spohr, "The First Danish-German Missionaries at the Cape of Good Hope, 1706," *Quarterly Bulletin of the South African Library* 21, no. 4 (1967).

34. Valentijn lived and worked in the Moluccas (1685-94) and in East Java and Ambon (1706-13). In the Netherlands he wrote *Oud en Nieuw Oostindien* (8 vols.).

35. Paul Fournier, *Voyages et découvertes scientifiques des missionnaires naturalists français à travers le monde pendant cinq siècles XVe à XXe siècle* (Paris, 1932), p. 230.

36. Petiver, "A catalogue of some Guinea-Plants, with their Native Names and Virtues; Sent to James Petiver, Apothecary, and Fellow of the Royal Society; with his Remarks on Them. Communicated in a Letter to Dr. Hans Sloane. Secret. Reg. Soc.," *Philosophical Transactions* [of the Royal Society] 19 (1695): 677-86.

37. Lodewijl Wagenaar, "Naturalia," in *Die Wereld binnen handbereik: Nederlandse kunst- en rariteitenverzamelingen, 1585-1735. Catalogus,* ed. Ellinoor Bergvelt and Renée Kistemaker (Amsterdam, 1992), pp. 41, 48, 127, 134.

lieved to alleviate kidney disease) or shavings from unicorns' horns (an effective remedy against poison).[38] The search for the unicorn, a prominent feature of biblical imagery, would continue to occupy missionaries well into the nineteenth century.[39]

Much of the enthusiasm that drove people to collect and order nature, and to diffuse their findings in expensive publications, found its impetus in natural theology. God's message could be read not only in the Bible, but also in nature, for nature was the product of his handiwork. Through his attention to the detail of nature, even the anatomy of insignificant insects, God showed his love for the world. "God's invisible nature," Christians could read in Romans 1:20, "that is, his everlasting power and deity, will be seen from the perception of his works, that is, the creation of the world." From this perspective, the fragile texture of a butterfly's wing or the design of a beetle's antennae emphasized God's care for the world; this view encouraged many to uncover and understand the laws through which God transformed nature and put it at the disposal of humankind. At the same time, the church and its institutions played an important role in the accumulation of knowledge both at home and abroad, and in its centralization in universities, museums, libraries, zoological and botanical gardens, and herbaria. The secular and the spiritual were enjoined in such intimate ways, in both individuals and their associations, as to make it difficult to distinguish a form of natural science untouched by Christianity and its practice. Collections served to display the wonders of God's creation while works on entomology or botany intertwined religious awe, emotion, and feeling with descriptions of God's handiwork.[40] Dutch painters particularly captured this spirit when, in the early seventeenth century, they abandoned biblical themes and produced finely detailed still

---

38. Kim Sloan, "'Aimed at Universality and Belonging to the Nation': The Enlightenment and the British Museum," and Ken Arnold, "Skulls, Mummies and Unicorns' Horns: Medicinal Chemistry in Early English Museums," in *Enlightenment: Discovering the World in the Eighteenth Century*, ed. Kim Sloan (London, 2003).

39. John Campbell, *Travels in South Africa* (London, 1822), 2:294; Rev. T. J. Bowen, *Adventures and Missionary Labours in Several Countries in the Interior of Africa from 1849 to 1856*, 2nd ed. (London, 1968), pp. 168-69. My thanks to Silke Strickrodt for this reference.

40. In the mid–sixteenth century the pioneering classifier and organizer of botanical specimens, Andrea Cesalpino, had worked as the physician to Pope Clement VIII and as a professor at the papal university. More than a century later the English clergyman John Ray developed new ways of classifying plants and wrote extensively on various animal species. At roughly the same time the revolutionary Dutch entomologist Jan Swammerdam used his observations of nature as a means of praising God and his works. Brienen, "Nicolas Witsen," p. 447. On Swammerdam, see Cook, *Matters of Exchange*, pp. 382-83.

lifes of flowers and fruit to which, later, they added shells, insects, butterflies, caterpillars, and other intricate products of God's hand. This spirituality led some to develop a form of Deism according to which "Nature" replaced the "Creator," or to see a transformation in the work of creation that could be called "natural history." It would lead others, like Ami Bost, the Swiss missionary who drew François Coillard to a missionary vocation, to regard learning with deep suspicion. "Science, the great golden calf of the academies," he would write in the early nineteenth century, "shows young people destined for the holy ministry that the gospel is only superstition . . . piety does not come from studying."[41]

Despite the strength of religious sentiment during the age of company expansion, the period saw a decline in missionary activity in Africa as the Portuguese lost their command of the seas and concentrated on the evangelization of more salubrious areas of their empire. French and British missionaries focused their energies on thriving colonies in the Caribbean, and Dutch missionaries invested their attention in the Sugar and Spice Islands. In Africa, this became the age of company botanists like Michel Adanson in Senegal and Palisot de Beauvois at the mouth of the Niger, the company soldier (Robert Gordon working for the VOC at the Cape), and the collectors sent out by wealthy patrons like Joseph Banks. Nevertheless, the hand of the church was not far behind many of their discoveries. Pierre Poivre was trained as a missionary and only abandoned this path when he lost an arm to the English in the war at sea. He went on to work for the Compagnie des Indes in Madagascar and, later, brought sugar and vanilla from the Caribbean to Île de France (Mauritius) and Bourbon (Réunion). Most importantly, he broke the VOC's stranglehold over the spice market when, on several occasions in the mid to late eighteenth century, he smuggled stocks of pepper, cinnamon, cloves, and nutmeg out of the Spice Islands (where this was strictly prohibited) and introduced them in the Mascarenes.[42] Even the irreligious Joseph Banks saw missionaries as informal collectors on the edge of empire and supported the establishment of their institutions in new colonies, such as the Cape at the end of the eighteenth century.[43]

During this period Johann Koenig, a student of Linnaeus, stopped at the Cape in April 1768 on his way to Tranquebar where he was to take up the post

41. Bost, *Mémoires* (Paris, 1854), II, p. 153.

42. Madeleine Ly-Tio-Fane, *Mauritius and the Spice Trade: The Odyssey of Pierre Poivre* (Port Louis, 1958).

43. John Gascoigne, *Joseph Banks and the English Enlightenment: Useful Knowledge and Polite Culture* (Cambridge, 1994); Gascoigne, *Science in the Service of Empire: Joseph Banks, the British State, and the Uses of Science in the Age of Revolution* (Cambridge, 1998).

Natural Science and Naturvölker

of medical officer to the Halle mission.[44] Inspired by Linnaeus and a number of leading British, German, and Dutch naturalists, a group of missionaries turned this center of evangelical activity on the Malabar coast into a global site for the study of the natural sciences. Several botanized at the Cape on their way to Tranquebar, from where they sent their findings to Europe to a transnational network of specialists, which included Joseph Banks.[45] João de Loureiro, a Jesuit father, paleontologist, and physician, botanized at Mozambique Island and Zanzibar on his return to Portugal from southeast Asia in the early 1780s.[46] In West Africa Henry Smeathman arrived in Sierra Leone where, instead of studying plants, as instructed by Banks, he spent three years examining the social behavior of termites and other insects.[47] Smeathman was a Swedenborgian whose entomological research (and his reluctant botanizing) fed into his desire to establish a utopian Christian community in Africa. Adam Afzelius (another of Linnaeus's students) and Carl Wadström were also Swedenborgians who visited Africa in the last decades of the eighteenth century to "make discoveries in botany, mineralogy, and other departments of science." Afzelius, serving as botanist to the Sierra Leone Company, received plants from Kew Gardens and dispatched bulbs to this center of imperial, botanical activity. Like Smeathman, he and Wadström hoped to establish a "primitive" Christian community in West Africa untrammeled by the corruption of modern life.[48]

---

44. Rookmaaker, *Zoological Exploration*, p. 18; for Valentijn, see Mary Gunn and L. E. Codd, *Botanical Exploration of Southern Africa* (Cape Town, 1981), p. 209.

45. Banks received about 500 botanical specimens from the Tranquebar missionaries between 1775 and 1780. John Gascoigne, "Joseph Banks and the Expansion of Empire," in *Science and Exploration in the Pacific*, ed. Marguerite Lincoln (Woodbridge, U.K., 1998), pp. 45-47. On the Cape, see the entry on Johan Rottler in Gunn and Codd, *Botanical Exploration*, p. 301. More generally, K. Hommel, "Physico-Theology as Mission Strategy: Missionary Christoph Samuel John's (1746-1813) Understanding of Nature," in *Halle and the Beginning of Protestant Christianity in India*, vol. 3, *Communication between India and Europe*, ed. A. Gross, Y. V. Kumaradoss, and H. Liebau (Halle, 2006); Mark Harrison, "Science and the British Empire," *Isis* 96 (2005): 62.

46. António de Figueiredo Gomes e Sousa, "Exploradores e Naturalistas da Flora de Moçambique," *Moçambique: Documentário trimestral* 18 (1939): 53-61.

47. Deirdre Coleman, *Romantic Colonization and British Anti-Slavery* (Cambridge, 2005); Starr Douglas and Felix Driver, "Imagining the Tropical Colony: Henry Smeathman and the Termites of Sierra Leone," in *Tropical Visions in an Age of Empire*, ed. F. Driver and L. Martins (Chicago, 2005).

48. Ray Desmond, *Kew: The History of the Royal Botanical Gardens* (London, 1995), pp. 96, 123; Robert Rotberg, "The Swedenborgian Search for African Purity," *Journal of Interdisciplinary History* 36, no. 2 (2005); Hugh Thomas, *The African Slave Trade* (London, 1997), p. 333.

At the Dutch colony on the southwestern tip of Africa, the Abbé Nicolas de la Caille observed the transit of Mercury in 1751, determined the positions of southern stars, measured the mean distances of the Moon and the Sun (in concert with colleagues in Europe), and calculated the shape of the Earth. He also gathered several plants that made their way to Benjamin Delessert's herbarium in Paris.[49] Churchmen also served as compilers of exotic knowledge. In 1728, two years after Louis XV ordered ships' captains operating out of Nantes to return home with seeds and plants, the former missionary and West Indian apostolic prefect Father Jean-Baptiste Labat compiled a long list of West African trees and plants taken from his reading of travel literature.[50] The Abbé Antoine Prévost, a Jesuit-trained Benedictine, excelled in this enterprise when he assembled texts on voyages in the same way that Buffon brought together a summary of all human knowledge under the title *Histoire naturelle*.[51]

Buffon was a passionate opponent of slavery — as were Wadström and yet another of Linnaeus's students in Africa, Andreas Sparrman. These *Aufklärer* combined their scientific forays into Africa with a determination to rid their work of the fantasy and fable that had marked earlier accounts of the continent. They also expressed a passionate denunciation of the slave trade; in the process they gave notice of the role that abolitionism would soon play in taking science and Christianity into the interior of Africa.

New Missionaries

Three weeks after the passage of the Abolition Bill in August 1807, a group of evangelical Anglicans played a prominent role in the establishment of the African Institution. Its members recognized "the enormous wrongs which the natives of Africa have suffered in their intercourse with Europe" and expressed a desire "to repair those wrongs" and "to promote their civilization and happiness." This included encouraging legitimate trade by collecting and diffusing information about the natural products and agriculture of Africa. At the same time, the gratification of curiosity that had marked earlier works

---

49. Harry Woolf, *The Transit of Venus: A Study of Eighteenth Century Science* (London, 1959); Rookmaaker, *Zoological Exploration*, p. 43.

50. J. B. Labat, *Nouvelle relation de l'Afrique occidentale*, 5 vols. (Paris, 1728).

51. Buffon's forty-four volumes compare with Prévost's fifteen. Buffon frequently quoted Prévost on, for instance, the efficiency with which central African bezoars countered poisons and other problems. Antoine François Prévost, ed., *Histoire Générale des voyages*, 5:83, cited in Buffon, *Histoire naturelle, générale et particulière avec la description du cabinet du Roi*, 12:244.

Natural Science and Naturvölker

on nature was increasingly replaced by a more systematic approach to its study.[52] A cocktail of concerns, stretching from scientific curiosity to moral reparation and commercial zeal, fired much of the exploration of the interior of Africa. Britain would also find a new empire in Africa to replace the one lost in North America and a new source of tropical goods to ease dependence on the politically volatile plantations of the Caribbean. Cape Town soon came to rival Freetown as a staging post in the adventure and excitement generated by the discovery of unexplored territories. In the early decades of the new century a posse of naturalists descended on the Cape to gather plants and animals for sale in Europe. Christian Hesse, the Lutheran minister in the city from 1800 to 1817, maintained a garden laid out with rare trees and shrubs, and sent plant and insect specimens to collectors in Europe, most notably Heinrich Lichtenstein at the new university in Berlin. He opened his home to visiting scientists and assisted their forays into the interior where they were helped by missionaries on both sides of the expanding imperial frontier.[53] On the eastern frontier of the colony, a missionary employed by the London Missionary Society (LMS), Johannes van der Kemp, drew up a description of the region at the turn of the century that included notes on its climate, geology, fauna, and flora.[54] George Thom, a Scottish Presbyterian who initially worked as a missionary for the LMS and later for the Dutch Reformed Church, sent plants to William Hooker, at that time regius professor of botany at Glasgow University, and purchased specimens on his behalf.[55] The botanical diversity of the Western Cape particularly dazzled collectors in Europe and led to a craze for its plants that attracted professionals to the region. These men lived off a commerce in "exotic" bulbs and plants until the 1850s when the development of glasshouses allowed the cultivation under controlled conditions of tropical species of plant life in Europe.[56]

The Royal Navy gave its support to the pursuit of science on the east coast

52. Robin Hallet, *The Penetration of Africa; European Exploration in North and West Africa to 1815* (New York, 1965), p. 351; Paul Hazard, *La Pensée européenne au XVIIIe siècle* (Paris, 1963), p. 424.

53. Cf. Lichtenstein et al., "An Early Cape Botanist," *Africana Notes and News,* June 1947; W. J. Talbot, "Pathfinders and Pioneers, Explorers and Scientists 1487-1976," in *A History of Scientific Endeavour in South Africa,* ed. A. C. Brown (Cape Town, 1977), pp. 14-15.

54. Johannes van der Kemp, "Specimen of the Caffra Language," *Transactions of the Missionary Society* 1, 2nd ed. (1795-1802).

55. Thom also collected geological specimens for Prof. Couper of the Hunterian Museum, Glasgow. Gunn and Codd, *Botanical Exploration,* p. 345.

56. Professor MacOwen, presidential address before the South African Philosophical Society, 28 July 1886, *Transactions of the South African Philosophical Society* 4, no. 1 (1884-86).

of Africa when it included a botanist on the hydrographic survey of East Africa undertaken by two warships operating out of Simonstown in the early 1820s; but it also allowed their commander, Captain William Owen, to report on the slave trade and to transport the Wesleyan missionary William Threlfall from Cape Town to his new posting on the southern shore of Delagoa Bay. The overlapping concerns of religion and science were also visible when in 1834 the Cape Town–based South African Institution organized a well-equipped scientific expedition into the interior. Led by Andrew Smith, this expedition aimed, among other things, to report on the religion of the natives they encountered and on the fragments of Christianity that had reached them.[57] Smith was helped by the LMS missionary at Kuruman, Robert Moffat, who, with a background as an estate gardener, would develop his own influential ideas on the relationship between deforestation and drought.[58] By this time, accounts of exotic plants, birds, and insects proved sufficiently attractive to a metropolitan readership for James Backhouse to include extensive descriptions of them in his narrative of a visit to the mission stations in South Africa.[59]

In the years after emancipation the abolitionist movement, frustrated by the Royal Navy's inability to halt the shipment of slaves to Brazil and Cuba, looked to science to harness the regenerative forces of West Africa. The ill-fated Niger expedition of 1841 carried two missionaries alongside a geologist, a mineralogist, a zoologist, and two botanists. Theodor Vogel gathered plants in Sierra Leone, on the Gold Coast, in Liberia, and along the Niger River and sent them to Kew Gardens where in 1849 William Hooker published *Niger Flora*.[60] Several botanical specimens were collected by further expeditions up the Niger in 1854 and 1857.[61] But by this time the high death rate among missionaries had caused the Church Missionary Society (CMS) to turn to a pol-

---

57. "Expeditions into the Interior of South Africa," *Journal of the Royal Geographical Society of London* 4 (1834).

58. These ideas particularly influenced the missionary John Croumbie Brown, who would go on to become the Cape's colonial botanist in 1862. R. Grove, "Scottish Missionaries, Evangelical Discourses and the Origins of Conservation Thinking in Southern Africa, 1820-1900," *Journal of Southern African Studies* 15, no. 2 (1989); William Beinart, *The Rise of Conservation in South Africa* (Oxford, 2003), pp. 99-116.

59. J. Backhouse, *A Narrative of a Visit to the Mauritius and South Africa* (London, 1844).

60. Lucile Brockway, *Science and Colonial Expansion* (New Haven, 2002), p. 131; David Turley, *The Culture of English Antislavery, 1780-1860* (London, 1991); Howard Temperley, *White Dreams, Black Africa: The Antislavery Expedition to the River Niger, 1841-1842* (New Haven and London, 1991).

61. Jean-Pierre Lebrun, *Introduction à la flore d'Afrique* (Paris, 2001), pp. 128-29.

icy of "native agency" that called on African missionaries to pioneer the spread of both Christianity and imported tropical plants in West Africa.[62]

The antislavery activities of the British succeeded in diminishing the number of slaves exported from West Africa, but, inadvertently, this strategy fostered a rapid growth in the slave trade along the east coast of Africa. The missionary explorer David Livingstone promised to combat this evil with a combination of commerce, Christianity, and science and, to this end, mounted a well-equipped expedition to penetrate the interior of east-central Africa. Although the evangelical endeavors of the Zambezi expedition of 1858-63 were foiled by a range of natural and human obstacles, its members were able to establish an experimental garden near Tête and, according to Livingstone, gather "considerable collections of plants, birds and insects." He felt that these "vegetable, animal and mineral productions" would make central Africa "better known in the world and thereby indirectly affect the slave trade." Livingstone also considered collecting to be a patriotic duty, for members of the expedition were honor-bound to offer any collections they took home to government museums so as to preserve their findings for the nation.[63]

Imperial institutions threw their weight behind the scientific aims of Livingstone's Zambezi expedition in a way that was still rare in the metropole. The Foreign Office provided Livingstone with consular authority and a salary of £500 a year; Parliament voted an annual sum of £5,000 to the enterprise; the Royal Navy's antislavery squadron (based at Simonstown) ferried missionaries along the coast; Kew Gardens, the British Museum, the British Association for the Advancement of Science, the Royal School of Mines, and, particularly, the Royal Geographical Society (RGS) assisted the project in a multitude of ways. It gained the backing of influential metropolitan intellectuals, such as Richard Owen (zoology) and Sir Roderick Murchison (geology).[64] Joseph Hooker drew up "the Principal Duties Expected of the Botanist" for John Kirk, the expedition's "Economic Botanist."[65] This remarkable

---

62. William Hooker, *Niger Flora* (London, 1849), p. viii.

63. Gary Clendennen, ed., *David Livingstone's Shire Journal, 1861-1864* (Aberdeen, 1992), p. 72.

64. Nicolaas A. Rupke, *Richard Owen: Victorian Naturalist* (New Haven and London, 1994), p. 364 n. 39; Robert A. Stafford, *Scientist of Empire: Sir Roderick Murchison, Scientific Exploration, and Victorian Imperialism* (Cambridge, 1989), pp. 174-79.

65. Lawrence Dritsas, "Civilising Missions, Natural History and British Industry: Livingstone on the Zambezi," *Endeavour* 30, no. 2 (2006); D. Liebowitz, *The Physician and the Slave Trade: John Kirk, the Livingstone Expeditions, and the Crusade against Slavery in East Africa* (New York, 1999).

civic and state support for missionary enterprise had started a few years earlier when Livingstone, a missionary of humble origins, had been turned into an icon of Victorian Britain after crossing the African continent on foot (1853-56). The RGS led this process by creating a media sensation about his geographical discoveries; the press built his reports on the slave trade into a reinvigorated moral crusade; and the leading publishing house of John Murray turned his account of the expedition into an international best seller.[66]

As a young man Livingstone had collected fossils and plants, and in the 1830s he had followed lectures in the natural sciences at Anderson's College (now Strathclyde University). He was a thoroughly modern missionary who scoffed at tales he heard in Africa of horned men three feet high, unicorns, or moon-blindness (other than the type caused by a lack of vitamin A).[67] His books, articles, and letters are replete with descriptions of climate, environment, geology, paleontology, mammals, birds, snakes, frogs, insects, and plants. He reported on the behavior of numerous species of wildlife, and documented for the first time the existence of both pygmy elephants and several new species of antelope. He was familiar with the findings of earlier naturalists such as William Burchell and Andrew Smith, and he counted the naturalist-hunter William Oswell as a close friend. Like Cavazzi, he was particularly fond of ants that, in their behavior, seemed to echo the actions of human beings. Livingstone found these insects to be "wise" when they calculated the effects of impending floods, "rapacious" when they devoured their food, and "tasty" when consumed by human beings. He wrote of "regiments of black soldier ants returning from their marauding expeditions . . . black ruffians . . . a grade lower than slave-stealers, being actually cannibals."[68] Yet he admired the pugnacity of driver ants as much as the "zeal and energy" of white ants (termites) whose building skills made them "little architects."[69] The extensive plant collections gathered by members of the Zambezi expedition allowed botanists at Kew to extend Hooker's *Niger Flora* into the first ex-

---

66. Felix Driver, *Geography Militant: Cultures of Exploration and Empire* (Oxford, 2001), chapters 2, 4.

67. David Livingstone and Charles Livingstone, *Narrative of an Expedition to the Zambezi and Its Tributaries* (London, 1865; new ed., 2005), pp. 148, 249, 437.

68. David Livingstone, *Missionary Researches and Travels in South Africa* (London, 1857), especially chapters 27, 30; Mackenzie, "Missionaries, Science and the Environment in Nineteenth-Century Africa"; H. H. Johnston, "Livingstone as a Man of Science," *Nature* 91 (1913): 89-90; H. Johnston, "David Livingstone: A Review of His Work as an Explorer and Man of Science," *Scottish Geographical Magazine* 29 (1913): 281-304.

69. Livingstone and Livingstone, *Narrative of an Expedition*, pp. 158-60.

tensive botanical survey of the continent. Edited by Daniel Oliver, the *Flora of Tropical Africa* depended on the collections of Afzelius, Smeathman, and Vogel, as well as material sent by Rev. W. C. Thomson from Calabar. It was completed by new collections of plants from south-central and southeast Africa assembled by Kirk, Livingstone, and other members of the Zambezi expedition, as well as by Charles Meller and Horace Waller of the associated Universities' Mission to Central Africa.[70]

Livingstone was not the only missionary explorer to call for science to aid the development of Africa, for in East Africa Johann Krapf appealed for "scientific men to explore the interior and to cultivate new resources to replace the slave trade." But the CMS missionary did not have Livingstone's skills as a naturalist, and his *Travels and Missionary Labours* presented an uncomfortable mix of scientific discoveries and easily disproved, classical myths about Africa. Whereas Livingstone wrote for a modern readership keen to uncover the rich diversity of human, animal, and plant life of Africa, Krapf addressed a public still eager to read of marvels and wonders in the Dark Continent. This led him to find Pygmies and troglodytes in East Africa, where they lived in the manner of animals, and to reproduce the ancient idea of a vast inland lake in the region feeding the Congo, Zambezi, and Benue Rivers.[71] Most importantly, unlike Livingstone, Krapf feared that the production of commercial crops would encourage the use of slave labor in Africa; and in general he was unwilling to subordinate his evangelical duties to "temporal benefits and improvements." Even in the short term, he feared that scientific and humanitarian interests would distract him from his religious mission. Hence, while Livingstone's prose was replete with references to natural history, Krapf's writings, like those of another great missionary explorer, François Coillard, said little about the subject.[72]

Clergymen in isolated postings in many parts of Europe had developed an engagement with nature as a means of communing with God while contributing to the scientific progress espoused by the learned associations in the

---

70. Daniel Oliver, *Flora of Tropical Africa*, I (London, 1868), pp. 10-11; B. Verdcourt, "Sir John Kirk's Field Drawings," *Curtis's Botanical Magazine* 4, no. 3 (2008).

71. Johann Krapf, *Travels and Missionary Labours in East Africa* (London, 1860), pp. 51-54, 58. Krapf's reports on the geography of East Africa appeared in the *Missionary Intelligencer* in the early 1850s and were criticized by W. D. Cooley, *Inner Africa laid open in an attempt to trace the chief lines of communication across the continent* (New York, 1852), pp. 21, 73-87.

72. R. C. Bridges, introduction to *Travels and Missionary Labours in East Africa*, by Johann Krapf, pp. 53, 66. For Krapf's critical views on the link between commerce and the slave trade, see p. 185.

capital.⁷³ Many missionaries took this tradition to Africa where they could study animal behavior *in situ* and where vast numbers of animal and plant species had yet to be discovered. Equally important, metropolitan organizers and explainers encouraged missionaries to send home evidence from the field in Africa. William Harvey and Charles Darwin were active in this regard in Britain, as were Auguste Forel, William Barbey, and Hans Schinz in Switzerland. In this way, the plant and animal species gathered by missionaries in various parts of Africa made an important contribution to the systems of classification and change developed by metropolitan intellectuals.⁷⁴ A talented individual like Livingstone, feted in the metropole and in the colonies, was able to raise the funding and political support needed to mount costly expeditions that combined science with Christianity and the fight against the slave trade. Yet the great explorer was also one of the innumerable missionary foot soldiers of science. The role of these men and women has remained hidden and to explore it would require a thorough examination of the archives of both scientific associations and missionary societies. It can only be mentioned briefly here. While some missionaries came to be recognized as important scientists, others played a more informal, supportive role in the gathering of evidence. But in general, missionaries played a significant role in the encounter around systematized knowledge that emerged in Africa as Europeans made their way into the continent.

Missionary Foot Soldiers of Science

In 1839 the Basel missionary Andreas Riis reported from Ghana that he would send collections of beetles and a number of stuffed birds to professors at the

---

73. Cf. Gilbert White, *The Natural History of Selbourne* (1788-89), and the work of the pioneering nineteenth-century entomologist Rev. William Kirby, J. F. M. Clark, *Bugs and the Victorians* (New Haven, 2009), pp. 14-33. See also Marc Weidemann, "Un pasteur-naturaliste du XVIIIᵉ siècle: Elie Bertrand (1713-1797)," *Revue Historique Vaudoise*, 1986; W. F. Cannon, "Scientists and Broad Churchmen: An Early Victorian Intellectual Network," *Journal of British Studies* 4 (1964); Charles J. Withers, "Geography, Natural History and the Eighteenth-Century Enlightenment: Putting the World in Place," *History Workshop Journal*, no. 39 (Spring 1995).

74. Robert Shanafelt, "How Charles Darwin Got Emotional Expression out of South Africa (and the People Who Helped Him)," *Comparative Studies in Society and History* 45 (2003); Patrick Harries, *Butterflies and Barbarians: Swiss Missionaries and Systems of Knowledge in South-East Africa* (Oxford, 2007); William Beinart, "Men, Science, Travel and Nature in the Eighteenth- and Nineteenth-Century Cape," *Journal of Southern African Studies* 24, no. 4 (1998): 793.

museum in Basel.⁷⁵ He also sent twelve cultural artifacts to Basel — including the earliest documented kente cloth in the world (now in the city's Museum der Kulturen). A few years later his colleague at the Akropong mission station, Georg Widmann, collected insects in the Akwapim Hills that he dispatched to Basel's new Natural History Museum. These included some startling specimens, such as a pair of Goliath beetles, the giant scarabs that are the largest known insects in the world. Widmann also included in his deliveries to Basel a number of fierce "drivers" or "visiting ants" that, he reported, had once gathered in a long column an inch wide and, invading his home, drove his family from the premises.⁷⁶ These ants (genus *Dorylus*) had been observed a few years earlier in Liberia where Thomas Savage, an American medical missionary, drew attention to their feeding habits and marching strategies. In 1847 he brought the attention of the world to these fearsome animals and their behavior when he published his observations in leading scientific journals in both Britain and the United States.⁷⁷ In the same year, Savage wrote to curators at the British Museum and the Natural History Museum in Paris about gorillas in Gabon and, a few months later, published in an American scientific journal the first detailed description of this new species of primate (that some would soon regard as a close relative of man).⁷⁸

The collecting of Hanna Bohner, the wife of a Basel missionary in Cameroon at the end of the century, was of a far more prosaic nature. With the help of mission schoolchildren, Frau Bohner first collected samples of algae in Cameroon that she sent to Mannheim where the mathematics teacher of her eldest son had been working on a collection of East African specimens gathered by Emin Pasha. She later dispatched a range of insects (which she described unfavorably as *Ungeziefer*, or vermin) to Mannheim where they were sold to raise the pocket money needed by her numerous school-going children. She also assembled a collection of snakes, some of which were venom-

---

75. Riis was in Ghana from 1832 to 1845. Seth Quartey, *Missionary Practices on the Gold Coast, 1832-1895* (Youngstown, N.Y., 2007), p. 56.

76. Ludwig Imhoff, "Über eine Art afrikanischer Armeisen," *Bericht über der Verhandlungen der Naturforschenden Gesellschaft in Basel* 10 (1852): 175-77, 180. Widmann was in Ghana from 1843 until his death in 1876.

77. Savage, "The driver ants of West Africa," *Proceedings of the Academy of the Natural Sciences* 4 (1847): 195-200; Savage, "On the habits of the 'drivers' or visiting ants of West Africa," *Transactions of the Royal Entomological Society* 5 (1847): 1-15.

78. T. S. Savage and J. Wyman, "Notice of the external characters and habits of troglodyte gorillas, a new species of orang from the Gabon River," *Boston Journal of Natural History* 5 (1847); Jürg Schneider, "Bruder oder Bestie? Die 'Entedeckung' des Gorillas im 19. Jahrhundert, in *Fotofieber: Bilder aus West- und Zentralafrika. Die Reisen von Carl Passavant 1883-1885* (Basel, 2005).

ous, that she preserved in spirits and sent to the Hungarian National Museum in Budapest.[79] Elsewhere in West Africa, Rev. W. C. Thomson and other missionaries of the United Presbyterian Church of Scotland engaged in botanizing after extending their endeavors from Jamaica to Calabar in 1846. They collected seeds and plants in (what today is) southeastern Nigeria and sent them back to Edinburgh where John Hutton Balfour, the professor of botany at the university, and keeper of the Royal Botanical Gardens, attempted to acclimatize and describe them.[80]

In southern Africa, French Protestant missionaries made their way from Cape Town into the interior where, in the 1830s-1840s, Jean Lemue and Thomas Arbousset documented numerous new species of plants and insects on the High Plateaux stretching from the Drakensberg to the Kalahari.[81] The next generation of missionaries in this region had a good grasp of Sesotho and, with the help of local assistants, Anna Dieterlen and Edouard and Hélène Jacottet noted the vernacular names of plants and collected information on their ritual, medicinal, and economic uses.[82] In the mid-1870s, Paul Berthoud left his colleagues in the Paris Evangelical Missionary Society in Lesotho to establish a French-speaking, Swiss mission in the foothills of the Zoutpansberg. He and his wife soon started to send home to Lausanne and Neuchâtel new species of interesting ants and beautiful butterflies. A few years after their mission extended its operations to southern Mozambique, it was joined in 1889 by Henri-Alexandre Junod. This missionary would amass a herbarium of well over 3,000 plant species in southeast Africa. He collected 384 different species of moths and butterflies and vast numbers of beetles, bugs, and other insects. From a makeshift "museum" outside his mission station, he sent these and many other specimens of nature to the Natural History Museum established by Louis Agassiz in Neuchâtel. Initially a pioneer in the fields of botany and entomology in southern Africa, Junod would later become the doyen of early anthropologists in the region.[83] Jean Borle would

79. Theodor Bohner, *Der Schumacher Gottes: ein deutsches Leben in Afrika* (Frankfurt, 1935), pp. 177-78. My thanks to Ulrike Sill for this source.

80. Particularly Hope Waddell and Hugh Goldie. J. Hutchinson and J. M. Dalziel, eds., *Flora of West Tropical Africa* (London, 1927), pp. 7-8. Balfour sent many of these plant specimens to Kew Gardens.

81. T. Arbousset, *Excursion missionnaire dans les Montagnes bleues* (1840; Paris, 2000), pp. 86, 109, 120-21, 133-34; J. Lemue, "Coup d'oeil sur le Kalagari: Les plantes," *Journal des missions évangéliques* [de Paris] 27 (1847): 67-80; Gunn and Codd, *Botanical Exploration*, p. 222.

82. E. P. Phillips, "A Contribution to the Flora of the Leribe Plateau and Environs," *Annals of the South African Museum* 16 (1917): 1-377; Gunn and Codd, *Botanical Exploration*, p. 200; Tim Couzens, *Murder at Morija* (Johannesburg, 2003), pp. 271-72, 468.

83. Harries, *Butterflies and Barbarians*, chapters 5, 8.

Natural Science and Naturvölker

carry his enthusiasm for the natural sciences into various parts of southern Africa in the early twentieth century.[84]

In Natal, Bishop John Colenso collected plants (some of which took his name, such as *Crinum colensoi* Hort) while his family botanized with passion and hunted for insects. The bishop's first cousin William, a CMS missionary in New Zealand, had supplied both William and Joseph Hooker with plants and had become one of Kew's most renowned collectors. In Natal, John's wife, Sarah Frances Colenso, collected ferns, mosses, orchids, and "new plants of all sorts"; she marveled at the land snails and other "treasures" found alongside the streams running through the kloofs leading from the escarpment. Inspired by Joseph Hooker, she captured the detail of flowers in her paintings. But while she approved of the devotion with which her daughter Agnes collected beetles for her brothers, she questioned the dedication with which her son Robert collected moths and butterflies, as this would distract him from the "serious things in life" at Oxford.[85] Yet, like her husband, she linked science indefatigably with progress. An interest in entomology and botany, believed Mrs. Colenso, indicated the superiority of her class. Because of "the dense ignorance of the people [and] their belief in witchcraft and the Devil, the fear of hell seemed all there was in the many who were above the mere animal."[86]

Although the Catholic Church was slow to return to the evangelization of Africa, Propaganda Fide encouraged its missionaries to "serve the different branches of science." "The missionary examines, sees, and compares," recorded its weekly bulletin in 1868; "applying new methods to strange phenomena, to unknown flowers, plants and trees, he thinks of the uses to be drawn by the mother country, and he addresses his notes to his superior or his friend."[87] In 1882 the Vatican's missionary wing, in the name of Pope

---

84. Gunn and Codd, *Botanical Exploration*, p. 100.

85. Wyn Rees, ed., *Colenso Letters from Natal* (Pietermaritzburg, 1958), pp. 139, 208-9, 219, 245, 357; Gunn and Codd, *Botanical Exploration*, p. 121. Mary Barber had offered to paint flowers for Hooker in the Eastern Cape; Beinart, "Men, Science, Travel," p. 795. On the botanizing of William Colenso, see Jim Endersby, *Imperial Nature: Joseph Hooker and the Practices of Victorian Science* (Chicago, 2008), pp. 49, 78-79, 87, 88ff.

86. Rees, *Colenso Letters from Natal*, p. 178. On Colenso's belief in the progress brought by science, see Jeff Guy, *The Heretic: A Study of the Life of John William Colenso, 1814-1883* (Johannesburg, 1983), pp. 166-67. The condescension of the educated classes was perhaps not a universal trait. Joseph Banks had learned a great deal from rustic bearers of local knowledge. Richard Drayton, "Knowledge and Empire," in *Oxford History of the British Empire: The Eighteenth Century*, ed. P. J. Marshall (Oxford, 1998), p. 237. See also Cook, *Matters of Exchange*, p. 135.

87. *Missions Catholiques* (1868), pp. 17-18.

Leo XIII, formally encouraged its members throughout the world to gather anything of value to natural history.[88] In fact, Catholic missionaries needed little encouragement to engage themselves in the taxonomy of botany, zoology, and other areas of scientific endeavor. French missionaries particularly led this field, for, as their country struggled to build a second colonial empire in Africa, their investigations of nature received the full support of the state's Natural History Museum in Paris.[89] In general, Catholic missionaries were not encouraged to move beyond taxonomy to speculate on the evolution of plants and animals; in a few instances, the Vatican took steps to prevent this.[90]

The Holy Ghost (or Spiritan) Father Charles Duparquet arrived in Libreville in 1855 and had soon gathered 400 plants, several of which represented new species and one a new genus. Eleven years later he moved to Mossamedes on the coast of southern Angola, from where he explored the Huila plateau and sent specimens of its plant life to the Natural History Museum in Paris. In 1871 he was stationed in the Congo, from where he sent home important observations in the fields of botany, geography, and ethnography. Eight years later Duparquet became the apostolic prefect of Cimbebasia, an area encompassing modern-day Namibia and Botswana. This allowed him to engage in extensive overland tours during which he gathered information on the climate, fauna and flora, geology, and human populations of the region. These tours allowed him to send plant specimens to the museum in Paris and both plants and rocks to the small museum run by the Marist Brothers in Cape Town. Duparquet also reported on his botanical findings to the Abbé Durand, the librarian and archivist of the Geographical Society of Paris who, in 1880, presented them to the French Association for the Advancement of Science. Six years later Duparquet explored Bechuanaland, where he discovered numerous new plant species in the Kalahari. During his career Charles Duparquet succeeded in sending large numbers of mammals, birds, and insects to France. A total of 1,372 of his plants arrived at the Natural History Museum in Paris; but this represented only a part of the botanical findings he sent to France before his death in 1888.[91]

---

88. Fournier, *Voyages et découvertes scientifiques,* p. 11.

89. Christophe Bonneuil, "Le Muséum national d'histoire naturelle et l'expansion colonial de la Troisième République (1870-1914)," *Revue française d'histoire d'outre-mer* 86 (1999).

90. M. Artigas, T. F. Glick, and R. Martinas, *Negotiating Darwin: The Vatican Confronts Evolutionism* (Baltimore, 2006); Paul Allen and Peter Hess, *Catholicism and Science* (Westport, Conn., 2008).

91. Fournier, *Voyages et découvertes scientifiques,* pp. 161-64; Abbé Durand, "Voyages du

Natural Science and Naturvölker

Another Spiritan, Father Théophile-Joseph Klaine, spent forty-five years in Libreville where he played a gargantuan role in the delineation and domestication of plants. In collaboration with the taxonomist Louis Pierre, famous for his work in Indo-China, Klaine uncovered 5 new families, 53 new genera, and around 200 new species of plants in this part of the "French Congo." In all, he sent 3,600 specimens to Pierre and, after the latter's death, to the museum in Paris. Klaine is today recognized as the pioneering collector of plants in Gabon.[92] Louis Pierre also encouraged Father Henri Trilles to gather plants and to send him specimens of the trees found northeast of Libreville. Trilles eventually dispatched up to 800 plants to Paris where, several taking his name, they found their way into the herbarium of the museum. He was also able to turn his knowledge of botany to the commercial production of rubber. As John Cinnamon points out in chapter 3 of this volume, Trilles is remembered principally today for his work in anthropology. But he was also a "physical anthropologist" who collected skulls of native peoples.[93] He was also familiar with minerals and, as an entomologist, sent to the museum in Paris large numbers of insects, particularly beetles and tsetse flies, some species of which also carry his name. Yet another Spiritan, Father Buléon, agreed in 1895, after ten years in Gabon, to establish himself at Aguma in the interior, south of Cape Lopez, to study chimpanzees and gorillas. He supplied the museum in Paris with the skins of various Quadrumana, mammals and birds, as well as samples of the mineral diversity of the country. He was also careful to take notes on the climate and people and to send these to the Central Meteorological Bureau and the Geographical Society in Paris.[94]

On the West African "slave coast" (Benin), Fathers Ménager and Chausse reported on local plants in 1874 and Father Courdioux wrote in 1883 on the area's contribution to medical and economic botany.[95] When the French made their way into the Uubangi-Chari region of northern French Equatorial

---

Père Duparquet dans l'Afrique austral d'après ses lettres [et] notice sur les diverses regions et tribus de la Cimbebasia," *Bulletin de la société de géographie* [de Paris], 1879, pp. 153-70, 275-92; Duparquet, *Viagens na Cimbebàsia* (Luanda, 1953).

92. Fournier, *Voyages et découvertes scientifiques*, pp. 165-66; J. Leandri, "Louis Pierre, botaniste de terrain et systématicien français," *Adansonia* 2, no. 3 (1963): 207-20.

93. Cf. the skulls he gave to A. Schenk, "Notes sur six crânes du Congo français," *Bulletin de la société neuchâteloise de géographie* 16 (1905).

94. Fournier, *Voyages et découvertes scientifiques*, pp. 166-70.

95. Ph. E. Courdioux, "Esquisse d'une flore médicale ou industrielle de la côte des Esclaves," *Missions catholiques*, 1883; D. Juhé-Beaulaton and A. Lainé, "Processus d'acquisition et de transmission des ressources thérapeutiques africaines dans les sources européennes du XVIIe au XIXe siècle," *Outre-mers* 346-347 (2005): 56.

Africa (present-day Chad), the Banda linguist Father Charles Tisserant collected both cryptogams and phanerogams. Established in the region in 1911, he collected some 500 species of moss, many of which were startlingly new, and sent 2,850 plants to the Natural History Museum in Paris.[96]

In Tanganyika, Spiritans such as Oscar Schweding, Yves Riou, and especially the Swahili linguist Charles Sacleux collected plants and maintained a correspondence with metropolitan institutions and experts. Once Sacleux had completed his linguistic work in 1886, he assembled a herbarium of 2,636 plants collected at Zanzibar and on the continent between Dar es Salaam and the equator. He also gathered a few mosses and mushrooms during his itinerations, and a herbarium of marine algae sent to the University of Montpellier. Sacleux also dispatched various fruits and vegetables to the museum in Paris; the glasshouses there once held 300 species that he had sent as seeds or young plants. He returned to Paris in 1898 to devote himself to determining the taxonomy of various botanical collections. Over 200 plants bear Sacleux's name today.[97] On the slopes of Kilimanjaro and elsewhere in the region, Monsignor Alexandre Le Roy collected insects, molluscs, Batrachia, and several hundred plants, while from the area east of Nairobi, Joseph Soul sent to the museum in Paris several new species of moss.[98] Cardinal Lavigerie's White Fathers also played a role in describing the natural history of this region of Africa. Members of the order sent molluscs from Lake Tanganyika to the French naturalist Jules-René Bourgignat, who produced an authoritative work on this subject in 1888. A decade later White Fathers stationed at Mpala supplied Edouard Foa, collecting for the Museum of Natural History in Paris, with numerous rare beetles and butterflies. Others collected minerals or, like Bishop Dupont at Chilubula (Nyassa), the venom of snakes, which was sent to the Pasteur Institute in Lille.[99]

In Mozambique the Jesuit missionary Ladislau Menyharth botanized in the Tête district in the 1890s while Junod collected plants in the south of the colony and in parts of neighboring South Africa. Both men sent specimens to the head of the Botanical Garden in Zurich, Hans Schinz, and published vari-

---

96. Fournier, *Voyages et découvertes scientifiques*, pp. 172-73.

97. J. A. Kieran, "The Origins of Commercial Arabica Coffee Production in East Africa," *International Journal of African Historical Studies* 2, no. 1 (1969): 53; Fournier, *Voyages et découvertes scientifiques*, pp. 174-75.

98. Fournier, *Voyages et découvertes scientifiques*, pp. 168, 173-74; Le Roy, *Au Kilimanjaro: Histoire de la foundation d'une mission catholique en Afrique orientale* (Paris, 1928), pp. 50-54, 263-71.

99. Aylward Shorter, *Cross and Flag in Africa: The "White Fathers" during the Colonial Scramble (1892-1914)* (Maryknoll, N.Y., 2006), pp. 192-93.

ous academic papers in collaboration with him.[100] In Natal, the Catholic missionary, Zulu linguist, and historian Alfred Bryant depended on Zulu assistants to collect medicinal plants and to explain their use. This led him to believe the average Zulu was "quite astonishingly learned in the domain of his own environment" and could "boast of a larger share of pre-scientific knowledge than the average European." This was a view shared with only slightly diminished conviction by Junod and others. Bryant would go on to work as a lecturer in Bantu studies at the University of the Witwatersrand (1920-23).[101]

Knowledge and Its Uses

Missionaries frequently commented on the ways in which the knowledge of plants and animals held by indigenous peoples took on a local value. In some cases, locals were able to sell the products of this knowledge to communities outside their home areas; in some instances this allowed them to pioneer the production of cash crops for the global market. In East Africa Charles Sacleux noted that communities west of Bagamoyo extracted a rich grease for lighting and cooking from the kernel of the fruit of the magnolia-like *Allanblackia sacleuxii* Hua. In southeast Africa, Henri-Alexandre Junod remarked that locals used a fat drawn from the nut of the *Trichilia emetica* in their cooking and as a body oil. Earlier in the century they had sold large quantities of these mafureira almonds to French merchants in Lourenço Marques (Maputo), who sent them to Marseilles to be processed into vegetable oil.[102] Junod also came across plants in the region that were known to combat migraines, gonorrhea, and other maladies; and he dispatched samples to Geneva for analysis.[103] On the lower Niger River, the Scottish Presbyterians remarked on the deadly efficacy of the Calabar bean in poison ordeals and in 1859 succeeded in sending a flowering specimen preserved in alcohol to Edinburgh. This allowed Prof. Balfour to name and classify the plant and lecture on it to the

---

100. Gomes e Sousa, "Exploradores e Naturalistas," pp. 78-81; Harries, *Butterflies and Barbarians*, chapter 5.

101. Bryant, "Zulu Medicine and Medicine Men," *Annals of the Natal Museum* 2, no. 1 (1909): 1; Harries, *Butterflies and Barbarians*, pp. 58, 138, 144.

102. Junod, *South African Tribe*, 2:18-19; Patrick Harries, *Work, Culture, and Identity: Migrant Laborers in Mozambique and South Africa, c. 1860-1910* (Portsmouth, N.H., 1994), pp. 8, 83, 86.

103. Botanical Conservatory, Boissier Herbarium, Geneva. Junod to Barbey, 5 July 1893. See also Junod's "pharmacy of the Ba-Ronga" and "collection of native medicinal roots" in the Neuchâtel Ethnographic Museum.

Royal Society in 1860. He later passed the bean to pharmacologists who extracted an alkaloid element (physostigmine) that could be used to constrict the pupil of the eye and alleviate glaucoma.[104] During the Zambezi expedition, John Kirk had come across arrows smeared with a poison that, he speculated, could serve to stimulate blood circulation. Livingstone secured information on the source of the poison, and the Scottish physician Thomas Fraser drew strophantin from its seed and eventually incorporated this strychnine-like alkaloid into a new drug used to counteract heart murmurs and poor circulation. By the end of the century the British Pharmacopoeia included both Calabar beans and the seeds of the *Strophantus kombé*.[105] Missionaries also commented on the distinctly local sartorial value given to a wide range of plants and animals. These extended from different varieties of bark cloth in East Africa to the chrysalis of the bagworm that served as a penis sheath in parts of southeast Africa.[106]

Several missionaries created botanical gardens and experimental plantations with a view to acclimatizing and cultivating imported foodstuffs. This was done most successfully by Pierre Poivre when he introduced various food stocks from the West Indies and southeast Asia to the gardens of Mauritius and Réunion. A century later Holy Ghost missionaries followed a similar path by cultivating new crops deemed to benefit the converts gathered at their mission stations, particularly freed slaves. In Libreville Father Klaine introduced and acclimatized various plants and fruit trees. Naval officers brought him specimens collected during their patrols along the coast, and the Natural History Museum in Paris sent him young vanilla, clove, and nutmeg stocks that adapted well to the region and climate. Klaine encouraged the commercial production of these plants and alerted entrepreneurs to the benefits to be

---

104. J. U. Lloyd, "Physostigma Venenosum (Calabar)," *Western Druggist* (Chicago), June 1897. It would later be used to counteract Alzheimer's disease. Alex Proudfoot, "The Early History of Physostigmine: A Tale of Beans, Great Men and Egos," *Toxicological Reviews* 25, no. 2 (2006).

105. Aneba Dove Osseo-Asare, "Bioprospecting and Resistance: Transforming Poisoned Arrows into Strophanin Pills in Colonial Gold Coast, 1885-1922," *Social History of Medicine* 21, no. 2 (2008): 271, 278-80. See also A. G. McKenzie, "The Rise and Fall of Strophanthin," *International Congress Series* 1242 (2002); Livingstone and Livingstone, *Narrative of an Expedition*, pp. 368-70. Livingstone had earlier reported on poisoned arrows and the remedy used to counter their effect in *Missionary Travels*, chapter 8. In East Africa Sacleux noticed that the Kambas and Somalis smeared their arrowheads with a poison extracted from *Acocanthera schimperi* Schweinf. Fournier, *Voyages et découvertes scientifiques*, pp. 174-75.

106. John Roscoe, *The Baganda: An Account of Their Native Customs and Beliefs* (London, 1911), pp. 406, 442; Harries, *Butterflies and Barbarians*, p. 137.

Natural Science and Naturvölker

gained from exploiting the wood of several species of trees growing in the tropical forests. Monsignor Hippolyte-Antoine Carries brought the Madagascan potato (*Coleus rotundifolus* Cheval. Et Pier.) from Brazzaville to Loango where this tuber made a significant addition to the edible plant life.[107]

As a young missionary, Alexandre Le Roy was posted to Gabon where he came across a hardy coffee bush on the banks of a river during one of his forays into the interior in 1885. The plant produced abundant fruit and, on investigation, was shown to mature quickly. He sent examples to Father Klaine in Libreville, who brought it to the attention of Louis Pierre in Paris, where the botanist described it as *Coffea canephora* Pierre (also known as *Coffea robusta*). Spread by the mission and its converts, the *robusta* variety soon replaced *arabica* in low-lying areas of equatorial Africa and, eventually, took on a global role as an important commercial crop in Java and, later, Brazil. In East Africa the Spiritans also played a major role in the spread of coffee when in 1877 they brought a "Bourbon" variety of *arabica* from their plantations in Réunion to their mission station at Bagamoyo. Coffee had been supplanted by sugar and vanilla on the French island and planters had already carried the *arabica* plant to Madagascar. Now, on the East African coast, the slaves freed by the mission cultivated the crop with such success that the Spiritans decided to plant it at their new stations on the uplands in the interior. By the turn of the century, the Spiritans had spread *arabica* into Kenya and Scottish missionaries had introduced Jamaican varieties of coffee into Tanganyika from Nyasaland. In many parts of East Africa, African peasants had traditionally grown indigenous *robusta* plants in their fields, alongside plantains or bananas. This form of cultivation produced coffee beans that were roasted and consumed as a casual snack. But as they recognized the importance of coffee as a drink, many farmers started to cultivate *robusta* as a cash crop, particularly after roads and railways linked them to an export market. By 1905 the production of coffee, which had started as a commercial venture initiated by struggling mission stations on the coast, had spread to northeastern Tanganyika and would soon enter Uganda.[108]

---

107. Fournier, *Voyages et découvertes scientifiques*, pp. 164-66.
108. Andreas Eckert, "Comparing Coffee Production in Cameroon and Tanganyika, c. 1900 to 1960s: Land, Labour and Politics," and Kenneth R. Curtis, "Smaller Is Better: A Consensus of Peasants and Bureaucrats in Colonial Tanganyika," in *The Global Coffee Economy in Africa, Asia, and Latin America, 1500-1989*, ed. W. G. Clarence-Smith and S. Tokik (Cambridge, 2003), pp. 291, 293, 315-16. While Curtis underlines the role of missionaries in the spread of coffee to Bukoba in northeast Tanganyika, Markus Boller stresses the part played by African peasants in the commercialization of indigenous *robusta* coffee in *Kaffee, Kinder, Kolonialismus: Wirtschafts- und Bevölkerungsentwicklung in Buhaya*

Coffee became a crucial element in the economy of some areas of East Africa, but it also encouraged class differences to emerge and at times brought African smallholders into conflict with European planters. This was perhaps why Henri-Alexandre Junod declined William Barbey's suggestion that he introduce coffee into southern Mozambique as a cash crop. However, the Swiss missionary was not averse to commercializing indigenous products that could be of benefit to the local population, and at one stage he tried, without much enthusiasm or success, to market the pith of a local palm tree as a substitute for cork.[109]

If the coffee introduced by missionaries into East Africa came to serve the interests of imperialism, their pioneering efforts in the cultivation of cocoa in West Africa served to stimulate the growth of an indigenous rural capitalism. In 1857 the first manager of the agricultural station attached to the Basel Mission's station at Akropong planted cocoa seeds imported from Surinam. Their blossoms were soon under attack from ants, perhaps members of the fierce species sent back to Basel by Georg Widmann, and the cocoa plants took ten years to establish themselves. In the meantime, missionaries sent pods to their other stations and imported new seeds directly from the West Indies. But the spread of cocoa cultivation succeeded only in the 1870s when Tetteh Quarshie, who had been trained by the mission as a goldsmith, returned home with a consignment of cocoa pods smuggled illegally out of Fernando Po. He planted the dried beans on his farm in Mampong and sold pods to neighbors who were not unfamiliar with ways to treat seeds and protect plants. In 1891 the Basel Mission Trading Company exported the first consignment of cocoa from Ghana. Twenty years later, native planters would turn the British colony into the most important exporter of cocoa in the world.[110]

Nature opened the eyes of missionaries to the glory of God. But some started to read new messages in the natural environment as Christian scholars like Charles Kingsley and Henry Drummond attempted to reconcile Christianity with natural selection. Drummond was a minister in the Free Church of Scotland, a celebrated lecturer and highly influential writer on nat-

---

(Tansania) in der deutschen Kolonialzeit (Münster, 1994), pp. 120-21, 135-48. See also, in the same volume, J. A. Kieran, "The Origins of Commercial Arabica Coffee Production," pp. 51-57, 62, 66; Roscoe, *The Baganda*, p. 434.

109. Harries, *Butterflies and Barbarians*, pp. 138, 140, 153 n. 100.

110. Gustaf Wanner, *The First Cocoa Trees in Ghana, 1858-1868* (Basel, 1962); Polly Hill, *The Migrant Cocoa-Farmers of Southern Ghana: A Study in Rural Capitalism* (Cambridge, 1970); Andrea Frank, *Wie die Schweiz zur Schokolade kam: Der Kakaohandel der Basler Handelsgesellschaft mit der Kolonie Goldküste (1893-1960)* (Basel, 2008), pp. 77-79.

ural history.[111] His views on evolution were strongly influenced by a trip he took in the footsteps of Livingstone in central Africa in the 1880s. On this journey, Drummond collected many animal and plant specimens, but he also commented on the analogy to be drawn between insect and human societies. When he observed termite colonies, he reflected on the industriousness with which these social insects raised ground to the surface and fertilized the land; and he described the mimicry practiced by insects as aesthetic rather than mechanical: "a system in the hands of natural selection [that] must ever increase in intricacy and beauty."[112] Unlike Darwin, Drummond saw God's distant hand behind the process of natural selection, and, to the relief of large swathes of the reading public, his theory of evolution invested change with both purpose and point.

In searching for reflexes and instincts in termite communities, Drummond and others, most notably Junod, sought to find the very origins of reason in the most primitive life-forms. Different animal communities exhibited a wide gradation in sociability that evolutionists interpreted as a hierarchy of behavior stretching from the simple to the complex. Amongst the more sociable insects (such as certain species of ants and wasps), the inmates of communities were able to adapt their behavior to changes in nature or social pressure in a way that indicated a certain intelligence rather than a simple, automatic instinct. Drummond discerned this same gradation in human societies that could be ranked from the simple, instinctual, and primitive to the complex, reasoning, and sophisticated.[113]

Botany and zoology had exerted a strong influence on the emergence of anthropology as a genre of knowledge. In Britain, the Association for the Advancement of Science had accepted ethnology as a science in 1846 only when its advocates (many of whom were involved in the attempt to revitalize Africa) agreed to abandon their political and religious ambitions by placing their discipline under the aegis of natural history in Section D. Although Murchison eventually freed anthropology from these constraints, by allying it

---

111. Henry Drummond, *Tropical Africa* (London, 1889); Anne Scott, "'Visible Incarnations of the Unseen': Henry Drummond and the Practice of Typological Exegesis," *British Journal for the History of Science* 37 (2002); James R. Moore, "Evangelicals and Evolution: Henry Drummond, Herbert Spencer, and the Naturalisation of the Spiritual World," *Scottish Journal of Theology* 38 (1985); David Bebbington, "Henry Drummond, Evangelicalism and Science," in *Henry Drummond: A Perpetual Benediction*, ed. T. E. Corts (Edinburgh, 1999).

112. Drummond, *Tropical Africa*, pp. 154, 176-79.

113. Drummond, *Tropical Africa*, pp. 25, 52, 105; Junod, *South African Tribe*, 1:126, 186, 214, 342; 2:55, 168 n. 1.

to geography, the subject remained the study of *Naturvölker,* of (primitive) man in his natural state.[114] Practitioners carried this definition into the field, and, when in 1903 they formed the South African Association for the Advancement of Science (SAAAS), anthropology and ethnology were grouped in a section with botany and zoology, geology, mineralogy, geography, and bacteriology. After a brief sojourn with philology, history, and education, anthropology and ethnology eventually settled in Section E with the sciences that would constitute the basis of African studies: archaeology, philology, and "native sociology."[115] The presidents of this section of the SAAAS were drawn uniformly from the field of missionary anthropology. By this time the missionary movement provided a solid institutional framework for the practice of anthropology as a discipline. As colonialism threatened to destroy the culture of the people amongst whom they worked, missionaries had turned to anthropology as a tool that would further their evangelical ambitions. Some had come to believe they could fashion a locally attractive form of Christianity by grafting imported beliefs onto acceptable indigenous religious practices and ideas. Many missionaries recognized that a knowledge of anthropology could be of service to their congregants and, at the same time, give them a new standing in the colonial state as experts on native affairs.

Wilhelm Schmidt, a Society of the Divine Word missionary, carried some of these ideas to *Anthropos,* the anthropological journal he founded outside Vienna in 1906. Alexandre Le Roy became an important and influential figure in the Catholic Church who, on his return to Europe, took up the chair in the history of religions at the Institut Catholique in Paris and in 1896 became superior general of the Spiritans.[116] The work of Le Roy and Schmidt gave a new respectability to the intellectual endeavors of Catholic missionaries and heralded Pope Benedict's overturning of antimodernism in 1914 and his encyclical *Maximum Illud* (1919), which called for missionaries to be trained in both the sacred and the profane sciences. A few years later Pius XI established a Vatican Missionary Exhibition that advertised the scientific achievements of Catholic missionaries by displaying books and maps, as well as fossils, plants, insects, shells, animals, and minerals from all over the world. In 1925 the Vatican created the Missionary Museum at the Lateran, in which it reorganized the earlier exhibition to include herbaria from different regions, showcases

---

114. Jack Morrell and Arnold Thackray, *Gentlemen of Science: Early Years of the British Association for the Advancement of Science* (London, 1981), pp. 283-86; George Stocking, *Victorian Anthropology* (New York, 1987), pp. 242-45.

115. Isaac Shapera, "The Present State and Future Development of Ethnographical Research in South Africa," *Bantu Studies* 8 (1934): 226.

116. Shorter, *Cross and Flag,* pp. 188-89.

Natural Science and Naturvölker

filled with insects, and native medicinal remedies. Headed by Wilhelm Schmidt, the museum also housed impressive ethnographic collections. It was soon accompanied by an African Missionary Museum in Lyon.[117] Protestant missionary societies had for many years attempted to organize knowledge in this way. Most missionary societies had their own libraries that included works on the natural sciences, and their own museums that sometimes included displays of botanical and entomological specimens.[118] They had close connections to regional museums and geographical societies that included clerics and missionaries amongst their founders, directors, and fellows.[119]

In their attempt to gain and maintain the acceptance of anthropology as a science, missionaries and others aimed to increase the objectivity and independence of the young discipline by bringing to it the methodological skills and narrative traditions associated with the study of natural history. At the same time, their interest in the names of plants and insects elided with a desire to understand the role and function of nature in the lives of "primitive" peoples; and several missionaries combined their investigation of tribal communities with an equally passionate study of nature. Henri-Alexandre Junod stands out in this regard; but so, too, do Alfred Bryant, Charles Tisserant, Henri Trilles, and a number of other missionaries, most notably Charles Duparquet and Alexandre Le Roy.[120]

---

117. Laurick Zerbini, "De l'exposition vaticane au musée missionnaire ethnologue du Latran," in *Une appropriation du monde: Mission et missions XIXième-XXième siècles,* ed. Claude Prudhomme (Paris, 2004). A list of the collections is contained in the *Revue de l'histoire des missions,* June 1925, pp. 213-311.

118. Cf. *Journal des Missions Evangéliques,* 1833, p. 192; Annie Coombes, "For God and for England: Missionary Contributions to an Image of Africa," in her *Reinventing Africa: Museums, Material Culture, and Popular Imagination* (London, 1994); J. Cannizzo, "Gathering Souls and Objects: Missionary Collections," in *Colonialism and the Object: Empire, Material Culture, and the Museum,* ed. T. Barringer and T. Flynn (London, 1998); Annegret Nippa, ed., *Ethnographie und Herrnhuter Mission* (Dresden, 2003); Patrick Harries, "Primitivisme au musée: La récolte des missionnaires en Afrique australe," in *Cent ans d'ethnographie sur la colline de Saint-Nicolas 1904-2004,* ed. Roland Kaehr (Neuchâtel, 2004).

119. Dominique Lejeune, *Les Sociétés de Géographie en France et l'expansion coloniale aux XIXe siècle* (Paris, 1993), pp. 96-97; J. M. Mackenzie, "The Provincial Geographical Societies in Britain, 1884-1914," in *Geography and Imperialism, 1820-1940,* ed. M. Bell, R. Butlin, M. Heffernan (Manchester, 1995), pp. 97-98, 102, 110-12.

120. Harries, *Butterflies and Barbarians,* especially chapters 5 and 8.

PATRICK HARRIES

Local Knowledge

By the 1920s missionary institutions and individuals had created a genre of anthropological writing, based on holistic surveys, which produced large databanks on the peoples to whom they brought the Christian message. These accounts of tribal life included long sections devoted to the knowledge of plants and animals exercised by people dependent on nature for their survival.[121] This encouraged anthropology to develop as a field science strongly influenced by African assistants and informants who knew where to find plants and animals, and who were familiar with the role played by these living organisms in the lives of local people. Many of these assistants were Christian converts with whom missionaries shared a social intimacy based on the trust and loyalty generated by belonging to a common community.[122] Various institutions supported this view of natural history as an integral part of the emerging discipline of anthropology. Many natural history museums reinforced this view when they incorporated the artifacts of primitive peoples into their displays of animals and plants; some anthropological journals even published essays on botanical subjects.[123]

As a genre of writing, field-based anthropological monographs contained substantial descriptions of the skills of native agriculturalists, hunters, herbalists, and doctors. They also included examinations of the very detailed ways in which locals distinguished between and named the fauna and flora of their regions, and attributed to plants and animals functions that could be pharmacological, medicinal, sartorial, and magical, as well as nutritional. As early as 1880, Duparquet had noted and named nine different tubers eaten by the population inhabiting the rocky plain north of Omaruru, and he had carefully described how the Ovambo exploited seven different, exotic species of fruit trees.[124] By the early twentieth century this concern with local views of

---

121. James Macdonald, "Manners, Customs, Superstitions, and Religions of South African Tribes," *Journal of the Anthropological Institute of Great Britain and Ireland* 19 (1890): 273-74; E. Gottschling, "The Bawenda, a Sketch of Their History and Customs," *Journal of the Royal Anthropological Institute* 35 (1905): 383.

122. For the "politics of knowledge" produced by this "affective sociality," see Nancy Jacobs, "The Intimate Politics of Ornithology in Colonial Africa," *Comparative Studies in Society and History* 48 (2006).

123. W. A. Norton, "Plants of Bechuanaland," *Man* 23 (1923): 121-24. A former missionary, Norton was at this stage professor of Bantu philology at the University of Cape Town. Interestingly, the Anthropological Survey of India remained a branch of the country's Zoological Survey until 1945. Verrier Elwin, "The Anthropological Survey: History and Development," *Man* 48 (June 1948).

124. *Les missions catholiques*, 1880, pp. 370, 407.

nature came to occupy an increasingly important space in the anthropological monograph. The CMS missionary John Roscoe noted that the Baganda had names for well over forty varieties of plantain, each adapted to a specific soil type. They also had names for sixty-six types of bark cloth used both as a means of apparel and as a currency.[125] The independent Methodist Edwin Smith named twenty-four wild fruits and forty-five species of birds, as well as dozens of vegetables, mammals, and fish eaten by the Ila of south-central Africa.[126] Junod wrote extensively about animals and plants in his monograph on the Thonga. Although he was quick to relegate much of their knowledge to "superstition," and thought their ways of ordering and systematizing nature old-fashioned, the Swiss missionary gave full credence to the knowledge and skills of Thonga specialists in the field of nature.[127] In southeastern Nigeria G. T. Basden, a CMS missionary at the center of chapter 4 of this book, was aware of the names given by the Ibo to several different palm trees and observed that they cultivated well over twenty varieties of yam.[128] In South Africa Alfred Bryant gathered a list of 240 medicinal plants that, he thought, constituted merely one-third of those known to indigenous specialists in Zululand and Natal; he devoted three long chapters to plants and animals in his historico-anthropological work *The Zulu People.*[129] This contribution of missionary studies to the fields of entomology and botany reached its peak in the 1920s-1930s. But as colonial dependencies started to develop their own centers of scientific achievement, the contribution of these amateurs to the production of scientific knowledge suffered an inexorable decline.

Conclusion

The professionalization of botany and entomology in Africa started at the turn of the century as the British brought science to bear on government in their colony of settlement at the Cape. Following the South African War, this process spread northward as the victors implanted a modern state in the region, including government and university departments of botany and entomology. While government departments focused on economic botany and a

---

125. Roscoe, *The Baganda,* pp. 403-6, 431, 434.
126. Edwin Smith and Andrew Dale, *The Ila-Speaking Peoples of Northern Rhodesia* (London, 1920), 1:149-51.
127. Harries, *Butterflies and Barbarians,* chapter 5.
128. G. T. Basden, *The Niger Ibos* (London, 1938), pp. 390, 393, 404-7.
129. Bryant, "Zulu Medicine," p. 76; Bryant, *The Zulu People: As They Were before the White Man Came* (Pietermaritzburg, 1949).

practical entomology, the universities placed a new stress on the laboratory sciences of plant anatomy and embryology, mycology, and bacteriology, and focused research on distinct categories of plants, such as phanerogams (seed-bearing plants) and cryptogams (plants that produce spores).[130] Missionary savants inevitably played a diminishing role in areas of research ever more dominated by scholars working with new technology in specialized areas of, increasingly, distinct scientific disciplines. A caste of professors and professionals emerged as bright young graduates from metropolitan universities came to the colonies to establish nodes of learning and scientific authority. Despite their dependence on British and American universities, these institutions quickly developed into centers of scientific research and teaching with their own growing, national autonomy.[131]

Joseph Burtt Davy stands out in this transnational network of learning. He trained at Kew Gardens and the University of California before joining the Botanical Section of the Department of Agriculture created in the Transvaal after the South African War. In laying the foundations of a national herbarium in Pretoria, Davy recognized the contribution of amateurs like Junod to its establishment. But he was openly critical of the missionary's amateur botanical skills and found his plant specimens "often scrappy and unfit for determination."[132] Criticism of missionary amateurs spread to the field of anthropology as its practitioners attempted to create a professional basis for their discipline. Alfred Radcliffe-Brown came to South Africa from Cambridge University in 1920 with the intention of bringing the practice of anthropology in the colony into line with modern theories in Europe, particularly those advocated by the editors of the *Année sociologique* in Paris. As the first professor of social anthropology at the University of Cape Town, he advocated an approach to the discipline critical of the missionary studies that dominated his field. Although he recognized their linguistic and fieldwork skills, Radcliffe-Brown tended to dismiss the work of missionaries as an "eth-

---

130. R. F. Lawrence, "Insects, Arachnids and Pripatus," and R. A. Dyer, "Botanical Research in South Africa in the Twentieth Century," in *A History of Scientific Endeavour in South Africa*, ed. A. C. Brown (Cape Town, 1977), pp. 114, 240-43; Howard Philips, *The University of Cape Town, 1918-1948* (Cape Town, 1993).

131. Cf. S. Schönland, "Some Aspects of Recent Progress in Pure and Applied Natural Science," in *Report of the South African Association for the Advancement of Science*, 1908. More generally, see Saul Dubow, *A Commonwealth of Knowledge: Science, Sensibility, and White South Africa, 1820-2000* (Oxford, 2006), chapters 4, 5.

132. J. Burtt Davy, "First Annotated Catalogue of the Vascular Plants of the Transvaal and Swaziland," in *Report of the South African Association for the Advancement of Science*, 1908, p. 232.

Natural Science and Naturvölker

nology" (based on outdated evolutionist ideas) that took insufficient account of "the general laws that underlie the phenomenon of culture."[133] His students would soon focus on specialized aspects of social life, such as tribal institutions and kinship structures, and introduce new concepts, such as "social change," that made the work of missionaries seem outdated and of little significance to pressing, current issues. The university-trained professionals who came to dominate anthropology in the years before the Second World War found the missionaries' holistic tribal studies too wide-ranging and imprecise, as Deborah Gaitskell shows in this volume, and cut back on the space allocated to botany and entomology in their monographs. As their interests moved from the means of production to the social relations generated by the production process, anthropologists would hand their interest in the natural sciences to the new discipline of ethnobotany. In their eyes, planting was more important than plants, and hunting and animal husbandry overshadowed the animals on which an earlier generation of missionary anthropologists had concentrated research.

Knowledge-producing institutions in the colonies built their authority and professionalism on their ties of sociability, training, and experience with metropolitan centers. International recognition cemented the authority of the professionals in the laboratory but increasingly separated them from the amateurs on the spot who were familiar with the languages and knowledge systems of native peoples. And in the process the university professionals built the strength of their discipline and institutions on an understanding of science that was increasingly divorced from native practitioners in the field. Eventually a knowledge and understanding of "Western science" became a litmus test for "civilization," as well as a resource used by politicians seeking to bring modernity and progress to their constituencies.[134] In time, "science" became a Western product that overlooked or hid the long contribution of "indigenous knowledge" to its development.

In this chapter I have attempted to outline some of the small ways in which missionary research in the related fields of entomology, botany, and anthropology contributed to an encompassing notion of science as a culturally diverse practice. Missionaries were pioneering figures in these fields on the edge of empire. The declining influence of missionaries in these emerging disciplines, I have argued, facilitated the emergence of a new concept of sci-

---

133. Cf. Radcliffe-Brown's presidential address to Section E of the SAAAS in 1923, "The Methods of Ethnography and Social Anthropology," in *Reports of the South African Association of Science*, 1923, p. 127.

134. Cf. Patrick Harries, "Missionaries, Marxists and Magic: Power and the Politics of Literacy in South-East Africa," *Journal of Southern African Studies* 27, no. 3 (2001).

ence and, with it, an accompanying discourse. This carried "Western science" from the imperial center to the colonial periphery, and from hubs on the outskirts of empire to a grateful hinterland. In the process, local ways of naming, ordering, and explaining nature were lost or ignored, and the power of "science" was irrevocably tied to a modernizing project underscored by a civilizing mission. In the process, the history of science concealed the work of missionary naturalists, as well as the knowledge provided by their indigenous assistants and informants.

Select Bibliography

Bonneuil, Christophe. "Le Muséum national d'histoire naturelle et l'expansion colonial de la Troisième République (1870-1914)." *Revue française d'histoire d'outre-mer* 86 (1999).

Cavazzi, Antonio. *Relation historique de l'Ethiopie Occidentale.* 1687. French ed., Paris, 1732.

Cook, Harold. *Matters of Exchange: Commerce, Medicine, and Science in the Dutch Golden Age.* New Haven, 2007.

Cooper, Alix. *Inventing the Indigenous: Local Knowledge and Natural History in Early Modern Europe.* Cambridge, 2007.

Dos Santos, João. *Ethiopia Oriental, e varia historia de cousas notaveis do Oriente.* Evora, 1609.

Driver, Felix. *Geography Militant: Cultures of Exploration and Empire.* Oxford, 2001.

Endersby, Jim. *Imperial Nature: Joseph Hooker and the Practices of Victorian Science.* Chicago, 2008.

Fournier, Paul. *Voyages et découvertes scientifiques des missionnaires naturalists français à travers le monde pendant cinq siècles XVe à XXe siècle.* Paris, 1932.

Grove, Richard. "Scottish Missionaries, Evangelical Discourses and the Origins of Conservation Thinking in Southern Africa, 1820-1900." *Journal of Southern African Studies* 15, no. 2 (1989).

Gunn, Mary, and L. E. Codd. *Botanical Exploration of Southern Africa.* Cape Town, 1981.

Harries, Patrick. *Butterflies and Barbarians: Swiss Missionaries and Systems of Knowledge in South-East Africa.* Oxford, 2007.

Harrison, Mark. "Science and the British Empire." *Isis* 96 (2005).

Jacobs, Nancy. "The Intimate Politics of Ornithology in Colonial Africa." *Comparative Studies in Society and History* 48 (2006).

Jardine, Nicholas, James Secord, and Emma Spary, eds. *Cultures of Natural History.* Cambridge, 1996.

Livingstone, David N. *Putting Science in Its Place: Geographies of Scientific Knowledge.* Chicago, 2003.

Natural Science and Naturvölker

———. "Scientific Inquiry and the Missionary Enterprise." In *Participating in the Knowledge Society: Researchers beyond University Walls*, edited by Ruth Finnegan. Basingstoke, 2005.

Livingstone, David, and Charles Livingstone. *Narrative of an Expedition to the Zambezi and Its Tributaries*. 1865. New ed., London, 2005.

Lobo, Jerónimo. *The Itinerário of Jerónimo Lobo*. Edited by M. G. da Costa. Translated by D. M Lockhart from the Portuguese manuscript, n.d. [1660s-1670s?]. London, 1984.

Rupke, Nicolaas A. *Richard Owen: Victorian Naturalist*. New Haven and London, 1994.

Stafford, Robert. *Scientist of Empire: Sir Roderick Murchison, Scientific Exploration, and Victorian Imperialism*. Cambridge, 1989.

CHAPTER 2

Missionary Linguistics on the Gold Coast: Wrestling with Language

ERIKA EICHHOLZER

The mastery of local language(s) in the mission field has been seen by Protestant mission societies as an important, if not the most important, tool for the successful evangelization of non-Christian peoples. This is largely because "the missionary is to share the spiritual home of language with the people" in order to reach them.[1] Language study was termed "language work" *(Spracharbeit)* to stress its practical nature. It was goal-oriented, aiming to create a religious literature centered on the Bible and hymnbooks, as well as language primers. It was not intended that missionaries pursue these studies to a higher end, let alone make a contribution to academic studies. Within the world of missionary linguistics, the Basel Mission occupies a prominent place.[2] This chapter considers the work of just two of the many linguists trained by the Basel Mission. Hans Nicolai Riis and Johann Gottlieb Christaller were sent to the Gold Coast by the Basel Mission to do basic language work but ended up making a significant contribution to linguistics as a scientific discipline. Riis is seen as a pioneer in the study of the Twi language, and Christaller, in his struggle to describe languages scientifically, is hailed as the founder of West African linguistics.[3] Al-

---

1. "[Der Missionar] muss darum auch die geistige Heimat der Sprache mit dem Volke teilen" (Johann G. Christaller, "Thoughts about Language Learning of the Missionaries and Transforming Pagan into Christian Languages," Manuscript, in the Mission 21 Archive, Holdings of the Basel Mission [hereafter: BMA], D-10.5,17 f.).

2. Adrian Hastings, *The Church in Africa, 1450-1950* (Oxford, 1996), pp. 242, 280, 341. Cf. also George E. Stanley, "Some Notes on African Language Grammars and Dictionaries Written between 1850 and 1900," *Anthropological Linguistics* 12, no. 3 (1970): 98-102.

3. See August Seidel, "J. G. Christaller und die afrikanische Sprachwissenschaft" (J. G.

though the acquisition of the local languages by the Basel missionaries was slow and imperfect in the period prior to Riis and Christaller's arrival in the second quarter of the nineteenth century, neither man received much encouragement to study from the mission's directors. It was only through their commitment and ability that past mistakes were grasped and advances were made.

The Linguistic Situation on the Mission Field

The linguistic situation in the southern part of the Gold Coast (Ghana), especially in the areas that today constitute Greater Accra and the Eastern Region, where the Basel Mission established its first mission stations, was rather heterogeneous. There was a high degree of linguistic diversification, so that a choice had to be made concerning which language(s) to use for evangelistic purposes.

Along the coast, between Accra and the river Volta, the Ga, Dangme, and Ewe languages were spoken,[4] and in the Akuapem Hills, Twi and the Guan(g) languages, Kyerepong-Guan and Larteh-Guan.[5] Significant numbers of people spoke the coastal languages, Ga and Dangme. In Akuapem, the Twi language was dominant. The Guan languages, representing the languages of the original inhabitants of Akuapem, were about to be superseded by the Twi language from the north, from Akyem.[6] By the nineteenth century, the inhabitants of the Guan towns were bilingual in Guan and in Twi.[7]

Language choice in the Ga-Dangme areas, however, was a much more debated issue. These two languages are linguistically interrelated but not mutually intelligible. The Ga language, the local language of Accra and its surrounding villages, was eventually chosen to become the mission and school

---

Christaller and African linguistics), *Zeitschrift für afrikanische und oceanische Sprachen*, no. 2 (1896): 267-70.

4. Other, early spellings for the Ga language are "Akra, Accra" or "Gã" (the nasalized *ã* is usually omitted in writing). Different spellings exist also for the Dangme language: "Adampe," "Adangbe," "Adan(g)me," and "Dan(g)me." The Ewe language with its various dialectal variants had the biggest number of all these three languages, but it was not a major language in the area where the Basel Mission operated.

5. All these languages are linguistically classified as belonging to the Kwa subgroup of the Niger-Congo language family; see John Bendor-Samuel, *The Niger-Congo Languages* (London, 1989).

6. See Michelle Gilbert, "No Condition Is Permanent: Ethnicity Construction and the Use of History in Akuapem," *Africa* 67, no. 4 (1997): 501-33.

7. See Sonia Abun-Nasr, *Afrikaner und Missionar. Die Lebensgeschichte von David Asante* (African and missionary: David Asante's biography) (Basel, 2003), pp. 22-23.

language, since it was believed to be spoken more widely than the Dangme language.[8] Subsequently, this attempt at language planning by the Basel Mission in Ga-Dangme was considered a mistake by Basel missionary linguist Johann Gottlieb Christaller, who wrote on the "future of the Gã (Akra) language" in 1883: "It was a fault to make Gã the language of the church and school. In Adanme the Twi would have found easier entrance than the Gã. The Twi has a future, and comprises many and important peoples, whereas the Gã is being decomposed [sic] and supplanted by English, which process we cannot stop by our endeavours to increase the existing Gã literature."[9]

The Twi[10] language was known to Europeans from works such as Thomas Edward Bowdich's *Mission from Cape Coast Castle to Ashantee,* first published in 1819.[11] This and other early travel accounts from the Gold Coast indicated the existence of a cluster of closely related dialects that the early Basel missionaries came to call "Ashante(e)."[12] From this cluster, the missionaries

---

8. Years later, the picture about the actual number of speakers of Ga and Dangme became more precise; see Mary E. Kropp Dakubu, "Notes on the Linguistic Situation on the Coast of Ghana during the Nineteenth Century," *Research Review,* n.s., 1, no. 2 (1985): 198: "Zimmermann estimated the numbers of Ga-speakers as 40 to 50,000, and of Dangme as 50 to 60,000. The latter figure was probably based primarily on the inland Krobo and Shai areas, with which he was more familiar than the coast. A few years later, Christaller and others estimated that only about 30 to 40,000 people spoke Ga while he numbered those who spoke Dangme at rather more, over 80,000. He believed that about three or four million people spoke the Akan language group that included Asante, Akyem and Akwapem as well as Fante."

9. See Johann G. Christaller, "On the Future of the Gã (Akra) Language," BMA D-10.22,18 (29.10.1883).

10. There were many different (mis)spellings of Twi over the course of time: (O)dschi/(O)ji, (O)tyi, Tshi/Tschi/Tswi/Tschwi, Chwee (etc.), as the sequence /tw/ represents a sound that is absent in Indo-European languages; in phonological terminology it represents a "labialised voiceless pre-palatal affricate"; see Florence A. Dolphyne, *The Akan (Twi-Fante) Language: Its Sound System and Tonal Structure* (Accra, 1988), p. 36. In "Grammatical Introduction to the Tshi Dictionary," Christaller explains the different spellings of the Twi language: "In the orthography devised for this formerly unwritten language, we write the name 'wi,' the true pronunciation of which might be rendered more exactly in letters of Dr Lepsius' Standard Alphabet by 'Tswì' and in English by 'Chwee'; but whilst the written 'Twi' may be justified by its simplicity and sufficiency and by reasons of analogy (with kw, dw, fw &c.), the translation 'Tshi' was chosen to avoid too much deviation for the former spellings 'Tyi, Otyi,' and the German writing 'Tschi' (formerly 'Otschi')." See Johann G. Christaller, *A Dictionary of the Asante and Fante Language Called Tshi (Chwee, Twi)* (Basel, 1881), p. xvii.

11. See Thomas E. Bowdich, *Mission from Cape Coast Castle to Ashantee, with a Descriptive Account of that Kingdom* (London, 1819 and 1873).

12. "It may be here remarked also, that the word Asante has been spelt in English erroneously as Ashante, and still more erroneously as Ashantee, putting the accent on the ulti-

would later choose one variety and turn it into the literary, standard language of the region. Why they chose one language form to serve as the written language, and the debates and divisions this produced, lie at the heart of the following section of the chapter.

The Basel Mission and the Language Question on the Gold Coast

The Basel Mission started its work on the Gold Coast in 1828 by sending out three missionaries who first settled in the Danish trading post Osu (also called Christiansborg). After some years the intention was to proceed farther inland, in order to settle more permanently. The coastal climate was considered lethal for Europeans, since many missionaries had died from tropical diseases shortly after their arrival. Missionary Andreas Riis,[13] who arrived on the Gold Coast in 1832, chose Akropong in the Akuapem Hills for the first inland mission settlement, and moved there in 1835.

In the early years at Akropong, language acquisition yielded few results, largely because the missionaries found it difficult to locate reliable "language assistants" *(Sprachgehilfen),* let alone to assess their linguistic proficiency. As Riis complained, "Without any language aid, learning a foreign language like Twi causes many difficulties. We have not seen our good Asante man for weeks now, the one who assists us in language learning, he only showed up again a few days ago. Through his miserable help we managed nevertheless to assemble about 1200 words and do not doubt their correctness."[14]

---

mate; it is to be accented on the penultimate: Asánte, and the s is no sh, but is distinguished from the common English s only by having a more palatal aspiration. . . . But speaking of the tribe, as connected not by political unity but by the ties of ethnological consanguinity, comprising all those who have the same vernacular idiom, the natives themselves will never use the term Asante, but they will speak of the *Oji-tribe* and the *Oji-language.* The word, as it is pronounced by the natives, ought rather to be spelt Tyi, Otyi, but we retain the other spelling, as Otyi is difficult for English organs to pronounce." See Hans N. Riis, *Grammatical Outline and Vocabulary of the Oji-Language, with Especial Reference to the Akwapim-Dialect, Together with a Collection of Proverbs of the Natives* (Basel, 1854), p. 2.

13. Andreas Riis, too, suffered from tropical illnesses but escaped death, which is attributed to the fact that he accepted treatment from local herbalists. He stayed on the Gold Coast from 1832 to 1839, and again from 1842 to 1845, when he was eventually withdrawn by the Basel Mission Committee; see Daniel Antwi and Paul Jenkins, "The Moravians, the Basel Mission and the Akuapem State in the Early Nineteenth Century," in *Christian Missionaries and the State in the Third World,* ed. Holger Bernt Hansen and Michael Twaddle (Oxford, 2002), p. 41. See also Wilhelm Schlatter, *Geschichte der Basler Mission,* vol. 3, *Geschichte der Basler Mission in Afrika* (History of the Basel Mission in Africa) (Basel, 1916), p. 27.

14. See Riis, Akropong, 6 July 1838, quoted from Sonia Abun-Nasr, "Von der

Due to Riis's political activities, which he pursued without the authorization of the Basel Mission, the committee made him return to Basel under the pretext of awarding him a furlough.[15] He brought with him a collection of linguistic notes on the Twi language that became the basis for a thirty-six-page primer called *Aschantekassa*,[16] which was printed in Basel in 1840/41.[17]

From a linguistic and also didactic point of view, however, that booklet was not useful for language learning, neither for the missionaries themselves nor for the future pupils in Akropong, as Twi words were listed under every corresponding letter of the Latin alphabet with no indication of their meaning in English or German. Nevertheless, this was the first print publication in Twi that can be attributed to the Basel Mission.

After considering their engagement in Africa, the Basel Mission Committee decided in 1841 to continue their work on the Gold Coast under a new strategy: the selected coworkers[18] for Andreas Riis were to be supplemented with Christians of African descent from Jamaica,[19] as well as freed slaves, who were believed to be more adjusted to the tropical climate. The presence of these black colleagues and assistants would, it was believed, most fully address the needs of Africans.[20]

The instructions[21] given to the four missionaries before their departure

---

'Umbildung heidnischer Landessprachen zu christlichen' — Die Anfänge von Schrift und Schriftlichkeit in Akuapem, Goldküste" (On transforming pagan into Christian languages — the beginnings of writing and literacy in Akuapem, Gold Coast), in *Wege durch Babylon: Missionare, Sprachstudien und interkulturelle Kommunikation,* ed. Reinhard Wendt (Tübingen, 1998), p. 196.

15. See Antwi and Jenkins, "Moravians," pp. 41-42.

16. Andreas Riis, *Aschantekassa A B Ch anna Kannehuma* (ABC of the Twi language or reading book) (Basel, 1840/41).

17. *Evangelisches Missions-Magazin,* 1846, p. 136.

18. Hermann Halleur (b. 1818) from Schwerin stayed on the Gold Coast from 1842 to 1845; Johann Georg Widmann (1814-76), from Tübingen, stayed on the Gold Coast from 1842 to 1876; and George Thompson (1819-89), who was born on the Gold Coast and taken to Basel as a ten-year-old boy and educated in the Basel Mission House, but was dismissed by the Basel Mission in 1845 due to moral misconduct (see Schlatter, *Geschichte der Basler Mission,* p. 39), one of the most common reasons for dismissals.

19. Twenty-four Jamaicans agreed to resettle to the Gold Coast; see Antwi and Jenkins, "Moravians," and also Ulrike Sill, "Encounters in Quest of Christian Womanhood: The Basel Mission in Pre- and Early Colonial Ghana" (Ph.D. diss., University of Basel, 2007), p. 404.

20. See Antwi and Jenkins, "Moravians," p. 43.

21. File "Instructionen & Contracte," BMA, Q-3-3,26, p. 27: "Instruktion für die nach der dänischen Goldküste in Guinea bestimmten Missionarien u. Missionsgehülfen: Br. Andreas Riis, Joh. Georg Widmann, George Thomson und Halleur" (Instruction for the

from Basel placed a considerable emphasis on language. Several paragraphs were dedicated to the way they should approach the "Ashantee" (= Twi) language. The language question was of special importance (1) to the formal education that the missionaries intended to introduce in Akropong and (2) for interaction with the non-Christian (adult) population. Two types of schools were planned, one for the children of the Jamaican Christians and one for those of the local Akuapem people: "The 'Ashantee' [Twi] language should be a teaching subject in the school to be established, and later, with growing mastery of the language, it should become the sole medium of instruction, and the two schools shall be combined into one."[22] There were also plans to build a Catechists' Seminary[23] in Akropong for the more promising pupils who should either become schoolteachers or catechists: "Catechists' Seminary Syllabus: Here as well, with growing mastery of the Twi language, English shall be replaced by Twi as a medium of instruction: The Subjects to be taught were: 1. Bible Stories and Reading, 2. Reading and Writing of the Twi Language, 3. Speaking of the Twi Language, 4. Singing, 5. Calculation, 6. Geography & History."[24] With regard to language for interaction with non-Christians,[25] learning Twi was deemed important for daily interaction with the local people in Akuapem, and the committee insisted on its quick and efficient acquisition: "The Committee hopes that the other three brethren (apart from Riis) will use their time well in the first few years to make sure that they will come to speak the country's language nicely and fluently." The ultimate goal of language learning, however, was evangelical work: "The Committee urges the dear brethren as far as their health permits it, to see to it that they will soon be able to preach without the help of interpreters, in order soon to replace sermons in English with Twi."[26] Not just oral skills were required since the local language was intended to be used as a literary language, and in order to lay a linguistic foundation, reference books for language learning were also needed: "The production of a — as complete as possible — dictionary (duty of all four missionaries) and a language manual (duty of Missionary Widmann)."[27] These instructions were clear but far too ambi-

---

missionaries and their assistants that are meant for the Danish Gold Coast in Guinea: Br. A.R., J.G.W., G.T. & H.).

22. "Instructionen & Contracte," 4, 20, 26.
23. This Catechists' Seminary was opened in Akropong Akuapem in 1848 (see Abun-Nasr, *Afrikaner und Missionar*, p. 88).
24. "Instructionen & Contracte," BMA, Q-3-3,26, §§28, 21.
25. "Instructionen & Contracte," BMA, Q-3-3,26, §28.
26. "Instructionen & Contracte," BMA, Q-3-3,26, §25.
27. "Instructionen & Contracte," BMA, Q-3-3,26, §24.

tious. They were goal-oriented with no indication of what methods should be used for the description of the language concerned, apart from collecting and writing it down, and systematizing its data.[28]

The Basel missionaries were not strangers to language study. During their training in the Basel Mission House, they had learned the biblical languages, Greek and Hebrew, plus Latin. In addition, they had to study English, as most of them came either from Switzerland or from southern Germany. However, they had not learned how to describe purely oral languages that had first to be reduced to writing and that, moreover, as it turned out later, were typologically very distinct from the Indo-European languages with which the missionaries were familiar.

The next group of missionaries, sent out in 1844, namely, Ernst Friedrich Sebald, Friedrich Schiedt, and Hans Nicolai Riis,[29] were instructed to study the unpublished collection of language notes drawn up by Andreas Riis, and his primer *Aschantekassa*, before and during their journey to the Gold Coast.[30] The committee stressed more clearly at this time that "no one of the dear brethren should abstain from learning the country's language Ashantee, and that they should consider it as one of their first duties to master this language."[31]

Hans Nicolai Riis was assigned to assist missionary Widmann with language work, the production of schoolbooks, the translation of the "Christian Holy Scripture," and — especially — to teach such boys and young men who could in the future be trained as schoolteachers.[32]

Twi remained the most favored dictionary, but the committee directed Widmann and Riis to add German to its English list as they considered a trilingual dictionary more useful.[33] Once again stress was put on the local language: "All missionaries should pay attention to learning the country's language *(Landessprache)* and to raising it to a written form," the committee decreed, in a way that linked literacy with social evolution. "It shall be maintained side by side with English. The country's language shall not be superseded by English, otherwise the already-converted Africans will become inefficient or even redundant as regards the conversion of their non-Christian compatriots who live further inland."[34]

---

28. See Abun-Nasr, "Von der Umbildung," p. 206.
29. Ernst Friedrich Sebald (1814-45), Friedrich Schiedt (b. 1819), and Hans Nicolai Riis (1822-90), a nephew to Andreas Riis, worked from 1844 to 1850 on the Gold Coast.
30. "Instructionen & Contracte," BMA, Q-3-3,26, §2.
31. "Instructionen & Contracte," BMA, Q-3-3,26, §36, p. 7.
32. "Instructionen & Contracte," BMA, Q-3-3,26, §10, p. 36.
33. "Instructionen & Contracte," BMA, Q-3-3,26, §12, p. 37.
34. "Instructionen & Contracte," BMA, Q-3-3,26, §12.

Language Choice in Akuapem

When the first mission station was founded in Akropong Akuapem, in a predominantly Twi-speaking town, it was only natural for the missionaries to learn the local language first and to translate some basic Christian literature into it. As Bowdich and others had already stated in their travel accounts, many languages from the coastal areas and regions dominated by the Asante seemed to be mutually intelligible: "The Ashantee, Fantee, Akim, Assin, and Aquapim languages are indisputably dialects of the same root, their identity is even more striking than that of the dialects of Ancient Greek."[35]

This raised the hope that this language cluster, which at that stage lacked a generic term under which all its (Twi and Fante) varieties could be subsumed, could be used as a literary language. Therefore much care had to be taken before choosing the most suitable linguistic variety for this purpose. Several important criteria were involved in this choice: these included the number of people who spoke the language form, as well as the extent to which it was believed to be "pure" (and as such to reflect the earliest condition of the language).

Concerning the criterion of "purity," Johann Gottlieb Christaller, who undertook thorough dialectological studies of the major Twi varieties, wrote in the introduction to his *Dictionary of the Asante and Fante Language:* "The Akan dialect is considered to be spoken purest [sic] in Ak(y)em but by its dainty and affected mode of expression, it appears less fit to become the common dialect of all Tshi [Twi] tribes."[36] As a linguist, he realized that the criterion of "purity" was not necessarily a weighty factor in the choice of an appropriate dialect to be raised to a literary form. But he nonetheless believed in a linguistic hierarchy and expressed this conviction in a clearly gendered form!

Of the language varieties in question, as already observed by Bowdich, Asante (Twi) had undoubtedly the largest number of speakers, but for politi-

---

35. Bowdich, *Mission from Cape Coast*, p. 180. The Asante, Fante, Akyem, Assin, and Akuapem varieties all belong to the Akan language, which was introduced in the 1950s as a cover term to refer to all those dialect forms; see Abun-Nasr, "Von der Umbildung," p. 194. In the nineteenth century, however, the term "Akan" did not include the Fante and the Brong; cf. Christaller's entry for "o-kànní": "A man of Akan descent, a man speaking the Akan or Tshi language. The name is used for the inhabitants of Akem, Akwam, Akuapem, Asen, Asante, Dakyira, Twuforo, Wasa, in contradistinction to the Fantefo and the Nnoṅkofo [slaves] and other potofo [people who do not speak 'proper' Twi]"; see Christaller, *A Dictionary*, p. 220.

36. See Christaller, *A Dictionary*, pp. vi-vii. By "the dainty and affected mode of expression," he meant the suffixes that were added to certain word classes.

cal reasons it was not possible to set up a mission station there (until 1896). The Fante variety, however, which followed Asante in number of speakers, "belonged" to the territory of the Wesleyan Missionary Society, and so for the Basel Mission the choice to be made was between Akuapem and Akyem Twi.

Not until 1866 was an official decision made on the language form that would serve as the standard variety of Twi. Christaller had been influenced by the following criteria in making this decision: (a) the political relevance of the dialect, (b) the number of people who spoke it, (c) its linguistic merits ("purity"), and (d) its potential links with other linguistic varieties of the language, this last point being a new aspect for the Basel Mission.[37] Christaller, who had previously favored Akyem, found Akuapem Twi to be the most "promising" among the Twi dialects. And the Akuapem District Conference, the regional decision-making body made up of the missionaries of the Twi stations, gave support to this pragmatic approach to the language question: "Since up to now the centre of our mission, in so far as it is an Otschi [Twi] Mission, is in Akuapem, since all our educational institutions are here and since parts of the Bible and other books are available in the Akuapem dialect, which is understood by all Otschi speakers, it is advisable that the Bible be completed in this [dialect]."[38]

The choice of Akuapem Twi did indeed prove to be a good, long-term decision for establishing an orthography for the Twi and Fante varieties. As late as 1995, the unified Akan orthography was published by the Bureau of Ghana Languages in a way that drew together the different ways of writing Akuapem, Fante, and Asante language forms.[39] This unified Akan orthography is mainly based on Akuapem Twi, the spelling rules of which had been established through the language studies of the Basel missionaries.

Wrestling with Language

In the propaganda employed by the Basel Mission, metaphors of fight were used to describe the process of language acquisition. This process was depicted like a wrestling[40] match between the learner and the language, with the

37. See Sill, "Encounters in Quest," p. 318.
38. Akuapem District Conference, no. 27, 13 June 1866, quoted from Sill, "Encounters in Quest," p. 31.
39. See the two publications by the Bureau of Ghana Languages: Akan Language Committee, *Akan Orthography (Spelling Rules)* and *Akan Nsɛmfua Kyerɛwbea* (How to write Akan words) (Accra, 1995).
40. See the title of Wilhelm Dilger's book *Wrestling with the Country's Language in In-*

intended result that the former should literally master the latter and make it a tool for conversion.[41] The reports sent to Basel showed an ambiguous picture about the mastering of Twi. The missionaries claimed to make good progress in language learning, but problems of communication were also reported. The two mission magazines, the *Evangelischer Heidenbote* and the *Evangelisches Missions-Magazin,* contained articles recounting the struggle.

In the *Evangelischer Heidenbote,* specimens of the Twi language were interspersed with the reports to give the reader an idea of the successful verbal interaction between the missionaries and the local people. In 1844, missionary Johann Georg Widmann reported that

> People are surprised to see that I already understand some Ashante [Twi], which is mysterious to them, as I have not stayed there yet. From time to time they brought different objects to me, and when I was able to name them, they laughed loudly and said: O nim kora! i.e. he knows it all. When I told them: Mi ko Akvapim mi ko asy Akvapim fo Jankupongasem, i.e. I go to Akuapem to teach the Akuapem people the Word of God, they were very amazed: Ampa! Very well! — Yet it will take us quite some time until we shall be able to express ourselves with ease in this language that has not yet been reduced to writing.[42]

By 1844 Widmann had spent just two years on the Gold Coast, during which time he had managed to understand some Twi. However, a close analysis of his account above suggests that he did not communicate in Twi as successfully as he believed he did. (The point here is not the orthography that had not been established yet but syntax and semantics.) In "proper" Twi: *Onim koraa* does not mean "he knows it all" but "he even knows [it]"; *koraa* should not have been rendered by "all" but rather by "even." Thus Widmann's Twi sentence was grammatically incorrect, and the following form would have been more correct, although still not elegant: *Mekɔ Akuapem, mekɔsua*

---

dian Mission Work; its German original: *Das Ringen mit der Landessprache in der indischen Missionsarbeit* (Basel, 1903).

41. In similar fashion, Birgit Meyer, in her article "Christianity and the Ewe Nation: German Pietist Missionaries, Ewe Converts and the Politics of Culture," *Journal of Religion in Africa* 32, no. 2 (2002), reports that the Bremen Mission prioritized language acquisition just as much as the Basel Mission did, by using even stronger metaphors, namely, metaphors of war: "Mastery of the Ewe language was considered the most important tool of the missionary. It was the 'weapon' in the 'war' the mission waged against 'heathendom'" (Meyer, p. 176).

42. *Evangelischer Heidenbote,* 1844, no. 3, p. 20.

Akuapemfo Nyankopɔn asɛm: "I go to Akuapem, I go to 'learn' the Akuapem people the word of God." He did not use the appropriate tense (the future tense), and the way he combined the sentence was also not elegant. To mean "I shall go to Akuapem to teach the Akuapem people the word of God," the sentence should have looked like this: *Mɛkɔ Akuapem akɔkyerɛ Akuapemfo Nyankopɔn*[43] *asɛm* (or: *Nyamesɛm*). *Ampa* is an adverb or interjection, which means "truly, really, indeed," "is that so," and can be used as a statement or a question. In the given context, it should be followed by a question mark rather than by an exclamation mark.

Widmann's audience must have had difficulty understanding what he intended to tell them, but they appear to have been fascinated by his attempt to speak the language. In the process, he failed to grasp the semantic field (or the meaning) of *ampa*, and did not realize that he was delivering a question, not a statement. Moreover, he failed to identify possible traces of surprise or even of irony in the sentence.

In another article in the *Evangelischer Heidenbote*, from 1846, missionary Friedrich Schiedt told readers about a conversation with his assistant Tette, a thirty-four-year old man, to whom he had been explaining the meanings of heaven and everlasting life. "And then, deeply moved, he [Tette] told me in his mother tongue: 'Massa, mi pä ko yamässa' (Massa, I want to go to Heaven). Tears started to come out of my eyes, when Tette added in bizarre English [Pidgin English] that: 'We Africans no know Heaven.'"[44]

The Twi phrase in the quotation is "broken Twi." The name "Tette" indicates that Schiedt's assistant was a native speaker not of Twi but rather of Ga. This would reflect the then-current practice[45] of the Basel Mission, which at the beginning recruited "language assistants" from the coastal areas because of their linguistic versatility, in that they spoke Ga, Twi, English, and sometimes Danish, too. In grammatically correct Twi, the utterance would have looked like *Mepɛ sɛ mɛkɔ nyameso* (or more common: *ɔsoro*).[46] Tette, who was

---

43. *Onyankopɔn*, one of the appellations for "God" (Onyame) in the Akan traditional religion, was early adopted to refer to the Christian God, for example, in the Fante translation of Luther's catechism in 1764; see Christian Protten, *Catechismus Lutheri, eller et Udtog af de Fem Parter: Den Første Part, de Ti Bud; paa Fante- og Acra-Sprog* (Luther's Small Catechism or an extract from the five parts, the first part, the Ten Commandments, in the Fante and Ga languages) (Copenhagen, 1764).

44. *Evangelischer Heidenbote*, 1846, no. 5, p. 34.

45. See Abun-Nasr, "Von der Umbildung," p. 189.

46. In the 1840s, establishing a Christian terminology in Twi was an ongoing process. The concept of heaven, for example, was initially rendered by *nyameso*, signifying "the upper (inward, invisible) part of heaven" (Christaller, *A Dictionary*, 1881, p. 343). In one of the

highly praised for his human qualities in the same article, did not seem to be proficient either in English or in Twi, which the missionary did not realize! Not all the specimens of the Twi language printed in the *Evangelischer Heidenbote* were ungrammatical or otherwise deficient. But these two examples illustrate the fundamental problems in language learning with which Basel missionaries were confronted; for they could not assess the proficiency of their assistants, and found it difficult to learn a language, without the aid of books that anchored (oral) languages in time and space.

In another article in the *Evangelischer Heidenbote*, from 1854, which presented a retrospective account of the last twenty years of mission work on the Gold Coast, the editor tried to explain to the readers why language acquisition took so much longer in the African mission field than in Europe:

> However, we want to talk about the acquisition of African languages and also about the fact that we had to master two of them in our mission field. Many believe that these studies are a mere bagatelle, as servants [in Europe] are used to learning English and French within a few months. Some people do forget that the sounds of African languages are partly somewhat more different, and thousands of those who pride themselves on speaking English and French, are neither able to read nor to write it, let alone to preach and to translate the Bible.... Seen from this point of view, it is indeed a great thing that our missionaries managed to compose grammars and dictionaries of the Twi and Ga languages, to translate Bible stories and considerable portions of the Old and New Testaments into these two languages, and that they can now go about preparing the needed school books.[47]

Missionary Hans Nicolai Riis

Hans Nicolai Riis had been a university student before joining the Basel Mission, and was therefore considered to be better at language learning and

---

early Twi translations, a selection of Bible stories, *Ojikassa Kannehuma: Yankupong Asem* (Basel, 1846), p. 159, *yamäso* (old spelling for *nyameso*) was the Twi term believed to render this Christian concept most accurately. But later on, as can be seen in the Twi Bibles in print, it was replaced by ɔsoro, "the upper part (of any object)," and also "the upper world, the sky"; a term that was not restricted to religious language only.

47. *Evangelischer Heidenbote*, 1854, no. 12, p. 75. See the Basel Mission publications in Ga and Twi up to the first edition of the Twi and Ga Bibles in Sill, "Encounters in Quest," pp. 315-16.

teaching than his fellow missionaries. He produced two Twi grammars, a German (1853) and an English version (1854), entitled *Grammatical Outline and Vocabulary of the Oji-Language, with Especial Reference to the Akwapim-Dialect, Together with a Collection of Proverbs of the Natives*. He stated in the preface that

> The author begs leave to state, that this volume must not in any way be considered as an attempt at a complete grammar and vocabulary of the Oji-language. His short stay in Africa, prematurely terminated by disease, did not permit him to acquire much more than the first rudiments of a language, which has never before been reduced to writing, and the learning of which was made extremely difficult, as well by the entire want of any assistance in the way of books, not to speak of teachers, as by the well-known weakening and depressing influence of the climate of those parts on the bodily system.[48]

In the German edition of his grammar (but no longer in the English version), he expressed the hope that his grammar would also be recognized in academic circles, as a contribution to the study of the so-called Hamitic[49] languages. "Of all tools, it is the tool of language that is needed to raise these people from the dire depths of their paganism through the renewing power of the gospel. Apart from that, these materials might be a welcome, yet modest contribution to the study of general linguistics that is collecting elements of language from the four corners around the globe. Especially since the Hamitic language family is still to a large extent a *terra incognita*, much more so than the hinterland of geographic exploration."[50]

Riis's attempt to describe the Twi language was not altogether erroneous, as quite a few of the elements he distinguished could still be used for further language studies, even though the way he presented the data in the book

---

48. See Hans N. Riis, *Grammatical Outline and Vocabulary*, p. iii.

49. The creation of the term "Hamitic languages" was an early attempt (in 1850) to classify African languages and is attributed to Johann Ludwig Krapf, a missionary with the Church Mission Society, who was also trained in the Basel Mission House. See Oswin Köhler, "Geschichte und Probleme der Sprachen Afrikas. Von den Anfängen bis zur Gegenwart" (History and problems of African languages: From its beginnings to the present time), in *Völker Afrikas und ihre traditionellen Kulturen*, vol. 1, ed. Hermann Baumann (Wiesbaden, 1975), pp. 276-77. See also Edith R. Sanders, "The Hamitic Hypothesis: Its Origin and Functions in Time Perspective," *Journal of African History* 10, no. 4 (1969): 521-32.

50. Hans N. Riis, *Elemente des Akwapim-Dialects der Odschi-Sprache enthaltend grammatische Grundzüge und Wörtersammlung nebst einer Sammlung von Sprüchwörtern der Eingeborenen* (Basel, 1853), p. iii.

made it difficult to learn the language systematically. Missionary Johann Gottlieb Christaller (cf. next section), one of Riis's Twi students in Basel, described the latter's approach to Twi metaphorically as "opening the path through an untrodden wilderness in the right direction,"[51] a judgment that carried no negative undertone.

One of the greatest shortcomings of Riis's grammar is his failure to recognize that Twi was a tone (or tonal)[52] language, which is the case for most African languages (apart from examples such as Swahili and Wolof). He assumed that it was also an accent language comparable to the German language. Because of this, he was unable to recognize the existence of two grammatical forms, which are only tonally distinct (as Christaller would find out later). These he named the negative and the potential moods (the latter being a grammatical mood that indicates a wish or a hope, which in modern linguistic terminology is called "optative"):

> Thus to the eye there is no difference between the negative and the potential. There seems to be in pronunciation a minute difference, which, however is difficult to express in writing, consisting merely in a various [sic] modification of the accentuation, which to the European ear is all but imperceptible. This similarity of the two forms cannot but be attended by serious inconvenience especially in the written language, where their distinction depends entirely on the context in which they occur, and it will probably become necessary here to adopt some mark or other to facilitate their distinction.[53]

Riis correctly observed that both of them are formed by prefixing a nasal consonant *(m-* or *n-)* to the verbal root but was unable to detect the underlying tonal pattern of the respective verb forms.[54] So he did not realize that the nasal consonant for the negative form carried a low tone, and the one for the optative a high tone.

In 1846, Hans Nicolai Riis had to seek medical treatment in Europe, and in

---

51. Johann G. Christaller, *A Grammar of the Asante and Fante Language called Tshi [Chwee, Twi]: Based on the Akuapem Dialect: With Reference to the Other (Akan and Fante) Dialects* (Basel, 1875), p. i.

52. The meaning of a word in Akan depends not only on the vowels and consonants of which the word is made, but also on the relative pitch on which each syllable of the word is pronounced; see Dolphyne, *The Akan (Twi-Fante) Language*, p. 52.

53. See Hans N. Riis, *Grammatical Outline and Vocabulary*, p. 44.

54. Example with *kɔ* ("go"); negative: ɔànàkɔá (Low-Low-High tonal pattern), "s/he does not go"; optative: ɔ́ánákɔ́á (High-High-High tonal pattern), "s/he should go."

1850 he was forced to return to Basel definitely due to poor health. He was made Twi instructor for those missionaries in training who were to be sent to the Gold Coast.

Missionary Johann Gottlieb Christaller

Johann Gottlieb Christaller[55] worked as an assistant to a town clerk in his hometown of Winnenden before entering the Basel Mission Seminary, where he was trained from 1848 to 1852. As his talent for languages became apparent, it was decided to send him out to India. Later, when progress in the acquisition of the Twi language continued to pose a major problem in Akropong Akuapem, he was assigned to the Gold Coast:

> The Inspector believes that a more talented brother than the existing one is necessary for the scientific description of the Twi language. The best philologist that we have here is Christaller who has already started to learn Twi with [Hans Nicolai] Riis. This brother is very capable and was already assigned before to serve in Africa. So Christaller will definitely be meant for Africa, especially for linguistic research on the Twi language at Akropong but he should spend another year in Basel and make very good use of Riis' Twi course.[56]

Christaller's main tasks[57] were still very much the same as those of his predecessors, namely, the production of schoolbooks in Twi and the translation of the Scripture, but he held a teaching position in the Catechists' Seminary as well. When he arrived at Akropong in January 1853, he already had a basic competence in the Twi language. He interacted a lot with the local people, to become fluent in Twi. With the help of his students, he was able to embark on the translation of the New Testament, even before he himself was sufficiently competent in Twi. He proceeded as follows: in a first stage, during the Bible studies, he presented his students with a portion from the English

---

55. Johann Gottlieb Christaller (1827-95) from Winnenden (close to Stuttgart) stayed on the Gold Coast from 1853 to 1858 and again from 1862 to 1866. For detailed information on his life and his motivation to enter the Basel Mission, see Erdmann Nöldeke, *Johann Gottlieb Christaller: 1827-1895. Ein Leben für die Afrika-Mission* (J. G. Christaller: 1827-1895; A life for the African mission) (Neuenbürg, 2000), 1:3-13.

56. See the Minutes of the Committee, no. 22, of the Basel Mission Society, 27 August 1851, p. 113, BMA Q-1.

57. See "Instruction f. Br. Christaller," in "Instructionen & Contracte," BMA Q-3-3,26.

Bible and had them translate it into Twi. The different Twi versions could be compared by discussing the grammatical and semantic difficulties in the Twi- and English-language versions respectively. By doing so, a mutual learning process resulted from this method; the teacher learned Twi from his students, whereas they themselves improved their competence in English. In a second stage, Christaller compared these Twi translations with the Greek (or later the Hebrew) original. In this manner, the Gospel of John was translated within the first seven months of his arrival.[58]

Moreover, Christaller collected language samples from the various Twi varieties, as the missionaries were still debating which of those language varieties would be *the* reference dialect or which one would be understood by all, in order to develop a literary language for all of them. After two years in the mission field, Christaller had achieved considerable progress in his analysis of the Twi language, and gave the following report on his studies: "As far as my progress in the acquisition of the country's language is concerned, there was and still is the task of solving the problems of the melodical intonation system in front of me (which differs from the so-called 'accentuation' in European languages). In the past we seemed to travel by night through this tropical country and unconsciously thought that its environment was identical with a European one."[59]

Christaller was the first to solve the mystery of the so-called melodical intonation system of the Twi language, something his teacher Hans Nicolai Riis had faltered over (see above). He reported to Basel:

> It was the natives who basically made me aware of it. David Asante thought as Miss. Mader let me know when I arrived here that I had the talent of pronouncing the Twi language quite acceptably and [David Asante] told me frankly after a long time that I would give quite something, if I spoke Twi like Adolf Mohr [son of missionary Mohr]. (The children of the missionaries born in this country speak like the natives of course, if they learn the language from them.) And shortly before he [David Asante] left for Akyem, . . . he told me that it was the "intonation" of the Twi language that caused most of the difficulties for us [the Europeans]. It is only after this statement that I became aware of the importance of the whole issue, even though I had thought about it

---

58. See Abun-Nasr, *Afrikaner und Missionar*, p. 102, and also *Evangelisches Missions-Magazin* (1854, Quarterly Reports, 01.07.1853–30.09.1853).

59. *Evangelisches Missions-Magazin*, 1855, Quarterly Reports, 01.07.1853–30.09.1853, p. 52.

before. If only this modest young man had told me about this a long time ago.[60]

After studying the tonal system of Twi, he soon developed a practical notational system to distinguish tones in writing. It was only in 1893 that he managed to put his insights into African tone languages into print, in a German publication called *The Tones of the African Languages and Their Names*.[61]

Due to poor health, Christaller had to leave Africa in 1858, but unlike his predecessors, he had accomplished almost all his linguistic assignments, such as the production of schoolbooks and a hymnbook. He also returned to Basel with a manuscript of the four Gospels.[62] On his return, he was made secretary to the Basel Mission Inspector, an occupation he disliked intensely, as he realized that his language talent was being wasted. He fought tirelessly for a position where he could make good use of his knowledge of African languages, but in vain. The committee decided that, "Concerning Christaller,"

> it is like this: He is convinced that he was not in his right position right now, his nerves are blank and he has become quite depressed. He is virtually possessed by the idea of having to finish the work he has started on African languages and that he cannot rest in his current position. . . . He wants another occupation and would like to have more leisure for his African language work. He even thinks of returning to the African mission field. The Inspector believes that this latter idea cannot be realised because of his illness, and about Christaller's proposition to publish a Twi grammar plus a dictionary, the Inspector thinks that this was one of his mad ideas, for the plans for these books were too extensive and thus not feasible.[63]

---

60. Christaller, from Akropong, 30.09.1855, quoted from Abun-Nasr, "Von der Umbildung," p. 207. David Asante (ca. 1834-92) first worked as Christaller's language and teaching assistant in 1856 in the Akropong Catechists' Seminary. The following year, Asante left for Basel to undergo further theological training. After his ordination in 1862, he returned to the Gold Coast, accompanied by Christaller, who returned to the African mission field for a second term (see Abun-Nasr, *Afrikaner und Missionar*, p. 229). As for the word "intonation" as used by David Asante in the quotation, he did not use the correct term to refer to the phenomenon of tone/tonal languages, as intonation is used in accent and in tone/tonal languages likewise (see Dolphyne, *The Akan [Twi-Fante] Language*, p. 52).

61. Johann G. Christaller, *Die Töne der Neger-Sprachen und ihre Bezeichnung* (The tones of the African languages and their names) (Basel, 1893).

62. Abun-Nasr, "Von der Umbildung," p. 210.

63. See the Committee Minutes 60, 28th meeting, p. 90, 12a, dated 11 July 1860, BMA Q-1.

It was not until 1862 that the Basel Mission allowed Christaller to return to the Gold Coast for a second term, even though he kept pleading for permission to go. He became increasingly depressed. Because the committee suspected that he was losing his mind, he was obliged to abandon his cherished work. "The proofs of the Gospel of Mark in the Gã language, of which I got 5 sheets so far, are a source of joy to me and I believe that nothing would be more conducive to the restoration of my health and of my general ability to work, if I could use some hours (e.g. 8-10 a.m.) before noon to work on the Twi grammar. If I understand you correctly, it is just that which I am not allowed to do and I have to hide my talent."[64]

In another letter to Inspector Josenhans, dated 26 September 1861, Christaller seemed to give in and was thus ready to abandon his much-cherished language work and also his hope to get a position within the Basel Mission where he could teach and do more research in African languages.

> I shall agree to all that the Committee will decide by God's grace for me.... I have just this one wish that I'll be able to put down the insights into the Twi language that I have gathered but have not yet been able to make good use of for other people. I'd like to assemble all those insights that the missionaries in Africa cannot and will not find, and put them into a concise grammatical system. This is what I would have liked to do within this year that is now ending for the restitution of my health, not to the disadvantage to my health rather to its promotion. That is what I meant in my letter of 16.11.1860, before I moved to Winnenden. That it could not be realised — I am not allowed to say "by me" but "by the Mission" — that the language could not be "crystallised," whilst the material and the possibility to do so were just lying in front of me. This saddens and humiliates me whenever I think of it, because I believe that God did not allow it for any other reason than I was not humble enough. Now that God — through the facts which I cannot deny — has declared me unworthy and unable for this work, as I do not have any hope left that anybody will do it successfully — I have completely buried this one wish, namely to put my insights into the Twi language into writing for the benefit of other people, in a forest at Teinach — in just the same manner as Abraham once sacrificed his own son Isaac.[65]

64. See letter by Christaller to Josenhans, Winnenden, 16 November 1860, quoted from Nöldeke, *Johann Gottlieb Christaller,* 2:140.
65. See letter by Christaller to Josenhans, Winnenden, 26 September 1861, quoted from Nöldeke, *Johann Gottlieb Christaller,* 2:153.

Quite unexpectedly, a short time later, Christaller obtained permission to serve for a second term in Africa. He set about the journey in 1862, together with David Asante, and missionary Johann A. Mader.[66] Christaller's family stayed back home, but his wife Emilie was to join him soon.

He was given the following instructions concerning his work:[67]

- Stationed at Aburi, he should continue the translation of the Bible into Twi;
- He should translate and revise schoolbooks when asked to do so by the District Conference or the committee;
- He should compile a Twi-English dictionary and a small Twi grammar for the use of schools, and later a grammar for the teachers;
- He should daily teach a lesson at the Girls' School at Aburi, the subject of which would be indicated to him by the school inspector after hearing the station conference;
- He should assist Br. Dieterle — as far as his health would permit — in preaching on the station and beyond.

In a letter to Inspector Josenhans, Christaller tried to rid himself of the teaching and preaching assignments, not because he disliked them but because he was convinced that he was the only one who was able to move ahead with language studies in Twi:

> Apart from the language work I do not have enough strength for other missionary work. I'd feel bad, if I felt the spiritual needs of the people and yet would not be able to help or assist them; why should I not concentrate my energy on the indispensable auxiliary task and dedicate myself exclusively to it for the years to come, in the same fashion as a wheelwright, a locksmith or an economist? I am convinced that the elaboration and presentation of the language building is almost as necessary as the construction of a church, the expansion of school buildings and the erection of seminaries.[68]

In 1868 he returned permanently to Europe, and even though he would have been allowed to serve in Africa for a third term, he decided against it. He

---

66. Johann Adam Mader (1826-82), from Mägerkingen (Germany), stayed on the Gold Coast with intervals from 1851 to 1877.

67. File "Instructionen & Contracte," BMA, Q-3-3,26, pp. 74-75.

68. See letter by Christaller to Josenhans, dated 8 May 1863, quoted from Nöldeke, *Johann Gottlieb Christaller*, 2:184.

instead returned to Schorndorf to live with his five children, who had become half-orphans after his wife Emilie died in Kyebi in 1866. He continued his linguistic work on the Twi language by correspondence with David Asante and with language assistants that he requested from the Basel Mission.

The Impact of Christaller's "Language Work"

Johann Gottlieb Christaller could not have carried out his language studies without the help of his assistants.[69] His most noteworthy "language assistant," with whom he worked for more than thirty years, was David Asante. Over the years, Asante stepped out from under Christaller's shadow; he became a translator and a writer in the Twi language in his own right.[70]

David Asante was born into the royal family at Akropong Akuapem and adopted by missionary Johannes Christian Dieterle. He belonged to a group of four Gold Coasters who were sent for further training to Basel and Stuttgart in 1857. After five years of training in the Basel Mission Seminary, he was ordained in 1862 and was to go back to his country to serve as a missionary.[71] Over the years, Asante became a close friend of Christaller and also an ally in his fight to justify his position as a missionary linguist, as their Twi correspondence,[72] among other things, bears witness. They started correspond-

---

69. According to Abun-Nasr, *Afrikaner und Missionar,* p. 102, the names of these assistants were William Hoffmann, Paul Staudt, Jonathan Palmer, and David Asante.

70. Here are the books David Asante translated into Twi (see Abun-Nasr, *Afrikaner und Missionar,* pp. 194-95): 1. *Kristofo nyamesom hõ kyerẹ* (*The Doctrines of the Christian Religion,* by Johann H. Kurtz) (Basel, 1872); 2. *Onipa koma (Man's Heart, Either God's Temple or Satan's Abode)* (Basel, 1874); 3. *Wiase abasẹm mu nsẹmma-nsẹmma* (*Stories from General History,* by Ernst Kappe) (Basel, 1874); 4. *Germane asase so kristosom terew* (*The Spread of Christianity in Germany,* author not indicated) (Basel, 1875); 5. *Kristoni akwantu* (*Pilgrim's Progress,* by John Bunyan) (Basel, 1885). Apart from his translation work, Asante wrote numerous reports, especially on his mission travels, in Twi, of which many were printed in the *Christian Messenger* that was founded in 1883 by J. G. Christaller.

71. See Abun-Nasr, *Afrikaner und Missionar,* p. 108.

72. I am very much indebted to Dr. Sonia Abun-Nasr (Basel), who drew my attention to this Twi correspondence in 1997, and also to Mr. Ebenezer Sakyi-Addo (Akropong), who translated the Twi letters into English. The whole (unpublished) correspondence is contained in the Basel Mission Archive and comprises about fifty letters, mostly written in Twi by David Asante, and a few in German by Christaller, over a span of almost thirty years, from 1862 to 1890 (BMA D-20.2,7). The matters they discussed with each other over the years were basically language questions, that is, Christaller wrote down specific questions on the Twi language, in German, which Asante answered in his Twi mother tongue. Apart from that, he provided J. G. Christaller with geographical information and sociolinguistic

ing with each other when they returned to the Gold Coast in 1862 and were posted in different mission stations, Christaller in Aburi and David Asante in Akropong.

Christaller's main linguistic task was still the translation of the Bible, which he gradually accomplished with the help of language assistants and students at the Akropong Catechists' Seminary. From 1863, individual books of the Bible were printed one after the other. In 1866, David Asante wrote a letter to Christaller on his reception of the Psalms and Proverbs that had just been published: "I got myself part of your latest printed translations — they appeal to me very much, especially the Psalms and also the Proverbs, but less so the Book of Genesis. The translation of the Psalms is excellent, even unique. Nobody can possibly read them without feeling their superiority. As they resemble the 'Twikwadwom' very much, the Twi people will like to read them. The Lord gives his blessing to them. Now, at last, I'd like to congratulate and thank you for them in the name of Africa."[73]

It is not known whether Christaller had studied the literary genre of *Twikwadwom* before, but since the Psalms were translated in that fashion, whether intentionally or not, the resemblance with this genre was crucial to its reception.[74]

In 1871, when the whole Bible could eventually be published in Twi, Christaller was informed from Larteh, where David Asante was still stationed, that the availability of the Twi Bible would have a positive effect on literacy. It also brought a new impetus to education in general:

> Both literates and illiterates welcomed its [the Bible's] arrival. Many illiterates in my congregation here are learning how to read. Our prayer now is that God will make people, Christians or Pagans, mightily hunger after His Word. We have also received the Bible History. We are so much pleased with that, too. I am aware that it is not your wish to be praised for your work, yet on examination of these two pieces of work,

---

observations that he collected on his mission travels, with the latest news from the various mission stations on the Gold Coast, with intimate information on former European and African coworkers concerning their conduct, but also about political and other events. All this makes this correspondence an invaluable source not only for linguists and theologians but also for historians and anthropologists.

73. Asante to Christaller, from Larteh, 1 November 1866, original in German; BMA D-20.2,7. A *Twikwadwom* was a song of mourning, a song expressive of sorrow and lamentation, delivered in a dramatic manner; an elegy (see Christaller, *The Dictionary*, p. 270).

74. In modern Bible translation, translators are required to study text or discourse types (such as narrative, poetry, etc.) of the receptor languages.

one cannot help thanking God, and then praising whoever made them. I am not alone in thinking this way. All others share my thinking.[75]

The Twi Bible, however, increased the rate of literacy in both Akuapem and the Fante area, as David Asante reported after one of his itinerations along the coast: "From there I went to Fante.... I did not only sell books, I also spread the gospel. If someone bought a book and expressed the wish to know how to read, I at once started teaching him how to read. After two or three hours, he would know how to read. The reason is that all those who wished to buy books were people who had once attended school, so they only needed some guidance to help them to read."[76] In the same letter, Asante narrated to Christaller how popular books in Twi had become, and that he himself was surprised at the extent to which he had been able to sell African-language books. He intended to advertise the list of available books in the journal *Gold Coast News*[77] and hoped to reach a wider (literate) audience, especially among the Fante-speaking population:

> Nobody thought that the books would be bought in that way.... The books that the people liked most were the Bible, the two Dictionaries, the book on the Heart of Man, the Primer, and the hymn books.... It looks as if the Wesleyans do not want the Twi books on Fante land.... I am sorry for the Fante. They are interested in Christianity but they do not have competent and interested people to help them. Wherever we arrive at, they ask for Basel Missionaries to come to help them, for they do not see what the Wesleyans are doing.[78]

---

75. "ebae, woṅ a wonim kaṅ nè woṅ a wonnim nnyina eyee woṅ fe, mā pii abo modeṅ resua keṅkaṅ ne wo m'asafom' ha. Nea afei yesere Onyame ara ne se, omā hõ kom kese mmra kristofo nè abosonsomfo mu. Anyamesem mu abakosem no nso ato yeṅ. eno nso so ani se biribi. Minim se wode wompe se woyi wo aye wo w'adwuma hõ, nso wofwe sā. Adwuma abieṅ yi a, na eṅka wo fwẽ se nea oyee woda Ony. ase a wuyi no aye kā hõ. Nea mekā yi nye me ṅkõ trim asem; nnipa nny. na ekā no sā." Asante to Christaller, from Larteh, 29 December 1871, Twi original, BMA D-20.2,7. The Bible history mentioned is *Dr. Barth's Bible Stories,* in German; see Christian G. Barth, *Anyamesem mu abakosem* (Basel, 1871).

76. "Na mefaa so mekoo Fante a wofi pūaa me se meṅko akye no,... Nso nye nhōma ṅkō na metoṅ. Meretoṅ ṅhōma no na mekā asem mefa ho. Nea ope se oto nhōma no bi na se ose onnim kaṅ a, na amonom' ho ara mede ne kyere mahyehye so, nnonhwerow 2 se 3 pe na oahū kaṅ. Efi se woṅ a woto ṅhōma no nnyina ako sukuu peṅ nti wonnye kyerenā." Asante to Christaller, from Anum, 2 June 1885, Twi original, BMA D-20.2,7.

77. A monthly journal published by W. C. Niblett, from March till August 1885; see K. A. B. Jones-Quartey, "The Gold Coast Press: 1822–c. 1930, and the Anglo-African Press — the Chronologies," *Research Review,* no. 4 (1967): 38.

78. "Obi ani nni so se wobeto ṅhōma no sa.... Ṅhōma a wopee titiriw nè Kyerew

The Wesleyan Methodist Society started their mission work along the coast around the same time as the Basel Mission in Akuapem (in the second half of the 1830s).[79] Like the Basel missionaries, the Methodists were encouraged "by the Home Committee to acquire a knowledge of the native languages," but their efforts proved far less successful.[80] The production of Christian literature in Fante began later than that of the Basel Mission, even though the Home Committee recommended that Methodist missionaries embark on the translation of the Bible as early as 1858. In 1874, the Methodist catechism was published as a bilingual Fante-English edition.[81] The four Gospels in Fante were published thirty years after the Twi edition had appeared in 1859,[82] which the historian Carl C. Reindorf considered to be a "great mistake":

> Had our [Methodist] missionaries fully recognised the importance of native literature, and encouraged such of the native ministers as were competent, ... to undertake the work of translation, our Mission would have been more progressive, our converts more intelligent, and gospel truths much more diffused amongst the masses. Latterly this mistake was seen and efforts put forth to meet the want, but though something has been done, we are still left far behind in this very important and indispensable department of our work by this fundamental error.[83]

Unlike Reindorf, Christaller was not happy about the Methodists producing their own Bible in Fante, as he had still hoped to integrate Fante into a single written form for all the Twi and Fante varieties. According to Thomas Bearth, this hope was thwarted when the Fante translation emerged, as it gave this language variety quasi-official recognition of its distinct and separate status.[84]

Kronkron, Dictionary horow 2 no, Onipa koma ṅhōma no, Primer nè Nnwom. . . . Wesleyfo no mpẹ sẹ yeṅ Twi nhōma yi ba woṅ maṅ mu họ. . . . eyẹ me yaw mā Fantefo sẹ wọpẹ anyamesẹm na wọannyā nnipa pa bi ammẹyẹ woṅ mu adwuma. Baabiara a yẹbẹdu na wọkā sẹ Baselfo mmra họ na woṅhū nea Wesleyfo rekyerẹ." Asante to Christaller, from Anum, 2 June 1885, Twi original, BMA D-20.2,7.

79. See Adrian Hastings, *The Church in Africa, 1450-1950* (Oxford, 1994), p. 179.
80. See Carl C. Reindorf, *History of the Gold Coast and Asante* (Basel, 1895), p. 244.
81. Wesleyan Missionary Society, *The First Catechism of the Wesleyan Methodists*, translated into the Fanti language (London, 1874).
82. The British and Foreign Bible Society, *Nsempa Anan: The Four Gospels in Fanti*, trans. Rev. A. W. Parker (London, 1886, but not published before 1888/89).
83. Reindorf, *History*, p. 245.
84. Thomas Bearth, "J. G. Christaller: A Holistic View of Language and Culture — and

As Christaller found it difficult to work without a language assistant, he repeatedly asked the Basel Mission Committee for help, but to no avail. David Asante, himself, would have been ready to come to Europe again.

> I have thought that were it not for my encumbrances — my wife and children — as well as my position here, I would have agreed to come over to work with you, if that would be sanctioned by the Basel Mission. I place greater premium on your work and teaching than any other sector of this mission work. Yet I do not think the authorities in Basel think the same as I do, otherwise your work would be given the same attention paid to the various schools. If they ignore your work and concentrate only on schools, it would amount to climbing a tree from the top. Probably they think that after the ministers have learnt the local languages, they would use books from their own country to teach in the schools here, and that would be all. But they would fail that way. Progress being made lately in our schools has its roots in the availability of books written in the Twi language.[85]

In another letter, Asante suggested that Christaller should have used more Akyem Twi: "If I had been at Akyem during the period you were doing the translation, I would have requested you to make it more Akyem than you did. The reason is that in spoken Twi here in Akuapem a speaker's performance is rated higher when his language has bits of Akyem thrown in here and there. Our Akuapem Twi lends itself to being mixed with Akyem and even Fante. Fante, too, could be treated likewise, but not Akyem, which will lose its charm that way."[86]

C. C. Reindorf's History," in *The Recovery of the West African Past: African Pastors and Africa History in the Nineteenth Century; C. C. Reindorf and Samuel Johnson,* ed. Paul Jenkins (Basel, 2000), p. 92.

85. "Mankasa manyā no sā nsusuwi sẹ, ẹnyẹ adwuma yi nè abusūasẹm (ọyere nè mma) nti a, na Baselfo pẹ no sā a, ankā wose mémmra nea wowọ a, mẹba. Efisẹ w'adwuma yi ne sukūkyerẹ yẹ me anyamedwuma yim' kẹse sen nea aka yi nny. Na me de, ẹnyẹ me sẹ Basel mpanyin no dwen no sa; ankā wọde onipa hẹfwẹ w'adwuma yi sẹ wọde fwẹ sukū horow yi. Sẹ wọanfa onipa anfwẹ wode yi, na wose sukū horow yi na wofwẹ dodo a, na ẹtesẹ wufi dua soro reforo. Wosusuw sesẹ sẹ, asọfo no sūa ọkasa no wie nam wọn kurom kasa nhōma so de kyerẹkyerẹ a, na ne yọ ara nen. Nso mọborọ! Wọn de wonnim sẹ ete. Nansā yi adesūa a ẹkọ so yi na efi nhōma a wọanā wọ Twi kasam." Asante to Christaller, from Kukurantumi, 30 December 1873, Twi original, BMA D-20.2,7.

86. "ẹne sẹ ẹhọbere no na maba Akyem a, ankā mẹkā na wayẹ no Akyem mu dodo asen sẹnea woyẹẹ no yi; efisẹ Akuapem, obiara kasa na wose ne kasa yẹ dẹ a, na ọde Akyem frafra mu. Yen Akuapem Twi wọ họ yi, wode Akyem ne Fante po fram' a, ẹyẹ yiye, na Fante

Asante himself continued to stress the importance of Christaller's language work and encouraged the enthusiasm with which he approached it. He even suggested that the Twi language would become more important in the future and could be introduced as a school and church language in other African countries:

> Go ahead. You are not labouring in or for only Akuapem and Akyem. Your work shall eventually cover much of African regions and countries, too. Today, Twi is understood and spoken in all farming communities, and it is their wish that Twi-speaking teachers work among them. And truly, Twi is spoken in a very wide area. Wherever you go, if you do speak Twi, you are at home. English and Twi are regarded as the two most important languages in this country. Alexander the Great made it possible for Greek to be used extensively as a missionary tool in his day. In like manner, Asante power has helped to make Twi a missionary tool for us today.[87]

"Asante power" is certainly one of the reasons for the spread of Twi during the last two centuries, but there are other reasons as well, namely, trade and migration.[88] Asante mentions the example of the Ewe traders who learnt Twi to promote their business:

> At the time of writing, the Twi language has become a licence with which you can travel to most of these towns with protection and safety. The Ewe people have accepted the fact that knowledge of the Twi language promotes trade because many people understand it. So your deci-

---

nso woyɛ no sā a, eyɛ yiye, Akyem na ɛn'de woyɛ no sā a, na ɛnyɛ dɛ." Asante to Christaller, from Kyebi, 20 September 1874, Twi original, BMA D-20.2,7.

87. "na kɔso ara. Nyɛ Akuapem & Akyem ṅkõ adwuma na wayɛ sɛ nso wugu so yɛ yi na ɛte sɛ Abibiri mu amaṅ ne nsase pii adwuma na woreyɛ yi. ɛnɛ kua maṅ nny. te kasa Twi pɛ sɛ aṅkā Twifo aky.kyerɛfo mmra wɔn ṅkyeṅ. Amaṅ nso a ɛkasa Twi wom' nohõa nyɛ adewa. ɛnɛ wonam babiara na wokasa Twi a wogye wo tom mma nny. Nɛ ɔkasa a aman nny. bu no sɛ nfaso wɔ hõ ne Eṅiresi ne Twi. Sɛ Helakasa yeɛ Alexander kɛseɛ bere so māa anyamesɛm kā asomafo bere so no sɛ Asantefo tumi bere no amā Twi kasa ayɛ amā nɛ yi asɛmpa kā neṅ." Asante to Christaller, from Kukurantumi, 20 February 1882, Twi original, BMA D-20.2,7.

88. See Eugen L. Rapp, "Zur Ausbreitung einer westafrikanischen Stammessprache (das Twi)" (On the spread of a West African language [Twi]), in *Afrikanistische Studien (Festschrift für Westermann)*, ed. Johannes Lukas (Berlin, 1955), pp. 220-30. For the wider context, cf. Judith T. Irvine, "Subjected Words: African Linguistics and the Colonial Encounter," *Language and Communication* 28, no. 4 (2008): 323-43.

sion to write a Twi book [the *Christian Messenger,* established in 1883] is most welcome because there will be so many people ready to buy and read it. You can guess the prospects yourself when you consider the vast Twi-speaking area and other areas I have written about including faraway Salaga and Gyaman. The spread of God's word to all corners in this country cannot be done without the Twi language. To top it all, the Twi people are the most powerful in this country and all others respect them and their language also.[89]

Christaller persevered against all odds and achieved his scientific goals by publishing prolifically in Twi and about Twi and other African languages as well.[90] Much of what he wrote is still of scientific value today, especially his *Twi Grammar* (1875) and also his *Twi Dictionary* (1881). This latter is still unmatched, compared to other works on Akan lexicography published over the last 130 years.

Christaller received scant recognition for his language studies from the Basel Mission, but, during his lifetime, his work did attract praise and attention in academic circles. For his years of scholarly work in philology, Christaller was twice awarded the prestigious Prix Volney[91] by the Institut de France, once in 1876 and again in 1882. Notably, it was the Basel Mission that submitted his works to the panel of judges.[92]

89. "Nɛ yi wode Twi nam emu hɔ bābiara a siwa nti wo na wɔakɔ aba. Hūafo nè pɔtɔfo a ɛwom' hɔ nny. sɛ Twi na ɛhō wɔ nfaso seṅ kasa nny. efi sɛ wode kɔ babiara a wunyā nea ɔte nè no kasa. Enti woyɛ Twi ṅhōma a amaṅ a woreyɛ amā woṅ nni ano. Wo ara fwɛ Twifo babraha dedaw yi na fwɛ nea merekyerɛ yi de siaṅ kɔfa Sraha dakɔpem Gyaman n. a yi anyamesɛm bɛko hɔ sɛ na yeṅ Twi ṅhōma yi ara na wode rekɔ. Yɛda Onyame ase sɛ ɔde wo mā Twifo. Nso ɛyɛ ṅwoṅwa sɛ Twifo ara na woṅ ani yɛ deṅ amaṅ a aka yi nny. mu." Asante to Christaller, from Anum, 29 May 1882, Twi original, BMA D-20.2,7.

90. Apart from his main works, as listed in the bibliography, Christaller was a regular contributor of scientific articles to newly founded Africanist journals: *Büttner's Zeitschrift für Afrikanische Sprachen* (edited by Carl G. Büttner, 1889-93) and *Zeitschrift für afrikanische und oceanische Sprachen* (edited by August Seidel). Seidel, in his obituary for Christaller, "Christaller and African Linguistics," highlighted the great help Christaller had been to him when he started in the same year that the latter died (1895).

91. See Joan Leopold, ed., *The Prix Volney,* vol. Ia, *Its History and Development for the Significance of Linguistic Research* (Dordrecht, 1999).

92. In 1876, the Basel Mission submitted the following three books for Christaller: the translation of the Twi Bible (1871, together with David Asante and Theopil Opoku), the English-Twi-Gā dictionary (1874, together with the missionaries C. W. Locher and J. Zimmermann), and his Twi grammar (1875). For all these entries, Christaller got an award of 300 francs that year (Leopold, *The Prix Volney,* pp. 335-36). In 1882, he submitted his Fante-Asante dictionary (1881) and was again awarded 300 francs (p. 346).

Conclusion

Even though Protestant missionary societies, such as the Basel Mission, put great emphasis on language acquisition in the mission field for educational and evangelization purposes, establishing a discipline called missionary linguistics was not the intention. Language studies for the propagation of the gospel were rather seen as a transient objective that should not divert (human and other) resources indefinitely from the major objective of evangelical work: the conversion of the heathen to Christianity. Research on language(s) and the thorough description of language forms, however, is an endeavor that takes years, if not decades. Missionary linguistics is thus a by-product or an auxiliary science — a strand of work that was seen to be essential to evangelization. Hans Nicolai Riis and Johann Gottlieb Christaller serve as examples of gifted linguists who fought against the odds for a position in the field of missionary linguistics. As I have shown in this chapter, Christaller especially paid a high personal price for the passion with which he invested his linguistic work. However, in the process he laid a good part of the foundations on which future generations would build the scientific study of West African languages.

Select Bibliography

Abun-Nasr, Sonia. *Afrikaner und Missionar. Die Lebensgeschichte von David Asante.* Basel, 2003.

———. "Von der 'Umbildung heidnischer Landessprachen zu christlichen' — Die Anfänge von Schrift und Schriftlichkeit in Akuapem, Goldküste." In *Wege durch Babylon: Missionare, Sprachstudien und interkulturelle Kommunikation,* edited by Reinhard Wendt. Tübingen, 1998.

Akan Language Committee. *Akan Orthography (Spelling Rules).* Accra, 1995.

Antwi, Daniel, and Paul Jenkins. "The Moravians, the Basel Mission and the Akuapem State in the Early Nineteenth Century." In *Christian Missionaries and the State in the Third World,* edited by Holger Bernt Hansen and Michael Twaddle. Oxford, 2002.

Bearth, Thomas. "J. G. Christaller: A Holistic View of Language and Culture — and C. C. Reindorf's History." In *The Recovery of the West African Past: African Pastors and Africa History in the Nineteenth Century; C. C. Reindorf and Samuel Johnson,* edited by Paul Jenkins. Basel, 2000.

Christaller, Johann G. *A Dictionary of the Asante and Fante Language Called Tshi-Chwee, with a Grammatical Introduction and Appendices on the Geography of the Gold Coast and Other Subjects.* Basel, 1881 and 1933.

———. *A Grammar of the Asante and Fante Language Called Tshi [Chwee, Twi]: Based on the Akuapem Dialect; With Reference to the Other (Akan and Fante) Dialects.* Basel, 1875.

Dolphyne, Florence A. *The Akan (Twi-Fante) Language: Its Sound System and Tonal Structure.* Accra, 1988.

Gilbert, Michelle. "No Condition Is Permanent: Ethnicity Construction and the Use of History in Akuapem." *Africa* 67, no. 4 (1997).

Kropp Dakubu, Mary E. "Notes on the Linguistic Situation on the Coast of Ghana during the Nineteenth Century." *Research Review*, n.s., 1, no. 2 (1985).

Leopold, Joan, ed. *The Prix Volney.* Vol. Ia, *Its History and Development for the Significance of Linguistic Research.* Dordrecht, 1999.

Meyer, Birgit. "Christianity and the Ewe Nation: German Pietist Missionaries, Ewe Converts and the Politics of Culture." *Journal of Religion in Africa* 32, no. 2 (2002).

Nöldeke, Erdmann. *Johann Gottlieb Christaller: 1827-1895. Ein Leben für die Afrika-Mission.* 2 vols. Neuenbürg, 2000.

Riis, Hans N. *Grammatical Outline and Vocabulary of the Oji-Language, with Especial Reference to the Akwapim-Dialect, Together with a Collection of Proverbs of the Natives.* Basel, 1854.

Sill, Ulrike. "Encounters in Quest of Christian Womanhood: The Basel Mission in Pre- and Early Colonial Ghana." Ph.D. diss., University of Basel, 2007.

CHAPTER 3

Of Fetishism and Totemism:
Missionary Ethnology and Academic Social Science in Early-Twentieth-Century Gabon

JOHN CINNAMON

This chapter assesses the contributions and impact of late-nineteenth- and early-twentieth-century missionary ethnographers as producers of anthropological knowledge about equatorial Africa. A second concern is to compare and contrast the theoretical orientations of missionary ethnographers, particularly in Gabon, and academic social scientists. How, during the early decades of European colonialism in equatorial Africa and during this transitional period before missionaries were largely excluded from professional anthropology, did missionary knowledge production and academic social science influence each other? The present chapter looks comparatively at the writings of two missionaries, American Presbyterian Robert Hamill Nassau and French Spiritan Henri Trilles. Nassau worked in present-day Equatorial Guinea, Gabon, and Cameroon from 1861 to 1906; Trilles worked in Gabon during several stays between 1893 and 1907. Both men learned African languages, traveled in the interior of present-day Gabon and Equatorial Guinea, claimed the sympathetic cultural understanding of Africans, and wrote prolifically about the peoples they sought to understand and convert. In addition to writing for church-based and popular audiences, they also sought to contribute to social science. In their ethnographic texts, they addressed already-circulating discourses and scholarly conventions of their day while contributing to ethnographic knowledge, albeit through the filter of the evangelizing imperative.

Elsewhere, I have explored Nassau's and Trilles's fieldwork experiences, their claims of ethnographic expertise, Nassau's unintended ethnography of the colonial missionary encounter, and Trilles's improbable but surprisingly prominent role in the genealogy of Fang ethnography.[1] Here I focus on Nassau's ethnological explorations of fetishism and Trilles's writings on totemism, important concepts respectively in the travel writing and anthropology of their day. By the time Nassau left Africa in 1906, the concept of fetishism had largely failed to catch on in the anthropology of religion.[2] The concept of "fetish" — as opposed to fetishism — nonetheless continues to play a role in both African and academic discourses today. Trilles published his major work on totemism, *Le Totémisme chez les Fân,* on the eve of World War I at the height of academic interest in the topic. Almost immediately, however, the concept of totemism came under attack from within anthropology and fell into decline. Rather than critiquing these concepts here, I situate Nassau's and Trilles's writings against the shifting background of popular and social science knowledge production. Together, their writings demonstrate how certain missionaries sought to draw on their long field experience to address important scientific debates of their day while at the same time remaining on the margins of emerging academic disciplines.

It is against the backdrop of popular ethnography on fetishism and spirited academic debate on totemism that I explore the ethnographic and ethnological contributions of Nassau and Trilles. Nassau, a New Jersey Presbyterian, had already embarked on his missionary career in Africa when anthropology began to develop in the United States; he never gained a foothold in academic anthropology. Princeton University, where Nassau com-

---

1. See John M. Cinnamon, "Social Science, and the Uses of Ethnographic Knowledge in Colonial Gabon," *History in Africa* 33 (2006): 413-32; Cinnamon, "Robert Hamill Nassau: Missionary Ethnography and the Colonial Encounter in Gabon," *Le Fait Missionaire* 19 (2006): 37-64; Cinnamon, "Colonial Anthropologies and the Primordial Imagination in Equatorial Africa," in *Ordering Africa: Anthropology, European Imperialism, and the Politics of Knowledge,* ed. Helen Tilley with Robert J. Gordon (Manchester, 2007), pp. 225-51.

2. Anthropologists have continued to draw inspiration from Marx's concept of commodity fetishism. See, for example, Michael T. Taussig, *The Devil and Commodity Fetishism in South America* (Chapel Hill, N.C., 1980), and David Graeber, *Toward an Anthropological Theory of Value: The False Coin of Our Own Dreams* (New York, 2001), pp. 66, 105. In a recent monograph on the Christian mission encounter and modernity in Sumba, Indonesia, anthropologist Webb Keane uses the term "fetishism" "to denote the imputation to others of a false understanding of the divisions between human and nonhuman, subject and object, an error that threatens human agency." Keane is not referring to Sumba religious practices or theories of agency but to missionary discourses of otherness; Webb Keane, *Christian Moderns: Freedom and Fetish in the Mission Encounter* (Berkeley, 2007), p. 27.

pleted both his undergraduate degree (1854) and his seminary training (1859), led the conservative U.S. reaction to evolutionary theory, a dominant anthropological paradigm in the late nineteenth century. Swiss physical geographer and geologist Arnold Guyot, who began teaching at Princeton in 1854, "recognised the progressive nature of the fossil record, the antiquity of the earth, the figurative language of Genesis, and the possibility of at least organic development," while seeking at the same time "to harmonize science and scripture."[3] Other leading Princeton figures, such as Charles Hodge, principal of Princeton Theological Seminary from 1851 to 1878, while not a biblical literalist in the sense of present-day creationists, nonetheless concluded that ateleological Darwinism, which rejected the idea of design, was tantamount to atheism.[4] James McCosh, who became president of Princeton in 1868, adhered to a sort of "evolutionary Calvinism" that sought to reconcile evolution and intelligent design. Through the late nineteenth century, while Nassau was in Africa, making periodic visits to New Jersey while on furlough, Princeton scientists and theologians continued in various ways to seek a balance between evolutionary theory, scriptural infallibility, and divine supervision. Only after Nassau's death in 1921, and after a half-century of growing accommodation with Darwinism, did Princeton theologians begin to dismiss evolutionary theory outright, anticipating the later positions of creation science.[5]

Between the time he finished theological seminary and the time he left for Africa in 1861, Nassau completed an accelerated M.D. degree at the University of Pennsylvania Medical School. This training may have contributed to his scientific spirit of discovery, but he never intended to practice missionary medicine. His main motivation was to look after his own health at a time when missionaries to Africa still experienced high mortality. His medical training nonetheless allowed him to provide medical assistance and first aid to his children and occasionally to others. He was also able to prepare and ship scientific specimens back to museums at Princeton and the University of Pennsylvania.[6]

---

3. Ronald L. Numbers, *The Creationists: From Scientific Creationism to Intelligent Design,* expanded ed. (Cambridge, Mass., 2006), pp. 21-23.

4. David N. Livingstone, "The Idea of Design: The Vicissitudes of a Key Concept in the Princeton Response to Darwin," *Scottish Journal of Theology* 37 (1984): 329-31.

5. Livingstone, "The Idea of Design," pp. 336-37. Livingstone concludes, "The vicissitudes of the idea of design . . . hold the key to the theory to understanding much of the orthodox Calvinist encounter with the theory of evolution in the late nineteenth and early twentieth centuries."

6. Raymond W. Teeuwissen, "Robert Hamill Nassau 1835-1921: Presbyterian Pioneer Missionary to Equatorial West Africa" (master's thesis, Louisville Theological Seminary, 1973), pp. 14, 54, 59.

Of Fetishism and Totemism

Nassau's writings on fetishism were part of a discursive and representational system that stretches back to fifteenth-century Portuguese mariners and continues to inform twenty-first-century west and west-central African religious and anthropological imaginaries. Trilles, criticized even during his lifetime for his exuberant imagination and interpretive leaps of faith, waxed most scholarly in his writings on Fang totemism. And Trilles, more so than Nassau, read and sought to engage the growing field of anthropology. In *Le Totémisme chez les Fân,* he cited key scholars on the subject, including McLennan, Tylor, Frazer, and Durkheim, discussed below. Trilles's 1914 paper on the subject was published in *Anthropos* in a special section on totemism alongside articles by Rivers and (Radcliffe-) Brown, (soon to be) major figures in British social anthropology.[7] Yet, although Trilles's speculations of Egyptian origins are still influential among Fang intellectuals, his writings on totemism seem to have had little lasting impact on "Fang studies" or anthropology. As Robert Alun Jones argues, by 1910 professional anthropologists were already turning away from totemism as a key anthropological concept.[8] Elsewhere in Africa, far away from the main sites of totemic ethnography (Australia and North America), scholars have occasionally made use of the concept to analyze the relations between clan structure, exogamy, and religion.[9]

Debates on the complex and often problematic relationship between missionaries and professional anthropology date back to the late nineteenth century when British anthropologist Edward Tylor complained of missionary bias.[10] This uneasy relationship has continued forward to the present. African philosophers, V. Y. Mudimbe and Fabien Eboussi Boulaga, for example, have underlined the commonalities between missionaries and anthropologists, while challenging anthropologists' claims of scientific objectivity.[11] In a 2004 volume on anthropology and missiology, Eboussi Boulaga posits that a critique of mission provides a necessary foundation for a reflexive African an-

---

7. The special section "Das Problem des Totemismus," *Anthropos* 9 (1914), included articles by Trilles, "Le totémisme chez les Fân," pp. 630-40; A. R. Brown, "The Definition of Totemism," pp. 622-30; and W. H. R. Rivers, "The Terminology of Totemism," pp. 640-46.

8. Robert Alun Jones, *The Secret of the Totem: Religion and Society from McLennan to Freud* (New York, 2005).

9. See, for example, E. E. Evans-Pritchard, *Nuer Religion* (New York, 1956); Alfred Adler, "Le totémisme en Afrique Noire," *Systèmes de pensée en Afrique Noire* 15 (1998): 13-107.

10. Christopher Herbert, *Culture and Anomie: Ethnographic Imagination in the Nineteenth Century* (Chicago, 1991), p. 152.

11. V. Y. Mudimbe, *The Invention of Africa: Gnosis, Philosophy, and the Order of Knowledge* (Bloomington, Ind., 1988), pp. 44-45, 65-67.

thropology in which Africans discover how they are viewed from the outside — "as an object or project for others, their knowledge, their power or their compassion."[12] At the same time, Eboussi Boulaga suggests that missionaries and anthropologists are "brothers, even when they behave as enemies." The missionary devotes himself to proselytism, while the anthropologist purveys "secular gospels as profane ideologies," which in turn have genuine consequences in "economy, politics, and culture." By leading Africans to see themselves as others, both anthropologists and missionaries have contributed to complex African identities that emerge as "strategic and dialectical responses" to the ethnographic and mission encounter. Such identities transform and displace the object of anthropological/missiological inquiry beyond the "capture" of anthropology and missiology.[13] Eboussi has also sought to subvert the meaning of the term "fetish," a key concept treated in the present chapter. In his work *Christianisme sans fétiche*, he does not argue that Africans "should give up the use of amulets or small images of the divine." Instead, he suggests that Christianity and God, as presented to Africans, have themselves "been reduced to fetishism, because the ultimate and transcendental have been understood as manageable" and under the control of missionaries and the church.[14]

Theologian and missiologist Anton Houtepens, while not directly addressing Eboussi's critique, argues instead for "an intensive collaboration between cultural anthropology and the theology of mission, leading to a comparative theological anthropology." Houtepens explores two possibilities for such collaboration. First, cultural anthropology can play a "descriptive and purely empirical role . . . but at a price of losing an essential aspect of religion." Second, anthropology and missiology can work together to address "human problems: poverty, violence, oppression and exploitation, inequality, sexual and marital conflicts, the destruction of social structures through modernity and processes of globalization . . . , while contributing to human happiness and religious freedom 'for the glory of God.'"[15] French historian of Christianity Jean-François Zorn also underlines the commonalities of anthropology and missiology, "born from the 'theoretical bricolage' of

---

12. F. Eboussi Boulaga, "Fétichisme et prosélytisme," in *Anthropologie et missiologie XIXe-XXe siècles: Entre connivence et rivalité*, ed. Olivier Servais and Gérard Van't Spijker (Paris, 2004), p. 62.

13. Boulaga, "Fétichisme et prosélytisme," p. 63.

14. Jan Heijke, "Fabien Eboussi Boulaga's Fight against Fetishism," *Exchange* 30, no. 4 (2001): 311.

15. Anton Houtepens, "Vers une anthropologie de la Pâque?" in *Anthropologie et missiologie XIXe-XXe siècles*, pp. 73-74.

fieldworkers," either by themselves or with the assistance of colonial "armchair" scientists who never ventured into the field. Anthropology and missiology thus form an "inseparable couple" that, in spite of the domination, conflicts, and ruptures, has produced "an original synthesis." The upshot is not to impose a dominating Christian universal, but rather to deliver the gospel to each human being in ways that escape dogma and institutions.[16] Here, the goal is to focus not on the relation between evangelization and anthropology, but rather on how two Africanist missionaries sought to contribute to anthropological knowledge production about African religious practices.

As prolific authors, Nassau and especially Trilles, albeit from marginal positions as missionary fieldworkers, sought to address important scientific debates of their day. Below, I briefly consider how they obtained ethnographic information from Africans and their institutional relations with both their respective missionary organizations and academic anthropology. I turn to a brief history of fetishism before discussing Nassau's writings on the topic. I then provide an outline of totemism in nineteenth- and early-twentieth-century anthropology to set the stage for Trilles. In the conclusion, I return to the ambivalent relation of Nassau and Trilles to professional anthropology and to the question of the contemporary relevance of totem and fetish in Africanist anthropology.

Methods and Institutional Affiliations

How did Nassau and Trilles use their positions as missionaries to gain access to cultural information on fetishism, totemism, and other subjects? How, in turn, was their knowledge production supported institutionally by their respective mission bodies and by academic anthropology? Methodological statements by both authors were underdeveloped, but they do provide some insight into how they collected information. For different reasons, both men had sometimes turbulent relations with their mission brethren and boards. At the same time, both remained marginal in the growing field of academic anthropology.

From 1893 until after Nassau had definitively left Africa in 1906, his relations with the mission board and fellow missionaries in the field were troubled in part by suspicions of his too close relationship with the Mpongwe

16. Jean-François Zorn, "Missiologie et anthropologie: un couple inseparable," in *Anthropologie et missiologie XIXe-XXe siècles*, pp. 77-80.

woman Anyentyuwe, educated at Baraka Mission, who had helped to raise Nassau's motherless daughter. As one of Nassau's principal informants, Anyentyuwe served as a principal source of Nassau's ethnographic knowledge and of his tensions with the mission. He wrote:

> Anyentyuwe was the only highly educated native Christian, male or female, in Libreville; she could look on those rejected beliefs from the native point of view, and at the same time was willing, from a point of literature, to talk about them; and, with her bright intelligence, she helped me very much. I often went to the house where she was living . . . where, in the presence of her daughter and other women, I took copious notes of her statements and explanations. I am indebted to her for much of what I published, ten years later in my "Fetishism in W. Africa."[17]

In 1899, following the publication of Mary Kingsley's *Travels in West Africa,* the Presbyterian Mission Board in New York encouraged Nassau to devote some of his energies to "block[ing] out . . . that Fetich book that Miss Kingsley says you ought to write."[18] That same year, while on furlough, Nassau received permission from the mission board to devote himself entirely to research and writing up "the garnered information of a generation of mission work."[19] While on leave, he also met with William Libbey, professor of physical geography at Princeton. At that time, academic anthropology was still in its infancy in the United States; a department of anthropology at Princeton would not be founded until decades later.[20] Franz Boas had joined the faculty of Columbia University in 1896, but Nassau seems to have had no contact with Boas or the anthropology department at Columbia.

Back in Africa, Nassau's colleagues in the West Africa Mission did not approve of his release from mission work to work on a book: "Without underestimating the value of the book of the West African folk-lore, we suggest that, in this Mission . . . , it is of doubtful propriety for a missionary of experience, who has also acquired more than one of the native languages, to sit down in the midst of the perishing heathen to write their folk-lore as his main business.

---

17. Nassau, "Autobiography" (unpublished manuscript, n.d.), pp. 1048-49.
18. Nassau, "Autobiography," p. 1244, letter from Sec'y Speer to Nassau, 4 November 1899 (included in autobiography).
19. Nassau, "Autobiography," p. 1246.
20. According to Professor James Boon (personal communication), the Princeton Department of Anthropology was not created until 1971. Note that Princeton theologians were writing about anthropology in the late nineteenth century; Livingstone, "The Idea of Design," pp. 330, 346.

We think this work might be done as an accessory to missionary and religious work, or even after a missionary has retired from the field."[21] Board members also brought up Nassau's "unfriendly" relations with missionaries stationed at Baraka (Libreville) and the "standing scandal" of his relation to "a certain native woman of Gaboon." Upon his return to Africa in 1900, Nassau was disappointed to be assigned to Batanga, 175 miles north of Libreville on the Cameroon coast. He nonetheless made periodic visits to Libreville during which he worked with Anyentyuwe. He also traveled across the estuary several times to work with King Andande. At Batanga, he purchased items he had promised Professor Libbey for the Princeton ethnological museum.[22]

Given his pressing duties at Batanga, work on his fetishism book advanced slowly. He nonetheless took advantage of available opportunities. After evening prayers at Batanga, people remained to tell him "all sorts of stories about native customs and beliefs. It was a valuable source of information, for the compilation of material for the chapters of my 'Fetishism.'" In November 1902, Nassau was transferred to Gabon in part "that I might have more time for my literary work." The ensuing months were a period of intense productivity. For example, in February 1903 he spent a week with King Andande "in the collection of Fetish information. At one village where I slept, I was surrounded by unusual superstition. Idols were in the room, and, off in the village, were the phallic songs of the women of the Njembe Society."[23] During the first half of 1903, Nassau wrote, "everything went happily. I wrote in the mornings." At the same time, Anyentyuwe's health was declining, leading to her death in November 1903. Nassau himself fell ill in June of that year and was sent against his will to the French Roman Catholic hospital. When he left the hospital on his own, his Baraka colleagues obliged him to go on "forced furlough," which he bitterly resented.[24]

Arriving healthy back in the United States, Nassau began "a year of travel" to give invited lectures and sermons. In late September 1903, he went to Princeton to spend a month with Professor Libbey reviewing the chapters of *Fetishism in West Africa*.[25] He was finally cleared to return to Africa in Octo-

---

21. Nassau, "Autobiography," p. 1248, letter from West Africa Mission to Dr. Brown, 1 March 1900 (included in autobiography).

22. Nassau, "Autobiography," pp. 1364, 1313, 1418, 1324, 1373-74.

23. Nassau, "Autobiography," pp. 1337, 1367, 1374, 1428, 1438-39.

24. Nassau, "Autobiography," p. 1451. Nassau wrote: "All my life, from childhood, I have detested the R. C. Church, its organization and its orders. My Protestantism is intense. I have never conversed with priest or nun; have avoided even saluting them; and refuse to have anything in any way to do with them."

25. Nassau, "Autobiography," p. 1470.

ber 1904 for what would be his final stay. In Batanga that year, he collected folktales:

> I thought it well to try to collect Folk-lore Tales. I invited a man, Epumbuwe, a skillful story-teller at the village evening entertainments, to come to my room with one or two companions. There, I dimmed the lamp, so that he might imagine himself out in the street, and had him tell his Story to the two (not to me) so that he might have all the reality of native surroundings, while I, by the lamp, rapidly took notes; which, next morning, while memory was fresh, I copied. I also employed Utonga, an educated man, taking his own time in his village, to write me a note-book full of stories in full, in Benga, which, later, I translated. During the subsequent year, I thus collected some 60 Tales. (Several years later, I published them under the title "Where Animals Talk.")[26]

While American Protestants were establishing mission stations on the western equatorial African coast and later inland, French Catholics pursued parallel endeavors. Initial efforts in the 1770s by French priests and Italian Capuchins to gain a foothold on the Gabon coast had been unsuccessful. French Catholic priests established a mission on the right bank of the Gabon Estuary (present-day Libreville) in the 1840s. The Catholics, after 1848 under the direction of the Holy Ghost Fathers (Spiritans), initially undertook mission efforts primarily in the estuary region. In the 1880s and 1890s, they expanded into the Ogooué River and along the Gabon coast. When Trilles arrived in Gabon in 1893, he initially served under vicar apostolic Alexandre Le Roy. Le Roy, who had worked on the Swahili coast of East Africa for eleven years before coming to Gabon, believed that "the scientific study of humanity must be integral to missionary work," including "the study of physical geography, axes of communication, resources, population density, relations that link or oppose peoples and families," and "the simple details of life."[27] At the

---

26. Nassau, "Autobiography," pp. 1537-38. Nassau repeated this information in the introduction to the Benga sections of *Where Animals Talk* (1912), in which he lays out several ways of obtaining stories, including those written out by "civilized" people. In the introduction to the Mpongwe section, he writes: "The following Tales were narrated to me, many years ago, by two members of the Mpongwe tribe (one now dead [Anyentyuwe?] at the town of Libreville, Gaboon river, equatorial West Africa. Both of them were well-educated persons, a man and a woman"; Nassau, *Where Animals Talk: West African Folk Lore Tales* (Boston, 1912), pp. 79, 11. See also Nassau, "Batanga Tales," *Journal of American Folklore* 28, no. 107 (1915): 24-51; and "Bantu Tales," *Journal of American Folklore* 30, no. 116 (1917): 262-68.

27. Philippe Labruthe-Tolra, "Pourquoi et comment un lien inextricable existe entre

same time, according to Le Roy, the missionary too often lacked a "scientific formation, critical spirit, habits of research and intellectual work, time, money, necessary encouragement," and institutional support.[28] Le Roy, who also wrote on Fang speakers, "Pygmies," and the missionary encounter, seems to have mentored and protected the controversial Trilles during Trilles's early years in Gabon, but returned to France in 1896 to become superior general of the Spiritans. Gabon's first priest and greatest priest-ethnographer, André Raponda Walker, was ordained in 1899.[29]

Trilles's career, both as missionary and ethnographer, was a troubled one. Eventually he ran afoul of both his Spiritan brethren and professional scientists. According to fellow missionary, author, and adversary Maurice Briault, he had already created difficulties for himself by 1897, only four years after his first arrival in Gabon, and returned to France. During his first furlough, from May 1897 to August 1898, Trilles gave talks and penned articles "but encountered, especially in his own congregation, much mistrust because he made a mass of affirmations that his fellow members did not accept." During his second return to France from 1901 to 1903, Trilles continued to write and speak a great deal, "but the mistrust toward him [crossed] the border of his congregation and spread out, especially among certain savants who [had] reservations." Following his third and final return from Gabon in 1907, Trilles continued to give "highly picturesque outlines of his stay in Gabon and often hasty conclusions in his favorite science, ethnography."[30] According to Briault, "the poor Trilles acted outside all control." He gave conferences, wrote articles and made new books, assembling old articles, sometimes borrowing from other authors (some of whom were angry), all without shame. He was "forty years old, in good health, full of force, even active, but disorderly, careless, indiscreet, and no one wants him." In short, he was an *homme brûlé* (burned-out man).[31]

Later, Trilles managed to gain the sponsorship of Father Wilhelm

---

anthropologie et mission chrétienne," in *Anthropologie et missiologie XIXe-XXe siècles,* pp. 20-21.

28. Labruthe-Tolra, "Pourquoi et comment un lien inextricable existe entre anthropologie et mission chrétienne," p. 22.

29. Jeremy Rich has explored André Raponda Walker's substantial contribution to Gabonese ethnography; see "Maurice Briault, André Raponda Walker and the Value of Missionary Anthropology in Colonial Gabon," *Le Fait Missionnaire* 19 (2006): 65-89.

30. Augustin Berger, "Henri Trilles (1866-1949)," *Hommes et destins (Dictionnaire biographique d'Outre-Mer),* n.s., vol. 2, no. 5 (Paris, 1977), p. 730.

31. Maurice Briault, "Notes sur le Père Trilles. Cas du Père Trilles et de son ouvrage sur les pygmées" (Archives C.S.Sp., Chevilly-Larue, France, 631 A.2D12, 1 à 3).

Schmidt, who played a leading role in fostering Catholic scientific ethnology in Europe, founding both the journal *Anthropos* in 1906 and the Ethnological-Missionary Museum in Rome in 1925.[32] Schmidt's sponsorship earned Trilles "the unhoped for honor" of spending 1929 at the Institut Catholique, where he gave "lectures of a particular ethnography that only attracted, thank God, a small audience." Briault also complained of Trilles's forged Pygmy ethnography through which he had somehow convinced Father Schmidt of his ethnographic expertise.[33] "Today," concluded Briault, "Father Trilles is 'demonetized' in scientific milieus and, by tacit agreement, most missionaries who write abstain from citing him and others, without naming or refuting him. One can go no further because he is a priest and one of ours."[34] Yet, in spite of his character and penchant for exaggeration, Trilles, more than Nassau, sought to engage the anthropology of his day, especially when it came to the question of totemism.

Fetish and Fetishism

In addressing fetishism and totemism, respectively, Nassau and Trilles were deferring to important anthropological constructs of their day. When they attempted to find explanatory models to arrange and interpret their experiences, they turned to then-current conceptual frameworks. This section sets out the broader historical contexts in which discussions of fetishism circulated in the late nineteenth and early twentieth centuries. It is also necessary to explore the intersecting but distinct histories of the concepts of fetish and fetishism.

The fifteenth-century Portuguese terms *feitiço, feiticeiro,* and *feitiçaria* "referred respectively to the objects, persons, and practice" of witchcraft.[35] *Feitiço* is derived from the Latin term *factitius:* "In the accepted usages of its

---

32. An Vandenberghe, "Entre mission et science: La recherche ethnologique du père Wilhelm Schmidt SVD et le Vatican (1900-1939)," *Le Fait Missionnaire* 19 (2006): 15-36.

33. A number of scholars have discussed Trilles's alleged forged pygmy ethnography; see Kurt Piskaty, "Ist das Pygmäenwerk von Henri Trilles ein zuverlässige Quelle?" *Anthropos* 52 (1957): 33-48; Jan Vansina, *Paths in the Rainforests: Toward a History of the Political Tradition in Equatorial Africa* (Madison, Wis., 1990), p. 17; Serge Bahuchet, "L'invention des Pygmées," *Cahiers d'études africaines* 129 (1993): 171; John M. Cinnamon, "Missionary Expertise, Social Science, and the Uses of Ethnographic Knowledge in Colonial Gabon," *History in Africa* 33 (2006): 422-23.

34. Briault, "Notes sur le Père Trilles."

35. William Pietz, "The Problem of the Fetish, II: The Origin of the Fetish," *RES: Anthropology and Aesthetics* 13 (1987): 24.

original adjectival forms, feitiço means, like the Latin term, 'artificial' and, beyond that, 'false, feigned, unnatural.'"[36] In modern Portuguese *feitiçaria* can be glossed as both "magic" and "witchcraft," underlining a terminological and conceptual confusion between occult agency and material objects (*feitiços*) as well as the vocabulary Europeans use to describe them. According to Pietz, the term "fetish" derives from the pidgin word *fetisso*, a derivative of the Portuguese *feitiço*, "which in the late Middle Ages meant 'magical practice' or 'witchcraft.'"[37] Pietz conceives of *fetissos* as material objects that "embody — simultaneously and sequentially — religious, commercial, aesthetic, and sexual values." Moreover, he argues that the fetish, "as an idea and a problem, and as a novel object not proper to any prior discrete society, originated in the cross-cultural spaces of the coast of West Africa during the sixteenth and seventeenth centuries," and was distinct from "Christian notions of idolatry, superstition, and witchcraft." In his estimation, the concept was not original to Africa, but emerged in the contact zone between "radically different social orders" — "Christian feudal, African lineage, and merchant capitalist systems."[38]

Before turning to more contemporary Africanist and African uses of the term "fetish," I first consider the development of the term "fetishism." Frenchman Charles de Brosses used the term *fétiche* in the mid–eighteenth century to refer to an inanimate object worshiped by "primitive peoples on account of its supposed inherent magical powers, or as being animated by a spirit."[39] In 1760, de Brosses coined the neologism *fétichisme*, which, along with the cult of heavenly bodies and natural forces, would have constituted the first religious sentiment to have emerged after the biblical flood. In the extreme isolation and precarious living conditions that followed the flood, people turned to fetishes — "objects with very limited protective functions, hence their multiplicity, that men adored to meet each of their needs."[40]

By the 1830s, the term "fetishism" had become more widespread through

---

36. Valerio Valeri, *Fragments from Forests and Libraries: A Collection of Essays by Valerio Valeri*, ed. Janet Hoskins (Durham, N.C., 2001), p. 15.

37. William Pietz, "The Problem of the Fetish, I," *RES: Anthropology and Aesthetics* 9 (1985): 5. Pietz traces *feitiço* to the "late Latin adjective facticious, which originally meant 'manufactured.'"

38. Pietz, "Problem of the Fetish, I," pp. 5-6, 11; "Problem of the Fetish, II," p. 24.

39. "Fetish, n." *Oxford English Dictionary*, 2nd ed. (1989). Consulted online, 30 January 2010, http://dictionary.oed.com.

40. Michèle Tobia-Chadeisson, *Le fétiche africain: Chronique d'un "malentendu"* (Paris, 2002), pp. 41-42. According to Tobia-Chadeisson, de Brosses, drawing on Scottish philosopher David Hume, prefigured later models of the evolution of religion: fetishism/sabeanism (worship of the sun, moon, and stars), polytheism, monotheism.

the writings of travelers, explorers, and continental thinkers. Thenceforth, the problem of fetishism was debated "in terms of progress, stagnation, or degeneration." August Comte, who posited the universal human capacity for progress, saw fetishism as the earliest form of religion. For Hegel, "fetishism was an exclusively African phenomenon and doomed its peoples to a [permanent] impasse." For others, including mid-nineteenth-century missionaries opposed to evolutionism, fetishism was "a corrupt practice inspired by the devil."[41] Nassau, who arrived on Corisco Island (present-day Equatorial Guinea) in 1861, would have been exposed to discourses of fetishism used to describe and typify African ritual practices and beliefs.[42]

Later Marx developed the concept of commodity fetishism "as a critique of capitalist culture" in which "social relationships are dismembered and appear to dissolve into relationships between mere things — the products of labor exchanged on the market — so that the sociology of exploitation masquerades as a natural relationship between systemic artifacts."[43] Finally, Freud considered fetishism a form of neurosis that entailed the "amorous overvaluation" of certain attributes (e.g., shoes, feet, underwear) substituted for normal sexual objects or body parts.[44] Freud sought to explain fetishism in light of the Oedipus complex, castration fear, and the splitting of the ego. Contemporary psychotherapists have abandoned Freud's Oedipal explanations but continue to define fetishes as objects that provide sexual gratification and fetishism as "a condition wherein non living objects are used as the exclusive or consistently preferred method of stimulating sexual arousal."[45]

By the end of the nineteenth century, even before Nassau published *Fetichism in West Africa* (1904), the concept of fetishism as religious system had come under serious attack. Already in 1889, German philologist and Orientalist Max Müller argued that fetishism "had taken on such disparate and even contradictory meanings as to render its elimination from the science of religion necessary." Müller, "who contributed more than anyone else to destroying the idea of a 'fetishistic religion,'" accused travelers, missionaries, and anthropologists of "'fetishizing' any religious phenomenon that they

---

41. Tobia-Chadeisson, *Le fétiche africain*, pp. 49, 51, 57.
42. John Leighton Wilson, *Western Africa: Its History, Condition, and Prospects* (New York, 1856); Paul Belloni Du Chaillu, *Explorations and Adventures in Equatorial Africa* (London, 1861).
43. Taussig, *Devil and Commodity Fetishism*, pp. 8, 31-32.
44. Valeri, *Fragments*, pp. 23, 26.
45. L. F. Lowenstein, "Fetishes and Their Associated Behavior," *Sexuality and Disability* 20, no. 2 (2002): 135.

did not understand."[46] Later, French sociologist Marcel Mauss claimed that fetishism was "useless as a scientific concept" that made no contribution to theories of African religions, and that the term "fetish" should be replaced by the central African concept of *nkoisi* (or *nkisi*).[47] Dutch anthropologist Peter Pels has suggested that anthropologists and folklorists discussed the "magic of Africa" in terms of the "fetish" until "witchcraft" emerged as a central problem in the twentieth century.[48] Along similar lines, Tobia-Chadeisson notes that fetishism, "weakened by its negative connotation . . . gradually disappeared from ethnographic language," having been replaced by World War I by the concepts of magic and sorcery, themselves pragmatic rites "on the margin of religion."[49]

*   *   *

In western equatorial Africa, where Nassau and Trilles worked, the term "fetish" continues to serve as a translation for composed power objects even to the present. Lima points out that in ethnographies of that region, "it is not unusual to encounter the term fetish applied to figurines used in magico-religious cults."[50] Anthropologist Wyatt MacGaffey, who has written extensively on Kongo religion, society, and politics, has periodically turned his attention to Kongolese understandings of the "fetish." MacGaffey has situated the "locus classicus of 'fetishism'" on the Loango coast (present-day Congo-Brazzaville) and "its hinterland (Cabinda and Western Zaire), inhabited by the Bakongo people, who use a kind of charm called *feitiço* in early Portuguese narratives." MacGaffey uses the well-known Kongolese term *nkisi* (pl. *minkisi*) to designate a broad class of composed objects used variously in healing, protection, cursing, and attacking witches. "The entire procedure," he concludes, "is conceptually far more complex than the conventional idea of 'fetishism' allows for." MacGaffey situates *minkisi* in a broader cosmology

---

46. Valeri, *Fragments*, pp. 26-27.

47. Mesquitela Lima, "Fetichism," in *The Encyclopedia of Religion*, vol. 5, ed. Mircea Eliade (New York, 1987) p. 315. I discuss the term *nkisi* below.

48. Peter Pels, "The Magic of Africa: Reflections on a Western Commonplace," *African Studies Review* 41, no. 3 (1998): 196. Pels notes that Evans-Pritchard's "*Witchcraft, Oracles, and Magic* arose from the desire of colonial administrators to be able to deal with 'witchcraft' as a political and legal problem. I still have to find out where the definition of the problem as 'witchcraft' comes from, and why this term replaced 'fetishism' in the ethnography of Eastern and Central Africa around 1900."

49. Tobia-Chadeisson, *Le fétiche africain*, p. 61.

50. Lima, "Fetichism," p. 315.

that includes ancestors, local spirits, ritual specialists *(nganga)*, ghosts, and witches (pl. *bandoki*) but does not refer to this broader cosmology as fetishism.[51]

MacGaffey also explains how Kongolese religious terminology changed under the influence of colonial officials and missionaries, who "took for granted the reality of a unitary idolatrous phenomenon called 'fetishism,' whose sinister promoter was the 'witchdoctor,' 'fetisher,' or 'sorcerer.'" The undertaking included the client, the specialist *(nganga)*, the *nkisi,* and in the case of destructive *minkisi,* the targeted witch. As private rather than communal undertakings, activation of *minkisi* was viewed with suspicion, as "very close to witchcraft *(kindoki),* from which it was distinguished only by the legitimacy of its aims, dubious though they might be."[52] Finally, MacGaffey notes that in contemporary Kongolese French, both *fétiche* and *médicament* operate as glosses of *nkisi*. In most cases, people sought out particular *nkisi* specialists to address "specific problems — pneumonia, childbirth, hunting luck, difficulty passing exams, and the like; to each such problem corresponds one or more *minkisi*."[53]

According to Belgian anthropologist René Devisch, sorcery and fetishes can be either benign or predatory, and are thus bivalent. "Benign sorcery, assisted by fetishes, seeks to disarm the misfortune of daily life and, in particular, stave off the threat of death." Predatory sorcery entails nocturnal gatherings at the "marketplace of sorcerers," where participants distribute and feast on human flesh in an atmosphere of "sexual inebriety, and delirious voluptuousness in a fantasized, hence fantasmic spectacle of rape, murder, and trade in the blood of relations" in ways that epitomize "the absolute negation of social constraint."[54] Like sorcery, the fetish (also *nkisi* in Yaka) is bivalent:

---

51. Wyatt MacGaffey, "Fetishism Revisited: Kongo Nkisi in Sociological Perspective," *Africa* 47, no. 2 (1977): 172-76; see also "The Eyes of Understanding: Kongo Minkisi," in National Museum of African Art, *Astonishment and Power* (Washington, D.C., 1993), pp. 21-103; and *Kongo Political Culture: The Conceptual Challenge of the Particular* (Bloomington, Ind., 2000).

52. MacGaffey, "Fetishism Revisited," pp. 180-81.

53. MacGaffey, "African Objects and the Idea of Fetish," *RES: Anthropology and Aesthetics* 25 (1994): 123-32.

54. René Devisch, "Sorcery Forces of Life and Death among the Yaka of Congo," in *Witchcraft Dialogues: Anthropological and Philosophical Exchanges,* ed. George Clement Bond and Diane M. Ciekawy (Athens, Ohio, 2001), pp. 105, 112-13. Drawing on his interest in psychoanalytic theory, Devisch also underlines the sexual dimension of predatory sorcery.

Of Fetishism and Totemism

It may therefore be the ally of both the harmless and predatory sorcerer as well as of the innocent commoner or average mortal. The fetish is constituted by a sculpture or pouch filled with sorcerous ingredients and thus invested with desire or libidinal energy. It provides a fantasmic support to malefic sorcerous action . . . [and] can ambivalently confer either death or vitality.

The fetish is a power object not only granting its owner access to the forces and flows of life but giving him the ability to intervene in the play of energies and in the vital web of beings and things. The predatory sorcerer allows his fetishes to arouse him and incites them to attack or do harm. . . . [T]here is price to pay for induction into sorcery, however, and the initiate is required to make a gift of a human life.[55]

Finally, in a portrait of Kinshasa, "the invisible city," De Boeck and Plissart liken the power of that city, with its continuous "evanescent push and pull of destruction and regeneration," to "the power of the fetish. Like the fetish, the city of Kinshasa is a constant border-crossing phenomenon, resisting fixture, refusing capture."[56] This brief history of fetish has thus moved from efforts by fifteenth-century Portuguese mariners and coastal Africans to explain one another in terms of power objects and ritual practices to contemporary cities as fetishes.[57] Where is Nassau's place in this long sweep of fetish history?

---

55. Devisch, "Sorcery Forces," pp. 116, 119. See E. C. Eze, "Epistemological and Ideological Issues about Witchcraft in African Studies: A Response to René Devisch, Elias Bongmba, and Richard Werbner," in *Witchcraft Dialogues,* pp. 264-82, for a strong critique of what he sees as Devisch's exoticizing discourse. Eze explores with no small irony how African witchcraft, sorcery, and fetishes closely parallel anthropology, which he characterizes as "a cross-cultural form of bewitchment of, and by, its African objects" (p. 265).

56. Filip De Boeck and Marie-Françoise Plissart, *Kinshasa: Tales of the Invisible City* (Ghent and Amsterdam, 2004), p. 19.

57. Contemporary discussion of fetishes in anthropology and African studies must be situated within Africanists' renewed fascination since the early 1990s with witchcraft, sorcery, and the occult. Sources include Jean Comaroff and John L. Comaroff, eds., *Modernity and Its Malcontents: Ritual and Power in Post-colonial Africa* (Chicago, 1993); Peter Geschiere, *The Modernity of Witchcraft: Politics and the Occult in Postcolonial Africa* (Charlottesville, Va., 1997); Isak A. Niehaus, *Witchcraft, Power, and Politics: Exploring the Occult in the South African Lowveld* (London, 2001); Stephen Ellis and Gerrie Ter Haar, *Worlds of Power: Religious Thought and Political Practice in Africa* (New York, 2004); Adam Ashforth, *Witchcraft, Violence, and Democracy in South Africa* (Chicago, 2005); Harry G. West, *Ethnographic Sorcery* (Chicago, 2007). For a recent brief critique see Terence Ranger, "Scotland Yard in the Bush: Medicine Murders, Child Witches and the Construction of the Occult: A Literature Review," *Africa* 77, no. 2 (2007): 272-83.

JOHN CINNAMON

Nassau and Fetishism

A principal argument put forth here is that Nassau and Trilles sought to contribute to some of the major scientific debates of their day. Nassau, for instance, published almost verbatim versions of several chapters from *Fetichism in West Africa* in two journals. Three chapters appeared in the *Bulletin of the American Geographical Society,* and a fourth in the *Journal of the Royal African Society.*[58] In *Fetichism in West Africa,* Nassau never elaborated a systematic theory of fetishism and its attributes. Instead, he presented chapters on customs, God, polytheism and idolatry, and spirits. Nassau also included a number of chapters on various dimensions of fetishism and the fetish: philosophy, charms and amulets, worship, witchcraft, government, family, secret societies, daily life, funerals, and two long chapters on "fetich tales." He drew on earlier and contemporary missionary accounts and histories, as well as his own anecdotes, classifications, and accusations of superstition, while neglecting anthropological sources.

In *Fetichism,* Nassau ignored the cultural evolutionism of Morgan and Tylor.[59] Nassau's writings on fetishism indicate that he was a proponent of degradation or degeneration theory, which he summarized in a chapter titled "Fetichism — Its Philosophy." As Nassau saw it, humans were originally monotheists but eventually came to represent God by using idols, which they "did not actually worship." Later, they began to worship such idols, thereby becoming idolators and polytheists. As humans lapsed ever further away from God, they stopped worshiping God and instead became animists, substituting for God "a multitude of spiritual beings." Finally, to provide local residences for spirits, any object whatsoever became acceptable. "Neither dignity, beauty, nor strength was any longer a factor in the selection." This,

---

58. Robert Hamill Nassau, "Fetishism, a Government," *Bulletin of the American Geographical Society* 33, no. 4 (1901): 305-17; Nassau, "Spiritual Beings in West Africa: Their Number, Locality, and Characteristics," *Bulletin of the American Geographical Society* 33, no. 5 (1901): 389-400; Nassau, "Spiritual Beings in West Africa: Their Classes and Functions," *Bulletin of the American Geographical Society* 35, no. 2 (1903): 115-24; Nassau, "The Philosophy of Fetishism," *Journal of the Royal African Society* 3, no. 11 (1904): 257-70.

59. Edward Burnett Tylor, *Primitive Culture: Researches into the Development of Mythology, Philosophy, Religion, Art, and Custom* (London, 1871); Lewis Henry Morgan, *Ancient Society* (New York, 1877). Nassau drew on a different set of writings, including those of his predecessor in Gabon, John Leighton Wilson, *Western Africa: Its History, Condition, and Prospects* (New York, 1856); Mary Kingsley, *Travels in West Africa, Congo Français, Corisco, and Cameroons* (London, 1904 [1897]); and biblical scholar Alan Menzies, *History of Religion: A Sketch of Primitive Religious Beliefs and Practices, and of the Origin and Character of the Great Systems* (New York, 1922 [1895]).

Of Fetishism and Totemism

Nassau concluded, was "bald fetichism." He noted that the "fetich worshipper" clearly distinguished "between the reverence with which he regards a certain material object and the worship he renders to the spirit for the time being inhabiting it."[60]

In a discussion of the widespread use of charms among "the Bantu," Nassau asserted the close link between fetishes and fetishism. Citing Menzies' *History of Religion,* he outlined the history of the term "fetish":

> [Fetishes] almost monopolize the religious thought of the Bantu Negro, subordinating other acknowledged points of his theology, dominating almost his entire religious interest, and giving the word "fetich" such overwhelming regard that it has furnished the name distinctive of the native African religious system, *viz.,* fetichism. "Fetich" is an English word of Portuguese origin. It is derived from feitico, "made," "artificial" (compare the old English fetys, used by Chaucer); and this term, used of the charms and amulets worn in the Roman Catholic religion of the period, was applied, by the Portuguese sailors of the eighteenth century, to the deities they saw worshipped by the Negroes of the West Coast of Africa.[61]

Continuing to cite Menzies, Nassau referred to de Brosses, who had coined the term "fetishism" to refer to "the type of religion of the lowest races." He also cited American missionary John Leighton Wilson, who had served in Liberia and Gabon, and who wrote of fetishes rather than fetishism. Nassau was now ready to propose his own definition of fetish:

> A fetich [sic], then, is any material object consecrated by the "oganga," or magic doctor, with a variety of ceremonies and processes, by virtue of which some spirit becomes localized in that object, and subject to the will of the possessor. . . . In preparing a fetish the oganga selects substances such as he deems appropriate to the end in view, — the ashes of certain medicinal plants, pieces of calcined bones, gums, spices, resins, and even filth, portion of the bodies of animals, and especially of human beings (preferably eyes, brain, heart, and gall bladder), particularly of ancestors, or men strong or renowned in any way, and very especially of enemies and white men.[62]

---

60. Nassau, *Fetichism in West Africa* (New York, 1904), p. 75.
61. Menzies, cited in Nassau, *Fetichism in West Africa,* pp. 80-81.
62. Nassau, *Fetichism in West Africa,* pp. 81-82. Although elsewhere Nassau used the

When Nassau was able to refrain from the constant, invidious comparison between enlightened Christian truth and degraded African wickedness, his observations contained glimmers of ethnographic insight. For example, his chapters "The Fetich — Witchcraft — a White Art — Sorcery" and "The Fetich — Witchcraft — a Black Art — Demonology" pointed to the moral ambiguity of "fetishes" and "occult power," widely noted in equatorial African ethnography. Referring to the "white art," Nassau described how substances that went into the composition of "medicines" were selected: "These are of both animal and vegetable origin, but mostly vegetable."[63] In the chapter on fetishes as a black art, he noted African efforts to compare beneficial and malevolent uses of fetishes to the "Christian use of firearms, — proper for defense, improper for unprovoked assault."[64] "The black art [the African] admits is wrong, its object being to kill or injure some one else; the white he thought allowable, because with it he acts simply on the defensive."[65]

In his chapter on fetishes as a white art, Nassau noted the power of the belief in fetishes, even among converted Christians.

> In emerging from his heathenism and abandoning his fetichism for the acceptance of Christianity, no part of the process is more difficult to the African Negro than the entire laying aside of superstitious practices, even after his assertion that they do not express his religious belief. From being a thief, he can grow up an honest man; from being a liar, he can become truthful; from being indolent, he can become diligent; from being a polygamist, he can become a monogamist; from a status of ignorance and brutality, he can develop into educated courtesy. And yet in his secret thought, while he would not wear a fetich, he believes in its power, and dreads its influence if possibly it should be directed against himself.[66]

---

standard English orthography ("fetish," "fetishism"), in *Fetishism in West Africa* he adopted a hybrid orthography ("fetich," "fetichism") that is neither English nor French (*fétiche, fétichism*). Except in direct citations, I use the standard English.

63. Nassau, *Fetichism in West Africa*, p. 108. Even here, however, Nassau could not avoid the temptation to denigrate: African-composed medicines, usually packed into hollow animal horns, "may be absurd from our civilized view, they may be disgusting and even filthy; but they are all ranked as 'medicine,'" and actually have "some fitness to the end in view."

64. Twenty-first-century Gabonese refer to nocturnal rifles (*fusil nocturnes*) as medicines or mystical devices that one shoots or throws at one's enemies to inflict harm.

65. Nassau, *Fetichism in West Africa*, p. 116. Here again, Nassau is obliged to condemn the use of fetishes, whatever the intentions of their user, as a dishonor to God.

66. Nassau, *Fetichism in West Africa*, p. 101.

Here, Nassau makes no pretense of suspending missionary judgment; he lays out his moral values while noting the African's capacity for moral improvement (as he defined it). At the same time, Nassau was forced to acknowledge that African beliefs in the power of ritually charged objects remained steadfast.

Fetichism in West Africa was reviewed in a number of prominent publications, including *National Geographic,* the *New York Times,* the *Nation,* and *Année sociologique.* Reviews were mixed and pointed to Nassau's marginal position vis-à-vis the scientific community. *National Geographic,* for example, lauded Nassau's expert treatment of "witchcraft, charms, blood sacrifices, and other forms of fetichism"; the reviewer hailed the book as an "important contribution to our knowledge of the religious beliefs and superstitions of the nations and French Congo and adjacent regions."[67] The *New York Times* review sought to educate the reading public on fetish objects, how fetishism and witchcraft led to African population decline, and how these practices made "the work of the missionary" more difficult. "The fetich," explained the reviewer, "is a material thing, and its use is so universal as to dominate much of negro native life and to form a large part of his religion, which we call fetichism. . . . The number of objects which may be converted into fetiches is countless. The author once saw an old coffee pot which was supposed to possess magical powers. The witches, male and female, are countless, and their power too terrible to be described. They bring about death whenever it pleases them."[68]

An anonymous review in the *Nation* was decidedly more mixed, in effect tacitly reproducing the dichotomy between amateur fieldworkers and academic theoreticians. The reviewer praised Nassau's partial "scientific instinct" as a "gatherer of facts," while referring to his stance on "the evolution of religion" as "the old, orthodox, conservative sort." The "book contains a large amount of interesting and valuable data, the result of [Nassau's] personal observations, and experiences." After outlining the volume's content based on the chapter headings, the reviewer astutely suggested that Nassau's broader personal position was circumscribed by "his narrower theology," before concluding that "the writer's facts are better than his theories. . . . There are fetishes and fetishes."[69] In effect, Nassau was never able to suspend missionary judgment in order to elucidate the underlying logic of the African cultural

67. A.W.G., "Fetichism in West Africa, Geographic Literature," *National Geographic* 16 (1905): 135.
68. N.A., "Fetichism: A Missionary's Book about the Native Customs and Superstitions of West Africa," *New York Times,* 14 January 1905, p. BR21.
69. N.A., "Review of Fetichism in West Africa," *Nation* 80 (1905): 465-66.

practices he described. Finally, the reviewer in Durkheim's *Année sociologique* reproached Nassau for giving the notion of fetish an "unlimited extension," by including such heterogeneous things as "the religious cultures of secret societies and families, magical practices, funerary rites, taboos, and superstitious customs."[70] This last review underlined Nassau's marginal position in academic social sciences.

Thus, while Nassau appears to have been admired as an expert in reviews destined for the general reading public, his theoretical position was questioned by the *Nation* and dismissed by *Année sociologique*. On one level, this dismissal may be as close as Nassau came to the academic anthropology of his day.

Totemism and Anthropology

In a recent, richly detailed exploration of totemism and Victorian evolutionist anthropology, Robert Alun Jones argues that during the half-century preceding World War I, social evolutionism and totemism were "joined at the hip."[71] Jones traces the intellectual history of totemism through the writings and spirited debates of major anthropological thinkers from the 1860s to 1913, including Lubbock, McLennan, Robertson Smith, Frazer, Durkheim, and Freud. Already in the 1860s, naturalist and archaeologist John Lubbock (1834-1913), an outspoken critic of degenerationist theories of religion, proposed an evolutionary schema that included both fetishism and totemism:

> His "lowest form of religion" ... was "a mere unreasoning belief in the existence of mysterious beings" (for example spirits invisible to others, who visit during dreams and nightmares). In fetishism, the second stage, this belief is more rational and methodical (the native now believes that by means of witchcraft the spirit can be compelled to serve human ends or purposes). At a still higher stage, we find totemism (the worship of animals and plants, which also serve as emblems of the clan or tribe), a form of religion that "can be shown to have existed, at one time or another, almost all over the world." Only at the fourth stage, Lubbock observed, do we reach ... "idolatry" ... with the higher, more abstract conceptions of religion following thereafter.[72]

---

70. R.H., "Review of 'Nassau (R.H.), Fetishism in West Africa,'" *Année sociologique* 9 (1904-5): 191. The reviewer, R.H., was probably Robert Hertz, a Durkheim student later killed in World War I.

71. Jones, *Secret of the Totem*, p. 58.

72. Jones, *Secret of the Totem*, p. 43.

For Lubbock, while the fetish was individual, the totem involved a "deification of classes."[73]

Scottish anthropologist John Ferguson McLennan (1827-81) also took an evolutionary approach. He saw totemism as "a transitional stage in the progress from savagery to civilization." "[A]ncient civilizations first progressed through the totem stage, then practiced the worship of animals and plants, and finally arrived at the origin of anthropological gods." McLennan, a rationalist more interested in social organization than religion, paid particular attention to the connections between totemism, exogamy, and matrilineal descent.[74]

Fellow Scotsman, Orientalist, and biblical scholar William Robertson Smith (1846-94) was strongly influenced by McLennan's ideas. In an 1880 lecture, "Animal Worship and the Animal Tribes among the Arabs and in the Old Testament," Smith noted that "'from the earliest times' and 'in the midst of widely separated races,' animals and plants 'were worshipped by tribes of men who were named after them and believed to be their breed.'" Smith concluded that in pre-Islamic Arabia, "ideas of god, animal, and ancestor were all brought into some kind of intimate connection — precisely like that found in Australian Totemism." In his 1889 *Lectures on the Religion of the Semites,* Smith came close to asserting that the early Semites had practiced totemism. "For Smith, totemism was a body of spiritual truths embodied in vulgar, material husks, evolving gradually with its related social institutions until . . . God had truly revealed himself" to the Old Testament prophets. According to Jones, "Smith's lectures also mark the beginning of that period of almost obsessively focused scrutiny of totemism that culminated around 1910 with Frazer's *Totemism and Exogamy,* Durkheim's *Les Formes élémentaires,* and Freud's *Totem und Taboo.*"[75]

In his 1887 volume *Totemism,* James Frazer (1854-1941) summarized the then-current knowledge on the subject. A totem was "a class of material objects which the savage regards with superstitious respect, believing that there exists between him and every member of the clan an ultimate and altogether special relation." Frazer identified three kinds of totems: "the clan totem, common to all members of a clan and passing by inheritance from generation to generation; the sex totem, common to either all the males or all the females of a tribe; and the individual totem, belonging to a single person and not passing to his or her descendants." The totem protected people, while they in

---

73. Jones, *Secret of the Totem,* pp. 54-55.
74. Jones, *Secret of the Totem,* pp. 45, 53, 58.
75. Jones, *Secret of the Totem,* pp. 73-74, 100, 103.

turn showed respect by not killing or otherwise harming it. According to Frazer, clan totems were the most important, "reverenced by a body of men and women who call themselves by the name of the totem, believe themselves to be of one blood, descendants of a common ancestor, and . . . bound together by common obligations to each other and by a common faith in the totem."[76]

During his long career, Frazer proposed three separate "rationalist and utilitarian" theories of the origin of totemism, including the idea that as a system, totemism had been "expressly devised for the purpose of procuring a plentiful supply of food, water, sunshine, wood, etc." In 1897, Frazer entered into correspondence with British-Australian biologist and anthropologist Baldwin Spencer (1860-1929), who studied the Arunta and other groups in central Australia. The Arunta case directly contradicted two defining features of totemism: "the (religious) prohibition against killing and eating the totemic animal or plant, and the (social) prohibition of marriage between individuals of the same totem." These revelations led Frazer to submit that the Arunta and other central Australian aborigines were at an earlier stage of evolution and that clan exogamy and totem food taboos had arisen later.[77]

Like Frazer, French sociologist Émile Durkheim (1858-1917) admired Spencer and Gillen's 1899 *Native Tribes of Central Australia* for its portrayal of a totemic religious system in its unity, completeness, and complexity. Frazer had explained totemism as a system designed to maintain or increase the alimentary resources of a society. Durkheim criticized this position, however, arguing that as Frazer saw it, totemism lost "nearly all its religious character," instead becoming "a sort of economic enterprise." According to Jones, if Frazer's four-volume *Totemism and Exogamy* (1910) was "the grand compendium of the evolutionary anthropological obsession with totemism," Durkheim's *Les Formes élémentaires de la vie religieuse* (1912) was the grand synthesis, bringing together an entire range of theories, "weaving them all together . . . within the framework of Durkheim's grand theoretical vision."[78]

Durkheim defined religion as "a unified system of beliefs and practices relative to sacred things, that is to say, things set apart and forbidden — beliefs and practices which combine into a single moral community called a Church, all those who adhere to them." For Durkheim, Australian totemism, "the most simple religion which is actually known," represented religion stripped to its bare essentials. The basic unit in Durkheim's analysis was the

---

76. Jones, *Secret of the Totem*, p. 83.
77. Jones, *Secret of the Totem*, pp. 150, 207, 148, 153.
78. Jones, *Secret of the Totem*, pp. 206-7, 232.

clan. Members of each clan were united by a common name or emblem, often passed down matrilineally, and usually taken from animals and plants, or less frequently places, celestial bodies, and natural phenomena such as rain.[79]

The totem was an emblem, similar to a flag or coat of arms, which affirmed the identity of the clan. It also had a religious character, for it was used in rituals and was considered sacred. Hence, the totem represented the clan and also forged the moral community without which clan life would be impossible.[80] The totem symbolized above all the clan — in other words, society itself — inspiring awe and exercising moral power over community members. Religion functioned to bind the individual to the community and to forge the moral community of the clan to whose will and superiority the individual must submit but which, at the same time, allowed him to partake in the force of the collectivity and the symbolic force of the totem.[81]

Like Durkheim, Freud approached religion from within the "evolutionary anthropological framework" and saw totemism as the "most primitive form" of religion. Both had been influenced by Frazer, although Durkheim had challenged Frazer's "rational, utilitarian interpretation of Australian totemism," while Freud had drawn on "Frazer's connection between totemism, exogamy, and incest taboo." They each considered religion "a vast, powerful system of human nature and society."[82] But while Durkheim saw religion as a collective and beneficial source of action and self-transcendence, Freud traced the origin of religion to the Oedipal complex, in filial "jealousy and hostility toward the father, . . . in the collective inheritance of guilt over his murder . . . [and] whose first sexual object is his mother." In *Totem and Taboo* (1913), Freud returned to "the two most important taboos in totemism . . . , that no member of the clan may kill the totemic ancestor, and that members of the same clan may not have sexual relations with one another." He linked these taboos to the primal Oedipal desires of the male child (to kill his father and have sexual relations with his mother).[83]

Paradoxically, both major works by Durkheim and Freud were published at the very moment when totemism — as a systematic, comparative construct — had begun to unravel as a new generation of anthropologists lost interest in social evolution.[84] In the United States, Franz Boas's student

---

79. Émile Durkheim, *The Elementary Forms of the Religious Life,* trans. Joseph Ward Swain (New York, 1915), p. 62.
80. Durkheim, *Elementary Forms,* p. 157.
81. Durkheim, *Elementary Forms,* p. 240.
82. Jones, *Secret of the Totem,* p. 289.
83. Jones, *Secret of the Totem,* pp. 277, 284.
84. Jones, *Secret of the Totem,* pp. 232, 290.

A. Goldenweiser (1910) challenged what had been considered the "invariable characteristics of totemism." In line with Boas's move toward historical particularism, Goldenweiser argued that totemism could only be understood "as the association of particular elements within particular contexts." Contrary to Durkheim and others, Goldenweiser also questioned the use of totemism "to designate a relationship between certain religious and certain social phenomena."[85] Boas himself chimed in to question the unity of totemic phenomena, the notion that totemism was "natural and objective," and the possibility of generalizing from specific cases to all totemic practices.[86] It was thus at the moment of this incipient paradigmatic shift away from totemism that Frazer, Durkheim, Freud — and also Trilles — published their definitive works on the subject.

Trilles and Fang Totemism

In 1912, the same year Durkheim published *Les Formes élémentaires*, Henri Trilles released his even longer but far less well-known study on Fang totemism. In a literature review on totemism, Trilles demonstrated his efforts to engage with the leading scholars on the subject, including McLennan, Robertson Smith, Lang, Frazer, Van Gennep, and (in passing) Durkheim. Following A. Lang, by way of Van Gennep, Trilles defined a totem as "an animal, vegetable, etc. ally of a kin group, clan, phratry, etc." Trilles cited Frazer, who had defined totem as "A class of material objects that the savage regards with superstitious respect, believing that there exists between him and each member of this class an intimate and very special relation." Trilles also cited Jean Capart's definition of totemism as "A sacred object, generally an animal, more rarely a plant or inanimate thing, whose entire species is the object of the veneration of a tribe or clan." Hinting at his usually much more evident propensity for sensationalism, Trilles took issue with Capart's use of the term "veneration": "[T]he black man *(le Noir)* does not venerate his totem: for him the ritual cult is founded on fear."[87]

In a shorter article on the subject, published in a thematic section on

---

85. Jones, *Secret of the Totem*, pp. 292-93; see A. A. Goldenweiser, "Totemism, an Analytical Study," *Journal of American Folklore* 23, no. 88 (1910): 179-293; Warren Shapiro, "Claude Lévi-Strauss Meets Alexander Goldenweiser: Boasian Anthropology and the Study of Totemism," *American Anthropologist* 93, no. 3 (1991): 599-610.

86. Jones, *Secret of the Totem*, pp. 301-2; Franz Boas, "The Origin of Totemism," *American Anthropologist* 18 (1916): 319-26.

87. Henri Trilles, *Le totémisme chez les Fân* (Münster, 1912), pp. 24, 27, 30.

Of Fetishism and Totemism

totemism in the Catholic ethnological journal *Anthropos* (1914), Trilles also drew on Father Wilhelm Schmidt's definition of the totemic system or phase as one in which animals (e.g., mammals, snakes, birds, fish, insects), or less often plants and inanimate objects, were deemed sacred. Totemic animals may not be killed or eaten; "'man believes himself united with them by intimate ties and sees in them either ancestors or allies or protectors.' . . . Precisely, totemism is 'the permanent alliance, real and effective (or so believed), between an organized human collectivity and another collectivity belonging to the animate non-human world.'"[88]

To determine whether totemism indeed existed among the Fang, Trilles set out a set of attributes, based on criteria posed by a number of scholars: (1) the clan has a totem, and (2) ordinarily bears the name of the totem; (3) it admits kinship with the totem if the totem is animate; (4) clan members and individuals bearing the same totem practice exogamy, and (5) they refrain from killing or eating the totem, "except in certain well determined cases, such as ritual communion."[89] On the basis of the above criteria, Trilles concluded that "integral totemism" existed among the Fang. He denied, however, that any "tribe or clan attributes to itself an animal origin." Trilles observed in the Fang "no real kinship whatsoever, in the sense of an effective filiation (contra Van Gennep, Durkheim), but a collateral kinship, real in the sense that this has been an exchange of blood, and equally spiritual, resulting in a mystical tie."[90] Trilles characterized the Fang as a Bantu people, but also as a "semi-Nilotic branch," and an "isolated island." On the basis of his earlier assertions of Egyptian origins of the Fang, he also speculated that the Fang might have "borrowed its totemic cult from ancient Egypt or another people influenced by Egyptian ideas."[91]

Trilles noted three related attributes of totems: (1) an ethnic attribute, the sign of the clan, (2) the name of the clan (and other totemic groups), and (3) the ancestor or kin (made of the same substance). He took issue with this last attribute, drawn from Loret and Déchelette,[92] which struck him as "false

---

88. Cited in Trilles, "Totémisme chez les Fān" (1914), p. 631.

89. Trilles, *Totémisme chez les Fân* (1912), p. 36; Trilles, "Totémisme chez les Fān" (1914), p. 633.

90. Trilles, "Totémisme chez les Fān" (1914), p. 637.

91. Trilles, "Chez les Fang: leurs moeurs, leur langue, leur religion," *Les Missions Catholiques* 30 (1898): 68; Cinnamon, "Colonial Anthropologies," pp. 323-35; Trilles, *Totémisme chez les Fân* (1912), p. 46.

92. Trilles, *Totémisme chez les Fân* (1912), p. 60. Here Trilles cites Loret, *L'Egypte au temps du Totémisme* (Paris, 1906), and Déchelette, *Manuel d'Archéologie préhistorique* (Paris, 1896).

for the Bantu clans." Trilles went on to distinguish between "the real totem" and "the totem symbol." The real totem included the tutelary totem itself and the concretized totem, materialized and in tangible form. The totem symbol included the clan sign in a figurative form and the name of the clan. Trilles also questioned Frazer's above-noted division of the totem into three classes: the clan totem, the sex totem, and the individual totem. While admitting the importance of Fang clan totems, Trilles preferred the broader notion of "totem of the 'organized collectivity,'" which could refer to family groups, clans, tribes, secret societies, and the nation, as well as heterogeneous villages populated by migrant workers and their families during the early colonial period. He was inconsistent about the existence of the totem of sex, dismissing it on the one hand and noting its presence on the other.[93]

As for the exchange of blood, Trilles noted that under normal circumstances human clan members and corresponding totemic animals must protect one another: hitting, wounding, killing, or eating one's totem is forbidden. Accidental killing of one's totemic animal constituted a serious but reparable transgression, one that required ritual cleansing — "an affair for the fetisher." It was also possible for a totemic animal, such as the leopard *(nze)*, to kill a protected individual. The animal could make a mistake, punish a serious ritual fault, or itself wish "to renew a sacrifice and commune with the victim, which is fantastic! To the fetisher to disentangle all these cases." In certain cases it was acceptable for a person to kill and eat his totemic animal, "when one must renew the alliance by a new brotherhood, exchange of blood and communion with the victim."[94]

In part because the French language term *totem* had not seeped into the Fang language, Trilles pointed to the difficulty in obtaining information about Fang totemism. The most general term he used for totem was *étotore*, which he glossed as "protector." The term refers, "in a general sense," both to the tutelary being or guardian and to the national or even individual totem, "because he is, par excellence, the guardian, the protector." Trilles introduced two other terms, *mvame* and *bian*. *Mvame*, as Trilles notes, referred to forebear or ancestor, "but in Fāñ country, and elsewhere, the ancestor protects the children, and watches over the family, so by extension the totem mvame signifies 'protector or guardian.'" Trilles thus glossed *mvamayôñ* as "totem of the nation or tribe" and *mvamayum* as "totem of the clan." In Fang opinion, according to Trilles, the *mvamayôñ* was the "totem ancestor," which could present itself in three distinct ways — as a "living being," as an "immaterial be-

---

93. Trilles, *Totémisme chez les Fân* (1912), pp. 60, 65-66.
94. Trilles, "Totémisme chez les Fān" (1914), pp. 638-39.

ing," or as a "natural phenomenon." The "national totem," which Trilles believes "probably existed," was the elephant or crocodile.[95]

When it comes to the "tribal totem," denoted by the prefix "Ye," Trilles outlined a number of tribes named after animals, plants, and even the rain. Examples include the following:

Ye-ngü (*ngü,* "bush pig")
Ye-mvin (*mvin,* "type of antelope")
Ye-ngôm (*ngôm,* "porcupine")
Ye-shôñ (*eshôñ,* "type of tree")
Ye-bikon (*bikon,* "bananas")
Ye-mvèñ (*mvèñ,* "rain")

Here, Trilles cited Robertson-Smith and Marillier to support his argument that Fang "tribes" were totemic: (1) they possessed the name of an animal, plant, or natural phenomenon; (2) their members traced their origin to this plant or animal; and (3) they venerated this species and normally refrained from eating it.[96]

In subsequent chapters of *Le Totémisme,* Trilles undertook an exhaustive elaboration of the features of Fañ totemism as he conceived of them: the nature of totems (national, tribal, clan, familial, individual, and secret societies), questions of antiquity and origins, totemic cults, the roles of family heads and sorcerers, rituals and laws, and totem symbols. A final chapter compared totemism and fetishism. Much earlier in *Le Totémisme,* Trilles referred to Dr. Nassau, who "only observed the individual totem, and not the familial or tribal totem." In Nassau's *Fetichism in West Africa,* Trilles noted, "all the totemic facts . . . are only considered as fetishistic acts."[97] In his chapter "Totémisme et fétichisme," Trilles cited Mary Kingsley's definition of fetishism as "the religion of the natives of the Western Coast of Africa, where they have not been influenced by Christianity or Mohammedanism." Trilles found this definition "so vague and so general" (although "not without a certain malice"), that he was obliged to deem it "true enough."[98]

Like other authors on fetishism, Trilles cited Charles de Brosses and provided Portuguese and Latin etymologies of the term "fetish." "The navigators of the fifteenth century had designated by this name all the objects that the

95. Trilles, *Totémisme chez les Fân* (1912), pp. 84-85, 106.
96. Trilles, *Totémisme chez les Fân* (1912), p. 118.
97. Trilles, *Totémisme chez les Fân* (1912), pp. 41-42.
98. Trilles, *Totémisme chez les Fân* (1912), p. 624; Mary Henrietta Kingsley, *West African Studies* (London, 1901 [1899]), p. 96.

natives seemed to adore, all the things or beings to which the blacks rendered a religious cult." Since that time, the general term had been extended to include "all the spiritual or corporeal beings, all the animals or vegetables, all the material things, even the most bizarre, to which the Black man had rendered any cult whatsoever." Trilles went on to review a number of perspectives, including Edward Burnett Tylor's definition of animism as "man's earliest outlook on Nature," and totemism as "the earliest social arrangement" characterized by exogamy. A. Lang distinguished between totems (generative heroes and protective ancestors or divinities produced by mysterious natural forces) and fetishes (inanimate objects imbued with "magical powers" by way of incantations or "occult virtues"). Trilles also cited Reinach "and his school" that distinguished between the fetish as an individual object and the totem as "a class of objects, considered by the clan as tutelary."[99]

Finally, Trilles referred to a hybrid category, "totemic fetishes," that included totems engraved on weapons, statuettes, and the remains of sacrifices consisting of ashes, calcined bones, and other small fragments carefully conserved in animal horns or small packets. Totemism thus entered into fetishism, "constituting one of its aspects." Trilles concluded that fetishism and totemism, "as different as they are, nonetheless have points in common and easily encroach upon each other's realm." Totems, for example, had their own particular fetishes while also using more general fetishes. The fetish, according to Trilles, might be "a statuette or any object, stone or tree, cranium or bone," but "only becomes something if it is 'influenced,' inhabited by a spirit, the depository of a mysterious force. . . . [B]efore its consecration, and after its execration, the fetish is nothing. The crude wooden statue that the black man carves for the European, even the fetish that has served, but that sold to the white man for his museums or his collections, no longer has any religious value, is no longer, properly speaking, a fetish."[100]

Rather than engaging in a sustained critique of Trilles's anthropology of Fang totemism, I have sought to show how he strove to situate his own scholarship in the early-twentieth-century ethnology of totemism. Nonetheless, while animal and plant images and symbols have surely played important roles in Fang imaginaries, Trilles overstates his case while confusing human ancestors, animals, and natural phenomena. In my own research on Gabonese Fang speakers, I have been unable to find the term *étotore* (protector). The term *mvam* indeed refers to grandparent or ancestor, and for many Fang speakers, ancestors continue to serve as protectors and moral arbiters.

---

99. Trilles, *Totémisme chez les Fân* (1912), pp. 624-26.
100. Trilles, *Totémisme chez les Fân* (1912), pp. 634-35, 628, 629-30.

Of Fetishism and Totemism

Most "clan" *(ayong)* names come from human founding ancestors. Thus, *mvamayoñ* would refer to clan ancestor rather than "totem." In some cases, as Trilles shows, clan names draw metaphorically on forest animals, forest and cultivated plants, or natural forces. But in no case, to my knowledge, did Fang speakers attempt to trace their genealogy back to the nonhuman. For example, during the clan reunification movement in post–World War II Gabon, members of the composite Ye-Mveng "tribe" ("people of the rain") claimed to have originated from mythical human ancestors rather than the rain. The Ye-Mveng might have been as prodigious and powerful as an equatorial deluge, but they did not consider themselves "children of the rain."[101] This is not to deny, however, that certain groups and individuals may have had significant metaphorical and ritual ties to certain natural species.

Conclusion

The careers of Nassau and Trilles coincided with the period of European colonization of much of Africa and the rise of professional anthropology. This transitional period still afforded amateur ethnographers (explorers, travelers, administrators, and missionaries) the opportunity to contribute to scholarly production both as providers of raw ethnographic data and, to a degree, as ethnological theorists. Jones notes a shift from the views of early-nineteenth-century missionaries, who were less educated and more aggressively ethnocentric, to "a more sympathetic view of the religions and cultural practices of those whom they sought to convert."[102] Along similar lines, Patrick Harries remarks that by the mid–nineteenth century, missionaries had begun to take a more scientific approach to understanding the populations among whom they worked.[103] In turn, many missionaries sought to publish accounts in anthropological and geographical journals as well as mission society publications.

Although both Nassau and Trilles wrote on a wide variety of topics, I have

---

101. I draw this example from the papers left by Menié M'Oyone Fabien (ca. 1909-82), French military veteran, president of the Ye-Mveng, and canton chief, near Makokou, Gabon, from 1952 to 1982. For a discussion of Menié's political career and his efforts to revitalize Fang ethnohistory in northeastern Gabon, see John M. Cinnamon, "The Long March of the Fang: Anthropology and History in Equatorial Africa" (Ph.D. diss., Yale University, 1998), chapter 7.

102. Jones, *Secret of the Totem*, p. 123.

103. Patrick Harries, "Anthropology," in *Missions and Empire*, ed. Norman Etherington (Oxford, 2005), p. 239.

focused here on their attempts to make ethnographic and ethnological contributions to the study of two problematic concepts, fetishism and totemism. Fetishism, having lost pride of place to animism and totemism, appears never to have been fully elaborated in nineteenth-century evolutionary anthropology. Moreover, the study of fetishism never gave rise to the kinds of debates and treatments that culminated in such major works as those of Frazer and Durkheim. Freud, of course, did write on fetishes as objects of displaced sexual desire and on fetishism as a form of neurosis. Marx's concept of commodity fetishism remains useful to contemporary materialist anthropologists. And in popular discourses and ethnographic accounts of invisible powers, fetishes remain prominent in representations of west and west-central Africa. This staying power is, at least in part, a legacy of missionary ethnography.

Totemism, on the other hand, largely disappeared from anthropological discourse as anthropologists abandoned evolutionist explanations and turned their attention to other kinds of questions. Although Trilles's credibility was seriously challenged even during his lifetime, his Fang writings have exercised formative influence on the Fang ethnographic imagination largely due to the enduring popularity of his controversial theory of Egyptian origins.[104] Trilles's writings on Fang totemism, however, have been largely ignored. In 1913, German ethnographer Günter Tessmann, who had also studied the Fang of southern Cameroon and Rio Muni, was highly critical of Trilles's writings. In particular, he accused Trilles of presenting "a completely false idea of the religious culture of the Pahouins."[105] Alexandre and Binet were considerably more generous to Trilles in their 1958 monograph, *Le Groupe dit Pahouin (Fang-Boulou-Beti)*. Without attempting any systematic analysis of totemism, the authors referred several times to Trilles's writing on the subject. They noted, for example, that according to Trilles, personal names had formerly conveyed "totemic signification," which was linked in turn to genealogy. They stopped short, however, of arguing that clans were totemic.[106] In a brief bibliographic entry they refer to *Le Totémisme* as follows: "This is the magnum opus of Father Trilles. As in all the works by this author, one finds beside keen and exact observations, conclusions that are sometimes risky and unexpected gaps, deriving

---

104. Trilles, "Chez les Fân"; Trilles, *Chez les Fang, ou Quinze années de séjour au Congo français* (Lille, 1912); Cinnamon, "Missionary Expertise, Social Science, and the Uses of Ethnographic Knowledge in Colonial Gabon."

105. Günter Tessmann, *Die Pangwe: Völkerkundliche Monographie eines westafrikanischen Negerstammes* (Berlin, 1913), cited in Philippe Laburthe-Tolra and Ch. Falgayrettes-Leveau, *Fang* (G. Tessmanm, *Les Pahouins*, Extraits) (Paris, 1991), p. 172.

106. Pierre Alexandre and Jacques Binet, *Le group dit Pahouin (Fang-Boulou-Beti)* (Paris, 1958), p. 93.

Of Fetishism and Totemism

perhaps from a certain professional deformation. In spite of which Father Trilles remains the grand authority on the Fang."[107]

As tempting as it might be, I have refrained here from making a sustained postcolonial critique of fetishism and totemism, or for that matter of Nassau and Trilles.[108] Instead, I have sought to gain deeper insight into how Nassau, Trilles, and their contemporaries understood, debated, and used such concepts to answer their questions, not ours. If anthropology, at least as it is taught in the United States, asks us to use cultural relativism as a means of gaining insight into the logic of cultural others, is it not also possible to gain parallel insights into late-nineteenth-century historical others, in this case missionary ethnologists?

Finally, I would like to suggest that these bygone concepts from nineteenth-century anthropology have not entirely disappeared either from anthropological discourse or from the African imagination. In a lengthy 1998 article on totemism in Africa, Alfred Adler reminds readers that Evans-Pritchard devoted considerable attention to Nuer totemism in his *Nuer Religion* (1956).[109] Adler also describes examples of totemism among the Dinka, the Baganda, and the group Adler himself studied, the Moundang of Chad. When it comes to the Moundang, Adler remains unrepentant in his reliance on totemism: "the Moundang have a clan system that it would be difficult if not impossible to describe without the notion of totemism."[110]

Turning to fetish, I cite one contemporary example from my own research on spirits in Gabon. This comes from a 2007 interview with Kouidi Marie-Françoise, a forty-six-year-old grandmother, part-time trader, and former healer *(nganga)* from northeastern Gabon. She had been initiated in 1985 by the famous ritual expert and healer Zoaka-Zoaka Pascal after she suffered bouts of insanity. Although the interview was recorded in Libreville, the capital, this case, which unfolded in sparsely populated northeastern Gabon, provides a rural example. Her narrative also maintains the long-term ambivalence over the terms "fetish/fetisher" in their capacities both to heal and to harm:

> Zoaka-Zoaka was a grand fetisher *(féticheur)* in our region. He removed medicines and treated crazy men and women. . . . I had bouts of insanity

---

107. Alexandre and Binet, *Le group dit Pahouin*, p. 146.

108. I do not mean to imply, of course, that evolutionary or degenerationist anthropology was unproblematic and did not somehow emerge in a context of European expansionism and colonialism.

109. Alfred Adler, "Le totémisme en Afrique noire," *Système de pensée en Afrique noire* 15, no. 4 (1998); E. Evans-Pritchard, *Nuer Religion* (Oxford, 1956).

110. Adler, "Totémisme en Afrique Noire," p. 16.

that started during a male circumcision ceremony.... I saw things as if on television.... The spirit, Mademoiselle, said, "Remove your clothes." I took off my dress. "Remove everything." I took everything off. I remained naked. The spirit directed me toward the latrine of a man in our neighborhood. The spirit told me, "There's something in the latrine there, enter." I removed the filth, the shit. Then I found a large bottle. There were many things inside: hair, needles, fingernails [and toenails], even papers and pieces of cloth *(pagnes)*. These had driven his children crazy and prevented his daughters from going into marriage. He blocked everything. And when I removed the bottle, they told me to explain [what it was].

Afterwards, my grandparents took me to Zoaka-Zoaka's village, seven kilometers from Mékambo. [She went on to detail how she was initiated by Zoaka-Zoaka, who had seen that she was called to be a healer.] That's how I learned to consult, to dance, to treat — I treated mad men and women.[111]

In this case, Zoaka-Zoaka, a powerful "fetisher," clearly provides healing, protection, and initiation, in part through his privileged access to the spirit, Mademoiselle.[112] At the same time, although Marie doesn't call the bottle she found in the latrine a "fetish," she is clearly referring to a harmful, composed "power object," designed to block others.

Even more than totemism, the terms *fétiche, fétichisme,* and *féticheur* have seeped into contemporary central African French. These problematic terms are sufficiently pliable to evoke aspects of nineteenth-century anthropological descriptions and polysemic African appropriations. The ethnography of colonial era missionaries such as Nassau and Trilles drew on both Christian and scientific understandings of their day as they sought to explain African religious practices through the lens of Christian evangelization.

Select Bibliography

Berger, Augustin. "Henri Trilles (1866-1949)." In *Hommes et destins (Dictionnaire biographique d'Outre-Mer)*, n.s., vol. 2, no. 5. Paris, 1977.
Boas, Franz. "The Origin of Totemism." *American Anthropologist* 18 (1916).

---

111. Kouidi Marie-Françoise, recorded interview (Libreville, 25 July 2007).
112. For a more detailed discussion of Zoaka-Zoaka and his relationship to the spirit Mademoiselle, see Joseph Tonda, *La guérison divine en Afrique Centrale (Congo, Gabon)* (Paris, 2002), pp. 65-84.

Brown, A. R. "The Definition of Totemism." *Anthropos* 9 (1914). (Special section "Das Problem des Totemismus.")

Cinnamon, John M. "Colonial Anthropologies and the Primordial Imagination in Equatorial Africa." In *Ordering Africa: Anthropology, European Imperialism, and the Politics of Knowledge,* edited by Helen Tilley with Robert J. Gordon. Manchester, 2007.

———. "Missionary Expertise, Social Science, and the Uses of Ethnographic Knowledge in Colonial Gabon." *History in Africa* 33 (2006).

———. "Robert Hamill Nassau: Missionary Ethnography and the Colonial Encounter in Gabon." *Le Fait Missionaire* 19 (2006).

De Boeck, Filip, and Marie-Françoise Plissart. *Kinshasa: Tales of the Invisible City.* Ghent and Amsterdam, 2004.

Devisch, René. "Sorcery Forces of Life and Death among the Yaka of Congo." In *Witchcraft Dialogues: Anthropological and Philosophical Exchanges,* edited by George Clement Bond and Diane M. Ciekawy. Athens, Ohio, 2001.

Durkheim, Émile. *The Elementary Forms of the Religious Life.* Translated by Joseph Ward Swain. New York, 1915.

Eboussi Boulaga, F. "Fétichisme et proselytisme." In *Anthropologie et missiologie XIXe-XXe siècles: Entre connivence et rivalité,* edited by Olivier Servais and Gérard Van't Spijker. Paris, 2004.

Harries, Patrick. "Anthropology." In *Missions and Empire,* edited by Norman Etherington. Oxford, 2005.

Kingsley, Mary Henrietta. *West African Studies.* London, 1901 (1899).

MacGaffey, Wyatt. *Kongo Political Culture: The Conceptual Challenge of the Particular.* Bloomington, Ind., 2000.

Nassau, Robert Hamill. "Bantu Tales." *Journal of American Folklore* 30, no. 116 (1917).

———. "Batanga Tales." *Journal of American Folklore* 28, no. 107 (1915).

———. *Fetichism in West Africa: Forty Years' Observation of Native Customs and Superstitions.* New York, 1904.

———. "Fetishism, a Government." *Bulletin of the American Geographical Society* 33, no. 4 (1901).

———. "The Philosophy of Fetishism." *Journal of the Royal African Society* 3, no. 11 (1904).

———. "Spiritual Beings in West Africa: Their Classes and Functions." *Bulletin of the American Geographical Society* 35, no. 2 (1903).

———. "Spiritual Beings in West Africa: Their Number, Locality, and Characteristics." *Bulletin of the American Geographical Society* 33, no. 5 (1901).

———. *Where Animals Talk: West African Folk Lore Tales.* Boston, 1912.

Pels, Peter. "The Magic of Africa: Reflections on a Western Commonplace." *African Studies Review* 41, no. 3 (1998).

Rich, Jeremy. "Maurice Briault, André Raponda Walker and the Value of Missionary Anthropology in Colonial Gabon." *Le Fait Missionnaire* 19 (2006): 65-89.

Taussig, Michael T. *The Devil and Commodity Fetishism in South America.* Chapel Hill, N.C., 1980.

Trilles, Henri. "Chez les Fang: leurs moeurs, leur langue, leur religion." *Les Missions Catholiques* 30 (1898). (This appeared in short installments throughout the year.)

———. *Chez les Fang, ou Quinze années de séjour au Congo français.* Lille, 1912.

———. *Le totémisme chez les Fân.* Münster, 1912.

———. "Le totémisme chez les Fãn." *Anthropos* 9 (1914). (Special section "Das Problem des Totemismus.")

Tylor, Edward Burnett. *Primitive Culture: Researches into the Development of Mythology, Philosophy, Religion, Art, and Custom.* London, 1871.

Vandenberghe, An. "Entre mission et science: La recherche ethnologique du père Wilhelm Schmidt SVD et le Vatican (1900-1939)." *Le Fait Missionnaire* 19 (2006).

CHAPTER 4

Missionary Ethnographers and the History of Anthropology: The Case of G. T. Basden

DMITRI VAN DEN BERSSELAAR

The history of the development of anthropology as an academic discipline during the first half of the twentieth century is well known. Key developments include the institutionalization, professionalization, and formalization of fieldwork and the rise of structural functionalism.[1] They also include a declining role for missionaries in knowledge production, as influential anthropologists such as Malinowski and Radcliffe-Brown began to consider the validity of data collected by missionaries as likely unsystematic and suffering from a Christian bias.[2] However, while this mainstream in anthropology was being forged in particular centers by influential individuals now celebrated for shaping the discipline, many other ethnographers had, or developed, different working practices and different conceptions of what anthropology was about. The ranks of "unfashionable" ethnographers included missionaries and colonial officers, as well as academic anthropologists. They may have

---

1. George W. Stocking Jr., *After Tylor: British Social Anthropology, 1888-1951* (Madison, Wis., 1995), pp. 367-426; Henrika Kuklick, *The Savage Within: The Social History of British Anthropology, 1885-1945* (Cambridge, 1991), pp. 182-241; Kuklick, *A New History of Anthropology* (Oxford, 2007); Adam Kuper, *Anthropology and Anthropologists: The Modern British School* (London, 1985); James Clifford, *Routes, Travel, and Translation in the Late Twentieth Century* (Cambridge, Mass., 1997), pp. 54-64.

2. Peter Pels, "Anthropology and Mission: Towards a Historical Analysis of Professional Identity," in *The Ambiguity of Rapprochement: Reflections of Anthropologists on Their Controversial Relationship with Missionaries*, ed. Roland Bonsen, Hans Marks, and Jelle Miedema (Nijmegen, 1990), p. 85; Patrick Harries, "Anthropology," in *Missions and Empire*, ed. Norman Etherington (Oxford, 2005), pp. 255-58.

been sidelined in the history of the development of anthropological theory and practice, but their works are often still valuable to current scholars because of the specific ethnographic detail they offer,³ or because their interpretations have been enthusiastically embraced in the localities they were documenting.⁴ It is therefore worth exploring what their motivations and influences were, why they ended up outside the mainstream history of anthropological knowledge production, and what this tells us about the process of knowledge production as well as about the reception of such knowledge.

One of these unfashionable ethnographers was the Anglican missionary George Thomas Basden (1873-1944), who published extensively on Igbo culture during his long and successful career as a missionary in southeast Nigeria. His publications, which span more than thirty years, show no evidence that he was influenced by the rise of structural functionalism, even though he was clearly aware of metropolitan initiatives that were shaping the discipline of anthropology. Basden never gained recognition as an important or influential anthropologist. However, his work was well known among missionaries, colonial officers, and ethnographers working in southeast Nigeria, and he was recognized as an expert on Igbo culture and society by the Nigerian colonial administration.⁵ Furthermore, his publications — especially his 1921 book *Among the Ibos of Nigeria* — have remained important for the study of southeast Nigeria.⁶ *Among the Ibos of Nigeria* is still frequently consulted by both foreign and Nigerian scholars, and the book has been reprinted several times, most recently in 2006.⁷ It has also gained popularity among a nonacademic Igbo readership who frequently refer to its contents. A cheap

---

3. See, for example, my discussion of Percy Amaury Talbot: Dmitri van den Bersselaar, "Establishing the Facts: P. A. Talbot and the 1921 Census of Nigeria," *History in Africa* 31 (2004): 69-102.

4. See, for example, the case of Henry Trilles discussed by John Cinnamon in this volume. See also Cinnamon, "Missionary Expertise, Social Science, and the Uses of Ethnographic Knowledge in Colonial Gabon," *History in Africa* 33 (2006): 413-32.

5. Dmitri van den Bersselaar, "Missionary Knowledge and the State in Colonial Africa: On How G. T. Basden Became an Expert," *History in Africa* 33 (2006): 433-50.

6. G. T. Basden, *Among the Ibos of Nigeria: An Account of the Curious and Interesting Habits, Customs, and Beliefs of a Little-Known African People by One Who Has for Many Years Lived amongst Them on Close and Intimate Terms* (London, 1921). Basden, in common with most writers of his time, uses the term "Ibo" instead of the phonetically more correct "Igbo." In this chapter the modern term "Igbo" is used throughout, but the spelling of older sources has not been altered.

7. G. T. Basden, *Among the Ibos of Nigeria* (Stroud, 2006), with a new introduction by Misty Bastian (page numbering differs from earlier editions; hereafter page numbers in references to *Among the Ibos of Nigeria* refer to the 1921 edition).

local paperback edition published in Onitsha was still available for sale in Nigeria in 2009.

This case study of G. T. Basden will argue that to understand the perspectives, methods, and theoretical frameworks employed in the production of anthropological knowledge by unfashionable ethnographers such as Basden, we need to contextualize their work not in the first place within the "official history" of anthropology, but rather within specific emerging localized traditions of anthropological knowledge production. This chapter will first introduce Basden, discuss his career, and describe and characterize his ethnographical output. It will then examine the changing ways in which he addressed the impact on Igbo culture of missionary work and the colonial economy. I will also consider the effect that this may have had on his ethnographic writing. The chapter will end with an evaluation of the various intellectual, social, and political factors that influenced Basden's ethnographical work.

George Thomas Basden was born in 1873. In his early twenties he attended the Church Missionary Society (CMS) Preparatory Institution at Clapham for four terms, where the curriculum included religious knowledge, English language and history, elements of Latin and Greek, arithmetic and bookkeeping, hygiene and elementary medicine, as well as technical training in carpentry and shoemaking. Following this he went to the CMS college at Islington, where he took the three-year course that mainly focused on Bible study and theology, and from which he graduated as an ordained missionary.[8] Basden then joined the CMS Niger Mission in 1900. At the time of his arrival, the Niger Mission was based in the trading town of Onitsha, situated on the river Niger. It had only very few mission stations, and these were situated in the vicinity of Onitsha and along the Niger. Although the CMS had been operating in southeast Nigeria for more than forty years at that time, they had achieved only limited geographical expansion and had made relatively few converts. This was about to change with the establishment of British colonial administration in the area. The colonial military activities were greeted with some enthusiasm by CMS missionaries, who expected that the eventual defeat of African resistance would result in the opening up of the interior, not only for colonial commerce, but also for missionary activities.[9] Around this time, CMS missionaries visited the town of Awka, about forty kilometers inland from Onitsha, and in 1903 the CMS decided to open a mission station there.[10]

---

8. Alison Hodge, "The Training of Missionaries for Africa: The Church Missionary Society's Training College at Islington, 1900-1915," *Journal of Religion in Africa* 4, no. 2 (1971): 85-86.

9. T. J. Dennis, writing in the *Church Missionary Intelligencer*, July 1900, p. 525; J. N. Cheetham, writing in the *Church Missionary Intelligencer*, December 1901, p. 931.

10. Birmingham University Library, Church Missionary Society Archives (hereafter

Basden spent most of his thirty-five years in Nigeria at this station. He was in Awka from the very establishment of the mission station onward, and later became the principal of Awka Training College, which trained schoolteachers for the mission.[11] During these years, Basden also continued his own training. In line with the Niger Mission's policy, he acquired a working knowledge of the Igbo language.[12] After his first tour in Nigeria, Basden returned to Britain on furlough, where he read for a B.A. degree at Durham University. This trajectory reflected a connection between the CMS and Durham University that went back at least to 1876.[13] During a later furlough Basden returned to Durham and completed an M.A. degree.

Basden saw himself as a "pioneer" missionary,[14] and in 1925 he tried to resist being moved to Onitsha on the grounds that "Onitsha has long ceased to be a 'bush' station."[15] Basden became the secretary of the Niger Mission in 1925 and acquired a Litt.D. in the same year.[16] He was appointed archdeacon on the Niger in 1928.[17] In 1930 he gave evidence as an expert witness in a high-profile inquiry into the causes and violent government suppression, in December 1929, of a protest movement of unarmed women in southeast Nigeria, called the "Aba riots" by the colonial government and locally remembered as the "Women's War."[18] The following year the colonial government asked him to become an unofficial member of the Nigerian Legislative Council as representative of the Igbo people.[19] He was awarded an OBE at the New Year's Honors of 1 January 1934.[20] Basden was married with four sons. He had met his wife, Eleanor C. Scott-

---

CMSA), G3 A 3/O 1903/54 Minutes of Niger Executive Committee, 23-28 February 1903. The influence of the language of colonialism is quite clear in such missionary reports: for instance, the term the missionaries used to describe the establishing of a mission station is "occupation." In 1910 the CMS decided to change the spelling of the town Oka to Awka, "in order to fall in with government spelling" (CMSA G3 A 3/O 1910/83 Minutes of Executive Committee, 1-13 August 1910).

11. CMSA Acc. 119 F1 Diary of Rev. Harold Taylor, Awka, 1918-1921.
12. CMSA G3 A 3/O 1902/74 Report of first language examination, 16 July 1902.
13. Hodge, "The Training of Missionaries," pp. 83, 89.
14. CMSA G3 A 3/O 1925/42 Basden to G. T. Manley, Awka, 18 May 1925.
15. CMSA G3 A 3/O 1925/74 Basden to Manley, Reigate, 12 November 1925.
16. CMSA G3 A 3/L8 Manley to Bishop Lasbrey, London, 12 May 1925; G3 A 3/L7 Hooper to Basden.
17. CMSA G3 A 3/L8 Wilson Cash to Bishop Lasbrey, 28 May 1928.
18. *Aba Commission of Inquiry. Notes of Evidence. Taken by the Commission of Inquiry into the Disturbances in the Calabar and Owerri Provinces, December, 1929.*
19. CMSA G3 A 3/O 1930/79 Archdeacon Basden to Hooper, Onitsha, 17 September 1930; Nigerian National Archive, Ibadan branch (hereafter NAI), CSO 26/1/27948 Basden to Colonial Secretary, 12 November 1935.
20. *Times*, 1 January 1934.

Lorimer Basden, in Nigeria where she worked as a medical missionary. They were married in Onitsha in 1906, but it appears that Eleanor mainly remained in the United Kingdom where she raised their children.[21] Basden formally retired from the mission on 30 September 1935 and returned to Britain in 1936.[22] He died at age seventy-one, on 30 December 1944 in Jevington near Eastbourne.[23]

Basden started his publishing career soon after his arrival in Nigeria, with articles in mission journals such as the *Church Missionary Intelligencer* and the *Church Missionary Review*. The topics he wrote on were typical for missionaries writing at the beginning of the twentieth century. They included the history and current state of CMS mission work in southeast Nigeria, eulogies of exemplary missionaries, and observations about the traditional religion and culture of the Igbo people in the area around Awka. From around 1914 he also wrote about the effects of Christianity and colonial modernity on Igbo culture, observing that "the old is in a state of decay and ready to vanish away."[24] The intended audience of these publications was ordinary Christians in Britain who supported the work of the mission with their donations.

In 1912, Basden published a brief article for an academic audience, "Notes on the Ibo Country and the Ibo People, Southern Nigeria," in the *Geographical Journal*.[25] The article consists of a map of the area around Awka, accompanied by a description of the landscape, vegetation, animal life, and people living in that part of Nigeria. The language used, the amount of detail provided, and the style of reasoning are similar to that employed in articles he wrote for a more popular audience. Basden modestly states that "no claim is made to having produced anything of great scientific value."[26] Many of his observations are indeed frustratingly brief and general, such as his comment that "in different towns" monkeys, fish, iguanas, crocodiles, pythons, tortoises, and others were "sacred animals" that could not be killed on any account. Sweeping generalizations include his description of the Igbo living to the west of the river Niger as "disposed to be fat, heavy, and lazy" compared to the "thin and scraggy" people that lived east of the Niger.[27] The sections de-

---

21. Misty L. Bastian, introduction to the modern edition of *Among the Ibos of Nigeria*, by G. T. Basden (Stroud, 2006), pp. 11 12.

22. CMSA G3 A 3/1 Basden to Hooper, 21 January 1936.

23. *Times*, 1 January 1945.

24. G. T. Basden, "Denationalizing a Primitive People," *Church Missionary Review*, October 1915, p. 597.

25. G. T. Basden, "Notes on the Ibo Country and the Ibo People, Southern Nigeria," *Geographical Journal* 39, no. 3 (1912): 241-47.

26. Basden, "Notes on the Ibo Country and the Ibo People," p. 242.

27. Basden, "Notes on the Ibo Country and the Ibo People," p. 244.

scribing the human population in the area focus mainly on outside appearances, including skin color, anatomy, dress, body painting, and tattooing. Apart from the occasional reference to commonly held assumptions about colonized peoples, such as the observation that the Igbo "possess all the inherent love of all things ornamental in common with other savage peoples,"[28] Basden rarely attempts to place his observations into a broader theoretical framework. Such framework nevertheless becomes apparent toward the end of the article, where a lengthy comparison of similarities between Igbo and Hebrew customs shows that Basden was influenced by an early version of the "Hamitic Hypothesis."[29]

This theme of the similarities between the Igbo and the Jews of the Old Testament reappears in Basden's first book, *Among the Ibos of Nigeria*, published in 1921. The book is subtitled *An Account of the Curious and Interesting Habits, Customs, and Beliefs of a Little-Known African People by One Who Has for Many Years Lived amongst Them on Close and Intimate Terms*. The claim to the book's reliability is thus based on an extended period of firsthand observation and interaction, rather than on a particular theoretical or political perspective, or a standardized methodology. In this respect, Basden is particularly defensive about the idea that missionaries may have found it difficult to understand and respect African religion, and he dismisses critics "who often trumpet forth their opinions, though some of them have never visited the country at all, and others have made but a sort of tour."[30] His apparently modest claim to "have simply striven to set forth in a plain way some of the things which the plain man may see and hear in Nigeria,"[31] thus mainly serves to convince the reader of the veracity of the text, and of the absence of an ulterior agenda. This point is repeated throughout the book. Following a comment about the alleged lack of zeal for Igbo traditional religion, for instance, Basden — aware of potential accusations of having a vested interest — considers it necessary to add: "This is a mere statement of fact, not a point of sentiment."[32] *Among the Ibos of Nigeria* aims to give a general overview of Igbo life and mainly narrates daily activities, work, trade, and pleasure of the Igbo groups in the area around Awka and Onitsha. It also contains many of Basden's personal experiences. The book starts with three chapters that offer a general outline and introduction to the Igbo area. This is followed by the

28. Basden, "Notes on the Ibo Country and the Ibo People," p. 245.
29. Basden, "Notes on the Ibo Country and the Ibo People," pp. 246-47. The "Hamitic hypothesis" will be discussed in more detail below.
30. Basden, *Among the Ibos*, p. 44.
31. Basden, *Among the Ibos*, p. 15.
32. Basden, *Among the Ibos*, p. 43.

ethnographical substance of the book: twenty-two short chapters organized around themes, such as polygamy and slavery, music, war and weapons, arts and crafts for women, and aspects of religion. Two final chapters, entitled "The Day of Better Things" and "Christianity and Islam," examine the spread of Christianity. The book is illustrated with about forty photographs. These had presumably been taken by Basden himself over the years, as photographs were widely used by the CMS (and by other missionary societies) to raise awareness and funds for mission work. Some of the photographs included in the book had been published previously in the CMS magazines or as postcards.

The topics are discussed in general terms. In a number of cases discussion is followed by Basden's reflections and by an explicit attempt to present the topic as seen through the eyes of the Igbo. For instance, Basden makes clear that he is no fan of polygyny because "the custom is productive of bestiality, and the dulling effect on the mind is such that a polygamist is rarely capable of any real mental attainment, and certainly of none demanding strain for a lengthened period."[33] Yet, he recognizes the practice as an integral part of Igbo social economy, desired by both Igbo men and women for sound reasons: "The ambition of every Ibo man is to become a polygamist, and he adds to the number of wives as circumstances permit. They are an indication of social standing and, to some extent, signs of affluence: in any case, they are counted as sound investments."[34] He also notes that "a woman is not content to remain the sole wife of a man. An only wife considers herself placed in an unenviable and humiliating position. It is also lonely, as the sexes are not companions to one another."[35] His discussion of kinship nevertheless remains superficial and unsystematic. Basden describes most topics in the "ethnographic present," but in some chapters he discusses changes brought about since the introduction of colonial rule. While Basden regards the spread of Christianity as a positive development, he laments what he perceives as the decline of traditional customs, a process he terms "denationalization." In his estimation this occurred not so much because of missionary activities, but because of colonialism and trade. In his discussion of arts and crafts for women, for instance, he notes that local spinning and weaving industries are doomed because they cannot compete with imported cloth on price or attractiveness. He then complains that "[a]gain, the missionary is held to be the culprit, as he is generally accused of introducing clothing for

33. Basden, *Among the Ibos*, p. 87.
34. Basden, *Among the Ibos*, p. 83.
35. Basden, *Among the Ibos*, p. 84.

his converts." He then points out that the missionaries did not in fact derive any benefit from the sale of imported goods in Africa (unlike the traders and — indirectly, through import duties — the colonial government).[36]

Basden's descriptions are lively and often provide great detail, but they lack essential information as to where and when he had observed specific events. This is where Basden's ethnographical writing can be frustrating. Basden was clearly very interested in the Igbo people, and he made quite some effort to gain an understanding of their society and their religion. He had already been in the area for twenty years when he wrote *Among the Ibos of Nigeria*, and for most of this time he could speak the Igbo language.[37] Yet, his writing style indicates distance from those described, and it is often unclear how far back his observations date. It is possible that some of it was indeed fairly old, because late in the decade 1910-1920 Basden had responsibilities that made him spend much of his time on management and financial issues. By this time Basden was based in Onitsha, and would come over to Awka at regular intervals to deal with financial and other matters relating to the training college.[38] At this stage in his career, he was perhaps not necessarily that "close and intimate" to the people he wrote about. Compared to an influential missionary anthropologist such as Henri-Alexandre Junod, Basden is remarkably silent about the process through which he collected ethnographic data.[39] Basden does not discuss his sources in any detail. He claims: "I have, for the most part, sought simply to put into readable English what I have learned from the natives themselves, as originally written or related by them."[40] However, he does not provide the names of his informants and gives no indication of their age, gender, geographical location, or social position. We have to assume that his informants must have mainly been people already associated with the mission in one way or another — as mission school pupils, churchgoers, catechists, servants, and so on. Basden does not discuss how he conducted fieldwork or evaluated contradictory sources. He claims authority as the man on the spot, who knows "his" people and has absorbed information about their culture for many years. His correspondence with the CMS headquarters in London does not contain any information about his fieldwork methods either.

36. Basden, *Among the Ibos*, p. 148.
37. CMSA G3 A 3/O 1901/51 letter T. J. Dennis, Onitsha, 17 April 1901; G3 A 3/O 1902/74 report of first language examination, 16 July 1902.
38. CMSA Acc. 119 F1 diary of Rev. Harold Taylor, Awka, 1918-21.
39. Patrick Harries, *Butterflies and Barbarians: Swiss Missionaries and Systems of Knowledge in South-East Africa* (Oxford, 2007), chapter 8.
40. Basden, *Among the Ibos*, p. 10.

Among the Ibos of Nigeria was the first book that defined its unit of analysis as the Igbo people. This was at a time when it was not always clear to whom this ethnonym referred.[41] Not only did many living in the area not accept the term "Igbo" as applicable to them, the region also shows significant linguistic, cultural, and sociocultural differences that made the exact definition of the Igbo area a matter for debate for a long time.[42] Local definitions of belonging tended to focus on the town or village group *(obodo)* and did not define the local as part of a broader pan-Igbo culture.[43] Basden shows an awareness of local differences, but generally brushes these aside in his attempt to capture the essence of Igbo culture. For the most part, when Basden talks about the Igbo, he presents the culture of one particular part of the Igbo area, that around Awka and Onitsha. Although often regarded as an "Igbo heartland," this region is certainly not representative of the cultural diversity of the wider Igbo area.[44] Basden apparently did not consider this very problematic. For example, it did not stop him from providing evidence as an expert witness after the Women's War,[45] even though the information he had to offer related to the north/central part of the Igbo area, while the disturbances had taken place in the very south, an area where, according to Basden, "pure unadulterated forms are not found" and "ideas of other tribes have been superimposed or intermingled with the ancient Ibo beliefs and practices."[46] Within the CMS, Basden gained a reputation for being a partisan to the interests of the Igbo from the Onitsha area, and he was accused of going against CMS policy in pushing the interest of Onitsha Igbo.[47]

41. Van den Bersselaar, "Establishing the Facts," pp. 69-102.

42. Dmitri van den Bersselaar, *In Search of Igbo Identity: Language, Culture, and Politics in Nigeria, 1900-1966* (Leiden, 1998), pp. 198-99.

43. Axel Harneit-Sievers, *Constructions of Belonging: Igbo Communities and the Nigerian State in the Twentieth Century* (Rochester, N.Y., 2006).

44. On "Igbo heartland": M. A. Onwuejeogwu, *An Igbo Civilization: Nri Kingdom and Hegemony* (London and Benin City, 1981). See also his earlier "The Dawn of Igbo Civilization in the Igbo Culture Area," *Odinani. The Journal of the Odinani Museum Nri* 1, no. 1 (1972): 15-56. See also A. E. Afigbo, *Ropes of Sand: Studies in Igbo History and Culture* (Nsukka, 1981); O. N. Njoku and F. N. Anozie, "High Points of Igbo Civilization: The Nri Period," in *Groundwork of Igbo History*, ed. A. E. Afigbo (Lagos, 1992), pp. 178-97. On diversity, see the following: Eli Bentor, "Aro Ikeji Festival: Toward a Historical Interpretation of a Masquerade Festival" (Ph.D. diss., Indiana University, 1994); Simon Ottenberg, *Farmers and Townspeople in a Changing Nigeria: Abakaliki during Colonial Times (1905-1960)* (Ibadan, 2005).

45. *Aba Commission of Inquiry.*

46. G. T. Basden, *Niger Ibos: A Description of the Primitive Life, Customs, and Animistic Beliefs, Etc., of the Ibo People of Nigeria by One Who, for Thirty-five Years, Enjoyed the Privilege of Their Intimate Confidence and Friendship* (London, 1938; reprint, London, 1966), p. xix.

47. CMSA G3 A 3/O 1913/78 letter T. J. Dennis, Onitsha, 16 August 1913; G3 A 3/O 1915/

Basden's first monograph was followed by another scholarly article in 1925, which was again titled "Notes on the Ibo Country" and published once more in the *Geographical Journal*. It presents another map, this time limited to Onitsha province, the area Basden knew best.[48] This is yet again accompanied by a general overview of the Igbo area as a whole, including many parts not covered by the map. There is a clear pattern in Basden's writings: he does not attempt to engage with an academic debate, but rather, as an expert, introduces "his" people to a wider audience. His publications are not in the first place about contributing to anthropological knowledge, but about representing the Igbo to the outside world. In this respect his ethnographic writings, his membership of the Legislative Council for the Igbo, and his willingness to act as expert witness for the colonial administration can all be seen to stem from the same impulse. Indeed, Basden claimed to have received the Igbo praise name "*Onu-nekwulu-ọra* = The mouth that speaks on behalf of the people = Advocate."[49]

In the summer of 1934, Basden attended the first International Congress of Anthropological and Ethnological Sciences in London as delegate of the CMS.[50] He presented a paper titled "How Far Can African Customs and Beliefs Be Incorporated in the Christian System?"[51] After reminding his audience that his contribution was based on observations during thirty-four years in Nigeria and that "one living in close contact with primitive heathenism cannot but be conscious of the inherent evil in the system," he discussed aspects of Igbo religion that could be incorporated in the local Christian church. These included the belief in the existence of a supreme being *(Chukwu)*, the belief that spirit can be invoked into material substance by priestly invocation, and the practices around naming and dedicating children and the "coming out" of the mother. It interested Basden especially that "many customs and beliefs have striking resemblances to the laws enjoined on the Israelites," where "the Christian teacher has much upon which to build."[52] The paper attracted a

---

40 correspondence between SPCK and CMS, May 1915. For a more detailed discussion, see Dmitri van den Bersselaar, "The Language of Igbo Ethnic Nationalism," *Language Problems and Language Planning* 24, no. 2 (2000): 123-47.

48. G. T. Basden, "Notes on the Ibo Country, Southern Nigeria," *Geographical Journal* 65, no. 1 (1925): 32-41.

49. Basden, *Niger Ibos*, p. xxii.

50. CMSA G3 A 3/L 8 Hooper to Basden, London, 5 March 1934.

51. G. T. Basden, "How Far Can African Customs and Beliefs Be Incorporated in the Christian System?" in *Congrès International des Sciences Anthropologiques et Ethnologiques. Compte-rendu de la Première Session, Londres 1934* (London, 1934), pp. 213-15.

52. Basden, "How Far?" p. 214.

large number of critical responses, most of which focused on his conception of Christianity rather than on his claims about Igbo religion. No one commented on Basden's observations about the similarities between Igbo and Hebrew laws. Jomo Kenyatta criticized missionaries for their methods of conversion, and also suggested that their knowledge about African traditional religions was incorrect because they "obtained most of their ideas of African customs from converts to whom their old gods have become devils."[53] This latter comment must have been particularly irksome to Basden, who had the previous day commented that anthropologists had inaccurate information because they took at face value the comments from informants who were merely trying to please the anthropologists, and because they attempted to discover features that corresponded with the custom of other peoples.[54] Here Basden indicated that he had no taste for structural functionalism and that information should be specific and based on long-term observation. He also made a number of other contributions to the discussions during which he presented aspects of Igbo culture, including one intervention in response to J. J. Williams's paper on "Ashanti cultural influence in Jamaica," where he suggested that what Williams had described as Asante influence might very well have been Igbo.[55] After the conference he complained to the CMS that he had experienced some very hostile criticisms of missionaries and their methods.[56]

In 1938, after his retirement from the mission, he published his second ethnographic book, *Niger Ibos: A Description of the Primitive Life, Customs, and Animistic Beliefs, Etc., of the Ibo People of Nigeria by One Who, for Thirty-five Years, Enjoyed the Privilege of Their Intimate Confidence and Friendship*. This second book, like the first, offers a general ethnographic description of the Igbo in the Onitsha-Awka area. It is longer and has more detail than the first book, but covers generally the same ground. It is also organized in the same way, and many sections are copied verbatim from the earlier volume. However, there are more references that compare his observations on the Igbo to published ethnography, there is less mention of Basden's own experiences, and it is less defensive about missionary enterprise. In all these respects it is a more scholarly book than *Among the Ibos of Nigeria*, though it does not engage with developments in anthropology as a discipline. The main contention of the book is that Igbo political and religious institutions had been destroyed by missionary activity and especially by colonial rule. The book

---

53. *Congrès International des Sciences Anthropologiques et Ethnologiques. Compte-rendu de la Première Session, Londres 1934* (London, 1934), p. 215.
54. *Congrès International des Sciences Anthropologiques et Ethnologiques*, p. 210.
55. *Congrès International des Sciences Anthropologiques et Ethnologiques*, p. 234.
56. CMSA G3 A 3/O 1934/62 Archdeacon Basden to Hooper, 14 August 1934.

therefore discusses the irretrievable past of traditional Igbo society: "It is chiefly in order to preserve some knowledge of old customs, beliefs and practices that this book has been compiled."[57]

Basden here offers a conservative definition of anthropology as documenting and understanding the "primitive beliefs" and "ancient laws and customs" of people "totally unacquainted with the white man,"[58] at a time when anthropological research began to develop an interest in understanding change in African societies.[59] In Britain, the 1930s marked a new rapprochement between missionaries and anthropologists, who each had become interested in researches with a focus on the change and destruction to traditional African culture brought by culture contact.[60] It was possible for missionaries to remain up-to-date of developments in anthropology thanks to the scholarships that were available to study courses in anthropology when on leave. For instance, when the missionary James Welch went on leave in 1931, he was awarded a studentship from the International African Institute as well as an extension of his leave by the CMS, to study anthropology. Welch worked with Dr. J. H. Oldham, Professor B. Malinowski, and others in London, and especially with Colonel T. C. Hodson at Cambridge, who was his supervisor. Welch concluded that his own, earlier studies of the Isoko people among whom he worked as a missionary were "amateurish" and "badly done."[61] In 1934 he published an article on the Isoko in *Africa*, in which he tried to work out some of his new insights.[62] Meanwhile, Basden's approach in *Niger Ibos* was not only out of step with developments in anthropology more generally, it was also old-fashioned compared to other monographs on the Igbo that were published around the same time, such as Meek's *Law and Authority in a Nigerian Tribe* (1937) and Leith-Ross's *African Women* (1939).[63]

57. Basden, *Niger Ibos*, p. xvi.
58. Basden, *Niger Ibos*, p. xii.
59. CMSA AF g O 28 Memorandum J. H. Oldham on the relation of the International Institute of African Languages and Cultures to missionary work in Africa (1936).
60. In contrast, Patrick Harries states that missionaries and professional anthropologists grew apart during the 1930s. As most of his examples are drawn from South Africa, the difference between the present interpretation and his may reflect the different ways in which anthropological traditions developed in Britain and South Africa during these years. Harries, "Anthropology", pp. 255-57.
61. CMSA G3 A 3/O 1932/41 Report (by J. W. Welch) of the work done while holding studentship from October 1931 to October 1932.
62. James Welch, "The Isoko Tribe," *Africa* 7, no. 2 (1934): 160-73.
63. C. K. Meek, *Law and Authority in a Nigerian Tribe: A Study in Indirect Rule* (Oxford, 1937); Sylvia Leith-Ross, *African Women: A Study of the Ibo of Nigeria* (1939; reprint, London, 1965).

Missionary Ethnographers and the History of Anthropology

Over a period of about thirty years, Basden's ethnographic writings were remarkably consistent. It appears that he regarded his writings to be those of an "advocate" for the Igbo, who explained their disappearing traditional way of life to general audiences back in Britain, to colonial administrators, and to anthropologists. In his later work he also includes Western-style-educated Igbo, whom he thought had little or no knowledge of traditional Igbo practices, among his intended audience.[64] A number of themes appear again and again in his writings. These include the standard discussions of Igbo traditional laws and customs (including polygyny and the roles of chiefs and elders), and religion (including shrines and sacrifices), but also two themes of great importance to Basden: "denationalization" and the similarities between Igbo traditions and the laws of the Israelites.

Basden was not the first to link the Igbo to the Jews. As early as 1789, Olaudah Equiano, the ex-slave and abolitionist activist, wrote in his autobiography that his people, now identified as the Igbo, descended from the ancient Jews. Equiano gave the same evidence for this assertion as Basden would later on, pointing toward similarities in customs.[65] The same claim was also made in 1868 by James Africanus Horton, a Sierra Leonean of Igbo ancestry. In his book *West African Countries and Peoples*, he stated that the Igbo were remnants of the "lost tribes" of Israel.[66] However, such claims were not just made for the Igbo. The idea that West African peoples were descendants from the Jews of the Old Testament was fairly widespread in missionary and in colonial circles, but also among local West African culture brokers, during the nineteenth century and the first half of the twentieth century.[67] The missionary J. J. Williams, for instance, suggested that the Asante had Hebraic connections.[68] Local historians made similar claims for the Efik.[69] In 1909, the Sierra

---

64. Basden, *Niger Ibos*, p. xvi.

65. Olaudah Equiano, *The Interesting Narrative of the Life of Olaudah Equiano, or Gustavus Vassa the African (with a New Introduction by Paul Edwards)*, 2 vols. (London, 1969), 1:34-36.

66. Robin Law, "The 'Hamitic Hypothesis' in Indigenous West African Historical Thought," *History in Africa* 36 (2009): 306.

67. Robin Law, "Constructing 'a Real National History': A Comparison of Edward Blyden and Samuel Johnson," in *Self-Assertion and Brokerage: Early Cultural Nationalism in West Africa*, ed. K. Barber and P. F. de Moraes Farias (Birmingham, 1990), pp. 78-100.

68. Philip C. Zachernuk, "Of Origins and Colonial Order: Southern Nigerian Historians and the 'Hamitic Hypothesis' c. 1870-1970," *Journal of African History* 35, no. 3 (1994): 444.

69. Ute Roeschenthaler, "A 'New York City of Ibibioland'? Local Historiography and Power Conflict in Calabar," in *A Place in the World: New Local Historiographies from Africa and South Asia*, ed. Axel Harneit-Sievers (Leiden, 2002), p. 97.

Leonean historian A. B. C. Sibthorpe claimed that the Yoruba were the "lost tribes" of Israel, which was only one among a number of theories of Middle Eastern origins for this particular group. Probably based on an older Islamic tradition was Muhammed Bello's 1812 suggestion that the Yoruba derived from Nimrod, a descendant of the cursed Ham, who had fled Mecca resisting Islam. The claim that was most frequently made, however — for instance, by Samuel Johnson, writing in 1897 — was that the Yoruba had migrated to West Africa from Egypt.[70] Similar claims to Egyptian origins were also made for the Asante.

Historians have used the Hamitic hypothesis to explain such diverse claims to Middle Eastern origins. The term "Hamitic hypothesis" denotes not one single, stable concept, but rather a set of different incarnations of an idea that dates back to the Jewish Old Testament. Use of the term is thus potentially confusing as our first association might be with what Robin Law called the "classic European racialist version" that had emerged in the nineteenth century:[71] the colonial idea that throughout the history of Africa lighter-skinned peoples had inspired civilization into black peoples. This interpretation was widely used in popular and scholarly literature as a justification for European colonial rule until World War II.[72]

However, this was not the version of the Hamitic hypothesis that inspired Basden's comparison between Igbo and Hebrew customs. Basden had been influenced, as other missionaries before him had been, by an earlier version of the hypothesis in which the Hamites were black. Taking as its starting point the Bible, this version held that the black peoples of Africa descended from Noah's youngest son Ham, whose offspring Noah had cursed into a life of servitude. Of course, the Bible does not state that Ham's descendants were black; this interpretation appears to have been recorded first in postbiblical Jewish traditions compiled between the fourth and sixth centuries C.E.[73] This interpretation was adopted also in Christian and Islamic discourse, and the idea that black people had descended from Ham persisted throughout medieval

---

70. Law, "Hamitic Hypothesis," p. 307. Samuel Johnson's *History of the Yorubas from the Earliest Times to the Beginning of the British Protectorate* was published long after it was written, in 1921.

71. Law, "Hamitic Hypothesis," p. 294.

72. Zachernuk, "Of Origins," pp. 427-55; on the use of the idea in colonial historiography, see A. E. Afigbo, "Colonial Historiography," in *African Historiography: Essays in Honour of Jacob Ade Ajayi*, ed. Toyin Falola (Harlow and Ikeja, 1993), pp. 39-51.

73. Edith R. Sanders, "The Hamitic Hypothesis: Its Origin and Functions in Time Perspective," *Journal of African History* 10, no. 4 (1969): 521-22; Law, "Hamitic Hypothesis," p. 296.

times into the eighteenth and nineteenth centuries. It was then picked up by Equiano and Horton, who, Philip Zachernuk suggests, found it useful as a way of locating Igbo history within a respectable broader history.[74] A more common use of the Hamitic hypothesis, especially during the seventeenth to nineteenth centuries, was as justification for the enslavement of black Africans.[75] This was not just the case in Europe and North America, but also in the Islamic world, including among African Muslims.[76] Nineteenth- and twentieth-century missionaries used yet another aspect of this version of the hypothesis. To them the idea that the particular people they were trying to convert had "originally" been Jewish was particularly appealing because this implied that their religion had originally been monotheist.

The concept that monotheism lay at the basis of the religious system of the particular ethnic group but had gradually been lost or diminished — for instance, as result of distortions brought about by a reliance on oral transmission of customs through the ages[77] — gave missionaries both a justification and a starting point for conversion.[78] This is indeed what Basden consistently did in his publications: he downplayed the importance the Igbo attached to local gods and shrines, and emphasized that they recognized the existence of a supreme being: "*Chukwu* (as He is called) is supreme, and at His service are many ministering spirits whose sole business it is to fulfil His commands."[79] By presenting local deities as intermediaries, he opened up the possibility that the Igbo were originally monotheist. Basden's interpretation thus implied the existence in indigenous culture of a basis for Christian monotheism. This is where Basden's frequent references to the Igbo people's alleged Jewish origins fit. In the chapter "Some Similarities between the Israelites and the Ibos" in *Niger Ibos,* Basden starts off with a discussion about the monotheistic beginnings of man, before discussing a long list of Igbo laws and customs that were similar to Jewish customs.[80] In both his books Basden refers to R. H. Nassau's *Fetichism in West Africa: Forty Years' Observation of Native Customs and Superstitions* as an important source for understanding "primitive religion." Nassau's book had been published in 1904, when the notion of fetishism was

---

74. Zachernuk, "Of Origins," pp. 435-36.
75. David Brion Davis, *The Problem of Slavery in the Age of Revolution, 1770-1823* (Ithaca, N.Y., 1975).
76. Law, "Hamitic Hypothesis," p. 296.
77. Basden, *Niger Ibos,* p. 413.
78. Birgit Meyer, *Translating the Devil: Religion and Modernity among the Ewe in Ghana* (Edinburgh, 1999), pp. 60-62.
79. Basden, *Among the Ibos,* p. 215.
80. Basden, *Niger Ibos,* pp. 411-23.

already being challenged. It had received a mixed response within the anthropological community upon publication, and by the time Basden was quoting in agreement from Nassau's work in the late 1930s, *Fetichism in West Africa* was generally regarded as outdated.[81]

Basden was similarly consistent in his opinion that Igbo traditions were disappearing and that what had emerged in their place was not always desirable. He appears to have felt ambiguous about the consequences of the disappearance of Igbo tradition. On the one hand, he did not romanticize Igbo traditional religion, and he undoubtedly regarded its decline as a good thing. Already in 1912 he noted with approval that "the savage customs of cannibalism, human sacrifice, infanticide, etc., are being gradually swept away."[82] On the other hand, he warned consistently against "denationalizing" the Igbo: the replacing of traditional crafts and customs with inappropriate Western customs. In 1912 he warned that "with the advance of education through the agency of the Government and missionary societies, a new civilization is springing up, but if the sociological upheavals are to prove really beneficial they must be directed into right channels."[83] Three years later, he still approved of the disappearance of traditional customs, but he also suggested that many Westernized Igbo were merely imitating inappropriate European customs, without any substance or beneficial results.[84] There is no indication in Basden's publications or in his correspondence with CMS headquarters that he ever regretted the work of missionaries; he attributes all the changes he deplores to the colonial state and the colonial economy, in particular to European traders who had introduced the Igbo to the imported spirituous liquors that were corrupting this otherwise "sober race": "To be offered whisky, or German beer, when paying a call upon a native chief, is an innovation greatly to be deplored. . . . This is denationalisation in one of its most pernicious forms."[85]

Igbo society as he had found it when he arrived at the turn of the twentieth century no longer existed when he wrote *Niger Ibos* in the late 1930s. Igbo customs, he argued, were "irretrievably lost," and the book mainly described the past of Igbo society. In contrast to Basden's earlier publications, *Niger Ibos* opens with a discussion of these issues, and it could be argued that the book's main point is that Igbo political and religious institutions had been destroyed by missionary activity and colonial rule. However, this does not necessarily in-

---

81. Cinnamon in this volume, pp. 112-13, 119-20. See also Cinnamon, "Missionary Expertise," pp. 413-32.
82. Basden, "Notes on the Ibo Country and the Ibo People," p. 247.
83. Basden, "Notes on the Ibo Country and the Ibo People," p. 247.
84. Basden, "Denationalizing a Primitive People," p. 731.
85. Basden, *Among the Ibos*, p. 25.

dicate that Basden had mellowed his stance on Igbo culture, or that he regretted what missionaries had done. Rather, he raises these issues in order to argue against the colonial policy of the time, which aimed to redesign its system of indirect rule into one based more closely on the traditional political and religious institutions of the people of southeast Nigeria.[86] This reorganization was done in the wake of the 1929 Women's War, at a time when the colonial government had come to realize that the local level of colonial administration did not correspond with the precolonial political organization of the area. In response, and in line with its stated ideology of indirect rule, the colonial government attempted to reconstruct traditional political organization. It appointed government anthropologists to conduct research and to help train district officers to do their own studies. The questions the government asked from anthropology included "Are the Warrant Chiefs, i.e. the members of the Native Courts, the true leaders of the people?" and "Are the areas of jurisdiction true ethnic ones?"[87] Meek's study *Law and Authority in a Nigerian Tribe,* which was published a year ahead of *Niger Ibos,* followed the government agenda and aimed to give an interpretation of Igbo society that could be used as the basis for administration and taxation. This is not surprising: when Meek had come to Nigeria as colonial officer in 1912, he developed an interest in anthropological research. He was appointed anthropological officer for the Northern Provinces in 1924, and was transferred to southern Nigeria in 1929.[88] His study of Igbo law and authority was his first assignment, having just arrived from northern Nigeria and unable to speak the Igbo language. He based his study on about 200 intelligence reports from colonial officers about the history, laws, and customs of the population living in the districts under their authority, and on nine months of field research. In the introduction to the book, after identifying the Women's War as direct cause for the project, Meek remarks that "It will have been gathered that, in instituting anthropological inquiries in Iboland, the Government of Nigeria was not actuated by any academic or antiquarian interest, but by the purely practical motive of bettering the administration."[89]

---

86. A. E. Afigbo, *The Warrant Chiefs: Indirect Rule in Southeastern Nigeria, 1891-1929* (New York, 1972); H. Gailey, *The Road to Aba: A Study of British Administrative Policy in Eastern Nigeria* (New York, 1970); Olufemi Vaughan, *Nigerian Chiefs: Traditional Power in Modern Politics, 1890s-1990s* (Rochester, N.Y., 2000), pp. 34-35.

87. Nigerian National Archive, Enugu Branch, RIVPROF 1/9/1 Confidential circular from F. Ruxton, Lagos, 12 February 1926.

88. NAI CSO 26 09258 Baddely to Secretary of State for the Colonies, 25 April 1929; Secretary, Northern Provinces, to the Chief Secretary, Lagos, 22 March 1930; Badely to the Secretary, Northern Provinces, 12 April 1930.

89. Meek, *Law and Authority,* p. xv.

Basden did not agree with this approach. He regarded the government's method for collecting and collating data superficial and a recipe for biased information. Furthermore, he did not believe it was still possible to reconstruct traditional Igbo society after thirty years — or more — of colonial rule. Most of all, he disagreed with the government's underlying project: to reorganize local administration according to the neo-traditions of indirect rule. By its very design, this project would strengthen the position of those African local leaders who claimed the sanction of tradition, while it was likely to limit the ambitions of African Christians to play leading roles in their local communities.[90] Indeed, by the mid-1930s some mission-educated men felt so frustrated in their attempts to have a say in local affairs that they accused the African local authorities of being corrupt and despotic "gerontocracies."[91] In his introduction to *Niger Ibos* Basden thus spoke out against government policy when he stated that it should be left to the Igbo to decide which traditional customs to retain, and that this should not be "dictated by the foreigner." In fact, he argued that "attempts to persuade the native to retain old ideas and customs are doomed to partial, if not total, failure."[92] That Basden chose to frame *Niger Ibos* in the context of colonial government policy, rather than the anthropological debates of the day, should not have come as a surprise. Within the Niger Mission, Basden was regarded as someone who was closer to the colonial administration than most missionaries. In 1925 Bishop Lasbrey observed: "he usually gets on well with Government men."[93] In addition, as mentioned above, Basden acted as expert witness and was a member of the colonial legislative council. It appears, however, that his engagement with the administration had been critical throughout, and in 1927 he was characterized as "a passive resister to Government on the whole" and "a nuisance."[94]

Walter Buchanan-Smith, in his foreword to *Niger Ibos,* notes that Basden reached some conclusions "which will not commend themselves to some of his readers in their entirety."[95] As lieutenant governor for southern Nigeria, he was particularly responding to Basden's criticism of indirect rule, which he further referenced when he commented that it was "pleasant to observe that even where Dr. Basden is least optimistic as to the future he has, at any rate,

---

90. Harneit-Sievers, *Constructions of Belonging,* pp. 210-16.
91. National Archive, London, Colonial Office Records, CO583 214/30018 Annual Report on Southern Provinces for 1935; CO583 299/1 record of second meeting of the Colonial Local Government Advisory Panel, 22 October 1948.
92. Basden, *Niger Ibos,* pp. xii-xiii.
93. CMSA G3 A 3/O 1925/7 Bishop Lasbrey to Manley, 2 January 1925.
94. CMSA G3 A 3/O 1927/44 confidential report by Alec Fraser (1927).
95. Walter Buchanan-Smith, foreword in *Niger Ibos,* p. v.

no doubts as to the intentions of the Administrative Officers . . . to do their best for the welfare of their people."[96] Basden's refusal to contribute to the colonial agenda did not go unnoticed. One reviewer characterized *Niger Ibos* as an impractical and "unwieldy" book, of not much use to the colonial administration: "while a general reader will luxuriate uncomplainingly among vast riches of novelty and surprise, the men and women who are carrying — or are about to carry — responsibility in administration or mission service in S. Nigeria and who turn at once to this book for information and aid, will be less well catered for."[97]

So while Basden was consistent in the themes he covered in his ethnographic writings and in the methodology he employed, his work was also part of a broader debate and did respond to new ideas. However, these were not the themes of the developing field of anthropology, which was reevaluating its relation with colonial and missionary ethnographers at this time. Rather, Basden engaged with the very local, colonial debates about the nature of Igbo society, the organization of local government, and the direction in which a modern, colonial Igbo society should develop. Here, Basden turned out to be a self-styled representative of the Igbo people, who spoke from decades of personal experience. Basden was not unique in claiming the right to represent and protect the interest of "his" African community: other missionaries and missionary anthropologists — including Henri-Philippe Junod — defended the same position.[98] Yet, compared to more intellectual missionary anthropologists such as Henri-Alexandre Junod and Edwin Smith, Basden was much less interested in dialogue with the anthropological mainstream, or in presenting the detailed sources and methodological considerations on which his conclusions were based: Basden's concern was much more local, and much more practical in what it aimed to achieve politically. It is thus not surprising that his works failed to make an impact on broader anthropological debates yet remained important to local debates on Igbo culture.

SELECT BIBLIOGRAPHY

Basden, George Thomas. *Among the Ibos of Nigeria: An Account of the Curious and Interesting Habits, Customs, and Beliefs of a Little-Known African People by One Who Has for Many Years Lived amongst Them on Close and Intimate Terms.* London, 1921.

96. Buchanan-Smith, foreword, p. vi.
97. Cullen Young, review of *Niger Ibos*, by G. T. Basden, *Man* 39 (1939): 132.
98. Harries, "Anthropology," p. 255.

———. *Niger Ibos: A Description of the Primitive Life, Customs, and Animistic Beliefs, Etc., of the Ibo People of Nigeria by One Who, for Thirty-five Years, Enjoyed the Privilege of Their Intimate Confidence and Friendship.* London, 1938.

Harneit-Sievers, Axel. *Constructions of Belonging: Igbo Communities and the Nigerian State in the Twentieth Century.* Rochester, N.Y., 2006.

Harries, Patrick. "Anthropology." In *Missions and Empire,* edited by Norman Etherington. Oxford, 2005.

Kuklick, Henrika. *The Savage Within: The Social History of British Anthropology, 1885-1945.* Cambridge, 1991.

Law, Robin. "The 'Hamitic Hypothesis' in Indigenous West African Historical Thought." *History in Africa* 36 (2009).

Meyer, Birgit. *Translating the Devil: Religion and Modernity among the Ewe in Ghana.* Edinburgh, 1999.

Stocking, George W., Jr., *After Tylor: British Social Anthropology, 1888-1951.* Madison, Wis., 1995.

Van den Bersselaar, Dmitri. *In Search of Igbo Identity: Language, Culture, and Politics in Nigeria, 1900-1966.* Leiden, 1998.

———. "Missionary Knowledge and the State in Colonial Africa: On How G. T. Basden Became an Expert." *History in Africa* 33 (2006).

Zachernuk, Philip C. "Of Origins and Colonial Order: Southern Nigerian Historians and the 'Hamitic Hypothesis' c. 1870-1970." *Journal of African History* 35, no. 3 (1994).

CHAPTER 5

From Iconoclasm to Preservation: W. F. P. Burton, Missionary Ethnography, and Belgian Colonial Science

DAVID MAXWELL

William Frederick Padwick Burton was a significant figure in two seemingly separate worlds. In religious circles he was regarded as a pioneer, the cofounder (along with James Salter) of the iconic Pentecostal faith mission in Mwanza, southeast Belgian Congo, in 1915: the Congo Evangelistic Mission. He associated with members of the renowned "Cambridge Seven": graduates who sailed to Shanghai with Hudson Taylor as members of the China Inland Mission and who epitomized late Victorian missionary earnestness.[1] By virtue of his stature and ability Burton became a progenitor of a Pentecostal missionary tradition that gathered pace throughout the twentieth century. His life and work are celebrated in various missionary and Pentecostal hagiographies.[2] He

---

1. Peter Kay, "Cecil Polhill, the Pentecostal Missionary Union, and the Fourfold Gospel with Healing and Speaking in Tongues: Signs of a New Movement in Missions," North Atlantic Missiology Project Position Paper 20 (1996).

2. H. Womersley, *Wm. F. P. Burton, Congo Pioneer* (Eastbourne, 1973); C. Whittaker, *Seven Pentecostal Pioneers* (Southampton, 1983).

An earlier version of this chapter was published in *History and Anthropology* 19, no. 4 under the title "The Soul of the Luba: W. F. P. Burton, Missionary Ethnography and Belgian Colonial Science." This chapter has benefited from comments by Hein Vanhee, Bogumil Jewsiewicki, Pierre Petit, Tom Reefe, Jean-Luc Vellut, and Richard Werbner, and from discussions with Patrick Harries, Allen Roberts, Léon Verbeek, and David Womersley. This research has been funded by the Nuffield Foundation and the Economic and Social Research Council Grant No. RES-000-23-1535.

is also remembered for his scientific research on southeast Belgian Congo. His collections of Luba material culture and ethnographic photographs, now held in the University of Witwatersrand, South Africa, and Le Musée Royal de l'Afrique Centrale (MRAC) in Tervuren, Belgium, helped form the basis of two successful exhibitions of Luba art in South Africa in 1992, and the USA in 1996.[3] His ethnographic research[4] has been used by two generations of historians and anthropologists working on the Luba and their neighbors.[5]

This chapter addresses two key issues. The first concerns the conundrum *why* missionaries engaged in ethnographic research when they were so intent on changing the customs and beliefs they described. The question is more compelling in the case of Pentecostal faith missionaries. African Pentecostals and their missionary forebears are renowned for their adversarial stance toward African possession cults and traditional healing, and are famed for their destruction of objects associated with these practices.[6] Indeed, Burton ac-

---

3. In South Africa the exhibition was curated by the University of Witwatersrand and moved to the University of Cape Town; see A. Nettleton, ed., *The Collection of W. F. P. Burton* (Johannesburg, 1992). In the USA it was organized and presented by the Museum for African Art, New York, and traveled to the National Museum of African Art, Washington, D.C.; see M. Nooter Roberts and A. Roberts, eds., *Memory: Luba Art and the Making of History* (New York, 1996). A "fairly representative section" of the Burton collection was exhibited earlier in the Africana Museum, Johannesburg, 1939-40; see N. Leibhammer and F. Rankin Smith, "Redemption and Reconstruction: The Burton Collection," in *The Collection of W. F. P. Burton*, p. 15. Some of Burton's collection is on permanent display in Tervuren, Belgium. Masks from his Tervuren collection illustrate a number of books on African art, Musée Royal de l'Afrique Central, Tervuren, Belgium (henceforth MRAC), file Burton. Some of this material was also used in a French exhibition presented in Musée Dapper, Paris, 1993-94; see F. Neyt, *Luba. Aux Sources Du Zaïre* (Paris, 1993).

4. His most significant publications were *Luba Religion and Magic in Custom and Belief* (Tervuren, 1961) and *The Magic Drum: London; Tales from Central Africa* (London, 1961). These were published 1939-40 in *Bulletin des juridictions indigènes et du droit coutumier Congolais* (henceforth *BJI*); see below. He also produced an extensive collection of proverbs: "Proverbes des Baluba," *BJI* 23, no. 3, to 26, no. 10 (1955-58), which were republished as *Proverbes des Baluba* (Elisabethville, 1958).

5. Jan Vansina, *The Kingdoms of the Savannah* (Madison, Wis., 1966); Tom Reefe, *The Rainbow and the Kings: A History of the Luba Empire to 1891* (Berkeley, 1981); Luc De Heusch, *The Drunken King; or, The Origin of the State* (Bloomington, Ind., 1982); Pierre Petit, "'Les Charmes du Roi sont les Esprits des Morts': Les Fondements Religieux de la Royauté Sacrée chez les Luba du Zaïre," *Africa* 66, no. 3 (1996), and "Ngoy, mère et fille, potières luba de Lenge (Katanga, Congo)," *Anthropos* 93 (1998).

6. David Maxwell, *Christians and Chiefs in Zimbabwe: A Social History of the Hwesa People, c. 1870s-1990s* (Edinburgh, 1999); Maxwell, *African Gifts of the Spirit: Pentecostalism and the Rise of a Zimbabwean Transnational Religious Movement* (Oxford, 2006); B. Meyer, *Translating the Devil: Religion and Modernity among the Ewe of Ghana* (Edinburgh, 1999).

tively pursued the familiar missionary strategy of iconoclasm and the exposure of what he believed to be religious fraud. His inspirational writings celebrate numerous "bonfire meetings" where what he describes as "fetishes" were burnt by converts to Christianity.[7] Moreover, given that Burton, like most Pentecostals, believed that he was living in *end times*, the imperative of evangelism should surely have consumed all his energies.

The second issue concerns academic recognition. Unlike some of his peers, J. H. Oldham, Edwin Smith, and Diedrich Westermann, Burton did not get the acknowledgment he deserved as an authority on his subject. Only after his death in 1971 were his writing, collecting, and photography taken up by the scholarly community. Once again this issue relates more generally to the work of missionary social scientists, many of whom were marginalized by academic anthropology in the 1930s.[8] The means to resolve questions regarding Burton's motives for researching and the eventual status of his research lie in reconstructing the various contexts and ideologies that shaped his thinking and practice.[9] These were the following: the intellectual domains of museums and university anthropology in Britain, Belgium, and South Africa; the dominant paradigms of missiological thinking; the expectations of Belgian colonialism; and the pressures of Luba society. Burton was caught up in networks of academic collaboration and patronage, and was profoundly influenced by the ethnographic genre. Against these influences ranged the contingencies of mission work in remote southeast Belgian Congo.

The chapter charts Burton's shifting attitude toward the Luba, showing how he moved from an aggressive, intrusive mode of research to a position of greater sympathy as he came to consider their cultural riches through study of language, proverb, and folklore. Consideration of the second phase of Burton's research opens up discussion of the missionary origins of the disciplines of African theology and religious studies.

---

7. W. F. P. Burton, *God Working with Them: Being Eighteen Years of Congo Evangelistic Mission History* (London, 1933); Burton, *When God Changes a Village* (London, 1933); Burton, *Mudishi, Congo Hunter* (Luton, 1947).

8. P. Harries, "Anthropology," in *Missions and Empire*, ed. Norman Etherington, Oxford History of the British Empire Companion Series (Oxford, 2005) p. 248; D. van den Bersselaar, "Missionary Knowledge and the State in Colonial Nigeria: On How G. T. Basden Became an Expert," *History in Africa* 33 (2006): 49.

9. Pierre Bourdieu, "Participant Objectivation," *Journal of the Royal Anthropological Institute* 9 (2003); Henrietta Moore and Megan Vaughan, *Cutting Down Trees: Gender, Nutrition, and Agricultural Change in the Northern Province of Zambia, 1890-1990* (London, 1994), pp. 1-19.

DAVID MAXWELL

Public School Boy, Pentecostal Firebrand and Missionary

Burton's upbringing was distinctly upper middle class. He was born in Liverpool in March 1886. His father was commodore of the Cunard fleet. His mother, whose maiden name was Padwick, was related to the Marlborough family of Shrewsbury. She was an accomplished artist, having studied under Thomas Linnell. She taught William the techniques of oil and water and of sketching in pen and pencil, and ensured that he learned carpentry. Meanwhile, a governess taught him French. Like many of the imperial class, Burton grew up in the home counties, attending public school at St. Laurence College, Ramsgate. At seventeen Burton took an engineering course at Redhill Technical College and then moved to Preston, Lancashire, where he worked for General Electric, completing his studies in engineering at Liverpool University.

Burton's mother was a devout Plymouth Brethren who brought him up on a daily diet of Bible study and prayer. He eventually followed his father's faith, and was confirmed as an Anglican by the archbishop of Canterbury. But Anglicanism had little immediate impact upon him. Reflecting upon his confirmation, he wrote: "It was just a meaningless, powerless rite, in which I promised things I had no ability to perform."[10] However, he remained open to his mother's religion and was drawn into the world of radical evangelicalism that would lead him and many others into Pentecostalism. In 1905 he attended the London revival campaigns of Torrey and Alexander, where he experienced a dramatic conversion. His move to Preston exposed him to a series of new influences. The famous Keswick Conventions impelled him to search for a greater sense of holiness and an empowerment by the Holy Spirit. Around 1909 he heard of the Pentecostal outpourings in Azusa Street, California, and Scandinavia, and joined a group of pious believers in Preston who sought the gifts of tongues and prophecy through prayer and Bible study. Early in 1911 Burton was baptized in the Holy Spirit.[11] It was an experience so profound that he henceforth renounced engineering and took up a peripatetic existence as an evangelist, walking great distances across Lancashire and the Yorkshire Pennines, holding meetings in cottages and preaching on village greens. He was happy to be known simply as "the tramp preacher."

Like that of many pioneering Pentecostals, Burton's temperament was not entirely appealing. The sense of certitude and absolutism that came from his dramatic conversion and profound experience of the Holy Spirit led to dogma-

10. Whittaker, *Seven Pentecostal Pioneers*, p. 149.
11. *Elim Evangel* 3, no. 12 (December 1922): 196-99.

tism and irascibility. In his early days he crossed swords with Polhill and Alexander Boddy over infant baptism, and he even fell out with his mentors Thomas Meyerscough and John Nelson Parr. All were influential Pentecostal leaders. At this stage, too, he renounced all sources of knowledge save the Bible. But this constricting aspect of his postconversion zeal soon disappeared, replaced by openness to what others could teach him.[12] When Burton set sail for Africa in 1914, he had already done some solid research on Livingstone (1857) and Cameron's (1877) travels in central Africa. Henceforth he was a voracious reader with an extensive library. Much of Burton's theology came from the evangelical stable — Hudson Taylor, Reuben Torrey — but he was profoundly influenced by Roland Allen's *Missionary Methods: St. Paul's or Ours?*[13] Allen was a High Anglican theologian with a restorationist yearning to recover the supernatural power and miracles of the New Testament. Allen's suspicion of things that smacked of modernism led him to view the contemporary mission station with its educational and medical infrastructures as a barrier to continuous gospel proclamation.[14] The task of the missionary was to plant a simple, self-supporting, self-propagating, self-governing church and then move on.[15]

Burton and Salter's vision was to camp in a village, preach till a nucleus of believers had appeared, and proceed to the next settlement — and do this until the whole mission field had been covered. But this proved impractical in the face of thousands of Luba communities. Moreover, to train a local leadership, a mission station had to be constructed. However, Burton remained a committed "tramp preacher," covering some two thousand miles each year on foot, inspired by his nearest missionary neighbor, the influential Brethren missionary Dan Crawford.[16] Burton's Luba praise name was Kapamu, "The Rusher Forth," with connotations of petulance and impatience.[17] Proselytism remained Burton's primary goal, and although he would come to use ethnography to inform his missiological strategy, the reasons for his encounter with ethnographic science lie beyond his Pentecostal theology.

12. University of Witwatersrand Art Galleries (henceforth UWAG), file, Burton Personal, Burton to Owen Saunders, South Africa, 8 July 1925.
13. Roland Allen, *Missionary Methods: St. Paul's or Ours?* (London, 1912); Womersley, *Wm. F. P. Burton*, p. 79.
14. Kay, "Cecil Polhill," pp. 8-9.
15. Tim Yates, *Christian Missions in the Twentieth Century* (Cambridge, 1994), pp. 59-67. Central African Missions, Preston, henceforth (CAM), file, Burton to Salter, 1930-40. Burton believed that modifications had to be made to Allen's model and was scathing about the Brethen's uncritical adoption of "Allenism." Burton to James Salter, 22 July 1934.
16. Burton, *Luba Religion*, p. 1.
17. Womersley, *Wm. F. P. Burton*, p. 15; interview with Ngoy Kabuya, Ruashi, DRC, 13 May 2007.

DAVID MAXWELL

Belgian Colonial Science and Catholicism

Science was an important source of legitimation for Belgian colonization of the Congo, functioning on a symbolic level as much as a practical one.[18] Leopold's renowned International African Association was in fact an organization of explorers and anthropologists founded at a geographical conference in 1876. Along with its aim to promote trade and its supposed mission to eradicate slavery, it also pledged itself to a program of discovery and education.[19] The association's mouthpiece was the journal *Le Mouvement Géographique*, which ran numerous articles on the Congo's peoples, flora, fauna, and geography alongside a cruder promotion of Leopoldian imperialism.[20] Science was also a means of Belgium's rehabilitation as an imperial power after the Red Rubber Scandal (ca. 1903-6) and the ensuing crisis of sleeping sickness. By 1906 Catholic missions and the episcopacy in Belgium had realized the danger of being too closely associated with the atrocities of the Congo Free State and had begun to add their voices to the denunciations of the regime. On the founding of the new Belgian colonial state in 1908, a group of academics based at the Catholic University of Louvain, advocating a reformist or social Catholicism, seized the opportunity to engineer an ethical colonialism. Two professors in the university's *Ecole Coloniale*, E. De Jonghe and V. Denyn, played a key role in Belgian colonial science, founding the influential journal *La Revue Congolaise* and its Flemish counterpart, *Onze Kongo*. These journals combined in 1920 to form the publication *Congo*, another important vehicle of social Catholicism.[21]

Johan Lagae argues that knowledge production in the Belgian Congo surpassed that of all other African colonies. It certainly received more financial backing than other colonies.[22] By the 1920s its level of administration was unequaled in Africa with the exceptions of Mauritania and Dahomey. Great emphasis was placed upon territorial agents visiting frequently far-flung parts of

---

18. For a recent extensive account of Belgian colonial science, see Marc Poncelet, *L'invention des sciences coloniales belges* (Paris, 2008).

19. J. Stengers, "King Leopold's Imperialism," in *Studies in the Theory of Imperialism*, ed. R. Owen and B. Sutcliffe (London, 1972), p. 260.

20. *Le Mouvement Géographique* was published by the Institut national de Géographie de Bruxelles.

21. J.-L. Vellut, "L'Afrique dans les horizons de l'université catholique de Louvain, XIXe-XXe siècles," in *Leuven-Louvain-la-Neuve. Kennis maken. Aller-retour*, ed. J. Rogiers (Louvain, 2001).

22. J. Lagae, "Sur la production du savoir et le rôle de la science dans le contexte colonial belge," in *La Mémoire du Congo. Le temps colonial*, ed. J.-L. Vellut (Tervuren, 2005), p. 131.

the territory under their authority and making contact with local subjects. Administrative officers were expected to spend twenty days per month in the bush and were encouraged to publish their ethnographic impressions in one of the Belgian Congo's numerous "native affairs" journals.[23]

Belgian colonial science had a strong applied character until 1945. The new regime sought to liberate the Congolese with the microscope, investing in medical development so that it could eventually claim that the Belgian Congo was the best equipped of all African colonies. There was also a good deal of agronomic research, drawing upon botany, zoology, and entomology, stimulated by the creation of the Public Agricultural Service in 1910. Colonial science did not develop autonomously but in dialogue with debates and movements in the metropole. A prestigious group of monographs on various Congolese peoples drawing upon the Belgian tradition of empirical sociology was published from 1907 onward by Cyrille Van Overbergh, founder of the Société Belge de Sociologie and an influential figure in social Catholicism. A strong impetus to collect and classify came from the Belgian museums, particularly the great engine for research, the colonial museum in Tervuren.[24]

The type of colonial science most relevant to this paper was ethnography. This too had a strong applied dimension, being knowledge for domination. From around 1915 onward, the Belgians embarked on a near impossible task of organizing an extremely heterogeneous and fluid African population into ethnicities, demarcated by geography but also supposed social, linguistic, economic, and cultural differences. This project was intensified under the influence of Louis Franck, Belgian colonial minister (1918-24) and apostle of indirect rule. District colonial officers did much of the groundwork, producing hierarchies of chieftaincies. Genealogies were collected to ensure that the rightful candidate succeeded and careful work was done on the separation of powers between chiefs and subchiefs, leaders and councillors. Work was also done on the direction of tribute and its nature. A good deal of ink was spilled trying to sort out inconsistencies and anomalies such as female chiefs and villages that were autonomous or had multiple loyalties.[25] Colonial officials had a particular dislike of new communities of *ouvriers*, former railway builders or porters who did not want to return to their villages, or groups of refugees

---

23. C. Young, *Politics in the Congo: Decolonization and Independence* (Princeton, 1965), pp. 10-12.

24. Lagae, "Sur la production," pp. 131-35; M. Bastin, "Belgium," in *Encyclopaedia of Africa South of the Sahara*, vol. 4, ed. John Middleton (New York, 1997), appendix A, pp. 436-37; Jan Vansina, "The Ethnographic Account as Genre in Central Africa," *Paideuma* 33 (1987).

25. MRAC, Dossiers AIMO, EA.0.01-753.

who gathered around mission stations for protection from powerful missionaries who expanded the range of local big men.[26] Many of the local identities constructed by the Belgian colonial state were as arbitrary as those constructed by Swahili slavers or African big men before them, but the Belgians remained strongly committed to the project and drew others into their work to help fill new tribal identities with ethnographic detail.

There was a great range of contributors to Belgian colonial knowledge, including many non-Belgians.[27] In the era of the Congo Free State, military personnel and adventurers such as H. von Wissmann, P. Le Marinel, Emile Franqui, Emile Storms, Jules Cornet, and Clément Brasseur filled the pages of *Le Mouvement Géographique* and its sister journal, *Le Congo Illustré*, with accounts of their geographical and ethnographic expeditions. But given their longevity in one particular location, missionaries played a pivotal role as colonial scientists. Franciscans were particularly prominent in Katanga. Theodoor Theuws did important ethnographic work on the Luba. Servaas Peeraer collected important pieces of art from Luba-Shyankadi for the University of Ghent in the 1930s. Ernest van Avermaet, with Benoît Mbuyà, published the *Dictionnaire Kiluba-Français* in 1954. And most renowned was Placide Tempels, author of *Bantu Philosophy* (1945).[28] Working on the eastern margins of the Luba empire, the White Father Pierre Colle wrote an influential study of the Luba-Hemba. Outside of Katanga, Missionaries of the Sacred Heart Gustaaf Hulstaert and Edmond Boelaert wrote about the Mongo. J. Van Wing and L. Bittremieux researched the Bakongo.[29] Other Catholics, such as the Jesuit Brother Justin Gillet, moved beyond the human sciences into botany, founding the famous botanical garden in Kisantu in 1898-99.[30]

Some Protestants, such as Karl Laman of the Swedish Mission — Svenska Missionsförbundet — in Bas Congo, also carried out ethnographic work, but given the sheer number of Catholic researchers, one might think that

---

26. Archives Africaines: Ministère des Affaires Etrangères, Bruxelles (henceforth AAB), file 625/5 Rapports avec l'administration. Politique Indigène. District commissioner, S. E. Jensen, to governor general, 8 February 1918.

27. Lagae, "Sur la production," p. 136.

28. C. Petridis, "Art et histoire des Luba méridionaux. Partie I: La Collection du Père Peeraer à l'Université de Gand," *Anthropos* 100 (2005): 7.

29. H. Vinck, "The Missionaries' Influence on Mongo National Consciousness and Political Activism, 1925-1965" (1996), at www.aequatoria.be.

30. For a useful overview of the ethnographic work of Belgian Catholic missionaries and the intellectual and political context that shaped their work, see Flavien Nkay Malu, "Missionnaires belges et recherche ethnographique au Congo," in *Anthropologie et missiologie XIXe-XXe siècles. Entre connivence et rivalité*, ed. Gérard van't Spijker (Paris, 2004).

ethnographic research was a Catholic enterprise.[31] Indeed, the colonial state actively sought out Catholic missionary researchers. In 1908 a guide to the collecting of ethnographic objects was sent to all Catholic missionaries in the Congo with the view of founding an ethnographic museum at Louvain. It encouraged them to collect full sets of objects relating to different spheres of human activity with descriptions of their uses and manufacture, augmented, if possible, by drawings and photographs. The objects were sorted into standard anthropological categories such as food, clothes, habitation, etc. Known as the "Trait-School" within the ethno-museological tradition, the exercise once again sought to map Congolese peoples in terms of the presence or absence of certain cultural elements.[32] The appendix was republished in 1920 by Edouard De Jonghe in an article entitled "L'Ethnologie, son objet, sa méthode" in the journal *Congo: Revue Générale de la Colonie Belge*.[33] He also encouraged missionary ethnography, translating into French the first part of Margaret Sinclair-Stevenson's *International Review of Mission* article (1920), "The Study of Anthropology on the Mission Field," exhorting his readers: "Nous devons coloniser scientifiquement."[34] Meanwhile, as director in the Ministry of Colonies, he produced ethnographic surveys and questionnaires for use in the field.

Along with the intellectual and missiological impetus to do ethnography, Catholic missionaries reaped large rewards for their collaboration with the Belgian colonial state. Leopold's 1906 concordat with the Vatican, which remained in force until 1960, ensured that the Catholic missionary enterprise would remain essentially Belgian. In return, the colonial state subsidized Catholic mission schools, contributed to the maintenance of missionaries, and granted two hundred hectares of land to each Catholic mission station.[35] Informally, Catholics were given first refusal of new territories and greater evangelical opportunities among workers in mines, towns, and sites of rail-

---

31. J. M. Janzen, "Laman's Congo Ethnography: Observations on Sources, Methodology, and Theory," *Africa* 42 (1972); W. MacGaffey, "Nationalisme Kongo et Ethnographie Coloniale," in *La Mémoire du Congo*.

32. E. De Jonghe, "L'ethnologie, son objet, sa méthode," *Congo* 1, 2, 2 (1920): 292-93.

33. In brief, the full list constituted the following: (1) general — knives, axes, etc.; (2) food; (3) clothes and hygiene; (4) habitation; (5) industry; (6) commerce; (7) arts and games; (8) religion; (9) law; (10) politics; (11) intellectual life; (12) physical anthropology. See De Jonghe, "L'ethnologie, son objet, sa méthode."

34. AAB, D61/3860/117. The first part of the essay, pp. 426-33, became "L'Etude de l'Anthropologie à la Mission Field: Comment il faut commencer?" For more detail on Sinclair Stevenson, see Deborah Gaitskell's chapter in this volume.

35. F. De Meeus and R. Steenberghen, *Les Missions Religieuses au Congo Belge* (Brussels, 1947).

way construction. Given the vast number of Catholic missionaries in the Belgian Congo, the Catholic Church was one of the holy trinity of powers that ran the colony, along with the administration and the corporations.[36]

Protestant Relations with the Belgian Colonial State

Protestant groups in the Belgian Congo, which were mostly from Britain, North America, and Scandinavia, were viewed as outsiders whose loyalty to the colony was always under suspicion. The colonial state preferred to deal with a monolithic Belgian Catholicism that sat well with its own homogenizing tendencies.[37] Its officials had read the conclusions of the commission into the Chilembwe Revolt in neighboring Nyasaland (1915) and subsequently determined that low-church Protestant missions financed and directed by people with no authority or competence were dangerous to the colonial order.[38] Small-scale Protestant enterprises were described as poor *petits rentiers* in comparison to the preferred large-scale Catholic enterprises such as the White Fathers.[39] Belgian officials believed that Protestantism with groups animated by zealous lay adepts had a tendency toward independency: "Sous l'influence de leur enseignement, de prophètes thaumaturges et visionnaires se multiplieront en Afrique." This prejudice was confirmed by the Kimbangu movement of the 1920s.[40] What the colonial state particularly feared was an African national church, a movement of multiethnic assimilation that cut across its ordered regime of ethnicities. Kimbanguism was banned, as was Ethiopianism and, later, the Watchtower. The American Church of Christ and the Seventh-Day Adventists remained near the top of the danger list, but the greatest obsession was the African Methodist Episcopal Church. There was a constant fixation with black American missionaries and the likes of W. E. B. Du Bois from the Pan African Congress, who represented a model of black autonomy the Belgians had no wish to see replicated in their colony.[41]

36. Young, *Politics in the Congo*, pp. 13-14.
37. While the regime sought after a monolithic Belgian Catholicism, there were tensions between Catholic orders and dissenting voices such as the Missionaries of the Sacred Heart.
38. AAB, 625/5/1. Personnel Missions Belges, "Conclusions de la Commission d'Enquête chargée par le Gouvernement du Nyassaland de rechercher les causes de la révolte suscité par John Chilembwe."
39. AAB, Pentecostal Missionary Union Kivu, 642 XXVIII, "Fait Particuliers," 30 May 1923.
40. AAB, General Council of the Assemblies of God, M641 XVIII, "Les Missionnaires de la 'Pentecôte' au Congo," 14, 11, 1922.
41. For insight into the Belgian colonial state's mentality toward evangelical Protes-

From Iconoclasm to Preservation

For those Protestant churches in the southeast of the Belgian Congo, relations with the state were even more fragile. Groups such as the British Baptists or the American Methodists with networks of missions that spanned colonial borders threatened the hermetic nature of Belgian colonialism. Remembering Rhodes's ambitions for Katanga, some officials believed the American Methodists and Plymouth Brethren in Katanga were a fifth column for British imperial interests, seeking to denationalize and then detach the region to prepare it for annexation to the British Copper Belt in Northern Rhodesia. District officers reported an unhealthy amount of English spoken in schools and mission stations. Protestant applications to work in towns and cities and teach African elites were viewed with great suspicion and often blocked. The commissioner general for Katanga wanted professional training schools in his territory, but only schools with a Belgian spirit *(des écoles d'esprit belge)*.[42]

As a Protestant mission in Katanga, the Congo Evangelistic Mission (CEM) was in a particularly precarious position.[43] It was not too dissimilar from the type of Protestant sect that aroused Belgium's greatest fears, and was similar to Pentecostal movements that had unnerved British colonial officials in adjacent territories.[44] Reports by colonial officials, based on a high level of surveillance, were far from positive. Officials read CEM's earliest publications such as *Missionary Pioneering in Congo Forests: A Narrative of William F. P. Burton and His Companions in the Native Villages of Luba-Land* (Moorhead, 1922), and went on discreet intelligence missions to Mwanza. What unnerved them was the mission's Pentecostalism. Divine healing undermined the regime's commitment to medical science. Tongues, intercessory prayer, and other pneumatic practices seemed to stir up African believers in a manner that ran counter to the Belgian desire to create disciplined colonial subjects fit for industrial labor. As Governor General Tilkens observed in a retrospective report (1934), the mission's "superstitious practices" produced trouble and

---

tantism, see P. Lerrigo, "The 'Prophet Movement' in Congo," *International Review of Mission*, 1922.

42. AAB, 625/5 Rapports avec l'administration, Politique Indigène, Commissioner General Katanga to Minister of Colonies, 7 August 1917. For a broader discussion of the Belgian fears about Anglo-American influence in Katanga, see B. Jewsiewicki, "Belgian Africa," in *The Cambridge History of Africa*, vol. 7, *From 1905 to 1940*, ed. A. Roberts (Cambridge, 1986), p. 471.

43. Extended treatment of the CEM's relation with the Belgian colonial state is found in D. Garrard, "History of the Zaire Evangelistic Mission/Communauté Pentecôtiste au Zaire 1915-82" (Ph.D. diss., University of Aberdeen, 1983; 2 vols.), pp. 289-359.

44. Maxwell, *African Gifts,* chapter 2.

excitement in the spirit of the black person.[45] A 1923 report recorded with approval that the catechists worked under European supervision with children learning to read and write in Kiluba. The carpentry shop at Mwanza and the introduction of basket making were noted with satisfaction. But Burton's claim to have healed Jimmy Salter's arm through prayer was met with incredulity, and his account of termites being chased from the house following a time of intercession was accompanied by a large exclamation mark in the margin from the provincial governor who received the report. It was also noted, somewhat coldly, that Burton and Salter's fellow pioneer, Armstrong, had fallen victim of his own belief in God's protection by not taking medicines and consequently dying of blackwater fever. "Certain members of the group," the official observed, "bordered on otherworldliness or neurosis" *(Certains d'entre eux frisent l'illuminisme ou la névrose).*[46]

Burton won himself few Belgian friends with his criticism of the migrant labor system. While neighboring American Methodists had been more measured in their petitions to the administration, Burton was characteristically forthright.[47] In a report submitted to the colonial government (1926), he observed that labor recruitment had been so abusive and extensive that vast regions of Katanga had been depopulated, undermining the work of missionaries.[48] Burton's letter was forwarded to the governor general, who extracted and copied his complaints to the minister of the colonies. It is doubtful whether they were received in good spirit, coming as they did from a "foreign mission." On receiving the 1923 intelligence report, the provincial governor had recommended that although the CEM's "bizarre practices" could not be banned and did not currently pose a threat to public order, the CEM should nevertheless remain subject to continued attention.[49] For all these reasons, the CEM was denied civil recognition *(personnalité civile)* until 1932. It was forced to exist in limbo, its churches, schools, and hospitals vulnerable to seizure. But one more factor needs to be considered: Protestant-Catholic rela-

---

45. AAB, 640, XIV CEM, Katanga, Governor General A. Tilkens to Minister of Colonies, 5 June 1934.

46. AAB, M640 XIV, CEM, Katanga, Governor p. i, G. Heenen to Governor General, Elisabethville, 5 July 1923; report 10 May 1923.

47. Archives of the United Methodist Church, Drew University, Madison, USA, file, 1001-2-5:01 Guptill, Roger S. and Constance Correspondence, 1917-21, Roger Guptil, Kabongo to the Commissioner, District Lomami, Kabinda, 20 February 1918.

48. AAB, M640 XIV, CEM, Katanga, W. F. P. Burton, Un Rapport des Activités de la Mission Evangélistique du Congo Belge, 10 January 1926.

49. AAB, M640 XIV, CEM, Katanga, Governor p. i, G. Heenen to Governor General, Elisabethville, 5 July 1923.

tions. Whenever the CEM made mistakes, Catholic missionaries happily stoked the fires.

In most respects, the struggle between the CEM and its Catholic neighbors — Scheutists, Spiritans, and Franciscans — was a microcosm of a global Christian conflict. The missionary movements in the ascendant in the Belgian Congo and in other parts of the world in the twentieth century were representative of the two most dynamic forces in world Christianity — crusading Roman Catholicism and its systematic opposite, evangelical Protestantism. The similarity of the movements contributed as much to the clash as their differences. The forces were theological opposites, but both were fundamentalist in their sense of mission. There were Protestant-Catholic conflicts in Anglophone Africa.[50] However, in the Belgian Congo, as in Lusophone Africa, the conflict intensified because the Catholics came to represent the forces of Belgian colonialism against an alien and threatening Protestantism.

In Katanga, Catholic missionaries complained about the aggressive proselytizing of their villages by CEM evangelists, and Burton had an altercation with a Franciscan priest that reached a magistrate, who wisely dropped the case. The Pentecostal missionaries were quick to dismiss Catholicism as a syncretistic heretical religion, often eliding it with African superstition. Burton wrote his own critique of Catholicism (and Anglicanism and Methodism for good measure) entitled *Babylon* (no date). However, somewhat ironically, Protestants could find common cause with anticlericals in Belgium and the Congo. Some of these anticlericals, also known as the "left" in Belgium, were also members of Masonic lodges and hence strongly anti-Catholic. There were also a handful of Protestants in the higher ranks of the colonial ministry.[51] It was through the intervention of these elements that the CEM was allowed to remain in the colony.

Burton, the CEM, and Missionary Science

Along with the tendency toward certitude and absolutism within the Pentecostal temperament, there is a countervailing impulse toward pragmatism, a desire "to do whatever is necessary in order to accomplish the movement's purposes."[52] Faced with the threat of the CEM's termination, Burton likely

---

50. Maxwell, *Christians and Chiefs*, chapter 3.
51. Personal communication, Jean-Luc Vellut.
52. Grant Wacker, "Searching for Eden with a Satellite Dish: Primitivism, Pragmatism

threw himself into scientific research to demonstrate his loyalty to the state and prove that Protestants were just as able as the numerous Catholic scientists working around him. In his first academic article published by the *Geographical Journal* in 1927, Burton cast himself as the "man on the spot":[53]

> Several writers, after a few weeks' journey through the country, have produced books in which they describe river travel, modern townships, and Europeanised natives. They have failed to recognise that they have not touched the real country or the real people. The few white men living in that part of the country are too much occupied with tax-collecting, tin-mining, or trading to worry about preparing maps. All existing maps that we have seen in print leave big blank spaces in Lubaland, with a few misleading names to mystify further. As a matter of fact there are villages scattered everywhere.[54]

Burton made his botanical data on the types and uses of timber available to the Belgians and gave them copies of his remarkably accurate map of central Katanga (although the latter raised suspicions that he was a spy).[55] He also furnished the administration in Elisabethville with intelligence on a neo-traditional association, Ntambwe-Bwanga, which he believed harbored strong antiwhite sentiments.[56] Likewise, the bulk of his scientific research was published in *Bulletin des juridictions indigènes et du droit coutumier Congolais (BJI)*. The appearance of this journal coincided with the reform of indigenous jurisdictions in 1933, whereby customary structures were incorporated into the colonial order and chiefs became civil servants. The *BJI* sought to improve the competence of native administration through publication of research of indigenous customs, crimes, and superstitions.[57] It was the same pragmatism that led Burton and his CEM colleagues to participate in the broader colonial project of health and education, despite the warnings of Allen.

---

and the Pentecostal Character," in *The Primitive Church in the Modern World*, ed. R. T. Hughes (Urbana, Ill., 1995), p. 142.

53. R. Thornton, "Narrative Ethnography in Africa, 1850-1920: The Creation and Capture of an Appropriate Domain for Anthropology," *Man* 18 (1983): 514; van den Bersselaar, "Missionary Knowledge," p. 433.

54. W. F. P. Burton, "The Country of the Baluba in Central Africa," *Geographical Journal* 70, no. 4 (1927): 322.

55. AAB M640 XIV, CEM, Katanga, Governor p. i, G. Heenen to Governor General, Elisabethville, 5 July 1923; report 10 May 1923; Womersley, *Wm. F. P. Burton*, pp. 92-95.

56. UWAG, File Burton Personal, Burton to Saunders, 14 October 1929.

57. Editorial, *BJI* 1 (1953): 1-4.

But expediency was only one of a number of reasons that led Burton into ethnography. He also had missiological goals. In the 1929 preface to his manuscript *Luba Religion and Magic in Custom and Belief,* he explained:

> Seeing that we *missionaries* are giving our whole lives, and at the expenditure of thousands of pounds, to uplifting the black, it is amazing that we know so little of the conditions from which we are striving to deliver him. The casual white may scarcely notice the startled cry in the darkness of the night, the small white mark upon a native's body, or the waving of a few leaves in the hand of one of his caravan porters, accompanied by a muttered spell. Yet a few judicious enquiries conducted in the right way, would lay bare a whole underworld of fearful custom, of which the white man has not even dreamed. We are convinced that for lack of such knowledge much missionary preaching is like a boxer striking the empty air instead of planting well-directed blows in the spot where they are most likely to take effect. . . .
>
> We need scarcely say that the more we know of this foul system, the more we hate and loathe it. We never yet saw a man, either black or white, who was made cleaner and better by seeking after the bad, but we have seen thousands who were wrecked in bodies, minds and morals. Thus while under the guise of "spiritualism" even prominent European men of letters have lent a hand to drag us back into the hideous depths which our forefathers left behind over a thousand years ago, those of us who have lived among it, and have first hand experience of the horrors of this foul cult and labour daily to deliver Africa from its hideous thraldom.[58]

Such observations were more than crude ethnocentrism. Burton's approach drew from theological and missiological authorities. His opinion that beliefs and practices surrounding Luba divination and so-called secret societies were spiritualism drew heavily from the work of Roland Allen. Allen contended that in spite of the great philosophers, Greco-Roman popular culture was depraved, reducing its peoples to lives of shame and fear. It was in this context that the apostle Paul preached a gospel of liberation.[59] Burton was writing in an age when many missionaries no longer viewed African culture

---

58. UWAG, Box W. F. P. Burton, File Correspondence with Wits, 1929. The manuscript was not published in English until 1961. See below. The image of a boxer striking the air is a well-known Pauline allusion about the effectiveness of Christian service. 1 Cor. 9:26.

59. Allen, *Missionary Methods,* pp. 26-40.

as diabolical but instead sought to graft Christian religion onto it in a manner that suggested Christianity was its fulfillment.[60] However, there was a spectrum of opinion regarding the concessions a missionary could make in this encounter. In Diedrich Westermann, the renowned German missionary linguist, Burton found some common cause. Although Westermann was not as far along the spectrum as Burton, he did reject any compromise on the issue of the Christian embrace of African religions: "However anxious a missionary may be to appreciate and retain indigenous social and moral values, in the case of religion he has to be ruthless. The missionary cannot be content with producing an amalgamation of old and new beliefs or with turning pagan views in a Christian direction, he has to admit and even to emphasize that the religion he teaches is opposed to the existing one, and one has to cede to the other."[61] Burton cultivated good academic relations with the University of Witwatersrand during his numerous furloughs to South Africa, and became friends with Westermann on one of these visits.[62] Significantly, Burton's missionary neighbor and friend, Dan Crawford, had come to similar conclusions in his influential book *Thinking Black* (1912).[63]

Burton's status as a Protestant Englishman left him at a considerable remove from the Belgian administration and more open to influences from Luba society. He was resocialized by the strident young male evangelists responsible for the founding of Christian villages beyond mission stations. In their hands, the gospel message took the form of a Christianized witchcraft eradication movement. Conversion was followed by the complete abandonment of practices associated with witchcraft and divination, and accompanied by the destruction of fetishes.[64] Burton collected Luba material culture for the Department of Anthropology in the University of Witwatersrand, and in his correspondence with one of its members, Winifred Hoernlé, he wryly related the following explanation of a recent fire at the university:

> Yesterday we had a bonfire service, around the equipment of four compounders of magic, who had recently given their lives to the Lord Jesus. I

---

60. Harries, "Anthropology."
61. D. Westermann, *Africa and Christianity* (London, 1937), p. 94.
62. UWAG, Box W. F. P. Burton, File, Correspondence with Wits. See also University of Witwatersrand Archives, Winifred Hoernlé Papers, AU8 HOE.
63. Dan Crawford, *Thinking Black: 22 Years without a Break in the Long Grass of Central Africa* (London, 1912).
64. W. De Craemer, R. Fox, and J. Vansina, "Religious Movements in Central Africa: A Theoretical Study," *Comparative Studies in Society and History* 18, no. 4 (1976); Maxwell, *Christians and Chiefs in Zimbabwe*.

had half thought of sending these equipments down to the museum, but our Christians begged me not to. They said "You will remember that last time you sent some down, the building in which they were stored was burnt down. If you send any more of this devil's stuff to people there, it will set on fire another building. You see!"

To pacify the Christians rather than for fear of setting fire to the museum, I desisted. But you now know where to trace the source of your mysterious university fire![65]

In the 1929 preface to his manuscript Burton observed: "How is it that the native evangelist can reach the hearts of his hearers so much more readily than his white superintendent? Often it is because of his knowledge of actual conditions. He has been delivered of the same dreads, superstitions and temptations as those to whom he preaches."[66] While ethnography was useful for unmasking and undermining the powers of diviners and their societies, it was used more constructively with regard to the institution of chieftainship. Chiefs were pillars of indirect rule and thus enormously important agents in the governance of the Belgian Congo. Through their compliance the gospel was more readily advanced, and missionaries lived under their protection. The goodwill of Mwanza chief Kazingu had been essential in overcoming Catholic opposition to the CEM's presence in the region.[67] Befriending chiefs and accumulating knowledge of their powers was one of Burton's key evangelical strategies.

Finding Inspiration:
The Geographical Society, Tervuren, and Witwatersrand

Whatever the cause of the fire at Witwatersrand, it destroyed important correspondence between Burton and the embryonic Social Anthropology Department, making it difficult to reconstruct where Burton's first academic encounters took place. They are likely to have begun in earnest in 1927 when Willie and his wife Hettie traveled to Europe on furlough. Although CEM workers collected anthropological data from their "earliest days" in the

---

65. UWAG, Box W. F. P. Burton, File Correspondence with Wits, Burton to Hoernlé, 7 August 1933.

66. UWAG, Box W. F. P. Burton, File, Burton's notes on the Luba, 1929, Interview Ngoy Kabuya, Ruashi, DRC, 13 May 2007 (Kabuya was the son of Abrahama Nyuki, the CEM's first convert and subsequent evangelist).

67. AAB, M640 XIV, CEM, Katanga, "Reconnaissance du terrain que la Pentecostal Mission demande à SOPE (Mwanza-Kazingu)," 21 November 1915.

Congo — a notebook was a vital piece of missionary paraphernalia — research was a secondary concern in the mission's pioneering decade.[68] In the first two years of the mission's existence Burton and Salter struggled to survive: to find food, to clear land and build accommodation and then schools, to overcome sickness and exhaustion, to train the first generation of local evangelists. The "war [World War I] and its aftermath were collectively a traumatic experience." The forced recruitment of porters and workers, the requisitioning of crops, the influenza pandemic of 1918-20, and the postwar price rises and shortages combined to take their toll.[69] As the millennia-long equatorial "tradition" was finally shattered, there followed a remarkable Christian conversion movement among the Luba, led by returned ex-slaves and labor migrants, but missionaries played an important part as well.[70] In the years 1917-25 more than thirty CEM missionaries entered Katanga, vastly expanding the mission field to the north and south of Mwanza.[71]

Burton's first recorded contact was with the British Geographical Society, which Burton addressed at the Pitt Rivers Museum, Oxford, in May 1927. His lecture, entitled "The Country of the Baluba," was primarily a description of climate, relief, fauna and flora, and mineral deposits. However, his allusions to Luba history and culture were noted by the museum's keeper, Professor Henry Balfour: "I would urge that we should take every opportunity of encouraging people like Mr. Burton who are willing to reside in the country more or less continuously and who are also willing to take a keen and sympathetic interest in the natives — that we should urge them to make a thoroughly intensive study and write it all down, so that the record of what will soon be 'bygones' may be permanent."[72]

It is possible that Balfour directed Burton to his colleagues at the museum at Tervuren, for that is where the correspondence trail first begins in 1928. But whatever the order of contact, two individuals in the museum would have a profound influence on Burton, drawing him into the ethno-museological tradition of anthropology. The first was Henri Schouteden, a zoologist and director of the museum from 1927 to 1946, who created inventories of ethnographic, archeological, and botanical material collected by Burton and other amateurs in the field.[73] The second was Joseph Maes, a geographer by

---

68. *Congo Evangelistic Mission Report (CEMR),* March 1959, p. 268.
69. Jewsiewicki, "Belgian Africa," p. 470.
70. J. Vansina, *Paths in the Rainforests: Towards a History of Political Tradition in Equatorial Africa* (London, 1990), pp. 239-48.
71. Garrard, "Zaire Evangelistic Mission," pp. 110-67.
72. Burton, "Country of the Baluba," p. 340.
73. Lagae, "Sur la production," p. 136.

training who had worked briefly in the Ministry of Colonies before his attachment to the museum in 1909 as Conservateur de la Section Ethnographique. Maes had led a collecting expedition to central Africa from 1912 to 1914 but afterward became an armchair academic — *intellectuel en chambre* — along with Schouteden, drawing information from men on the spot.[74] Like Burton, Maes was a remarkable polymath with interests that were both pure and applied: history, ethnography, geography, agriculture, material culture, meteorology, botany, and race policy.

Burton met with Schouteden and Maes when he was in Europe in 1927, sending them a collection of Luba artifacts soon after. Under their influence he was steadily drawn into the trait-school of collecting, and was asked to locate objects that would complete the museum's collection of sculptures on Katanga. He was asked to discourse on the makers, users, and purpose of the objects he collected, and to identify analogous objects. And, of course, he was asked to identify the tribe they belonged to. Maes sent him one of the museum's catalogues and asked him to find explanations for the use of sculptures such as the *kitumpo* (for divination), informing him that he was doing the museum a great service.[75] Burton willingly complied, illustrating his letters with splendid sketches and diagrams, and augmenting the collections with a set of approximately 174 photographs.[76]

Captured by a Genre: Burton's Ethnography

Under Maes's influence Burton was captured by the Tervuren ethnomuseological genre. He did not write about what was happening around him but what he imagined precontact Luba society looked like. His ethnography was characterized by a bounded timelessness in which his observations were rarely given an orientation in time or space. There was little indication of where, when, and from whom he had derived his data, but rather he gave the impression that the Luba lived in an unchanging, unified culture.[77] The style was descriptive, with little progression of argument. The use of the passive voice, the impersonal "we," and generalized statements created the impres-

---

74. AAB, A25/61, Papers, J. Maes; Vansina, "The Ethnographic Account," p. 438.
75. This was probably E. Coart, E. de Haulleville, and A. de Haulleville, *Notes Analytiques sur les Collections Ethnographiques du Musée du Congo, Tome 1, Les Arts — Religion* (Brussels, 1902-6). I am grateful to Rik Ceyssens for helping me identify this text.
76. MRAC, Burton Correspondence, Dossier 473.
77. However, it is possible to derive data on dates, places, and informants through fieldwork and research on Burton's correspondence and missionary writings.

sion of scientific authority, although Burton could not resist intervening in his texts to condemn certain practices as "vile," "filthy," or "immoral." He had a specific interest in religion and magic, particularly as practiced in the Bambudye (the largest Luba association). It is difficult to fit his work into a single theoretical school. At times he took a historical/diffusionist perspective, but he also employed notions and terminology from functionalist anthropology, writing about "types" within a Luba "social system."[78] This varied approach was also manifest in his collecting and photography. Apart from traditional leaders and craftsmen, few individuals were named in his writings or photographs. Instead, once again, he wrote about and photographed "types" involved in traditional activities such as dancing or hunting. He only collected objects associated with traditional religion and traditional modes of production. And his ethnographic photographs, those for Tervuren, Witwatersrand, and scientific journals, contained few images of modernity: Western clothes, brick houses, motorcars, bicycles. Those modern images that impinged were relegated to the background, not alluded to in accompanying commentaries, and sources of conflict such as labor recruitment were never mentioned.[79] At that moment, the Luba-speaking peoples were experiencing rapid social and economic change through labor migration, urbanization, cash-crop agriculture, and modernizing Christianity.[80]

Burton was well aware of change. His 1927 Geographical Society lecture had begun with the premise of social and economic transformation — railways, mining, and steamboats — and he also noted the fluidity of identities and polities under Swahili slavers, Msiri, and the Belgians. Published in the *Geographical Journal* before he embarked upon his ethnographic writing, the lecture was ironically one of his most sophisticated and enlightening pieces. The CEM's bimonthly journal, *Congo Evangelistic Mission Report (CEMR)*, also had an explicit narrative of progress from darkness to light, savagery to civilization, with stories of the transforming effect of a modernizing Christianity on individuals and communities. However, an essentialized version of

---

78. Burton, *Luba Religion and Magic in Custom and Belief*; A. Barnard, *History and Theory in Anthropology* (Cambridge, 2000), pp. 27-79; A. W. Hoernlé, "New Aims and Methods in Social Anthropology," *South African Journal of Science* 30 (1933).

79. Thornton, "Narrative Ethnography," p. 513.

80. J.-L. Vellut, "Rural Poverty in Western Shaba c. 1900-1930," in *The Roots of Rural Poverty in Central and Southern Africa*, ed. R. Palmer and N. Parsons (London, 1977); Vellut, "Mining in Belgian Congo," in *History of Central Africa*, vol. 2, ed. D. Birmingham and P. Martin (London, 1983); B. Jewsiewicki, "Rural Society and the Belgian Colonial Economy," in *History of Central Africa*; B. Fetter, *The Creation of Elisabethville, 1910-1940* (Stanford, 1976).

the Luba appealed to Burton's sensibilities. He had collected birds' eggs and fossils for his local museum in Reigate Surrey and, like many people with an organized mind, found it "pleasant to collect."[81] Moreover, collecting was an act of preservation of a culture that changed rapidly in the decade after he first encountered it in 1915. In 1929 Burton informed Schouteden that European enamelware and cloth were replacing "the really indigenous pots and clothes" and that he would be "delighted to collect what in a few years time will be relics of a past age."[82] Under his mother's tutelage, Burton had developed a deep sense of aesthetics that led to an admiration of Luba material culture. He had a fascination with cicatrization and coiffures, and photographed these on people and sculptures. His subjects were often beautiful men and women whom he would subsequently paint. His gouache paintings of headdresses in Tervuren and his watercolors at Museum Africa, Johannesburg, were not diagrammatic representations like the sketches accompanying his letters to curators and anthropologists. They were illustrative rather than technical, more abstract than representative, and highly personal. In 1930 Burton informed colleagues that he had "an immense compilation of notes almost ready for print" concerning not only "religion and superstition" but also "Baluba aesthetics."[83]

It was evident from Burton's remarks on the effects of labor migration that the world of sedentary communities under the rule of chiefs suited his purposes. He was aware that the Belgian administration discouraged Christian villages because they undermined the authority of chiefs and subdivided its neatly ordered regime of customary jurisdictions.[84] But Burton's 1933 inspirational text *When God Changes a Village*, an extended account of the conversion of Chief Penge of Bunda, makes clear that his ideal was a *Christian* village under a *Christian* chief. He preferred that new converts were isolated from the "contaminating" influences of "heathenism" and urban life. Better still, the compliance of a sympathetic traditional leader gave missionaries

---

81. UWAG, Box W. F. P. Burton, File, Correspondence with Witwatersrand, Burton to Professor and Mrs Hoernlé, 27 September 1938. On the poetics of collecting see S. Pearce, *On Collecting: An Investigation into Collecting in the European Tradition* (London, 1995), chapters 13 and 14.

82. MRAC, Burton Correspondence, Dossier 473, Burton to Schouteden, 9 May 1929. In the 1940s the *CEMR* ran a series of articles entitled "Curious Congo Customs: You Will Never See It Again."

83. MRAC, Burton Correspondence, Dossier 473, Burton to Schouteden, 7 February 1930.

84. L. Le Grand and Editorial, "De la légalité des villages chrétiens," *Congo. Revue Générale du Congo Belge* 3, no. 1 (1922).

more license to bring about the wholesale social engineering they desired. In a Christian village, missionaries could teach, change landscape and architecture, and introduce literacy, schooling, and Western notions of hygiene.[85]

Burton's essentialized model of the Luba brought him publishing woes. His 1929 manuscript was eventually translated and published in 1939-40 as a series of articles entitled *L'Ame Luba — the Soul of the Luba* — in the Belgian native affairs journal *Bulletin des juridictions indigènes et du droit coutumier Congolais*. His title was probably inspired by the work of the professor of missions at Hartford Seminary, USA, W. C. Willoughby. Burton's agenda for researching African religions resembled that advanced by Willoughby in the opening pages of his 1928 monograph *The Soul of the Bantu: A Sympathetic Study of the Magico-Religious Practices and Beliefs of the Bantu Tribes of Africa*. Burton would have also liked to publish his research as a monograph in English. In 1938 he informed Audrey Richards that, "despite kind offices of Professors Schapera and Westermann," they had not able to find a publisher for his book on Luba ritual. Such a task should not have been that difficult. Burton's connections with the Social Anthropology Department at the University of Witwatersrand were more personal and intense than those with Tervuren. Burton and Salter had launched what became the CEM from South Africa after a year's work in the country. And Burton's wife, Hettie, came from a respectable South African farming family. Together they built a good personal friendship with Winifred Hoernlé and her distinguished philosopher husband, Alfred. The trail of archived correspondence with Witwatersrand begins in 1932, but it would have commenced prior to 1930 when Burton's article on secret societies was published in the Witwatersrand journal *Bantu Studies*. It was for Winifred Hoernlé that Burton built up a remarkably full collection of Luba material, seemingly on the principles he had learned from Tervuren. He also sent Witwatersrand a far more extensive set of photographs (approximately 420) than he sent to Tervuren.

The problem with Burton's research was that he embraced the notion of the bounded, unchanging precontact tribal people when Anglo-Saxon anthropological research on southern and central Africa was moving away from such notions to consider urban life and social change. Moreover, he had turned himself into a missionary ethnographer when Isaac Schapera was busily marginalizing missionaries in an attempt to professionalize the discipline. Burton's work on the Luba, rural themes, ritual, and magic would certainly have interested Schapera, but they parted ways in the latter's insistence on studying the unitary social field that included missionaries, traders,

---

85. Burton, *Mudishi, Congo Hunter*, pp. 125-26.

and administrators alongside so-called tribes. Even Hoernlé was known to be privately critical of missionaries, but her friendship with the Burtons complicated matters.[86] While Hoernlé remained committed to functionalist analysis, she was increasingly interested in how societies functioned in the light of change.[87] She encouraged Burton to write about change and social networks that extended beyond the bounded community of the tribe. She asked him about shifts in technology, new types of currency, and regional trade, and he responded with richly detailed notes. He also sent other historical data on hunting, fishing, and the slave trade.[88] None of this material ever found its way into his scientific work. Hoernlé was a great positive influence on Burton, the only person who received acknowledgment in his preface to *Luba Religion and Magic in Custom and Belief* when it was eventually published by Tervuren in 1961. It was thus unfortunate that Hoernlé left Witwatersrand in 1937 to pursue a career in social work.[89] Audrey Richards, who replaced Hoernlé, continued to encourage Burton, complimenting him on the high standard of his photography, but she was never the patron her predecessor had been. Indeed, Richards seems to have preferred photographs that essentialized the Luba rather than those that portrayed social change, perhaps because she desired comparative data to strengthen her own homogenous model of the Bemba.[90] Burton also lost his Belgian patron, Maes, who appears to have collaborated with the Nazis and hence disappeared from public life after 1945.[91]

Burton's research would also have been more publishable if he had used conventional academic apparatus such as footnotes and references to scholarly authorities. But the enduring issue was that his research on Luba religion and magic was out of favor with the anthropological and missiological fashions of his day. In 1947 Burton penned a critique of an unnamed book by Edwin Smith.[92] He began by noting that Smith's books on Africa were the

---

86. Harries, "Anthropology"; P. Pels and O. Salemink, "Introduction: Five Theses on Ethnography as Colonial Practice," *History and Anthropology* 8 (1994): 4.

87. Hoernlé, "New Aims and Methods in Social Anthropology."

88. UWAG, Box W. F. P. Burton, File, Burton's notes on the Luba.

89. Harries, "Anthropology."

90. Moore and Vaughan, *Cutting Down Trees,* pp. 3-10. UWAG, Box W. F. P. Burton, File, Correspondence with Witwatersrand, Burton to Richards, 7 January 1940; Richards to Burton, 16 March 1940. See also brief interview with Richards in S. Van der Geest and J. Kirby, "The Absence of the Missionary in African Ethnography," *African Studies Review* 35, no. 3 (1992): 86-87.

91. AAB, A25/61, Papers, J. Maes.

92. The Smith text may have been *Knowing the African* (London, 1946), published the previous year.

most enlightening that one could read. He recommended *The Golden Stool* (1926) and *Aggrey of Africa* (1929).[93] But then he wrote:

> There is one matter, however, in which I disagree with him radically. He paints a picture of the African's religion climbing up from something elementary, through dim gropings, toward our full-orbed revelation, towards salvation through the Lord Jesus, and of God revealed in His Son.
> Begging the gentleman's pardon, the Bible does not teach that, neither does experience.

Burton observed that in many places CEM personnel were the first whites the Luba had encountered; hence the missionaries had been in the prime position to reconstruct Luba beliefs before they were changed by Christian teaching. He acknowledged that the Luba had a "recognition" of the following: God, who had a son, a God-man mediator; the notion of substitutionary sacrifice; baptism and new birth; and God's return. He explained these beliefs as evidence of "a previous preaching of the Gospel and a strong Jewish influence in Lubaland."[94] However, he believed that what missionaries first encountered amongst the Luba was a "decadence from the previous knowledge of Christian truth": "One thing after another was added to that simple old testimony, either through man's imagination, or through a wrong idea of expediency . . . ornate clothing perpetuated in the witchdoctor's regalia; the worship of the dead . . . the veneration of relics as seen in the use of human bones for the medicine-man's charms." Authorizing his argument with Scripture, Burton cited Romans 1:18-32: "They knew God, but did not glorify him as God, changed God's truth as a lie, worshipped the creature instead of the Creator, changed God's glory into images of men and beasts, did not like to retain God in their knowledge, and have been given over to unnatural lusts."[95]

Smith was the most influential missionary thinker of his day and the only missionary ever to be elected president of the Royal Anthropological Institute.[96] It is probable that in his rebuttal of Smith's work, Burton was too ex-

---

93. E. Smith, *The Golden Stool: Some Aspects of the Conflict of Cultures in Modern Africa* (London, 1926); Smith, *Aggrey of Africa* (London, 1929).

94. W. F. P. Burton, "There Has Been a Previous Preaching of the Gospel in Lubaland," parts 1 and 2, *CEMR,* August-September 1947. The idea of the diffusion of Jewish influence was not uncommon; see van den Bersselaar, "Missionary Knowledge," p. 440.

95. Burton, "There Has Been a Previous Preaching of the Gospel in Lubaland."

96. W. J. Young, "'They Had Laid Hold of Some Essential Truths': Edwin W. Smith (1876-1957), a Wise Listener to African Voices," in *European Traditions in the Study of Religion in Africa,* ed. F. Ludwig and A. Adogame (Wiesbaden, 2004).

treme even for Westermann. It certainly appears that neither Westermann nor Schapera tried too hard to find Burton an Anglo-Saxon publisher. Both were influential figures with access to funding for research. Indeed, Westermann was the first director of the International African Institute. Notably, only a small part of Burton's material on secret societies found its way into *Bantu Studies*.[97] Burton's ecclesiological inclinations also stymied his opportunities for patronage and inspiration. His strong antiestablishment, anticlerical credentials made him suspicious of ecumenism and clerical hierarchies. When John R. Mott, chairman of the International Missionary Council, addressed Protestant missionaries in Elisabethville in 1934, Burton's response to Salter was characteristically pious: "though Mott may wield a big influence, yet I feel we must look to a Higher and Greater force than any little man, for the undertaking of our cause."[98]

Whether Burton was overly concerned that his work did not reach a broader academic readership is a moot point. An audience was not mentioned in the 1929 unpublished preface to *Luba Religion and Magic:* "We write that the white man, the missionary, the government official and the interested public may be enlightened as to the true conditions, but we write also in order to reach a sympathetic hand to the native."[99] Robert Thornton has argued that while the format and rhetoric of ethnographic texts were influenced by the natural science monograph, their content was derived largely from travelogues and missionary letters and bulletins.[100] This is certainly the case for Burton and other CEM researchers such as Harold Womersley, as much of their research began as articles for the *Congo Evangelistic Mission Report*.[101] Burton's research agenda was guided by two principles: first, utility to mission work; and second, utility to the colonial state. He researched so-called secret societies because he saw them as bitter opponents of the gospel. One of the most prominent themes in the *CEMR* was the opposition Luba Christians encountered from secret societies, whose drumming and dancing often drowned out church services.[102] Burton viewed their activities as brutish, cannibalistic, and debauched. He argued that members joined out of fear or

---

97. W. F. P. Burton, "Secret-Societies of Lubaland," *Bantu Studies* 4 (1930).
98. Central African Missions (henceforth CAM, formerly CEM) file, Burton to Salter 1930-40, 1 July 1934.
99. UWAG, Box W. F. P. Burton, File, Burton's notes on the Luba, preface to *Luba Religion and Magic in Custom and Belief,* circa 1929.
100. Thornton, "Narrative Ethnography," p. 502.
101. See Tom Reefe's editorial introduction to H. Womersley, *Legends and History of the Luba* (Los Angeles, 1984), pp. vi-vii.
102. See, for example, *CEMR*, February 1922; May 1922; October-December 1929.

compulsion and that Christian converts who left them were subject to torture and intimidation. He did not fully grasp the political function of the *budye* association to initiate political candidates into the rules and regulations of royal authority, or interpret *kasandji* association as doctors who dealt with malevolent spirits and witchcraft accusation through spirit possession.[103] While contemporary liberal missionaries were willing to acknowledge the vital social function of certain practices even if they were not theologically *true*, Burton remained too staunchly evangelical to take such a line.[104] In this endeavor to expose secret societies he found common purpose with the influential Belgian researcher Edouard De Jonghe and numerous local administrators who viewed them as clandestine, and powerful, sources of alternative authority to the colonial state.[105]

It is a shame that the historical material Burton produced for Hoernlé never found its way into his scientific publications. Nevertheless, Burton was a recycler, a man who wrote in different genres for different audiences.[106] He was profoundly influenced by colonial science but also by the texts produced by his famous missionary neighbors. Both Springer and Crawford had written propagandist accounts of their pioneering work for the Christian faithful at home who supported the mission enterprise financially, and Burton did likewise. The photographs, conversion narratives, travelogues, letters, and ethnographic data that formed the basis of the *CEMR* became mission history.[107] To this material Burton added historical data on hunting, fishing, and the slave trade, to make compelling hagiographies of native evangelists that combined the grisly details of nineteenth-century travelogues with affectionate and uplifting elements of the missionary story.[108] The transfer of data between genres, as observed by Thornton, was not unidirectional. Scientific material was put at the disposal of the gospel message. Indeed, although Burton

---

103. M. Nooter, "Luba Art and Polity Creating Power in a Central African Kingdom" (Ph.D. diss., Columbia University, 1991), p. 12.

104. P. Forster, "Politics, Ethnography and the 'Invention of Tradition': The Case of T. Cullen Young of Livingstonia Mission, Malawi," *History and Anthropology* 8 (1994): 301.

105. E. De Jonghe, "Les sociétés secrètes en Afrique," *Congo* 4, 2, 3 (1923). This approach toward secret societies persisted until the 1950s when Vanden Bossche acknowledged that some were not "secret" at all and posed no threat; *Sectes et Associations Indigènes au Congo Belge* (Leopoldville-Kalina, 1954).

106. Thornton, "Narrative Ethnography," p. 506.

107. Burton, *God Working with Them*.

108. W. F. P. Burton, *When God Changes a Man: A True Story of This Great Change in the Life of a Slave Raider* (London, 1929); Burton, *Mudishi, Congo Hunter;* Thornton, "Narrative Ethnography," p. 504.

understood the power of different textual genres, it is unlikely that he conducted his research in a compartmentalized manner. Notebook always at hand, he simply recorded what he found useful and interesting.

Vernacular as the Gateway to the Soul of the People

Burton's work did not end with *Luba Religion and Magic*. In the 1940s he embarked on a new project on the vernacular, with the help of African assistants,[109] which helped him make the transition from an aggressive, intrusive approach toward the Luba to one that was more empathetic. In doing so he was following a trajectory made by other "amateur" colonial social scientists.[110] In 1943 he published a second article in the Witwatersrand journal *African Studies* (previously *Bantu Studies*) entitled "Kanya Oral Literature in Lubaland." The piece began: "Until recently Congo Natives had no books or writing. Even now practically all their books have been introduced by Europeans. Thus they represent the best and purest in Native languages. The language student who wishes to get authentic indigenous expression is therefore forced to seek classic examples in other fields, but specially that of oral literature."[111] He then outlined a classification of oral data: stories (history), fables, proverbs, riddles, and various rules of life and conduct relating to religion, hunting, politics, and geography. This type of research caused Burton to write more positively about Luba religion and culture. Thus he observed:

> God is described in many ways, some of which show a remarkable knowledge of his attributes, seeing they were in use a long way before the missionary came....
> *Bumbilebumbo. Leza mukata kyabumbile Bantu nepano Ukibwejya* (The Moulder, God the great, who forms men, and even now He continues to do it).... *Kongolo Mwine-bisaka, Katende Mwine-dyulu* (The Rainbow, Lord of the earth, the peaceful One Lord of the heavens)....[112]

---

109. In particular, Isaac Lupichi, the son of a leading councillor within the Mwanza chieftaincy. This is the subject of another paper. Interview, Banze Kalumba Shayumba, Mwanza, DRC, 23 May 2007.

110. For instance, Marcel Griaule, who worked among the Dogon; see J. Clifford, "'Power and Dialogue in Ethnography': Marcel Griaule's Initiation," in *Observers Observed: Essays on Ethnographic Fieldwork*, ed. G. W. Stocking (Madison, Wis., 1983).

111. W. F. P. Burton, "Kanya Oral Literature in Lubaland," *African Studies* 2 (1943): 95.

112. Burton, "Kanya Oral Literature," p. 95.

In 1955-58 he published a long series of articles in the *BJI* listing and classifying Luba proverbs. The proverbs were subsequently brought together, translated into French and English, and published in one volume of *Editions de la Revue Juridique* by the Société d'Etudes Juridiques du Katanga (1958). The collection of proverbs amounted to approximately 1,800 sayings, which Burton claimed was the largest such collection gathered in any African language.[113]

This second sequence of research on the vernacular arose from a similar set of motivations as the work on religion and magic. First, it had an evangelical impulse. In a 1959 *CEMR* article, Burton took a selection of the proverbs to demonstrate "their value in presenting the Gospel message." Citing the proverb "When called before the judges take one of your elders. When asked for an explanation, let him give the answer," Burton made the following connection: "He who would conduct his own defence he will find himself in difficulties. 'If any man sin we have an advocate with our Father, Jesus Christ the righteous, and He is the propitiation for our sins.' 1 John 2:1-2."[114] The research was also policy-driven, contributing to the increasing bureaucratization of customary rule under Belgian colonialism. The impetus to republish the material in *Revue Juridique* had come from Belgian judges and magistrates who sought to bolster "tradition" as a bulwark against African nationalism.[115] Impetus also came from certain African elites. As Bogumil Jewsiewicki argues: "many Luba found it appealing to cooperate with European missionaries and researchers in selecting and assembling cultural elements in order to elaborate a Luba theodicy and philosophy as a system of thought and to work with European researchers and administrators in constructing a judicial system that conformed to their expectations."[116] This was a broad project, involving a number of researchers, religious and secular (including Burton), who had worked in and around Elisabethville, which culminated in Placide Tempels's classic *Bantu Philosophy*, first published in 1945. As Jewsiewicki observes, it was "no accident" that such a work should first appear in connection with the Luba, given the density of research on them.[117]

Although the book was based on the study of just the Luba, the title *Bantu*

---

113. Burton, *CEMR*, March 1959.

114. Burton, *CEMR*, March 1959. Elsewhere Burton described proverbs as "handmaids to gospel preaching"; *God Working with Them*, p. 97.

115. Burton, *CEMR*, March 1959.

116. B. Jewsiewicki, "The Formation of the Political Culture of Ethnicity in the Belgian Congo, 1920-1959," in *The Creation of Tribalism in Southern Africa*, ed. L. Vail (London, 1989), p. 331.

117. Jewsiewicki, "The Formation," p. 331; P. Tempels, *Bantu Philosophy* (Paris, 1953).

Philosophy suggested much wider claims, highlighting a new trajectory in missionary science. After the Second World War missionary research was criticized by African nationalists who objected to the disparagement of African beliefs as idolatrous. Henceforth the missionary tradition, already marginalized from academic anthropology, evolved into what J. D. Y. Peel calls "African theology."[118] But the roots of African theology stretched back into the 1920s. As early as 1925, J. H. Oldham, the founding editor of the influential journal *International Review of Missions* and longtime secretary of the International Missionary Council, had identified the central importance of the study of African languages, pronouncing the vernacular to be "the gateway to the soul of a people and the expression of what is distinctive in their national character and traditions."[119] Oldham was also one of the initiators of the International Institute of African Languages and Cultures, part of the same circle as Westermann and Smith.[120] But it was Edwin Smith who did most to push the trajectory forward with his final work, *African Ideas of God*,[121] doing much to emphasize the "common Africanness" of "African traditional religion," highlighting a shared notion of a creator God at the apex of belief.[122] Institutionalized by the likes of Geoffrey Parrinder, the pioneer of religious studies at the University of Ibadan, Nigeria, African theology and philosophy usefully combined the applied aspects of missiology with missionary ethnography.

Burton also published other kinds of oral data in more popular form. In 1961 Methuen published his research on fables in a collection aimed at children and adults entitled *The Magic Drum: Tales from Central Africa*. The first draft of his preface (deposited at Witwatersrand) was an impassioned defense of Luba civilization:

> The following fables will doubtless come as a surprise to many. There are still those who imagine that the Central African is an ignorant and degraded savage.

---

118. J. D. Y. Peel, "African Studies: Religion," in *International Encyclopaedia of the Social and Behavioural Sciences*, ed. N. J. Smelser and P. B. Baltes (London, 2001), p. 260.

119. J. H. Oldham and H. Vischer, "Memorandum on the Place of the Vernacular in Africa Education and on the Establishment of a Bureau of African Languages," Spring 1925, in SOAS, IMC/CBMS, Box 204, cited in W. Young, "'They Had Laid Hold of Some Essential Truths': Edwin W. Smith (1876-1957), a Wise Listener to African Voices," in *European Traditions in the Study of Religion in Africa*, ed. F. Ludwig and A. Adogame (Wiesbaden, 2004), p. 172.

120. K. Clements, "'Friend of Africa': J. H. Oldham (1874-1969), Missions and British Colonial Policy in the 1920s," in *European Traditions in the Study of Religion in Africa*, p. 178.

121. Edwin Smith, ed., *African Ideas of God* (London, 1950).

122. Ludwig and Adogame, *European Traditions*, p. 10.

> In Europe, in the past we have set up an artificial standard of education, often not in the remotest degree fitted to the requirements of after life, and have considered all who were not educated by our standards were "uncivilised" and barbarians. . . .
>
> **The Central African Has His Own Standard of Education**
> Now for centuries the Congo native has had a most accurate and efficient school system, and it is probable that the education now being introduced by European missionaries will have to go through much adjustment and change *before it fits a native for after life as thoroughly as does his own system,* the product of the needs of Central African youth.
>
> His education fits him in the scheme of public life, and responsibility to the community. It gives him an accurate knowledge of the trees, animals, and insects of the forest in which he lives. He receives the rudiments of geography, tribal history, medicine, and many other branches of knowledge and handicraft.[123]

Although he remained critical of liberal theology, Burton's thinking shifted. Through the passage of time, the study of language, and the guidance of research assistants, he arrived at a more balanced and sympathetic view of the Luba society. Like many other post–Second World War missionaries, he came to believe that underneath the "superstitious" superstructure of Luba religion lay a deeper metaphysics discerned in fables and proverbs, which could be marshaled and Christianized.[124] Furthermore, his modernizing instincts were not necessarily at odds with his research on tradition. His significant contribution to the *BJI* put him at the heart of a *Katangeseit* led by Belgian legal practitioners who believed it was possible to lead the subjects of customary jurisdictions into modernity without cutting them off from their roots.[125] Finally, on reflection, Luba society did not compare unfavorably with the society Burton had left behind in England. He had been greatly disturbed by Europe's path toward war in the 1930s and increasingly felt out of place in the West, choosing to retire to South Africa in 1960. Setting out his

---

123. UWAG, File, Burton Personal, Burton, Preston, England to Owen Saunders, South Africa, 26 December 1936; "Preface" (n.d.). The final published preface differed little except that lines 3-8 were less emphatic.

124. J. Fabian, "Religious and Secular Colonization: Common Ground," *History and Anthropology* 4 (1990): 350-51. See W. F. P. Burton, *Congo Sketches* (London, 1950), pp. 117-18.

125. I am indebted to Bogumil Jewsiewicki for this observation. The notion is also apparent in the closing pages of Vanden Bossche's *Sectes et associations*.

credentials as an ethnographer in the 1961 preface to *Luba Religion and Magic,* he reflected on his forty-three years of "intimate contact" with the Luba as "their confident [*sic*] and friend" and concluded that "I am a stranger elsewhere. Lubaland is home."[126]

Conclusion

There is a danger in exaggerating the significance of Burton's marginalization from anthropological circles. Professional anthropology was still in its infancy when he did most of his writing, and African history was not yet considered an academic discipline. In the preface of his 1949 *West African Religion,* Parrinder expressed a hope that the text might be of interest to students of comparative religion and identified other interested parties as missionaries and colonial officials.[127] Burton's research was driven by the contingencies of Christian mission in a remote corner of Katanga Belgian Congo, a desire to win converts and to placate a hostile colonial state. He had grown up in a Victorian and Edwardian world in which amateur science was viewed as an educational and recreational activity at almost all levels of society.[128] And because the boundaries between those different types of knowledge were more porous, he did not feel obliged to stick to one field or genre. But Burton did differ from more widely recognized missionary scientists such as Oldham, Smith, and Westermann in two ways. First, while the latter left the mission field to pursue academic careers, Burton chose to remain in missionary service in the Belgian Congo for forty-five years, unable to develop networks of support and patronage and keep in touch with academic fashions. Secondly, while Burton was an atypical missionary scientist, he was representative of a growing and increasingly dominant trend in the twentieth-century missionary movement. This evangelical strand fought fiercely to maintain the distinction between advanced Christian and primitive pagan religion, viewing the former as a religion of the book.[129] The missionary maintained a central role in preaching a christocentric message that required a public confession

---

126. Burton, *Luba Religion,* p. 1.
127. G. Parrinder, *West African Religion* (London, 1949); Andrew Walls, "Geoffrey Parrinder (1910) and the Study of Religion in West Africa," in *European Traditions in the Study of Religion in Africa,* p. 208.
128. J. Mackenzie, "Missionaries, Science, and the Environment in Nineteenth-Century Africa," in *The Imperial Horizons of British Protestant Missions, 1880-1914,* ed. A. Porter (Grand Rapids, 2003), p. 107.
129. Forster, "Politics," p. 300.

of sin and repentance toward God, and a rejection of practices relating to ancestor religion, possession cults, divination, and witchcraft. While the evangelical imperative was not the only force organizing Burton's life, it was his major passion, shaping his practices and organizing his priorities.

Select Bibliography

Burton, W. F. P. *Luba Religion and Magic in Custom and Belief.* Tervuren, 1961.
———. *Proverbes des Baluba.* Elisabethville, 1958.
Jewsiewicki, B. "The Formation of the Political Culture of Ethnicity in the Belgian Congo, 1920-1959." In *The Creation of Tribalism in Southern Africa,* edited by L. Vail. London, 1989.
Ludwig, F., and A. Adogame, eds. *European Traditions in the Study of Religion in Africa.* Wiesbaden, 2004.
MacKenzie, J. "Missionaries, Science, and the Environment in Nineteenth-Century Africa." In *The Imperial Horizons of British Protestant Missions, 1880-1914,* edited by A. Porter. Grand Rapids, 2003.
Nettleton, A., ed. *The Collection of W. F. P. Burton.* Johannesburg, 1992.
Nooter Roberts, M., and A. Roberts, eds. *Memory: Luba Art and the Making of History.* New York, 1996.
Peel, J. D. Y. "African Studies: Religion." In *International Encyclopaedia of the Social and Behavioural Sciences,* edited by N. J. Smelser and P. B. Baltes. London, 2001.
Poncelet, M. *L'invention des sciences coloniales belges.* Paris, 2008.
Reefe, T. *The Rainbow and the Kings: A History of the Luba Empire to 1891.* Berkeley, 1981.
Smith, E. W. *The Golden Stool: Some Aspects of the Conflict of Cultures in Modern Africa.* London, 1926.
Tempels, P. *Bantu Philosophy.* Paris, 1953; 1st ed. 1945.
Thornton, R. "Narrative Ethnography in Africa, 1850-1920: The Creation and Capture of an Appropriate Domain for Anthropology." *Man* 18 (1983).
Vansina, J. "The Ethnographic Account as Genre in Central Africa." *Paideuma* 33 (1987).
Vellut, J.-L., ed. *Le Mémoire du Congo. Le temps colonial.* Tervuren, 2005.

CHAPTER 6

Dora Earthy's Mozambique Research and the Early Years of Professional Anthropology in South Africa

DEBORAH GAITSKELL

In 1933 the International Institute of African Languages and Cultures, at that point "the most important anthropological publisher in the world,"[1] with the assistance of a subsidy from South African universities, published a book entitled *Valenge Women: The Social and Economic Life of the Valenge Women of Portuguese East Africa; An Ethnographic Study*. The author was E. Dora Earthy, who had been a missionary with the Anglican Society for the Propagation of the Gospel (SPG) in Mozambique between 1917 and 1930.

A. C. Haddon, the eminent Cambridge anthropologist and early mentor of Winifred Hoernlé (the "Mother of Social Anthropology in South Africa"),[2] provided the short introduction. The Cambridge lineage of Dora's helpers (Haddon, Radcliffe-Brown, Hoernlé) is worth highlighting at the outset (and merits more attention than can be given here), not least because of Haddon's pivotal role in the creation of anthropology as a discipline in Britain in the wake of his leadership of the "watershed" expedition to the Torres Straits in 1898.[3] Haddon had first encouraged Dora's research back in 1921, when she wrote asking for advice:

---

1. A. Kuper, *Anthropology and Anthropologists: The Modern British School*, 3rd ed. (London, 1996), p. 100.
2. The phrase of tribute used in the Kriges' 1943 dedication of *The Realm of a Rain-Queen* to Hoernlé; see introduction in Winifred Hoernlé, *The Social Organization of the Nama and Other Essays*, ed. Peter Carstens (Johannesburg, 1985), p. xi. Hoernlé was head of anthropology at the University of the Witwatersrand, Johannesburg, 1923-37.
3. See Henrika Kuklick, "The British Tradition," in *A New History of Anthropology*, ed. Henrika Kuklick (Malden, Mass., Oxford, and Carlton, Australia, 2008), pp. 52-78, and her

I recognized that with her knowledge of the language, her sympathetic character, and the close contact which her professional duties implied, she was in a peculiarly favourable position to undertake such investigations. . . .

Studies of this kind can be accomplished only by women. And though there are many women with equal opportunities, there are very few who have sufficient enthusiasm, training, and catholicity to undertake them. Readers of the monograph will recognize the extraordinarily conscientious care with which the observations are recorded, and cannot but feel that they can fully rely on their accuracy. Miss Earthy also collected a large number of native texts, rituals, and formulae, which confirm her conclusions and have converted oral tradition into material available for students.[4]

This was warm praise, not least because Dora Earthy's "training" might appear to be largely self-acquired. Nevertheless, it is worth tracking in more detail the way in which the scientific community in South Africa offered her guidance, induction courses, a platform for conference presentations and journal publication, and finally, research funding and a book subsidy. It was crucial that the infancy of British and South African social anthropology so absolutely dovetailed with Dora's move to Mozambique and her scholarly awakening. This certainly made space for such a gifted amateur — even if it ultimately intensified the disadvantage of one outside the very small magic circle of that fledgling academy. She was not to know, either, that her attempt at a fairly pure "recovery" type of anthropology was going to be almost immediately superseded by a new wave of scholarship trying to take on a much wider context of culture contact, integration, and change, drawing on the formal professional training she never had, and concluding that the missionary was a "compromised observer," actually by rights forming part of the new discipline's object of study.[5]

The Savage Within: The Social History of British Anthropology (Cambridge, 1991), especially pp. 39-40, 130-139, 308, and (for a reference to Haddon as one of the "strong supporters" whom feminists found in the universities) 53.

4. A. C. Haddon, introduction to *Valenge Women: The Social and Economic Life of the Valenge Women of Portuguese East Africa; An Ethnographic Study*, by E. D. Earthy (London, 1933), p. v.

5. For "the emergence and decline of missionary contributions to anthropology" (p. 238), circa 1913-34, in the very years of Dora's research prime, see Patrick Harries, "Anthropology," in *Missions and Empire*, ed. Norman Etherington (Oxford, 2005), pp. 238-60. For Isaac Schapera's misgivings about "the compromised position of the missionary," see p. 253.

Dora Earthy's Mozambique Research

While the final parts of this chapter look at the reception and use of her monograph, alongside the theological and missiological innovations to which Dora's research led her, the first two sections seek to plot fairly carefully the two strands in the making of this female missionary anthropologist: the mission setting, including her personal inclinations and "formation" on the one hand; and the actual input from South African anthropology on the other. Dora Earthy's later career is of less relevance here, though my initial overgloomy and pitying assessment[6] took insufficient account of her extensive contacts with Save the Children in the 1930s, after her valued contribution to their 1931 international conference in Geneva on African children.[7]

Mission Skills and Motives for Dora Earthy's Research

Earthy's career with SPG gives evidence of that "knowledge of the language," "sympathetic character," and "close contact" with African women commended by Haddon as her unique contribution to scholarship.[8] First, regarding knowledge of languages, Dora was an avid and gifted linguist, unlike most of her female mission contemporaries (though long-serving American Board wife, Clara Bridgman, for instance, was remembered as very fluent in Zulu). In her lengthy previous employment,[9] indexing and cataloguing papers at the Royal Society in London, Earthy's command of several European languages also came in handy for scientific translations. (She had, by 1910, tried French,

---

6. See the final section, "Accounting for Dora Earthy's Obscurity," in Deborah Gaitskell, "Religion Embracing Science? Female Missionary Ventures in Southern African Anthropology: Dora Earthy and Mozambique, 1917-1933" (paper presented to conference on science and society, Sussex University, September 1998; also available as Basel Afrika Bibliographien, Working Paper 5, 1998). This was prompted by material in her personal files, such as the 1942 note, "Invalid (heart) since 1931. Living with invalid sister in large house belonging to her brother — rent free — V poor." Archives of the United Society for the Propagation of the Gospel (hereafter USPG), London, Dossier 2640. (Apart from this biographical dossier and one other, all USPG material referenced in this article is held in Oxford.)

7. See Deborah Gaitskell, "Mission by Other Means? Dora Earthy and the Save the Children Fund in the 1930s," in *Protestant Missions and Local Encounters in the Nineteenth and Twentieth Centuries: Unto the Ends of the World,* ed. Hilde Nielssen, Inger Marie Okkenhaug, and Karina Hestad Skeie (Leiden and Boston: Brill, 2011). For enlightenment and help on this issue, I am indebted to Dominique Marshall, "Children's Rights in Imperial Political Cultures: Missionary and Humanitarian Contributions to the Conference on the African Child of 1931," *International Journal of Children's Rights* 12 (2004): 273-318.

8. See quote for note 4 above.

9. That job lasted seventeen years, from age eighteen to age thirty-five; she offered relatively late for the mission field, and was forty-three when she arrived in Mozambique.

German, Latin, Portuguese, and Spanish, but was most proficient in Spanish, having been to Spain four times.)[10] In South Africa, she learned Dutch, Xhosa, and Tswana; later in Mozambique, Chopi and Shangaan;[11] in addition, she brushed up on her Portuguese in Portugal en route home one year.[12] Other languages beckoned in "retirement."[13]

Secondly, in terms of "her sympathetic character," the warmth of Dora's affection for Africa and its people repeatedly shines through her letters and jaunty reports. When she was running women's classes in the downtown slums of Doornfontein, Johannesburg, between 1911 and 1914, an SPG visitor pronounced her "charming, gentle, steady, persevering, daunted by nothing, acquiring the languages with great rapidity, loving her work, & a missionary out & out."[14] A colleague considered her "a most keen and valuable worker . . . her gentle ways have won the natives' hearts. She is indefatigable in language study, & has a good grasp of Sixhosa."[15] When Latimer Fuller, the pioneer leader of Rand Anglican mission work under the Community of the Resurrection, was made bishop of Lebombo (the diocese for Mozambique), Earthy was keen to respond to his request for her to come and do "women's work" there, but leaving Potchefstroom in 1916 was a real wrench: "These last few weeks have been a very painful time for me, for I have loved the natives,

---

10. USPG, London, Dossier 2640, application form.

11. She hunted about for Shangaan books in England before leaving, and was delighted to find on arrival that the Swiss mission had produced a Bible, a grammar, and a "vocabulary." At that stage she spoke the men's language (Shangaan) to the women, arguing that Xilenge, the women's language, was dying out, whereas Shangaan was more important: 100,000 "natives" in the Transvaal and 50,000 in Portuguese East Africa spoke it, while Junod claimed close to a million Africans were Shangaan. Rhodes House Library, Oxford, USPG, Committee of Women's Work papers (hereafter CWW), Earthy to Miss Saunders, 20 January 1918.

12. When Save the Children sent her to West Africa in 1932 to investigate children's lives there, she could not resist trying to acquire Kru in Sierra Leone. See Rhodes House, X1172 (Miscellaneous Series), Krepoh Kru, Notes, etc. by E. Dora Earthy. This is a twenty-six-page handwritten booklet of vocabulary, sentences, and notes on verbs and grammatical construction. She also made notes on the Kisi dialect of Liberia, which seem to have provided a basis for a later Austrian doctoral thesis. See H. G. Mukarovsky, "Die Sprache der Kisi in Liberia. Abriss einer Grammatiek mit Texten und Vokabular, bearbeit nach Aufzeichnungen von Dora Earthy" (Ph.D. diss., University of Vienna, 1948 — xerox in SOAS library). For her notes, which she said she had been encouraged to make by Dr. Westermann of the International African Institute (IAI), see manuscripts on "Kisi vocabulary" and "Grammar of the Kisi language, Liberia," in Rhodes House, X1177.

13. She dabbled in Arabic, Greek, and Hebrew in old age. See USPG, Dossier 2640.

14. USPG, CWW, Miss Phillimore to Miss Gurney, 21 March 1913.

15. USPG, Series E (Annual Reports), Theodora Williams, 31 December 1913.

and they have been so very sweet to me. They have simply been showering little farewell gifts upon me. It is all I can do to keep from breaking down. . . . I feel so ashamed to think I did not love them more & serve them better while I still had the chance. One woman did say very sweetly this week: 'She came from a far land to make herself one with us, we black people.'"[16] While on furlough back in Britain, she "longed to see them with a longing which was really pain,"[17] exclaiming from Cape Town on her return, "Oh! It is *so* delightful to be back again in beloved Africa!"[18]

Sympathy with and closeness to the women reached a new depth in Mozambique as Dora settled in for more than a decade of predictable routine in one place. She was giving religious instruction to prepare women for the various laid-down stages of progression through church membership: hearer, catechumen, baptized, confirmed — and was also teaching quite a bit of sewing![19] But her early letters from Maciene named specific women in her classes and asked for prayer for them in a personalized way much less evident in her South African postings.[20] Her "close contact" with the people, which Haddon valued for its scientific potential, took on greater intimacy and was sustained by stronger individual and communal ties than hitherto.

Crucially, Dora soon spotted a possible opening for a new development, to protect Christian widows from the levirate — which entailed being "inherited" by a "heathen" brother-in-law. In 1920 she was dreaming of a sort of secular "Order of S. Anna"[21] on a small scale, where Christian widows "could live together & work for their living (which they do in any case) & attend Church services & classes as much as possible; instead of being at the beck & call of a heathen husband who has already a superfluity of wives. They should be free to make a second Christian marriage if they choose." Three Christian widows in a nearby hut could form the nucleus, while a young widow recently arrived from the Zandamela district had been explicitly directed by her dying husband to seek their protection from "heathen" remarriage in this way.[22]

---

16. USPG, CWW, Earthy to Miss Saunders, 26 November 1916.
17. USPG, CWW, Earthy to Miss Saunders, 9 June 1917.
18. USPG, CWW, Earthy to Miss Saunders, 17 July 1917.
19. Three times a week in 1919. See USPG, E, Lebombo, Earthy, 29 November 1919.
20. USPG, CWW, Earthy to Miss Saunders, 9 January 1914, is a rare example of a request for intercession for four named women confirmation candidates. A couple of other early letters mention women prayer-group leaders by name (perhaps clergy wives).
21. An elderly widow and prophetess constantly worshiping in the temple, Anna (like Simeon) recognized the infant Jesus as redeemer. See Luke 2:36-38.
22. USPG, CWW 140, Earthy to Miss Saunders, 31 July 1920. This appeared as D. Earthy, "Widows in Africa," *Mission Field*, January 1921, pp. 14-15.

These were women without men, many of them mature women closer to Dora in age. They became women on whom she leaned for practical and emotional support, initially in church work but subsequently in her anthropological research as well.

By 1923, she had fifteen women in her Band of Anna and listed them all by name, distinguishing the special circumstances that had brought each to the mission;[23] by 1927, there were nineteen of them, Rhoda and Mara being especially involved in Dora's church work, coming on trek with her: "We have often slept in native huts and eaten native food, and have thus been brought into closer touch with the life of the women."[24] Mara lived with her little boy Ananias in one of the widows' huts at the mission, and was "of the greatest service" on trek, being "most unselfish and hard-working" with "surprisingly refined perceptions." Rhoda, though also a widow, was "under discipline" (which may mean she had had a baby since bereavement, but out of wedlock?). Dora gave her, a "beautiful needlewoman," a "regular occupation of sewing" and found her very helpful on trek when Dora had large sewing classes and could not give individual attention to all the members. Rhoda could read the Bible too.[25]

It is the evangelistic itineration of this exact trio of Dora, Mara, and Rhoda in the late 1920s, visiting more distant Christian homes to pray and teach the Bible to women and girls, which a Mozambican scholar singles out to exemplify how women's church mobilization long predated the formal constitution of the Mothers' Union in southern Mozambique.[26] Indeed, Alda Saúte goes so far as to argue that her thesis "demonstrates that while the Mozambican miners were the founders and nourishers of Anglicanism in the Maciene district, women and children were the keepers of the faith in the absence of the men."[27] Her extensive oral interviews document the skilled teaching and preaching of African women involved in the *União das Mães* (Mothers' Union) in the 1940s, and how, under their tutelage, members of the girls' guild of St. Agnes *(Grémio de Santa Inês)* competed enthusiastically "to master the Bible, catechism, prayer and hymn books." The guild served not

---

23. USPG, E, Earthy, 12 December 1923.
24. USPG, E, Earthy, December 1927.
25. See D. Earthy, "A Guild for Widows," *Mission Field,* July 1928, p. 166.
26. Miss Earthy, "A Little Visit to Mafangeni," *Lebombo Leaves* 27, no. 56 (Fourth Quarter 1929): 16-17, cited in Alda Romão Saúte, "The African Mission Encounter and Education in Mozambique: The Anglican Mission of Santo Agostinho — Maciene, 1926/8–1974" (Ph.D. diss., University of Minnesota, 2000), p. 162. Thanks to Eric Morier-Genoud for loaning this to me.
27. Saúte, "The African Mission Encounter," p. 10.

only to reinforce their Anglican faith, "but also constituted a place where girls learned and practiced the skills of reading, speaking, arguing, singing and leading a group or community."[28] Such female "fellowship groups" played a "critical role" in the rooting of Anglicanism in the district. Women and girls not only provided "eight out of ten congregants but also in their interchange visits were preaching and converting people to the Anglican faith. Church participation was a means of self-protection and mobilization; it re-gendered, and encroached upon, the public social sphere of human activity."[29] So Dora's evangelistic and teaching tours with her two local female companions in the late 1920s set a pattern for women's ongoing spiritual ministry. But such travels, she later realized, could also be systematized for academic study.

Dora Earthy's relocation from the relatively "Westernized" urban southern Transvaal to the very different setting of southern Mozambique clearly brought her up short. She had previously worked largely with far more "Westernized" and Christianized Africans in and around urban areas. When two Ndebele women came to a country church service at Middelbult for Xhosa Christians in 1912, for example, she was more interested in them than all the others because they were "raw" and it was "the first time" she had "had an opportunity of speaking to heathen women." Visiting them next morning, she was keen to communicate — and, seemingly, to acquire cultural artifacts — but she "did not get on very far with them" as the "only things" she "could say, which they could understand were: 'I want to buy a bead-necklace! What pretty babies! What nice mealies'!"[30] The unfamiliar but distinctive culture around Maciene got her thinking in a new way, stimulating her powers of observation and evoking a flood of writing. Although her interest in local custom and social organization was fostered, as we shall see, by academics in South Africa, her own curiosity and ready pen were first encouraged by Miss Saunders of the Committee for Women's Work (CWW) at SPG, on the lookout for likely items for publication in the mission literature.

Dora had been corresponding with Miss Saunders since at least 1914,[31] but there *may* have been an additional reason for the notable — indeed, extraordinary — expansion of her letter writing once she reached Mozambique. It seems very likely that this Miss Saunders was the same Agnes Saunders who had spent a decade or more in southern Mozambique herself, at the turn of

---

28. Saúte, "The African Mission Encounter," p. 164.
29. Saúte, "The African Mission Encounter," p. 218.
30. USPG, CWW, Earthy to Miss Gurney, 13 April 1912.
31. See n. 20 above and USPG, CWW, Earthy to Miss Saunders, 8 June 1915; 31 May 1916.

the century, before taking up responsibilities with CWW. The daughter of the dean (later bishop) of Peterborough, Agnes Saunders offered herself in 1894 as an "honorary missionary" (i.e., self-supporting — she had £200 per annum) to the SPG Ladies' Association after nine years of church work in Natal, six of those among Indian women and girls at St. Aidan's Mission.[32] She was sent to Inhambane in the pioneering diocese of Lebombo, only created the previous year, learning "a smattering" of the Tonga language[33] while acting as housekeeper to the clergy. The bishop hinted at her enterprise: "As soon as she felt she could get on alone, she began going over to Chilambi . . . for a few days at a time,"[34] starting a boys school there in 1895. She and her friends bore almost all its expense until 1898, including the purchase of the site. It developed into a residential college within two years, which they "hoped would supply the future teachers and catechists of the Tonga-speaking districts." The relatively well heeled Miss Saunders also "helped in the erection of the church at Chilambi," at whose opening in 1897 "all the known native Christians in Inhambane, other than Roman Catholics," were invited "to join in a great act of worship."[35] Her willing lack of pretension, however privileged her background, is suggested by the manner in which she lived when she opened an outstation at Churaneni that year, fourteen miles from Inhambane. "During her visits she occupied a small hut, which drew from the Bishop [W. E. Smyth] the exclamation, 'Oh! if I only had as good accommodation for my fellow workers as my father has for his horse in England, I should be so thankful!'"[36] Agnes Saunders's efforts at *female* mission education were more fraught with challenge, and ultimately unsuccessful: her girls' boarding school was short-lived, once the parents realized she hoped to substitute a church "dowry fund" for customary bride wealth *lobola* payments, in order to free girls from compulsory marriage (arranged by parents) to heathens or Muslims.[37] Miss Saunders seems to have worked in Mozambique until about 1905, when she went on furlough,[38] after which she appears not to have re-

---

32. USPG London, Dossier 2715. I am extremely grateful to Catherine Wakeling, London USPG archivist, for her helpful investigations on Miss Saunders.

33. Indeed, Agnes learned the language well enough to translate Tonga reading sheets, published by SPCK, and a short reading book, published locally. See C. F. Pascoe, *Two Hundred Years of the SPG* (London, 1901), p. 813a.

34. Bishop of Lebombo to the Committee of the SPG Women's Missionary Association (WMA), 27 May 1899, in WMA, *Annual Report* (1899), p. 66.

35. Pascoe, *Two Hundred Years*, p. 346e.

36. Pascoe, *Two Hundred Years*, p. 346e.

37. Saúte, "The African Mission Encounter," pp. 178-79.

38. E-mail Catherine Wakeling to author, 2 December 2009, having consulted lists of missionaries in SPG reports.

turned to Africa. But should Agnes indeed have been a keen predecessor in the very same region as Earthy, only a decade earlier, that circumstance would further explain the liberty Dora felt to fill pages of manuscript with detailed observations from southern Mozambique.

Dora's account of her journey to Maciene and first impressions of her new posting reached London early in 1918, was published in the *Mission Field*, the SPG periodical,[39] and was later drawn on for the prologue to her monograph. Her portrayal of the women missionaries on the little jolting steamer crammed with Rand labor-migrants bearing earnings and booty, and the journey past the WNLA labor depot at Chai Chai amid lovely scenery, highlights both her sharp awareness of the social and economic links between past and current areas of her church work, and her appreciation of the physical beauty of Africa. The close of the extract reveals her initial, rather wide-eyed reaction to the "mysterious rites" in this "stronghold" of "heathen" Africa, so different outwardly from the urban Transvaal locations. While the collection of Anglican buildings — mission house, church, and huts of converts — stood out on the tropical hilltop,

> All around are heathen kraals. It is a Mission station in the very strongholds of heathenism. The witch-doctors pass and re-pass on their way to magic heathen ceremonies in the kraals. There are women witch-doctors too — bold, handsome, half-naked women with red-ochred hair, their arms and ankles laden with bangles and bracelets.
>
> Many and mysterious are the rites performed by the witch-doctors on the occasion of births, illnesses, marriages, funerals, or the occupation of new kraals.

But the article ended with an attempt (partly edited out by SPG) to show how Christianity could build on the deep inherent sense of worship of the people, and offer true rites of purification to those whose existing beliefs emphasized such rites.[40] So from the outset, she was seeking to make links with prior beliefs, the better to accomplish her missionary evangelistic aim.

Improved language acquisition, greater cultural grasp, and better Christian instruction all worked together. In mid-1920, Earthy wrote: "I am teaching constantly, both here and at the out-stations. I am trying to improve my

---

39. "Women and Girls in Gazaland, Mozambique," *Mission Field*, January 1919, pp. 9-11.

40. "Women and Girls in Gazaland, Mozambique," filed next to Earthy letter of 23 August 1918 in USPG, CWW 137.

knowledge of the language also, and am learning a good deal more about native customs & modes of thought by travelling about in the kraals, & trying to pick up native idioms & words which have no equivalent in English, or at least, only a very round-about one. This is very fascinating work, & helps me in my teaching afterwards."[41] Her 1920 report was full of material on traditional beliefs and how Christianity could be grafted on: "I have culled a few examples from the great mass of heathen superstitions, which I think are interesting, as they show with what we have to deal, and how we try to teach the people that what they believe are in many cases perversions of the truth."[42]

Early in 1921 she sent the Women Candidates' Secretary the first installment of a long piece about their women:

> I only hope the length of it will not dismay you. But when once I start writing about them, I feel as if I should never cease. The first part of the letter is a sort of general account. Succeeding parts will be about the native religious rites, marriage and burial customs, dances, native medicines, etc. etc. (Always supposing you care to hear about them!)
>
> I am fortunate in having a native Catechist who is a keen Christian, & who knows all the customs of the country, to help me with various kinds of information.[43]

That she found a good informant was only part of the story (we will consider her larger group of informants later); the mission and scientific streams came together fruitfully at just this time to encourage her to be more systematic and comprehensive in her research.

In 1921 Dora Earthy began reflecting more fully on the roots and mission potential of her anthropological interests, thanking the Women's Committee for the "very interesting" copy of the *International Review of Missions (IRM)* with its "illuminating article on anthropological work in the Mission Field, by Mrs Stevenson." Thus another woman missionary, though from the very different field of India, provided Dora with inspiration, practical guidance, and the imprimatur of mission approval for scientific exploration. In her two-part paper, "The Study of Anthropology on the Mission Field," which had appeared in 1920, Mrs. (Margaret) Sinclair Stevenson, M.A., Sc.D., an Oxford graduate who had been in India twenty years, encouraged detailed study of the religion of those the missionary worked among — for more ef-

---

41. USPG, CWW 140, Earthy to Miss Saunders, 31 July 1920.
42. USPG, E, Earthy, 29 December 1920.
43. USPG, CWW, Earthy to Miss Saunders, 6 February 1921.

fective understanding. Using Indian examples and in a very enthusiastic, accessible, practical, enabling style addressed at women missionaries, Mrs. Stevenson urged them to ask lots of the right questions, find good informants, and take a life history of relevant ceremonies and stages, do their "prep" before attending relevant temples, make detailed notes, and even consider "weaving it into a thesis for a research degree." To begin with, they should "buy, borrow or beg at least four books: R. R. Marett's *Anthropology* (Home University Library); *Notes and Queries on Anthropology* (British Association); V. Gennep's *Les Rites de Passage;* Tylor's *Anthropology.*"[44] The aim was to enlarge one's loving sympathy for the people and deepen insight into their character.

Dora's scholarly appetite was well and truly whetted, though she explained the relevance of her past employment also:

> I am looking forward extremely to the arrival of the second number [of *IRM*], which you kindly promise to send. My first interest in anthropology as a science was aroused when I was working at the Royal Society, & had to catalogue and index anthropological papers among others. Anthropology studied in connection with missionary work, seems to me to be of thrilling interest, and I must try to get some books on the subject, especially those recommended by Mrs Stevenson, when I come to England next year. Meanwhile, I must go on studying and recording native customs.[45]

In the event, she couldn't wait — within the next fortnight, after getting the second article, she sent to England "for some of the handbooks on anthropology for beginners. This study seems to open out ever-widening vistas of research and work, and will be so extremely useful to one in one's missionary work."[46] But as this was coupled with an account of a "quite thrilling Lenten campaign in the heathen kraals," during which she took "hasty pencil notes" of the "very eloquent" Shangaan preaching, it was clear her missionary focus was undimmed. Further lengthy installments on Gaza women followed: "I do hope I am not boring you with all these papers! I seem to be only at the beginning of them."[47]

In fact, the first contacts with South African anthropologists seem to have

---

44. Margaret Sinclair Stevenson, "The Study of Anthropology on the Mission Field," *IRM* 9 (1920): 428.
45. USPG, CWW, Earthy to Miss Bewley, 6 February 1921.
46. USPG, CWW, Earthy to Miss Bewley, 27 February 1921.
47. USPG, CWW, Earthy to Miss Saunders, 3 April 1921; 30 April 1921.

been virtually simultaneous with these other developments of distant mission inspiration (from Mrs. Stevenson in India) and increased local documentation (on the ground in Mozambique), so they can now be woven in. The vital figures appear to have been Radcliffe-Brown and Winifred Hoernlé, while the relevant supportive institutions were the South African Association for the Advancement of Science (SAAAS), its journal the *South African Journal of Science (SAJS)*, and the Transvaal Museum, with its *Annals* publication. By the end of the decade, Mrs. Hoernlé's Witwatersrand University (Wits) would be making significant grants to enable Dora to consolidate and expand her findings.

Encouragement from South African Anthropologists

How Dora first made the acquaintance of various key scholars remains obscure. But early in 1921 she was pleased to report to Miss Saunders that "some few months ago,"

> Prof. Radcliffe-Brown, the newly-appointed professor of social anthropology at Cape Town University, asked me to collect some ethnological specimens for the Transvaal Museum at Pretoria, as he is the honorary curator of the ethnological department there. So I sent off some odds and ends last month when I went down to Delagoa Bay for my holiday; and I have received a very kind letter from the Acting Director of the Museum. He writes: — "The very interesting description you gave of each specimen is most welcome. . . . Your collection in that respect is one of the very best, and will help us in our ethnological studies very much indeed, and furthermore, when exhibited will also be of great interest to the general public."[48]

---

48. USPG, CWW 145, Loose sheet filed before letter of 6 February 1921. See also Kuklick, "The British Tradition," p. 62, for how "Haddon's lobbying, in particular, persuaded South African and Australian officials to endorse the creation" of anthropology professorships in 1921 and 1925 at the universities of Cape Town and Sydney — with Radcliffe-Brown the first occupant in both cases. W. D. Hammond Tooke, *Imperfect Interpreters: South Africa's Anthropologists, 1920-1990* (Johannesburg, 1997), chapter 1, is also good on this formative period, though he suggests (p. 33) that the vacation schools for administrators and missionaries "were not a success" (even though Dora clearly loved hers). Furthermore, while Radcliffe-Brown's "direct influence on South African anthropology was minimal," his "indirect influence on succeeding generations of English-speaking anthropologists was immense."

Dora continued, "It seems very conceited of me to tell you this, but I shall be very glad indeed if I have helped in ever so small a way, to make the 'general public' interested in the productions of our beloved native people!"[49] Radcliffe-Brown (1881-1955), some seven years Dora's junior (she was born in 1874), corresponded with the Transvaal Museum later that year about substantial further specimens that Dora had collected for them (bowls, musical instruments, girls' initiation ornaments, baskets, dancing gear).[50] In 1922, he even expressed the hope that the museum might give her a commission of from £20 to £30 to spend: he feared that all the best ethnological specimens had already been "collected into the museums of Europe" and they would "have to make haste in order to get anything at all." He had "ventured to promise" Dora that the Transvaal Museum would refund her the £10 that two carved figures and a small drum used in initiation ceremonies had cost her; he did this, Radcliffe-Brown explained, "because she had opportunities to sell them in England at a profit, and I wished to secure them for South Africa. Photographs have been taken of them at the Cambridge Ethnological Museum." (So Dora had presumably sought informed guidance from Haddon on the value of her specimens when back on furlough.) "With Miss Earthy" he hoped to "write few notes" for the museum's *Annals*.[51] Subsequently, in continuing to encourage the museum to carry some of her scholarship, Radcliffe-Brown seemed to keep her papers for quite some time, aiming to clarify them in copying them out for publication — though they appeared under her own name alone in the end.[52]

One thing led to another. It was presumably the contact from the collecting that resulted in an invitation to present a paper at the SAAAS meeting at Bloemfontein in July 1923. Dora reported to London:

---

49. USPG, CWW 145, loose sheet filed before letter of 6 February 1921.

50. Transvaal Museum, Pretoria, Box 536, TM 126/21, Radcliffe-Brown to Swierstra, 27 September 1921. Earthy had spent roughly £15 (a significant sum), which they would reimburse. Radcliffe-Brown to Swierstra, 4 August 1922, concerns the safe storage of her collection (and the regrettable admission that one of her dolls had been damaged "by rolling off a table"; he had "patched it as well as [he] could but it was a difficult job").

51. Transvaal Museum, Pretoria, Box 536, TM 126/21, Radcliffe-Brown to Swierstra, 15 October 1922.

52. Transvaal Museum, Pretoria, Box 536, TM 126/21, Radcliffe-Brown to Swierstra, 17 July 1923, noting the appropriateness of the *Annals* carrying Earthy's piece on girls' initiation as the specimens referred to there would all be in the Transvaal Museum. Also, though "of some length," it was "the most complete study yet made of the initiation ceremonies of any South African tribe" and was "a very important contribution to ethnography"; for the delayed paper, Radcliffe-Brown to Swierstra, 19 May 1924. Many thanks to Dr. Heidi Fourie of the Transvaal Museum for sending me copies of this correspondence.

I was extremely busy at the time, but thought it would be a pity to miss the opportunity. So I put together a few notes, and entitled my paper: — "The Social and Religious Preparation for Initiation among VaChopi and VaLenge women." The President of the Anthropological Section wrote to me afterwards, congratulating me on having carried out a difficult piece of work — and he kindly remarked that my paper had aroused a good deal of interest, and was the most satisfactory account of the Initiation of *women* as yet received from any part of Central or S. Africa.[53]

A short snippet on girls' initiation appeared in the journal *SAJS* that year.[54]

The following year Earthy renewed her links with SAAAS, but first had some concentrated academic teaching, which she clearly relished, on six aspects of African life. Early in 1924, Dora was on a social and scholarly "high":

I am having a most delightful holiday in Cape Town, attending a vacation course at the University [which would have been run by Radcliffe-Brown] — in phonetics; philology; native law and administration; problems of native education; customary law of the Bantu; social anthropology & ethnology. It all belongs to the "Department of African Life and Languages" in the University. We study in the morning, and rest in the afternoon, or make excursions, & go out to tea with friends.... I wish we could give you some of the warmth & sun-light [of Cape Town].[55]

She was back in Cape Town six months later, to help at the Missionary Exhibition, and "had a most delightful time, altogether." She stayed on afterward with Dorothea Bleek, daughter of the philologist of "Bushman" language, in order to attend the SAAAS meetings, reading a paper on the subject of tribal marks before the Anthropological Section, then stopped off for an enjoyable two days with old colleagues at Buxton Street on the Rand.[56]

The 1924 SAAAS paper received a much higher profile than the one the previous year: an article nearly fifteen pages long in *SAJS*.[57] Dora already dis-

---

53. USPG, E, Lebombo, Earthy, 12 December 1923.
54. "Initiation Rites for Girls in the Masiyeni District, Portuguese East Africa," *SAJS* 20 (December 1923): 512-13.
55. USPG, CWW 148, Earthy to Miss Saunders, 4 February 1924.
56. USPG, CWW 148, Earthy to Miss Saunders, 27 July 1924. For Bleek, see USPG, CWW 148, 13 January 1925.
57. E. D. Earthy, "On the Significance of the Body Markings of Some Natives of Portuguese East Africa," *SAJS* 21 (1924): 573-87.

played at this early stage of her "academic" career an arresting turn of phrase. Of bodily incisions, she commented:

> The Va Chopi write the story of their lives on their own flesh. The ink is their life-blood, and their pen the razor. But because the written story sometimes grows dim, it has to be re-written at intervals, until the marks are ineffaceable. And why do they do this, absolutely regardless of the inconvenience and physical suffering which such operations occasion? . . . these practices, which seem to us so degrading, have evidently had in the past among the Va Chopi and Va Lenge a high ritual and social value, and have become intimately connected with all the great crises of the lives of these people.[58]

In publication output, 1925 marked a high point: it was only then that she finally had three pieces in succession published in the same issue of the Transvaal Museum's *Annals* (a substantial one on female initiation; shorter notes on carved bowls; and one on ritual objects);[59] a brief item on kinship appeared in *SAJS*;[60] and two linked, fairly short notes on agriculture for *Bantu Studies*,[61] her third local scholarly journal within three years. Back in the U.K. on furlough in 1926, Dora was glad to have been asked "to write a paper (on the sublimation of native customs) for the International Review of Missions. It is a rather difficult subject, but I am going to do my best."[62] The piece made reference to the work of Junod and Radcliffe-Brown, while enthusiastically endorsing Raymond Dart's 1925 remarks to the SAAAS about soul-stirring African music and dance. Its overall thrust was to suggest ways in which ritual practices associated with women's lives could be adapted to Christianity, and Christian spiritual teaching could build on existing patterns

---

58. Earthy, "On the Significance," pp. 577, 587.
59. All in *Annals of the Transvaal Museum* 11, no. 2 (1925): "Initiation of Girls in the Masiyeni District, Portuguese East Africa," pp. 103-17; "Notes on the Decorations on Carved Wooden Food-Bowls from South Chopiland, Portuguese East Africa," pp. 118-24; "On Some Ritual Objects of the Vandau in South Chopiland, Gaza, Portuguese East Africa," pp. 125-28.
60. "The Role of the Father's Sister among the Valenge of Gazaland, Portuguese East Africa," *SAJS* 22 (1925): 526-29.
61. "Notes on Some Agricultural Rites Practised by the Valenge and Vachopi (Portuguese East Africa), Pt. 1," *Bantu Studies* 2, no. 3 (1925): 193-97; "Pt. 2," *Bantu Studies* 2, no. 4 (1925): 265-67.
62. USPG, CWW 148, Earthy to Miss Saunders, 28 May 1926. This was published as "The Customs of Gazaland Women in Relation to the Christian Church," *IRM* 15 (1926): 662-74.

of thought, because Christ himself was the one who bridged all gulfs, whether that separating heathenism and Christianity, or the passage "from sin to holiness, from death to life." Thus, despite a serious foray into academic anthropology, Earthy was still holding her evangelistic and church-building goal to the fore.

It is therefore somewhat ironic that it was Winifred Hoernlé now whose sponsorship became pivotal and whose help in preparing her book manuscript Dora Earthy acknowledged. In her original research a decade and a half earlier among the Nama (which made her the first trained woman anthropologist to undertake field research anywhere),[63] Mrs. Hoernlé repeatedly portrayed Christian missions as inherently antipathetic to anthropological concerns. Her candid Namaqualand field diaries of 1912 argued that missions erased pure Nama culture and were therefore to be deplored:

> Think it will be better to get away from the mission station, the people will be freer then [she mused, after an old woman refused to undress to be photographed, saying she was too dirty]. . . . Decided to move on, influence of Mission station too strong here. They say the other people are more savage and have as little to do with the Mission as possible, probably they will be better for my purpose. . . . Dreadful to think how dull religion can make a people. . . . They seem to have no songs nowadays except hymns, and in spite of constant observation I have not been able to catch them singing to their children. . . .
>
> Their old traditions have all gone out and they now accept in a hazy way the beliefs of the missionaries. . . . As their utensils and material customs have given way to those of the white man, so also have their mental traits. . . . Dutch culture has penetrated very deep and it is really a marvel that as much of the Hottentot culture has remained as is the case.[64]

Yet at the same time Hoernlé confessed that "There is no doubt that the life of these people centres around their church," and — somewhat inconsistently — pronounced the Old Testament "admirably suited to a shepherd race" to whose conversation pastures and flocks were ever central.[65] To the SWA mandate administration in 1923, Hoernlé vented her frustration that missionary

---

63. Hammond Tooke, *Imperfect Interpreters*, p. 37.

64. Hoernlé in Peter Carstens, G. Klinghardt, and Martin West, eds., *Trails in the Thirstland: The Anthropological Field Diaries of Winifred Hoernlé* (Cape Town, 1987), pp. 32-33, 40, 48-49, 58.

65. Hoernlé in Carstens, Klinghardt, and West, *Trails in the Thirstland*, pp. 61, 49.

activity of over a hundred years "has done its work here and stamped out the inheritance from their forefathers . . . the pure Hottentot with his culture is doomed already . . . drawn irresistibly by things European." On that last field trip, she reminded herself how artificial the life led on mission stations was, and berated the missionary determination to make the Hottentots sedentary — it had had such detrimental, eroding effects.[66] Mrs. Hoernlé was in touch with Dora from at least 1924, when she wrote a long, chatty, affectionate letter, thankful for a copy of Earthy's notes on the agricultural rite (to be published in *Bantu Studies*) but largely pressing her to ask detailed questions about the plants, prayers, and sacrificial rituals used by medicine men.[67]

In 1928, with church permission, Earthy received a six-month grant from the University of the Witwatersrand to do research,[68] which seems to have quite rejuvenated her. Her personal relationships with the two widows with whom she had already been doing church visitation were crucial to the project, as her long and fascinating account of her method makes clear:

> On Easter Monday I started my ethnological research work, and continued it for several weeks without a break, leaving Masiyeni early Monday morning, and coming back every Saturday, and sometimes on Friday afternoon, for the week-end services. (Incidentally, I was glad to come back, too, for my letters and to get some hot baths and regular meals.) Mara looked after me splendidly in the kraals, and under God, I owe my good-health to her. She would tuck in my mosquito-net at night when we slept in the native huts; light log fires, cook vegetable dishes, and prepare early tea and hot water. Often I have wakened on cold winter nights and found Mara piling more wood on the fire. She herself slept on a reed mat, quite close to my camp-bed, as did also another widow, Rhoda, and one of the S.P.G. scholarship pupils, Nyankwavane, the leper's daughter. These three went with me everywhere, and slept in my hut, accommodation in all the kraals being limited. Sometimes we had to share the hut with other women. There were times when I found the lack of privacy very trying, but my companions were very good to me, and generally slipped out of

66. Hoernlé in Carstens, Klinghardt, and West, *Trails in the Thirstland,* appendix A, pp. 177, 182; also 119, 113.
67. School of Oriental and African Studies (hereafter SOAS), Special Collections, MS 380515, Dora Earthy Papers, File 1, W. Hoernlé to E. D. Earthy, 27 October 1924.
68. See University of the Witwatersrand (Johannesburg), Historical and Literary Papers (hereafter Wits), AD843/RJ/Kb32.2.1.3, E. D. Earthy to Mrs Hoernlé, 26 February 1928, 15 March 1928, and the accompanying application form, which may still be misfiled in Wits, AD843/RJ/Kb32.2.1.15, Bantu Affairs Research Committee 1930-31.

the hut as soon as they awoke in the morning and had said their prayers, and went off to warm themselves at some fire in a cooking-hut.

If we happened to be in a kraal where there was a native catechist, we attended a very early Matins in his little reed church, but if not, then I generally read prayers for the women. Then after breakfast, I had to watch and familiarize myself with all that went on in the kraal, taking as many notes as I could. Naturally, the natives could not understand my being among them in any other capacity than that of a missionary who had come to teach them, so my time was very fully occupied all day long, with one thing and another. In every fresh district I visited I went to greet the Chief, and to give him a small present. Of course, it was an unheard-of-thing for a white woman to be living among natives, in this part of the world, and many of them could not understand it at all, so I deemed it wise to hurry to see the chief as soon as I arrived, tired or not. I was well received except sometimes when I went to places which were closed to us as regards Church purposes. After a few weeks I thought it advisable to obtain the consent of the local magistrate to visit these areas for scientific purposes, — the permission being cordially granted.

Many miles we tramped through the Bush, visiting one village after another. My carriers were Mara, Rhoda and Nyankwavane, and occasionally others. Nyankwavane carried a paraffin-tin full of our tank rain-water on her head, for the drinking water in the kraals is not good, as a rule, and I could not face it. In the evenings we used to sit round the fire, and listen to folk-stories, which were quite thrilling. Then, when I thought they had had as many fairy-tales as were good for them, I said evening prayers, and we went to bed. In order to gain their confidence and to draw them out, I would generally start off with some story like "The Three Bears" or "Little Red Riding-Hood."

The results of my researches during those six months, will, I hope, be handed over to the Witwatersrand University early in February, with the exception of most of the folk-lore, which takes a long time to write up in the native language according to the recommended orthography (International Institute of African Languages and Culture). (USPG, Series E, Earthy, 26 December 1928)

Earthy even got an additional grant from the University of the Witwatersrand in 1929 to follow up on peoples farther north,[69] and published some of those

---

69. See Wits, AD843/RJ/Kb 32.2.1.15, Bantu Affairs Research Committee 1930-31, E. D. Earthy to Prof. Hoernlé, 30 January 1930, from which it is clear she used their £30 to travel

findings in a longish piece and two shorter notes in *Bantu Studies,* the anthropological journal based there, plus a short item in the IAI journal, *Africa.*[70]

The centrality of the physical and emotional support of Rhoda and Mara to Dora's anthropological research raises the question of their possible input into her findings — and how much her informants (and other anthropologists' informants) took part in and shaped the content of ethnographic research, a general issue on which Schumaker and others offer fascinating insights.[71] While lacking the personal papers and local experience that so aided Bank,[72] the monograph contains a wealth of internal evidence on Dora's use of informants, more than can be explored here. Alongside historical accounts from named old men and chiefs, and stories of complicated birth or of possession attributed to named women, there are many scattered references to "A Tchopi woman told me . . ." or "All my informants agree. . . ."[73]

In the heart of the book, though, it would appear that the faithful Mara (if she is indeed "M," as I suspect) actually greatly facilitated Dora's learning about female initiation and her physical access to supposedly secret ceremonies. First, there is a one-and-a-half page description of M's own experience of initiation prior to her marriage to a man from Johannesburg to whom she had been "lobolaed," after which she took a name meaning "in father's power," for "she did not want to be taken by her husband . . . but was going to resign herself to her father's will about the marriage." As an informant, she had her shortcomings: Dora admitted that "she was (and is) very nervous, and was far too frightened to take notice of details" in the opening activities.[74]

---

to Beira from Johannesburg (return), hire a motor launch to Sofala, and travel from Umtali to Melsetter (return), as well as pay photographic expenses and for ethnological specimens. Presumably this was a short trip, not the six months envisaged (April to September) and asked for in her application for a Grant in Aid of Research, Wits AD843/RJ/Kb32.2.1.3, since she had noted in her mission correspondence that her local priest would not permit another six months' absence.

70. D. Earthy, "Sundry Notes on the Vandau of Sofala, P.E.A.," *Bantu Studies,* June 1930, pp. 95-107, and "Notes on the 'Totemism' of the VaNdau," *Bantu Studies* 5, no. 1 (1931): 77-79; "A VaNdau Ordeal of Olden Times," *Bantu Studies* 9, no. 2 (1935): 159-61.

71. See Lyn Schumaker, *Africanizing Anthropology: Fieldwork, Networks, and the Making of Cultural Knowledge in Central Africa* (Durham, N.C., 2001); Andrew Bank, "The 'Intimate Politics' of Fieldwork: Monica Hunter and Her African Assistants, Pondoland and the Eastern Cape, 1931-1932," *Journal of Southern African Studies* 34, no. 3 (September 2008); Helen Tilley with Robert Gordon, eds., *Ordering Africa: Anthropology, European Imperialism, and the Politics of Knowledge* (Manchester and New York, 2007), p. 1 and part II, "African Ethnographers, Self-Expression and Modernity."

72. Bank, "The 'Intimate Politics' of Fieldwork."

73. For examples, see Earthy, *Valenge Women,* pp. 3, 7, 70-75, 106, 200-204, 211.

74. Earthy, *Valenge Women,* p. 131.

Then follow a rich few pages of Dora and M going to some initiation dances in July 1928, with M excitedly exclaiming each time she saw "a fully-fledged debutante or initiation candidate, her hair and her body flame-red with ochre." They arrived late at night, "accompanied by a boy with a storm-lantern," in a clearing near Zandamela. Group astonishment at seeing a white woman, "for they keep these performances strictly secret," yielded to "a little murmuring and a little debating" after "M. explained politely that I had heard about the dances and would like to see them." The group then agreed to their staying (and Dora confessed that the dances "did not strike one as being vulgarly done").[75]

They were less lucky a couple of days later with a more anxious old woman, who would not let them see the ceremony there, with a hundred or so involved — even though the local chief told Dora and M they should have been allowed to.[76] Yet, just as the caring intimacy with which Mara "mothered" Dora on the research treks could segue into a version of domestic service, so the racial and ecclesiastical hierarchy of these "constant companions" was inevitably subtly demonstrated on public occasions, as when the duo went to one of the winter dance contests. As the only European there, Earthy was "received very politely and a chair was brought from a hut for me and placed in the front row, likewise a mat for my native woman companion." As for the dancing, "In a savage kind of way the scene was a brilliant one."[77]

Scholarly Reaction to Valenge Women

The International African Institute (IAI) was diligent in trying to get Dora's book widely appraised, listing two dozen newspapers and periodicals — from scholarly German journals to the *Rhodesian Herald*! — that were sent copies for review.[78] The book was delightfully reviewed in *Africa*, the IAI's in-house journal, by Monica Hunter, at that stage writing up her fieldwork among the Pondo. She highlights the due prominence given to "the daily routine of women's work, the elaborate methods of preparing food and beer, the making of domestic utensils, baskets, and pottery — all matters which have hitherto received but scant attention in monographs on African communities." She notes the careful observation, "charmingly translated" folktales, and illustra-

75. Earthy, *Valenge Women*, pp. 133-35.
76. Earthy, *Valenge Women*, pp. 135-36.
77. Earthy, *Valenge Women*, p. 177.
78. IAI office, SOAS, Earthy file (hereafter IAI), "Earthy *Valenge Women*" (typed list), 1 September 1933.

tions of artistic design in domestic utensils, hairdressing, scarification, and "tatuing." Hunter comments with interest on a suggestion that a form of birth control is practiced, and declares the chapter on girls' initiation "the best account yet published" for the southeastern Bantu. While gently suggesting that "some slight modifications in the material [on religion] might have made it clearer," she commends Earthy's inclusion of valuable data on a woman's duties toward her brother's children and her active part in the rich ancestor cult; unusually full coverage of early childhood education (the review quotes material on the care of dolls with engaging relish); the extensive use of religious and other texts; and the impressive identification of plants used for medical and magical purposes. She quickly picked up the parallel Valenge/Pondo explanation of increased spirit possession as a result of contact with Europeans, Earthy seeing it as a "hysterical religious movement . . . due to disturbance . . . in tribal life." Hunter playfully concludes her raft of questions provoked by the "tantalising glimpses" of dance contests, with, "Would you tell me please," said Alice, a little timidly, "Why — ?"

This mild expression of frustration at explanatory gaps follows an observation of Earthy's focused approach that readers of *Reaction to Conquest* would recognize *its* author took care herself to avoid, Hunter being keen to foreground in her own monograph the textured detail of "culture contact": "Reference is frequently made to changes resulting from contact with Europeans. The country is under Portuguese administration, men go to Johannesburg to work for periods, money is the usual medium of *ukulobola*, there are Indian traders' stores throughout the country, manufactured goods are worn, roads have been built, and many customs are being dropped or modified. There is, however, no discussion of the part played by new elements such as school, or church, in the community."[79] Nevertheless, it is an unusually favorable review (and Hunter was not to know that Earthy originally seems to have included more of precisely this sort of material, but was forced to cut it, along with vernacular folk tales).[80]

---

79. M. Hunter, review of *Valenge Women*, by E. D. Earthy, *Africa* 7, no. 1 (January 1934): 110-12.

80. IAI, D. G. Brackett to D. Earthy, 20 February 1932, suggests there *was* a chapter on the Valenge in transition which, in IAI discussion with Audrey Richards, it had been felt was very interesting but at the same time did not "fit in with the rest of the book." They suggested she give it up and use it for an article in the *International Review of Missions* instead. Earlier correspondence about cuts focused on removing the large number of vernacular texts that Hoernlé and Haddon thought "rather [overweighted] the book"; plus the list of plants, which Earthy argued the government botanist in Pretoria said was of "outstanding scientific interest" and the keeper of botany at the Natural History Museum

Other fellow scientists were fulsome in their praise of *Valenge Women*. In *Man*, "T.C.Y." (presumably missionary anthropologist T. Cullen Young) described it as "a veritable storehouse of a book, and a very great piece of work," with three outstanding features: "Women's whole life" was "dealt with — intimate, domestic, economic — and full use . . . made throughout of native text in translation," while the illustrations were excellent and the "botanical identification of medicinal and ritual materials" invaluable. Possibly the "marshalling and co-ordination of knowledge" needed more time — and the book was incomprehensibly pricey, while the "brief concluding section on folk-lore, enigmas and proverbs" was "rather too slight to be useful."[81] In *Nature,* the way Dora's work complemented and extended Junod's was again stressed, with her accounts of marriage and puberty rituals most prized. The journal *East Africa* also lamented the price: "A book like this needs a wide, not an exclusive, circulation," but enthused how it "does help one realise how different is the angle when anthropology is studied by a woman among women."[82]

Both the quality Cape Town papers reviewed the book favorably, while South African novelist abroad, William Plomer, in a dual appraisal in the *Spectator,* commended Earthy ("She has written a monograph of which she may well be proud") and Alice Werner (for *Myths and Legends of the Bantu*) for their "warm hearts and clear heads," their "love of learning and a love of life." Plomer argued that "the scientist" had made the point of view of "the average Victorian missionary" (with his talk of "savages" and "heathen") "untenable if not contemptible. The educated man of today approaches primitive peoples not to teach them but to learn from them." He passed on Dora's summary of the people as "both religious and scientific, musical and artistic, . . . lazy only when bored, . . . unmoral but by no means incapable of making of their sex 'a spiritual achievement,'" and liking money and clothes. He con-

---

was also interested in. IAI, Brackett to Westermann, 7 February 1931; Earthy to Brackett, 2 October 1931. Articles by Earthy on some of the folktales appeared elsewhere, albeit a couple with an undue time lag: "A Chopi Love-Song and a Story in Ki-Lenge," *Africa* 4, no. 4 (October 1931): 475-82; "A Specimen of the Folklore of Gazaland," *Bantu Studies* 6, no. 3 (1932): 265-66; "An Analysis of Folktales of the Lenge, Portuguese East Africa," *Ethnos* 18, no. 1-2 (1953): 73-85; "A Probable Creation- and Flood-Myth in Portuguese East Africa," *Numen* 4, no. 3 (1957): 232-34; "Social Tension Themes in Folktales of the Lenge, Portuguese East Africa" (paper sent to XV Congrès International de Sociologie, Istanbul, 1952). The last two and several other articles referenced in this paper are held in Rhodes House, X1175, E. D. Earthy: Offprints of various articles, 1923-1957.

81. Review by T.C.Y., *Man*, July 1934. SOAS, IAI holds a batch of *Valenge Women* reviews.

82. IAI, *Nature,* 10 March 1934, p. 367; extract from *East Africa,* recd. 31 January 1934.

cluded by stressing the West's unexpected points of contact with Africa, even in the arts and literature.[83]

The *Times Literary Supplement* commended "without reserve a piece of research at once sound in the way of science and serviceable in the cause of humanity," stressing that, while "planned and executed in so scientific a spirit" as to be "quite objective in method and style," Dora's "straightforward account of the feminine aspect of this simple life" would "appeal by the sheer force of the intimacy and homeliness of its details to any reader whose interest in the human soul extends beyond the borders of his own parish." Earthy was praised for keeping her views on Christianizing and civilizing Africans separate from her anthropological findings, just as Junod kept his strong opinions on such matters "clean away, as in another compartment, from his descriptions of native life, which, nevertheless [was] interpreted as much from the inside as is possible by means of a disinterested introjection."[84]

In the same issue of *Africa* in which Earthy's book was reviewed by Hunter, there was also a statement by Edwin Smith, *the* international church statesman who embodied the new direction that Christianity and anthropology would increasingly take. Smith said the IAI originated in 1924-26 as a desire for more systematic study of African languages in order to facilitate African education "through the medium of their own forms of thought." This inaugurated "a new era of international co-operation in the service of Africa." From 1932, however, its research was geared more explicitly to practical purposes using scientific methods. The IAI's aim was to help toward Africa's orderly progress, its successful negotiation of potentially calamitous and disintegrative changes threatening its cohesion via "the interpenetration of African life by the ideas and economic forces of European civilization." To assist the development of "the anthropology of the changing native," which Malinowski was declaring the new priority, "the study of the diffusion of Western cultures among primitive peoples" was the goal, rather than simply "the reconstructive study," which Smith argued could be "inadequate if not misleading."[85] It was ironic that the IAI had just helped Earthy publish a detailed study that was open to criticism on precisely this count, but which had been cast largely in such "reconstructive" terms precisely in order to qualify as "proper" social anthropology.

The book's 1968 reissue by Cass was reviewed by John Blacking in 1974 in surprisingly similar terms to Hunter's. He concluded: "In spite of its inevita-

83. IAI, extracts from *Cape Argus*, recd. 31 January 1934; *Cape Times*, recd. 27 May 1934; *Spectator*, 8 December 1933.

84. IAI, *Times Literary Supplement*, 19 October 1933.

85. Edwin W. Smith, "The Story of the Institute: A Survey of Seven Years," *Africa* 7, no. 1 (January 1934): 1, 21, 20.

bly old-fashioned style and its lack of theoretical orientation, it might have qualified as compulsory reading for anthropological students of South-east Africa, and it contains rich, though regrettably inadequate, material for students of ethnoscience."[86]

But who remembers and uses the research of Dora Earthy today? My estimation a decade ago was unduly downbeat, perhaps, but reflected the neglect and ignorance of that time. The copy of *Valenge Women* in the School of Oriental and African Studies library was taken out only four times in the four decades following publication (1935, 1946, 1966, and 1971) — the book clearly did not become, Blacking's praise above notwithstanding, "compulsory reading for anthropological students of South-east Africa." *Valenge Women* was neither in the bibliography of Newitt's fairly recent tome on Mozambique nor, despite its pioneering female focus, does it appear in Henrietta Moore's feminist exploration of anthropology — though, understandably perhaps, it *is* listed by the *Oxford History*.[87]

However, more detailed recent research on southern Mozambique *has* taken Earthy's findings onboard. The work of the late David Webster obviously warrants further investigation,[88] but Sherilynn Young makes brief reference to Earthy for female agricultural labor, as do Vail and White for Chopi origins, music competitions, migrants, and chiefs, and Penvenne for the hinterland context of Lourenço Marques.[89] Patrick Harries refers at several points to Earthy's various publications (not just her book) in his opening chapter and discussions of migrant labor and mine culture,[90] while his recent

---

86. J. Blacking, review of Cass 1968 reprint of *Valenge Women*, by E. D. Earthy, *African Studies* 33, no. 1 (1974): 65-66.

87. Malyn Newitt, *A History of Mozambique* (London, 1995); Henrietta Moore, *Feminism and Anthropology* (Oxford, 1988); Monica Wilson and Leonard Thompson, eds., *The Oxford History of South Africa*, vol. 1, *South Africa to 1870* (Oxford, 1969).

88. David J. Webster, "Kinship and Cooperation: Agnation, Alternative Structures, and the Individual in Chopi Society" (Ph.D. diss., Rhodes University, 1975), and "Migrant Labour, Social Formations, and the Proletarianization of the Chopi of Southern Mozambique," *Africa Perspective* 1 (1978).

89. Sherilynn Young, "Fertility and Famine: Women's Agricultural History in Southern Mozambique," in *The Roots of Rural Poverty in Central and Southern Africa*, ed. R. Palmer and N. Parsons (London, 1977), nn. 40-42, 45; Leroy Vail and Landeg White, "The Development of Forms: The Chopi *Migodo*," in *Power and the Praise Poem: Southern African Voices in History* (Charlottesville, Va., 1991), nn. 4, 52, 54, 58; Jeanne M. Penvenne, *African Workers and Colonial Racism: Mozambican Strategies and Struggles in Lourenco Marques, 1877-1962* (Portsmouth, N.H., 1995), chapter 1, nn. 21, 33.

90. Patrick Harries, *Work, Culture, and Identity: Migrant Laborers in Mozambique and South Africa, c. 1860-1910* (Portsmouth, N.H., 1994), chapter 1, nn. 6, 22, 40; chapter 6, nn. 124, 129, 150, 162, 185, 186, 188, 189; chapter 8, nn. 34, 86.

book on Junod lists her monograph in the bibliography and contains four references to her in the index.[91] She is, however, absent from the index of the important recent collection on missions and empire (though perhaps understandably, as her prominence came from work outside Britain's direct realm).[92] Yet she may be unique as a female missionary anthropologist writing in scholarly detail on the women of a non-Western society before the Second World War.

Alcinda Honwana, a Mozambican anthropologist who herself did fieldwork in the south of the country in the late 1980s and early 1990s, has recently paid generous tribute to the rich detail and "extraordinary" quality of the information presented in *Valenge Women* (while critiquing its omissions on the impact of migrant labor and Christian conversion on gender relations). She suggests that "it provides a useful starting point for any anthropological research project in the region" — but offers no documentation that it has indeed done so, for herself or others.[93] The scholar of Mozambique — and women — who has really finally used Earthy to good effect is Kathie Sheldon; she cited Earthy five times in her index, and listed eleven articles plus the book in her bibliography.[94]

The 1930s, as is well known, was something of a heyday for women anthropologists.[95] But Dora Earthy's early start, in the closing stages of the First World War, put her over a decade in advance of Malinowski's women students — Monica Hunter, Hilda Kuper, and Audrey Richards. Dora Earthy is not the only neglected early female pioneer in the scientific study of southern African society. Hansi Pollak and Erika Theron should have their work from the 1930s published. Even the pivotal impact on Hilda Kuper, Max Gluckman, Isaac Schapera, Eileen Krige, and Ellen Hellmann of the gifted Winifred Hoernlé — so underplayed in Adam Kuper's otherwise invaluable account[96] — was only fairly recently being rediscovered.[97] Yet Dora Earthy had eleven

---

91. Patrick Harries, *Butterflies and Barbarians: Swiss Missionaries and Systems of Knowledge in South-East Africa* (Oxford, 2007).

92. Etherington, *Missions and Empire*. However, her 1926 *IRM* article is footnoted (p. 251 n. 23) by Harries, "Anthropology."

93. Alcinda Honwana, draft introduction (to projected IAI reprint of *Valenge Women*, 1998).

94. Kathleen Sheldon, *Pounders of Grain: A History of Women, Work, and Politics in Mozambique* (Portsmouth, N.H., 2002), pp. 280, 305.

95. See D. Gaitskell, introduction to special issue on women in southern Africa, *Journal of Southern African Studies* 10, no. 1 (1983).

96. Kuper, *Anthropology and Anthropologists*.

97. See Hoernlé, *The Social Organization of the Nama and Other Essays*; Carstens, Klinghardt, and West, *Trails in the Thirstland*, especially the introduction; Hilda Kuper,

publications, one of them a book, listed in Schapera's bibliography,[98] to Hoernlé's ten (although included in the latter were two substantial chapters in the Schapera landmark volume *Western Civilization and the Natives of South Africa*)![99]

Dora Earthy's personal story raises larger questions about the shifting relations between Christian missions and scientific anthropology in the early twentieth century, as well as issues of gender and power in the historical sociology of knowledge. Whose research gets remembered and publicized, and why? What advantages for individual scholarship and career paths were there to studying peoples in the *British* (rather than Portuguese) African empire? How are scientific canons created and intellectual pantheons assembled, and which scholars get sidelined in the process? How significant is the impact of such ebbs and flows in scientific endeavor on the actual fortunes of the societies and peoples being analyzed? And how much amnesia is there in mission circles about outstanding women? Let us remember that the SPG *did* say to Dora's brother, on her death, after paying tribute to Dora's "true humility and humour," that they had seldom, if ever, had a missionary "of such real scholarly ability."[100]

Mission Theology from Anthropology

But it would be a shame to end by bewailing Dora Earthy's relative obscurity. Far more important, in a consideration of "the secular in the spiritual," is the

---

"Function, History, Biography: Reflections on Fifty Years in the British Anthropological Tradition," in *Functionalism Historicized: Essays in British Social Anthropology*, ed. G. W. Stocking (Madison, 1984). The sparkling array of key articles by Hoernlé's former students in their 1935 *Bantu Studies* tribute issue for her fiftieth birthday confirms the extent of the discipline's debt to this "brilliant, inspiring, and warm-hearted teacher." See M. Gluckman and I. Schapera, "Dr. Winifred Hoernlé: An Appreciation," *Africa* 30 (1958): 262.

98. I. Schapera, comp., *Select Bibliography on South African Native Life and Problems* (London, 1941).

99. On Hoernlé's various articles and book chapters, see Hammond Tooke, *Imperfect Interpreters*, p. 38: "The work of a clear thinker and lucid writer, with a strong bent for synthesis, these papers are all important milestones in the development of a comparative ethnography." A gifted teacher, Hoernlé was also "blessed with outstanding students" who went on to distinguished careers in international anthropology. Dora had no opportunity to nurture younger scholars and acolytes.

100. USPG, Dossier 2640, Secretary for Women Candidates to G. Earthy, 19 August 1960.

spiritual in the secular — the way in which Dora built a new theology of mission on her anthropological findings, in almost as pioneering a manner (for a *woman* missionary, certainly) as her detailed recording of key aspects of the lives of Valenge women and girls.

It is frustratingly hard to discover much about Dora's theological framework and presuppositions when she first went to Africa, and thus how much and in what ways they changed as she moved from the Transvaal to Mozambique. While explicitly spiritual feedback from some of her contemporaries survives, we have none of Dora's replies to the standard doctrinal questions put to candidates. "Her application form is [in the personal file], with the questions printed at the bottom and the instruction to write the answers on a separate sheet of paper. Either Dora Earthy's answers have been lost or she never answered the questions."[101] Tantalizingly, the questions she was posed back in 1910 were:

> Why do you consider you are called by God to be a missionary?
> What considerations have led you to offer yourself to this Society?
> What are the fundamental doctrines of the Christian Faith?
> State briefly what you understand by a) Sin b) The Atonement c) The Work of the Holy Spirit d) The Church e) The Sacraments.
> What has been your plan with regard to Bible Study?
> Name books you have read on a) The Bible b) The Prayer Book c) Christian Doctrine d) Church History.

Instead, we only know what church work Dora had mostly been doing before offering to SPG: thirteen years of Sunday school teaching (she went to church in Wimbledon), including a lot of visiting the children's homes, and playing the harmonium or piano. She had also distributed collection boxes for the South London Church Fund for three years (a task requiring great persistence, a local priest commented), and had given two lantern lectures to children in the Band of Hope. She was not a member of the Missionary Preparation Union, but had gone to a Study Band on China shortly before applying to SPG. Another clergyman testified that she was "always in deadly earnest" and not daunted by difficulties, though her eagerness not to be left out and to take part in every effort to help others "often caused her to do more than her time and strength really permitted." Once Dora got over her shyness and fear of doing the wrong thing when at the missionary training home in Wandsworth for a year prior to going to Africa, they found her very conscien-

---

101. E-mail, Wakeling to author, 2 December 2009.

tious and sincere, "Giving herself very readily to study," and the most missionary-hearted of the students.[102]

At work in the Transvaal mission field, Dora rarely offered doctrinal reflections or comments on spiritual behavior. Rather, she might foreground the complicated travel arrangements by train, foot, and ox wagon to visit scattered members of their Women's Help Society (WHS),[103] even though such trips were often a "delightful adventure."[104] She might feature the moral struggles of the mothers joining up not to brew beer or let their children go to tempting "heathen" dances, but instead to contribute regularly to the church and qualify to wear the WHS cross.[105] Once, though, when (unexpectedly) conducting a rural all-night service, Dora betrayed her spiritual preferences in her gratitude that the ten women from Boksburg accompanying her, when asked to speak in turn about their weekly prayer meetings and "all the advantages" of WHS, "really spoke very nicely & sensibly. . . . I am thankful to say there was no 'emotionalism' at all. All the service was quiet & restrained."[106] Unusually, on another occasion (after more accounts of intrepid visits, including walking for eight miles along a railway track in the dark because the goods train had been canceled), Dora assured Miss Saunders that "It is very necessary that native women should be taught the practice of Sacramental confession. Their idea of sin is so very vague. But the women are very anxious to do the right thing."[107]

Studying the religious beliefs of the local women in Mozambique led to much more coherent attempts to see how traditional practices and Christianity might interact. It is unclear how much Dora was aware of the ways in which international mission thinking about other faiths was changing in her own time, just as she set out for Johannesburg. The World Missionary Conference in Edinburgh in 1910 (despite its marginalization of Africa) particularly signaled this shift. Cracknell argues that replies from serving missionaries to questions from Commission IV, "The Missionary Message in Relation to Non-Christian Religions," reveal a greater attitude of sympathy and respect toward other religions than harsh condemnation of heathen idolatry. Those

---

102. USPG, London, Dossier 2640, references from H. Lovell Clarke, 22 January 1910; A. D. Ottaway, 21 January 1910; and M. R. Kirkpatrick, Summer and December 1910.

103. USPG, CWW, Earthy to Miss Saunders, 8 June 1915.

104. USPG, CWW, Earthy to Miss Saunders, 9 January 1914.

105. USPG, CWW, Earthy to Miss Gurney, 21 December 1915; USPG, E, Earthy, March 1915, on how "very bad" it was for "our Church girls to be the constant witnesses of the drinking, swearing and fighting . . . among the semi-heathen in the location."

106. USPG, CWW, Earthy to Miss Gurney, 13 April 1912.

107. USPG, CWW, Earthy to Miss Saunders, 31 May 1916.

who castigate the conference for a low estimation of African traditional religion are taken to task by Friesen, who insists missionaries displayed a variety of models of theological understanding of the relationship of "tribal" religion to Christianity.[108] Yet Stanley's authoritative overview makes clear that the few missionaries from Africa who were consulted did not find the points of contact with Christianity or preparation for it in traditional religion that "more liberal missionaries were eagerly identifying in Hinduism." Indeed, they often disputed the existence of either a religious system or a body of orthodox belief — rather, communal ritual took priority. Thus the much-studied Commission IV report "strained the evidence in its anxiety to accommodate Africa missionaries" into its "dominating theological paradigm which wished to show that, whatever errors needed correction by the light of the gospel, 'all that was noblest in the old religions was fulfilled by Christ.'"[109] So "fulfillment" theology was spreading — but not easily to Africa.

Nevertheless, one of the key outcomes of the conference, the *International Review of Missions (IRM)* (founded in 1912 by J. H. Oldham, so influential at Edinburgh and beyond), "saw anthropology as a tool that would enable missionaries to understand the cultures, and come to love the people to whom they had been assigned by their calling."[110] Around the time of Dora's first article for *IRM*, very much seeking to build on "points of contact" between two religions,[111] the journal published three others on similar lines from male missionaries, since a "growing number of missionaries believed that, through the 'retention and sublimation' of indigenous cultural practices, they could construct a form of Christianity adapted to the needs of local peoples."[112] Indeed, the conference at Le Zoute in Belgium the same year (1926), organized by the International Missionary Council (yet another — delayed — offshoot of Edinburgh 1910), asked for a reconsideration of mission attitudes "towards

---

108. K. Cracknell, *Justice, Courtesy, and Love: Theologians and Missionaries Encountering World Religions, 1846-1914* (London, 1995), and J. S. Friesen, *Missionary Responses to Tribal Religions at Edinburgh, 1910* (New York, 1996), as cited in B. Stanley, "Church, State and the Hierarchy of 'Civilization': The Making of the Commission VII Report, 'Missionaries and Governments,' Edinburgh 1910" (North Atlantic Missiology Project Consultation paper, April 1998), p. 1.

109. Brian Stanley, *The World Missionary Conference, Edinburgh 1910* (Grand Rapids and Cambridge, 2009), pp. 243, 240.

110. Harries, "Anthropology," p. 246.

111. See n. 62 above.

112. Harries, "Anthropology," p. 251, and n. 23, for W. Vincent Lucas, "The Educational Value of Initiatory Rites," and J. Raum, "Christianity and African Puberty Rites," both in *IRM* 16 (1927): 192-98, 581-91; W. C. Willoughby, "Building the African Church," *IRM* 15 (1926): 450-56.

some aspects of the African's life, so that the Church might become more deeply rooted in the nature of the people — more truly African."[113]

In the mid-1930s, in her second *IRM* article, Dora Earthy was still doing anthropology with at least one eye on its Christian implications. She seemed to be catching the wave of the time in her very positive and inclusive 1933 assertion in her monograph of the potential for adapting Valenge ritual to the detailed progress believers made through the catechumenate, baptism, and Christian marriage. She was sure from her own long experience among the Lenge of their deep understanding and acceptance of notions of sin, the practice of confession, the ceremony of confirmation, Christ's atoning sacrifice, and remembrance of the dead. She even returned to her (1926) metaphor of the bridge, but in a more encompassing fashion, suggesting that the cultural resources of pagan society might also be reaching across the gap: "Between African paganism and Christianity there is a gulf, the spiritual counterpart of the Victoria Falls. Only the Master Architect and Builder can bridge that gulf, but His workmen can help by finding the materials wherewith to build the bridge and span the gulf, under His direction. Tribes and classes of people have each their own contribution to bring."[114]

The Christian message had to be made "both intelligible and welcome to those to whom it is taken," which required the church to be as mobile and adaptable as the early church had been. Anglicanism would not "fulfil all an African's religious needs" if the "Anglo-Saxon temperament" were too "dominant" (her concerns two decades earlier for restraint and no emotionalism seem to have ebbed!); while when Nonconformity banished all ritual, it could not "appeal to a race to which ritual has been the breath of life."[115] By comparison with her concern in 1916 at the women's "very vague" sense of sin, Dora voiced now a much more understanding view of the communalism that gave meaning to sin (as upsetting the equilibrium of communal life) and conceded far more warmly, "The sense of sin is something which has always required education, even among Christians."[116] Ancestral spirits were a conception linking the dead to the living "in the same [unproblematic] way" as the church at rest was linked with the church militant. There was "nothing inherently difficult" to an African in the year's teaching necessary for catechumens

---

113. Edwin Smith, *The Christian Mission in Africa* (his account of the conference), p. 106, as quoted in W. John Young, *The Quiet Wise Spirit: Edwin W. Smith, 1976-1957, and Africa* (Peterborough, 2002), p. 123.

114. E. D. Earthy, "An African Tribe in Transition from Paganism to Christianity," *IRM* 22 (1933): 367.

115. Earthy, "African Tribe in Transition," pp. 367-68.

116. Earthy, "African Tribe in Transition," p. 370.

— he "readily" absorbed teaching on prayer, and found baptism most appealing if he wished to be a Christian: it was "his chief aim in life," and might sublimate some of his old *rites de passage.* Initiation, while encompassing much that "Christians must deplore," could help the Lenge understand their initiation into the church, while "the fundamental idea of the need for moral or rather sex education for the young people" had "much to commend it."[117]

Unlike Miss Saunders at the turn of the century, Dora had no problem with *lobola* as "sacramental," an "outward and visible sign" of the solemnity of marriage, existing alongside church blessing. The complexities of justice for widows were also explored, something of which she had much experience. The positive spin on the offerings of conventional High Church Anglicanism continued — the sacrament of penance was found a great help, and "large numbers" came to the priest to confess before the church festivals; teaching about confirmation was "well received and understood," with the "Holy Spirit's coming at baptism to give life and at confirmation to bestow strength" welcomed by a people who put "life and strength in the forefront of things prayed for to the ancestral spirits." Valenge church members understood well "the solemnity and sacredness of the holy eucharist; all the more because of their own ceremonial meals," while the "sacrificial side of the Atonement could never be too much stressed to an African," since sacrifice was "of the essence of their old religion." Many Lenge were finding the efficacy of "the Great Sacrifice in which types and shadows have their ending." The doctrine of the communion of saints should encompass even heathen ancestors — she had "found African women in a Bible class extremely interested" in the fact that Jesus went to preach to the souls in prison (1 Pet. 3:19), and they were glad they might "say a prayer for (although not to) their heathen ancestors." Christians were evolving new forms of hut blessings by the church or priestly exorcism of evil spirits via a special kraal service.[118]

Overall, she was confident that "Belief is easy to most Africans," while drily observing, "The difficulty is to show forth that belief in daily life (this difficulty is, of course, not confined to Africans)." The upshot was that the "pagan religion of the Valenge" was "suffering a change 'into something rich and strange' under the influences of Christianity"[119] — but at every point, she had been suggesting, could build on, and be shot through with meaning from, their prior beliefs and practices.

---

117. Earthy, "African Tribe in Transition," p. 371.
118. Earthy, "African Tribe in Transition," pp. 372-76.
119. Earthy, "African Tribe in Transition," pp. 375-76.

Conclusion

Three areas of broader significance, relating to gender, transnationalism, and mission theology, stand out in this exploration of the dealings of a serving woman missionary with the beginnings of social anthropology in South Africa. First, Dora Earthy was a pioneer of both female fieldwork and female subject-matter in anthropology. Both of these aspects of her monograph merit acknowledgment. Lyn Schumaker has commented recently that, in many ways, "the history of anthropology in the twentieth century has been the story of women's entry into the discipline and the interaction of this phenomenon with anthropology's defining methodological moment, the emergence of participant-observation fieldwork." While the latter got a lot of attention "thanks to Malinowski's talent for self-promotion," the "revolution in anthropology's self-perception effected through the inclusion of women proceeded much more quietly," although she argues that "women have profoundly changed the discipline's identity," as well as its trajectory and valuation of fieldwork in ways still to be properly analyzed historically.[120] Perhaps the projected second reissue of Earthy's monograph will help remedy the earlier disadvantages of her location in a non-British territory and on the fringes of academia, and reinstate her as a female pioneer fairly well networked into patronage relationships and major journals of the 1920s in South Africa, a woman who published more anthropological scholarship at the time than did Winifred Hoernlé, and hoped on retirement from the mission in 1931 to return to South Africa for a government post in anthropological research.[121]

In addition, Dora Earthy was plugged into more than merely South African webs of scholarly communication. Helen Tilley's recent exploration of African anthropology and the politics of knowledge particularly draws attention to transnational networks, institutions, and exchange, as well as the proliferation of research institutes and scholarly "clearinghouses" in Europe and Africa influencing "not only anthropology, but also wider intellectual and administrative debates."[122] Earthy's trajectory exemplifies these phenomena. Dora was enthused by the anthropological injunctions of a missionary to India, then advised by a South African scholar and her British mentor in Cambridge, while living in a Portuguese territory where a Swiss missionary was the most authoritative anthropologist. She studied at a Cape Town University

---

120. Lyn Schumaker, "Women in the Field in the Twentieth Century: Revolution, Involution, Devolution?" in *A New History of Anthropology*, p. 278.

121. See note pinned on Earthy's application form in USPG, London, Dossier 2640.

122. Helen Tilley, "Introduction: Africa, Imperialism, and Anthropology," in *Ordering Africa*, p. 26.

summer school, was funded by Wits, and had her work published not only in three South African scholarly journals but also in the journals of the International African Institute and the International Missionary Council, while her involvement with Save the Children in the 1930s illustrated how the new international philanthropy drew on and valued both her missionary experience and her anthropological skills.

Finally, beyond its relevance to thinking about women and anthropology, and the significance of transnational academic connections, Earthy's scholarship aimed to go full circle — from spiritual to secular and back to spiritual once more. Mission needs compelled an understanding of the culture of those one was trying to reach; with that new knowledge, the missionary could transform theological approaches. Understanding local customs in relation to the African church (to paraphrase Dora's *IRM* article titles) could enable the missionary to help Africans make the necessary "transition from paganism to Christianity." Anthropology should enlighten mission theology and practice, to build up the church in Africa, which remained her prime goal.

SELECT BIBLIOGRAPHY

Bank, Andrew. "The 'Intimate Politics' of Fieldwork: Monica Hunter and Her African Assistants, Pondoland and the Eastern Cape, 1931-1932." *Journal of Southern African Studies* 34, no. 3 (2008).

Carstens, Peter, G. Klinghardt, and Martin West, eds. *Trails in the Thirstland: The Anthropological Field Diaries of Winifred Hoernlé*. Cape Town, 1987.

Earthy, E. Dora. "An African Tribe in Transition from Paganism to Christianity." *International Review of Missions* 22 (1933).

———. *Valenge Women: The Social and Economic Life of the Valenge Women of Portuguese East Africa; An Ethnographic Study*. London, 1933.

Gaitskell, Deborah. "Mission by Other Means? Dora Earthy and the Save the Children Fund in the 1930s." In *Protestant Missions and Local Encounters in the Nineteenth and Twentieth Centuries: Unto the Ends of the World*, edited by Hilde Nielssen, Inger Marie Okkenhaug, and Karina Hestad Skeie. Leiden and Boston: Brill, 2011.

Hammond Tooke, W. D. *Imperfect Interpreters: South Africa's Anthropologists, 1920-1990*. Johannesburg, 1997.

Harries, Patrick. "Anthropology." In *Missions and Empire*, edited by Norman Etherington. Oxford, 2005.

———. *Work, Culture, and Identity: Migrant Laborers in Mozambique and South Africa, c. 1860-1910*. Portsmouth, N.H., 1994.

Hoernlé, Winifred. *The Social Organization of the Nama and Other Essays*. Edited by Peter Carstens. Johannesburg, 1985.

Kuklick, Henrika. "The British Tradition." In *A New History of Anthropology*, edited by Henrika Kuklick. Malden, Mass., Oxford, and Carlton, Australia, 2008.

———. *The Savage Within: The Social History of British Anthropology*. Cambridge, 1991.

Kuper, Adam. *Anthropology and Anthropologists: The Modern British School*. 3rd ed. London, 1996.

Saúte, Alda Romão. "The African Mission Encounter and Education in Mozambique: The Anglican Mission of Santo Agostinho — Maciene, 1926/8–1974." Ph.D. diss., University of Minnesota, 2000.

Schumaker, Lyn. "Women in the Field in the Twentieth Century: Revolution, Involution, Devolution?" In *A New History of Anthropology*, edited by Henrika Kuklick. Malden, Mass., Oxford, and Carlton, Australia, 2008.

Sheldon, Kathleen. *Pounders of Grain: A History of Women, Work, and Politics in Mozambique*. Portsmouth, N.H., 2002.

Stevenson, Mrs. [Margaret] Sinclair. "The Study of Anthropology on the Mission Field." *International Review of Missions* 9 (1920).

Tilley, Helen, with Robert Gordon, eds. *Ordering Africa: Anthropology, European Imperialism, and the Politics of Knowledge*. Manchester and New York, 2007.

CHAPTER 7

Ideology in Missionary Scholarly Knowledge in Belgian Congo: Aequatoria, Centre de recherches africanistes; The Mission Station of Bamanya (RDC), 1937-2007

HONORÉ VINCK

The Aequatoria Center, situated at Bamanya near Mbandaka (Democratic Republic of the Congo), was founded in 1937 with the intention of arriving at a comprehensive understanding of the language, history, and culture of the local people (Mongo). Mbandaka (until 1969, Coquilhatville) is located at the intersection of the geographical equator and the Congo River. Between 1937 and 1962, the Aequatoria Center was the source of a host of publications, expressing vanguard ideas on the detrimental effects of colonization on local society. Magazines and pamphlets published by Catholic missionaries, such as *La Page Chrétienne, Pax,* and the scholarly journal *Aequatoria*[1] with an international audience (associated with a research library), were destined for a European readership. Others, such as *Le Coq Chante, Etsiko,* and *Lokole Lokiso,* were printed in the Lomongo language and were intended for Congolese readers. These local publications served to popularize the ideas of the leading figures in the Aequatoria Center, with the very active collaboration of important Congolese. The Center's outlook was dominated by two exceptional figures, Gustaaf Hulstaert (1900-1990) and Edmond Boelaert (1899-1966),[2] who attracted a large group of sympathizers and collaborators of vari-

1. *Aequatoria* was published from 1937 to 1962 and relaunched in 1980 as *Annales Aequatoria*. In both series the Mongo people are a particular concern.

2. Numerous biographical notices have been published on Gustaaf Hulstaert since his death. The most important are H. Vinck, "In Memoriam Gustave Hulstaert," *Annales Aequatoria* 12 (1991): 7-76; H. Vinck, "Gustaaf Hulstaert: Missie en wetenschap," *Land van*

ous backgrounds. A large number of them, published in *Aequatoria*, acting as a "colonial conscience." Beside missionaries, other groups who participated were magistrates, then administrators, and finally colonialists. With the approach of independence, some *évolués* published in the journal. From 1947 to 1958 the journal was distributed to all 250 districts and territories of the colony, to all the public libraries, and to the offices of the civil service; a great number went to Catholic mission stations and some went to Protestant mission stations. The philosophical and political position of all these publications was clear: civilization and evangelization had to be based on a rigorous respect of the local people, their political and social structures, their languages and cultures. This *indigéniste*[3] stance can be called, with the benefit of more than a half-century of hindsight, the "School of Coquilhatville." This chapter examines the ideological roots of the protagonists, Hulstaert and Boelaert, and of their *indigéniste* philosophy. It considers how they were shaped by Flemish nationalism, and it explores the sources of their compassion for the victims of colonialism. The intention is to reveal the forces that impelled these missionaries into an exceptional activism.

The Editors, Contributors, and Critics

As editors of the *Aequatoria* journal, Edmond Boelaert and Gustaaf Hulstaert, both Catholic priests in the Congregation of the Missionaries of the Sacred Heart (MSC), were central to debates on colonial policy. Although neither had been formally trained in Belgian colonial institutions,[4] their research and publications met high scholarly standards. Yet, scientific knowledge was never their final goal: they always remained missionaries and viewed research as a means to improve their missionary praxis. In the colonial era, their work had a real but limited influence on colonial practices. Their legacy

---

Beveren 49 (2006): 202-33. For literature on Edmond Boelaert, see M. Storme, *Bulletin des Séances de l'Académie Royale des Sciences d'Outre-Mer* (1967), pp. 167-92; G. Hulstaert, *Biographie belge d'Outre-Mer* (1973), VII A., pp. 53-58; and H. Vinck, "Edmond Boelaert," in *International Dictionary of Anthropologists*, ed. C. Winters (New York, 1991), pp. 69-70.

3. The French word *indigéniste* was used by the protagonists as a term for characterizing their attitude and action in favor of Africans and African culture. Below, I use translations such as "indigenist" and "indigeneity" *(indigénisme)*.

4. Colonial policy was part of the curriculum in the colonial institutes in Belgium. It included the following: colonial deontology, ethnography, and languages of the Congo; customary law and colonial legislation; comparative methods of colonization; administrative organization; and the history of Belgian colonization.

includes an enormous number of publications, constituting a lasting contribution to the present-day understanding of the language and literature of the Mongo people and of Bantu linguistics in general. They were both members of prestigious institutions of colonial affairs. In Belgium they participated in the Colonial Academy in Brussels and in the Commission for African Linguistics in Tervuren (Musée Royal du Congo belge). Hulstaert was, moreover, a member of the Colonial Commission pour la Protection des Indigènes (1953-60), established in the Congo, and a consultative member of the Institute of Scientific Research in Central Africa (IRSAC). He was awarded a Doctorate Honoris Causa by the Universities of Mainz (1972) and Zaïre (1973) for his scholarly publications on Bantu linguistics and ethnological fieldwork. Boelaert was also a member of the Council of the Equateur Province, a body that assisted the governor.

The great impetus came from Father Gustaaf Hulstaert, who lived and worked in the Congo from 1925 to 1990 and acquired an encyclopedic knowledge of the region's language, people, and natural history. His extreme curiosity pushed him to scrutinize and study every aspect of the human and natural environment. He was consecutively headmaster (1927-34), inspector for the diocesan schools, and finally local superior of his missionary association, from 1936 to 1946. In 1931 he started publishing on Congolese affairs. Father Hulstaert had a Catholic vision of the world but combined this with certain humanist ideas. He preferred to engage with the broader cultural, social, and political issues debated in Western academic circles in the thirties such as democracy, the characteristics of Western civilization, and the legitimacy of colonization. The major influence on his early ideas came from Catholic authors such as Léon Bloy, Jacques Maritain, Daniel Rops, Alexis Carrel, Georges Bernanos, Jacques Leclercq, Gilbert Keith Chesterton, Arthur Beales, and a few others like Christopher Dawson, Constantin Virgil Gheorghiu, and Oswald Spengler. During that same period, Hulstaert thought he was progressive and even in the vanguard: "Do you know," he wrote to Mgr. Égide De Boeck, the bishop of Lisala, an adjacent town, "that I adhere to modern and revolutionary tendencies that in the eyes of some, seem to touch on heresy?"[5] Although this chapter focuses on Hulstaert's contribution to the disciplines of history, ethnography, and customary law, he made considerable contributions to other areas of secular knowledge such as zoology and botany, mostly related to the equatorial forest.[6]

---

5. Letter from 7 June 1941. H. Vinck, "Correspondance G. Hulstaert–E. De Boeck," *Annales Aequatoria* 15 (1994).

6. Entomology was his first love. The list of his early publications on this subject is im-

Edmond Boelaert was active in the Belgian Congo from September 1930 to September 1954 as a teacher at the junior seminary at Bokuma and as a "traveling father." At the same time, he took charge of the Catholic Action Movement and supervised the mission's printing office at Coquilhatville. He was also a talented author, writing plays and poems. He deserves special recognition for his popular works on the language, the history, and the customs of the Mongo people. His name will remain linked with the study, translation, and publication of the national epic of the Mongo, *Nsong'a Lianja*.[7] Boelaert belonged to the radical wing of the Flemish nationalist movement. In the report marking the end of his studies for the priesthood, the superior concluded that "he is very radical on the Flemish question."[8] Later on he manifested a radical pacifism that led him to refuse military service. He justified his stance with a six-page statement to the military authorities in Congo, arguing that he was "convinced that military service is against natural law."[9] In Congo Boelaert was committed to defending native peoples against colonial conditions, especially the problems brought about by the uprooting of people through obligatory labor laws and industrialization, which caused several population groups to die out.[10] He published about twenty articles on depop-

---

pressive: 11 in 1923, 9 in 1924, 1 in 1925, and 1 in 1926; all told, 130 pages. In 1926 appeared a tablet of 13 pages and in 1931 a book of 212 pages: *Lepidoptera rhopalocera. Fam. Danaididae. Subfam. Danaididae + Tellervinae,* Tervuren, Genera insectorum, fasc. 193. Missionaries from New Guinea and Indonesia sent him specimens of butterflies. He placed Congolese specimens in the Musée Royal du Congo Belge in Tervuren. In the Congo, Hulstaert recorded in small black pocketbooks, notes on everything that lived and moved around him. Much of this evidence came from native informants encountered during his itineration. He developed an intense correspondence with specialized institutions: Institut pour l'étude agronomique du Congo (INEAC) in Yangambo, the Botanical Gardens in Eala and Kisantu, the Botanical Gardens in Meise and Brussels, and the botanical and zoological section of the Tervuren Museum. He sent thousands of specimens for determination that today constitute an herbarium of several hundred plants. He shared his knowledge with the pupils, for in 1933 his first reader contained thirty-nine lessons on the fauna and the flora of the equatorial forest. In 1966 he published a remarkable synthesis: *Notes de botanique Mongo,* Sciences naturelles et médicales, n.s., XV-3 (Brussels, Académie Royale des Sciences d'Outre-Mer).

7. E. Boelaert, "Nsong'a Lianja. L'épopée nationale des Nkundo," *Aequatoria* (Coquilhatville) 12 (1949): 1-76.

8. Verslagen over de scholastieken. Archief MSC (Congregation of the Missionaries of the Sacred Heart) Borgerhout, Dossier Scholastikaat Leuven.

9. Undated and unmarked document, presumably written by Boelaert on 2 October 1940 to De Vré. Archief MSC, Borgerhout, Belgium, Boelaert Papers.

10. E. Boelaert, "Ontvolking door kolonisatie?" *Aequatoria* 8, no. 3 (1945): 92-94; Boelaert, "Het ontvolkingsvraagstuk door de industrie in Afrika," *19e Nederlandse*

ulation and declining birthrate in the colony. A second area of concern was the legislation on the land rights of the natives.[11]

Hulstaert and Boelaert were not the only MSC missionaries devoted to researching and publishing on what they defined as the Mongo culture. Father Joris Van Avermaet (1907-86) also participated as the director of the junior seminary at Bokuma and published on the making of a Lomongo school terminology for use in primary and secondary levels. Albert De Rop (1912-80) was awarded the first doctorate in African linguistics at Louvain University in 1954 and became in 1957 a professor at the newly founded Lovanium University at Léopoldville. Frans Maes (1922-2005) was also important. He had studied pedagogical sciences at the University of Leuven and, upon arrival in the Congo in 1948, immediately started to investigate the local school system. He also edited a new style of schoolbook, drawing upon local data, and elaborated an African language terminology for biology and zoology teaching. In addition, he produced learned publications on African education.[12] Gust Wauters (1898-1950) prepared a survey on the Pygmies of the Mongo region and left a valuable manuscript[13] on this subject.[14] In the sphere of the arts, Alfons Walschap (1903-38), Paul Jans (1886-1962), and Jules De Knop (1906-85) broke new ground in the theory and application of Bantu church music.[15] Walschap was also well known for his novels about the destructive effects of Western culture.[16] Jos Moeyens (1899-1955), Petrus Vertenten (1884-1946),[17] and Jos Yernaux (1882-1986) were recognized and found inspiration as portrait and landscape painters of indigenous subjects.[18]

The "Aequatoria philosophy" expanded on and merged with existing ten-

---

Missiologische week (Nijmegen), 1948, pp. 80-83; Nancy Rose Hunt, "Rewriting the Soul in a Flemish Congo," *Past and Present* 198 (February 2008): 185-215.

11. E. Boelaert, *L'Etat Indépendant et les terres indigènes,* Mémoires de la Classe des Sciences morales et politiques, Nouvelle série, Tome 5, fascicule 4 (Brussels, Académie Royale des Sciences Coloniales, 1956).

12. H. Vinck, "In Memoriam Frans Maes," *Annales Aequatoria* 26 (2005): 503-7.

13. Archives Aequatoria, Bamanya, Box 120, Envelope 1; Microfiches 5/113-119.

14. H. Vinck, "Gust Wauters, Bio-bibliographie," *Annales Aequatoria,* 1980, pp. 489-90.

15. P. Jans, "Essai de musique religieuse pour indigènes dans le Vicariat Apostolique de Coquilhatville," *Aequatoria* 19, no. 1 (1956): 1 16, 37 43.

16. H. Vinck, "Alfons Walschap. Le convertisseur et le converti," in *Approche du roman et du théâtre missionnaires,* ed. Pierre Halen, Collection: Recherches en Littérature et Spiritualité, no. 11 (Bern, 2006), pp. 191-200.

17. His paintings and drawings are preserved in the Koninklijk Instituut voor de Tropen in Amsterdam. Yernaux's paintings are preserved in the Archive of the Missionaries of the Sacred Heart in Borgerhout (Belgium).

18. H. Vinck, "Les tableaux des missionnaires-peintres coloniaux: Petrus Vertenten, Jos Yernaux, Raymond Carlé, Edward Van Goethem," *Annales Aequatoria* 22 (2001): 435-36.

dencies in the Belgian colony. Placide Tempels first discussed many of the ideas in his *Bantu Philosophy* with Hulstaert, and he published his introductory chapter in *Aequatoria* in 1944. These names could be supplemented with a host of less famous but significant scholars who engaged with missionary and colonial issues in *Aequatoria*, such as Basiel Tanghe, the *indigéniste* bishop of Molegbe, one of the pioneers of the study of the peoples of the Ubangi, and Jozef Van Wing, the eminent Jesuit of the *Etudes Bakongo*, both of whom were great allies of Hulstaert.

There were not only supporters and associates. Among the fiercest critics of the School of Coquilhatville were the *Frères des Ecoles Chrétiennes* and many Scheutist Fathers in Lisala and in Léopoldville. A formidable opponent was Giovanni Dellepiane, the *Délégué Apostolique*. This leading cleric had the best intentions and wanted to protect the new Christians against the "turpitude of heathenism" that, according to him, was bound up in Bantu language and culture. The best means to reach this goal was the "latinization" of the local culture. In this task, he was supported by the bishop of Elisabethville, Mgr. Felix de Hemptinne, and Égide De Boeck, Scheutist bishop of Lisala. The latter suggested in his reader published in 1920 that children should "speak the language of the Whites."

There were also nonmissionary figures associated with *Aequatoria*. While judges and magistrates required knowledge of customary law, civil servants (governors, commissioners, and administrators) had to engage with local traditional political and economic structures as they attempted to maintain order and bring about the economic progress of the colony. A few of these people were open to challenging colonial attitudes and behavior. A prime example was Emile Possoz (1888-1969),[19] whom Hulstaert considered the cofounder of *Aequatoria*. He was the somewhat curious *Substitut du Procureur du Roi* (deputy state prosecutor) in Irumu, Coquilhatville, Elisabethville, and finally Inongo. He undertook the first translation, from Flemish into French, of Tempels's *Bantu Philosophy*, and wrote the foreword. With Hulstaert he discussed some parallels between Roman law and African customary law, which resulted in the concept of *paternat*, a neologism from the

---

19. Much has been written on Emile Possoz and his numerous essays, published and unpublished. See Mubabinge Bilolo, "La Philosophie nègre dans l'œuvre d'Emile Possoz. I. de 1928-1945," *Revue Africaine de Théologie* 5, no. 10 (1981): 197-225; Mubabinge Bilolo, "L'impact d'Emile Possoz sur P. Tempels. Introduction au destin du possozianisme," *Revue Africaine de Théologie* 11 (1982): 27-57; H. Vinck, "Les papiers Possoz aux archives Aequatoria," *Annales Aequatoria* 7 (1986): 327-31; and H. Vinck, "Emile Possoz (1888-1969). Bio-bibliographie," *Annales Aequatoria* 10 (1989): 298-320. See also http://www.aequa toria.be/BiblioPossoz.html (October 2009).

Latin word *paternitas* used in some writings in that period, and subsequently the key idea in Possoz's *Elements de droit coutumier nègre* (1942). Hulstaert was also in regular contact with Antoine Sohier, former *Procureur Général* (general state prosecutor) in Elisabethville, who after 1951 served as a member of the Colonial Council in Brussels.[20] Hulstaert engaged with these magistrates in his endeavors to promote customary concepts and practices as the best guarantee for the stability of indigenous society.

Not only were many European colonial officials eager to impose on the local people their own culture, they even drew up a hierarchy of different, local traditions. People considered more likely to submit to the colonial order, such as the Bangala in Léopoldville, were favored. Reactions against cultural and political imperialism in the Belgian colony are at present better known than before independence when they were hidden by colonial propaganda. Some of these reactions came from Congolese grouped around *Aequatoria*. They took every opportunity to express themselves in missionary journals and pamphlets. Among the Mongo, three names deserve special mention. Louis Bamala was responsible for the version of *Nsong'a Lianja* published by the Musée Royal du Congo belge at Tervuren.[21] Pierre Mune was the first African to win an award offered by the Belgian Royal Academy of Overseas Sciences, for his survey *Le Petit Ekonda*.[22] But Hulstaert's most important "discovery" was Paul Ngoi (1924-97), a teacher at the junior seminary of Bokuma in 1934, with whom he worked until the 1970s. Paul Ngoi was his most important informant in Mongo linguistics and oral literature and embodied Hulstaert's idea of the "truly modern African": the person with deep respect for his own language, and love for his culture and history, who was a convinced Christian.[23] Hulstaert also attracted one of the first indigenous scholars, European style, the Rwandan priest Alexis Kagame, who wrote his first scholarly article in *Aequatoria*.

Not all Africans appreciated the policies propounded by *Aequatoria*. Jean-François Iyeki, a prominent *évolué* and publicist, argued in favor of French in

---

20. H. Vinck, "Correspondance G. Hulstaert–A. Sohier: 1934-1960," *Annales Aequatoria* 18 (1997): 9-238 and http://www.aequatoria.be/BiblioSohier.html.

21. Bamala's dates of birth and death are unknown. See http://www.aequatoria.be/BiblioBamala.html (October 2009).

22. Pierre Mune, *Bonanga wa Ekonda ea Bompou ou Le groupement de Petit-Ekonda*, Mémoires in 8° de la Classe des Sciences Morales et Politiques, Tome XVII, fasc. 4 (Brussels, Académie des Sciences Coloniales, 1959).

23. Hulstaert to Kagame, 14 August 1946, AeqArch: MF ch 4-5, *Annales Aequatoria* 16 (1995): 524. H. Vinck, "Tradition et modernité mongo: Bio-bibliographie de Paul Ngoi (en collaboration avec Lonkama Bondengo)," *Annales Aequatoria* 19 (1998): 335-90.

the schools and a greater access to the "superior culture of the Whites." There were certainly many other Africans, such as the host of *évolués* writing in *La Voix du Congolais*, the secular Léopoldville magazine, who shared these sentiments.

The Mongo

The Mongo people can be described as a conglomerate of human groups occupying the Congolese Central Basin. They exhibit patrilineal and segmental kin structures. Some groups lived in symbiosis with Pygmies of varied origins. All spoke dialects of one Bantu language. The region was partially touched by Arab incursions, and a system of domestic slave trade oriented downstream existed before the colonial period. The colonial occupation of the Mbandaka region started in 1883, spread slowly toward the interior, and was completed by 1910. The Leopoldian system of exploitation undermined the livelihood of the people, and in combination with imported illnesses (sleeping sickness and syphilis), it decimated the population. The fertile disposition of the region meant that many rubber, coffee, and cocoa plantations spread over the country, dominated by the Société Anonyme Belge (SAB) from 1888, and by the Huileries du Congo belge (HCB, Lever Company) from 1924 onward.

English Baptists first arrived in the region in 1883 but were quickly replaced by Disciples of Christ in the south and by the (English) Congo Balolo Mission in the north. Catholics made their entry with the Trappists of the Belgian abbey of Westmalle in 1895, followed by the London-based Mill Hill fathers in 1905 in the north. Other Catholic orders would soon move into surrounding areas. Trappists began timidly with the study of local customs and some of them published valuable essays on topics such as age groups.[24] The superiors in Europe judged missionary life incompatible with the monastic vocation of the Trappists and replaced them in 1924 with the Belgian Missionaries of the Sacred Heart. This brought a rapid change to the region and its people. The new apostolic prefect, Mgr. E. Van Goethem (1873-1949), who had spent twenty years as a missionary in British New Guinea, took a positive attitude toward Mongo culture and applied himself to studying the language and customs of the people, and soon published several ethnographic studies.[25] This did not accord with the general antipathy in the colony toward lo-

---

24. Alois De Witte, "Indongo," *Onze Kongo* 3, no. 1 (1912): 57-74.
25. See G. Hulstaert, "Goethem (Van) (Eduard)," *Belgische Overzeese Biographie*, VII, C (Brussels, Académie Royale des Sciences d'Outre-Mer, 1989), pp. 181-92.

cal African cultures, particularly when these were considered incompatible with Christianity.

Ideology, Theology, and Nationalism

The ideology at work in the Aequatoria Center could be described as the ideology of the natural, based on an essentialist vision of reality. Applied to the field of sociology, this perception became known, through the publications of Edmond Boelaert, as the theory of the "people's community." It was considered the basis of all political organization. Flemish nationalism found its historical expression, translated into a colonial situation, as *indigénisme*,[26] which in its turn generated anticolonialism. A religious extremism that supposed the superiority of Christianity merged with these ideological options. Recent work by Michael Meeuwis and Joseph Errington links the theory of the "people's community" to the romanticism of J. G. Herder.[27] When applied to ethnography and linguistics, it became the belief that "Mongo" and "Flemish" (or any other language) were clearly separate categories distinct from others and were not the cognitive product of representation, but had an independently physical existence in the natural world. These categories were like stones in the fields, created separately by God or by nature, which were simply "discovered" by scientists. It followed that these natural categories were primordial and should be preserved as such.[28]

The ideology of the natural was implicit in a good deal of nineteenth- and twentieth-century thought, and Flemish nationalism emerged from this context. Hulstaert may not have explicitly encountered this theory, but he was nevertheless influenced by it, particularly through notions of cosmology[29] or the "philosophy of nature" in his philosophical training as a Catholic priest.

---

26. The translation into English of the French word *indigénisme* is not straightforward. We define "indigeneity" as "a nexus of cultural identity, human rights, environmentalism, and specific political claims." See Katherine Martineau on http://www.culanth.org/?q=node/116 (10 October 2009).

27. Michael Meeuwis, "Flemish Nationalism in the Belgian Congo versus Zairian Anti-imperialism: Continuity and Discontinuity in Language Ideological Debates," in *Language Ideological Debates*, ed. Jan Blommaert, Language, Power and Social Process 2 (Berlin, 1999), pp. 381-423; Joseph Errington, "Colonial Linguistics," *Annual Review of Anthropology*, 30 October 2001, pp. 19-39.

28. Communication from Michael Meeuwis.

29. Cosmology is an area of science that aims at a comprehensive theory of the structure and evolution of the entire physical universe. It was part of the curriculum in Catholic theological schools.

In Hulstaert's case this was accentuated by his interest in the field of natural science (especially entomology) where he applied a "natural," Linnaean, rank-based classification of natural organisms to cultural phenomena. An unmistakable illustration of this doctrine is Hulstaert's assertion of the difference between languages and dialects as expressed in his *La carte linguistique du Congo Belge:*

> We know the opinion of some linguists who do not accept the existence of "languages," but only of "dialects" (beside the common languages). As a reaction against some mistakes, their argument is worth taking into consideration. But taken as an unrestricted statement we cannot agree with it. Denying the existence of [standard?] languages is as good as, in our view, denying the existence of species and genera, or pretending that there are no forests, but only trees. We therefore retained the distinction between languages and dialects; these are considered as species which can be grouped into genres: the languages.[30]

Boelaert highlighted this concept in an article published in 1939 when he responded to the objection that the communities composing the Mongo people did not have full awareness of their political and cultural unity: "The whole question can be summarized as follows: is it possible to go against this natural cohesion, because the constituent groups are not yet conscious of it? Even sleeping nature cannot be violated without impunity."[31]

When applied to the field of sociology, the "philosophy of nature" generated the concept of the people's community. This idea was systematized and propagated by Jacques Leclercq (1891-1971), professor at the University of Louvain who inspired Boelaert and Hulstaert. In his *La communauté populaire* (1938), Leclercq outlined the difference between the state, a legal concept, and the nation or the people's community, a concept based on a natural reality. He saw the people's community as the natural form of society, and portrayed the state as an artificial intervention that was "against nature." In 1941 Hulstaert clarified his vision:

> This concept of the people's community is opposed to the identification . . . of State and Nation. . . . In the concept of the people's community,

---

30. G. Hulstaert, *La carte linguistique du Congo Belge* (Brussels, 1950), p. 4 (translated from French).

31. Translated from Dutch. Quotation from Boelaert, "Koloniale krabbels: Volk en staat," *Nieuw Vlaanderen* 5, no. 33 (1939): 8.

the fatherland is the people's community.... What the author thus understands by people's community is the ethnologists' ethnos . . . : a group of populations speaking the same language, recognizing a common origin, having the same habits and social system.... But this thesis, while of importance for peace in Europe, is of a general application. It is also true for the colonies and the peoples under mandate.[32]

In articles written after 1940 — more precisely, in "De Nkundo-maatschappij" (The Nkundo society) — Boelaert located these concepts in the context of contemporary world history: "The question of people's ethnic communities brought Europe to a volcanic explosion. And this question of the new order will only be solved when justice has been given to each of these forces: i.e. ethnic (family and people's community), economic (trade, class, social categories) and policy (organization of the State)."[33]

Inspired by the history of the Flemish people within the framework of the Belgian state in the nineteenth–early twentieth centuries, Boelaert and Hulstaert made an easy transition from Flemish nationalism to African indigeneity. Both men were traumatized by the abuses of the colonial system around them. They noticed that the colonial administration showed no respect for the cultural practices of the people, while they saw a spectacular fall in the birthrate among the Mongo. Rapacious colonial companies dispossessed the people of their ancestral grounds and recruited their laborers by force. They even managed to deport whole populations in mobilization for the *effort de guerre*, "a war made by the whites." Africans were uprooted in their own country and cut off from their social, cultural, and environmental milieux. Finally, Boelaert describes colonization as the "white plague," evoking memories of the black (bubonic) plague in Europe.[34]

In their response to a destructive and dominant Belgian colonialism, Hulstaert and Boelaert drew inspiration from the recent history of Flanders where Flemish nationalists had drawn strength and built unity on the image of a glorious past resting on a firm cultural and linguistic basis. The saying "Be Flemish, you whom God created Flemish" was transformed into "Be Mongo, you whom God created Mongo." This romantic nationalism gener-

---

32. *Aequatoria*, 1941, pp. 59-60. The article is anonymous but is under a heading (Documenta) usually used by Hulstaert. An article by Boelaert starts with a *citation-définition*: "The people's community results primarily from a spirit manifesting itself in its own particular uses and its own way of life"; "Coups de sonde," *Aequatoria* 5, no. 11 (1942): 26-30.

33. E. Boelaert, "De Nkundo-maatschappij," *Aequatoria* 4, no. 3 (1941): 41-44.

34. E. Boelaert, "Ontvolking door kolonisatie?" *Aequatoria* 8, no. 3 (1945): 92-94.

ated an attitude of aversion to the Belgian colonial state in the Congo, and a forceful anticolonialism. In an interview in 1957 Hulstaert traced the historical contours of these insights: "The Mongo had to become aware of the fact that they were a great nation, far beyond the borders of our vicariate, with only one language, one spirit, one way of life and one history.... But as a missionary and a Fleming, I am firmly convinced that the future lies only in the use of the mother tongue as a common language. As Christian Flemings we know the force of solidarity which is in the attachment to one's own language and culture, for the conservation of national values and spiritual wellbeing."[35]

The ideology of the natural, the experience of Flemish nationalism, and the concept of the people's community, when applied in a colonial context, fostered a sense of racial consciousness or *indigénisme*, and an accompanying anticolonialism.

Indigeneity and Anticolonialism

Indigénisme (indigeneity) is a word often used by Hulstaert to express an a priori positive attitude toward all aspects of local cultures, including the acceptance of a fundamental equality between human beings — an equality that excluded any domination, by the colonizer as much as by another African people. Hulstaert wrote to Walpert Bühlmann, expert in Catholic mission studies: "To me, there is only one logical and coherent position for an *'indigenist'*: the pure position, without compromise: indigeneity as it really is and not as we would want it to be; therefore, we opt for the ancestral language and customs, and not for those of another African people."[36]

By virtue of their missionary experience and their research into modern colonial history, Boelaert and Hulstaert threw themselves into an intense struggle against the abuses and injustices meted out to the Mongo people by the Belgian colonial regime. Boelaert quickly moved to a more fundamental anticolonialism. As early as 1939 he proclaimed "colonialism to be the greatest horror of history."[37] Under his influence, Hulstaert also began to adopt a tough anticolonial rhetoric. In 1947 he wrote in a letter to Antoine Sohier:

---

35. I quote from the typescript, Archives MSC, Borgerhout, Boelaert-Biographica. The interviewer was Boelaert. This paragraph has been left out of the printed version in *Annalen van O. L. Vrouw van het H. Hart* (Borgerhout, 1957), pp. 108-9.

36. Vinck, "In Memoriam Gustave Hulstaert," p. 43.

37. The expression is in a book review of Sylva De Jonghe's *Het Koloniale in de Literatuur* (The colonial factor in literature), *Boekengids* 17 (January 1939): 6-7.

The more I grow old in Africa, the more anchored in me is the conviction that colonialism has nothing to do with idealism. It is a soft way to attract money and capital and a mask to trick the broad public. It is as it always was: a form of exploitation, a capitalist and an imperialist enterprise.... It is sad to say, but personally I am more affected by the effects of our actions on the natives, after all innocent people. We pulled them by force into our orbit. We painted our civilization for them in the most beautiful colours. We benefited from their naivety, and committed, in my opinion, a sin which shouts for revenge to the sky. It is finally (although rarely so in the conscience of the authors and instigators) an exploitation of the weak — that is characteristic of this kind of sin.[38]

Hulstaert shared the vision of the Catholic and ultramontane world that dated from the end of the nineteenth century. The only solution to the "evils of the time" was *Instaurare omnia in Christo* — the superiority of Christianity — the motto of Pius X (1903-14). In this single sentence, Hulstaert characterized his holistic approach toward the problems encountered in missionary work. In 1941, he wrote to Mgr. Égide De Boeck: "For me, it is all one reality: language problem, mission, school education, parochial ministry, politics, etc.; all turn around the same point and depend on it. It is the radicalism of the new movement which Pius X already provided with its 'Omnia instaurare in Christo.'"[39] Hulstaert subscribed to a view of anthropology that rested on Christianity as an essential aspect (necessary and integral) to the human condition. A prime example of this notion of the superiority of Christianity was Hulstaert's epistolary discussions with Alexis Kagame in 1946-47: "One can say that Christianity is a factor of civilization.... A civilization cannot be perfect if it is not Christian."[40]

Nevertheless, in Hulstaert's mind, a clear distinction had to be made between Christianity and Western civilization. Under the influence of C. Virgil Georghiu's work *The 25th Hour* and Oswald Spengler's *Der Untergang des Abendlandes* (The decline of the West) (1918-23), Hulstaert cultivated a gloomy pessimism about Western civilization. Also in this letter from 1941 to a colleague: "My dear Father, ... an out-of-date, or rather: a rotten civilization which must be replaced by a very new world.... These ideas are confirmed by all modern Catholic thinkers. Read Leclercq, Rops, Maritain,

---

38. Vinck, "Correspondance G. Hulstaert–A. Sohier"; http://www.aequatoria.be/BiblioSohier.html.
39. Vinck, "Correspondance G. Hulstaert–E. De Boeck," p. 557.
40. H. Vinck, "Correspondance Kagame-Hulstaert," *Annales Aequatoria* 16 (1995): 541.

Dawson, Chesterton, Van Duinkerken, Carrel, Schulte, Rademacher, Bernanos, and so many others. If civilization is bringing about the death of Europe, how can we expect Blacks to profit from it?"[41]

Thus his intention was not to convert Africa to European civilization but rather to bring a pure version of Christianity to the continent. He did not hesitate to praise the high level of African morals and culture, as illustrated in another letter of 1949 to the Rwandian priest and philosopher Alexis Kagame: "For my part I even believe that your views of society are PHILO-SOPHICALLY and MORALLY higher than those current in modern Europe. . . . I even feel that in patriarchal Africa the individual was INDEED freer than in European societies. . . . And I say that, since Europe does not want to learn from the catechism, it can learn from the example of primitive people!!"[42]

Boelaert expressed exactly the same opinion when he wrote that only Catholicism could ennoble a culture without using violence to bring about this change.[43]

Ideologies and Scholarly Practices

The ideological influences outlined above penetrated all aspects of Hulstaert and Boelaert's academic research and its practical applications: in the field of linguistics, through the creation of an integral, neatly limited linguistic universe; in the field of cultural anthropology, considering ethnicity as the expression of a creative will of God; in the field of history, the search for a primordial unity; in the field of law via the study and protection of the customary law of the people; in the field of pedagogy by deducing theories from ethnic data; in the field of governance and politics by connecting the concepts of "people" and "nation" in a way that distinguished them from the concept of the modern pluralistic nation-state.

They considered the study of the language as a particular service to the people. Language was part of human nature, a gift of God to the people, and therefore its essential expression. Thus a language's location and geographical delimitation over and against other languages were axiomatic. As early as

41. Letter to Father Romanus Declercq à Mbingi-Mutembo, 30 January 1941. The term "new world" suggests another one with a more political resonance: "new order," used in several other texts by Boelaert. Archives Aequatoria, Correspondance Hulstaert, Boîte 61, microfiche CH 160.
42. Vinck, "Correspondance Kagame-Hulstaert," pp. 532-33.
43. E. Boelaert, "Volk en staat in Kongo," *Kongo-Overzee* 5, no. 3 (1939): 125.

1935, Hulstaert wrote in a reader: "God has given people a language so they can communicate with family, friends and others on earth, so they may teach each other all kind of good things."[44] He declared in a letter to De Boeck, the bishop of Lisala, in August 1940: "Unlike others, I have as a principle: to unify as much as possible. When in doubt, I give preference to unification. Of all the elements, I give priority to the language. It is therefore based on an axiom, an apriorism if you like."[45]

He clarified his reasoning in a subsequent letter to Mgr. De Boeck in 1941:

> You see how important the language question is and how it forms part of the whole world vision. For me and for those who are of our tendency, the language is an element which deserves respect, also on behalf of the Church. It is a value, a being entering the intention of God; something with which the people cannot play around, that people must preserve and respect like all that exists in and for God. Language is thus an object of the love of God according to the first commandment. Consequently an individual or a group does not have the right to change its language, neither does one have the right to do with one's body whatever one wants.[46]

The corollary of this idea was that the announcement of the word of God to the people, in a language that God did not give to them, was blasphemous.

The search for the great linguistic units of the colony served an ideological goal. Boelaert and Hulstaert wanted to prove that Lomongo was a language sufficiently important to be used as a medium of general communication.[47] The creation of a unified language required scientific concessions. The selected dialect supplanted a great number of linguistic forms, which one still finds in the footnotes of the *Grammaire du Lomongo*. It is irrefutable that this intervention, codified in *Etsifyelaka*, the school textbook of the Lomongo

---

44. *Buku ea mbaanda*, lesson 17. This schoolbook was compiled by Gustaaf Hulstaert. Translation and comments in French on http://www.abbol.com/commonfiles/docs _projecten/colschoolbks/bukuea.php (October 2007). Click on "African colonial schoolbooks project." See H. Vinck, "The Influence of Colonial Ideology on School Books in the Belgian Congo," *Paedagogica Historica* 23, no. 2 (1995): 355-406. See also H. Vinck, "A l'école au Congo Belge. Manuels scolaires de 1933-1935. Introduction et Textes," *Annales Aequatoria* 23 (2002): 21-196.

45. Vinck, "Correspondance G. Hulstaert–E. De Boeck," p. 512.

46. Vinck, "Correspondance G. Hulstaert–E. De Boeck," p. 557.

47. E. Boelaert, "Vergelijkende taalstudie," parts I and II, *Aequatoria* 1, no. 3 (1937-38): 1-5; *Aequatoria* 1, no. 6 (1937-38): 1-8.

grammar, in the *Katakisimo* (catechism), in the *Bosako w' oyengwa* (sacred history), and in the translation of the Bible, brought a notable modification to the spoken language. The ultimate terminus was the formation of a literary language that would be accessible to the greatest number of citizens. As early as 1936, Boelaert had outlined its contours in a series of articles in *Kongo-Overzee*.[48] Quoting Vendryes,[49] he advanced the conservation of the morphological structure of the local language chosen as the source of the new common language, as sufficiently respectful to it. Hulstaert would repeat it ten years later in the journal *Zaïre*, adding a number of other criteria, like syntax, tone structure, vocabulary, and phonetics.[50]

The *Carte linguistique du Congo Belge,* designed by Hulstaert in 1950, has its origin in an effort to prove that the Congo was not a country with over 400 languages. Boelaert and Hulstaert were however not afraid to manipulate the linguistic data with the clear purpose of further extending the borders of Mongo territory. In his discussion with Mgr. De Boeck, Hulstaert declared that all these languages were so close to Lomongo that they could be replaced by the latter.[51] This included the idea that Lingala was based on Lomongo.[52] In a letter to Boelaert, Hulstaert wrote in September 1937: "It is therefore that I advise you to launch the idea that Lingala is based on a Mongo dialect.... Although one needs to 're-bantuize' the language. In that case, it is not a literary language, because not spoken by a real people. The solution will be to take a language already at a literary rich level: the Lomongo, which is a related dialect."[53]

He used a similar tactic toward the Lokonda, Lontomba, Londengese, and Longando languages, which could be found on consecutive maps. Boelaert

---

48. E. Boelaert, "Naar een nationale inlandsche taal in Kongo?" *Kongo-Overzee* 2, no. 4 (1935-36): 245.

49. See reference to J. Vendryes, *Le Langage, introduction linguistique à l'histoire* (Paris, 1921), p. 360.

50. G. Hulstaert, "Taalèènmaking en dialektenstudie," *Zaïre* 1, no. 3 (1947): 885-901.

51. The dispute grew in their correspondence and articles in *Aequatoria:* G. Hulstaert, "Lingala," 3 (1940): 33-45; E. De Boeck, "Lingala," 3 (1940): 124-27; G. Hulstaert, "Mise au point," 3 (1940): 127-30; E. De Boeck, "Un dernier mot," 3 (1940): 130-31.

52. Via the Bobangi and several other languages close to Lomongo. On the origins of Lingala as a vehicular or trade language, see W. J. Samarin, "Protestant Missions and the History of Lingala," *Journal of Religion in Africa* 16 (1986): 138-63; Samarin, "Language in the Colonization of Central Africa, 1880-1900," *Canadian Journal of African Studies* 23, no. 2 (1989): 232-49. For a fascinating debate about the cultural and political effects of African lingua francas in the Belgian Congo, see J. Fabian, *Language and Colonial Power* (Cambridge, 1986), and a response by G. Hulstaert, *Annales Aequatoria* 12 (1991): 527-33.

53. Archives MSC, Borgerhout, Fonds Boelaert. Translated from Dutch.

was equally unafraid of a certain expansionism. He suggested that the Bombesa, Bongando, Lalia, Yasanyama, Booli, Bosaka, and Boyela peoples should all be attached to the Mongo. In 1938 he wrote to Hulstaert about incorporating the Bambole into the Mongo group: "You see that you should not lock up [Mongo] within too narrow limits, as I always have told you."[54] In a short article published in 1939, he included the Atetela and related peoples.[55] Hulstaert summarized the whole approach and the final goal, in a letter written in 1941: "If my idea, which is not only mine, far from it, were universally accepted and put into practice, we would have in the centre of the Congo a group sufficiently large, to resist Europeanization, commercial languages etc. . . . and to allow an indigenous civilization, an indigenous literature."[56] In 1935, Hulstaert inculcated his belief about the value of pristine, authentic languages into the heads of schoolboys when he wrote in his abovementioned *Buku ea mbaanda*:[57] "Each region has its language. There are several languages in the world. Each language has its own system. All of them are good. We have our language, Lonkundo. . . . From one village to another, our speech has dialects. But we understand ourselves clearly."[58]

He believed there were authentic languages, as well as foreign and forged languages. He wrote in the same reader:

> Certain people, both Whites and Blacks, speak other languages. A certain kind of speech found among the Whites and their associates, has stretched as far as our territory. This language is Lingala. Even if certain people have a good appreciation of Lingala, we only appreciate our tongue, Lonkundo. This, our language, is very lovely, it expresses many realities based on reason. We much prefer our own tongue transmitted to us by our ancestors. Our language has its beauty. We can express all reality through it. We appreciate our language and we remain lovingly attached to it.[59]

54. Correspondance Hulstaert-Boelaert, Coquilhatville, 16 June 1938, Archives Aequatoria, Microfiches 123-127. Translated from Dutch.

55. E. Boelaert, "Batetela: Zuid-Mongo," *Kongo-Overzee* 5, no. 2 (1939): 77-81.

56. Letter to D. Brown from 25 February 1941, Archives Aequatoria, Correspondance Hulstaert MF 17. Translated from French.

57. Vinck, "A l'école au Congo Belge," pp. 21-193.

58. From lesson 17. Translated from Lomongo original: "Wengi ese ele la lolaka lokae. Ndaka ile buke nd'okili. Wengi lolaka lole nk'eleng'ekae. Ik'iuma ile nk'olotsi. Iso tole la lolaka lokiso jwa lonkundo. Bamo batanga loko lina lomongo. . . . Nd'ese l'ese lolaka lonko lokiso lole la bitsikwana. Lolo tswokana o fombo."

59. From lesson 17. Translated from the Lomongo original: "Banto bamo, la bendele la boindo, batefela ndaka imo. Lolaka lomo lotefela bendele l'ant'akio lookita l'endo ek'iso.

In his desire to discover the essential ethnic and linguistic unity of the Mongo, Boelaert spent his furlough in 1939 at the Africa Museum in Tervuren where, supported by the conservator Jozef Maes, he studied the cultural characteristics of the people of the Central Basin[60] of the Congo. The result of this work was a massive manuscript, with the title *Kulturele kenmerken der volksgroepen uit de Middenkuip* (Cultural characteristics of the people of the Central Basin).[61] He found in the material life of the Mongo a sufficient number of indices to constitute — according to the definition of Leclercq — a "people's community." In the field of social anthropology, Hulstaert's preferred author was Evans-Pritchard. He also drew on the work of Malinowski, Levi-Bruhl, Radcliffe-Brown, and Westermann without taking their theoretical or methodological stance.

Hulstaert's ideological concerns led him to make assertions that were at least very debatable, and often disputed by other anthropologists. Thus, he believed that the absence of a worship of God among the Mongo was a deviation from earlier traditional practice. The original cult activities had been replaced by ancestor worship. He never advanced the slightest proof in support of this assertion, but it allowed him to represent monotheism as the original faith of the Mongo. According to this idea, missionaries were merely aiding the Mongo to find their original, authentic belief in one God. He presented the concept of God among the Mongo as being of a pure spiritual nature, deprived of any anthropomorphism and thus perfectly fitted to the Christian representation of the deity. But even a surface reading of the "national epic," *Nsonga' a Lianja*, contradicts this. Another example is encountered in his handbook: *Les Mongo. Aperçu general*, where he wrote: "The rules which govern the authority are attributed to God."[62] This does not have any basis in reality. In fact, for the Mongo, power and authority are related to the ancestors. The argument he advanced was merely an abstract deduction with an apologetic purpose from the words of St. Paul: "All authority comes from God" (Rom. 13:1).

He believed that the loss of culture and traditions, under the influence of

---

Lolaka lonko wate lingala. La nkuma banto bamo basima l'otefela lingala, iso tosima o lolaka lokiso jwa lonkundo. Lolaka lone lokiso lole o bolotsi Mongo, lole la baoi buke ba wanya. Tosima loko buke loki bafafa bakiso ototsikelaka. Lolaka lokiso lole la jeli likae. Tokusa l'otefela baoi bauma. Tosima lolaka lokiso ko toakema o nda loko la lolango."

60. Geographical term for the region in the northern bend of the Congo River.
61. Papiers Boelaert, MSC-Archives Borgerhout (B).
62. G. Hulstaert, *Grammaire du Lomongo. Première Partie: la phonologie*, Annales du Musée royal d'Afrique centrale, Sciences humaines 39 (Tervuren, Musée royal d'Afrique centrale, 1961), pp. 39-42.

Belgian colonization, could destroy the physical basis of the Mongo, specifically in terms of a visibly declining birthrate. As we can read in *Bosako wa Mongo* (The history of the Mongo):[63] "The responsibility of the Whites lies in the fact that they have distorted our traditions. We accepted that by disavowing the way of thinking of our ancestors is to degrade and reject the basis of our very existence. Here the alliance with the forbears in our community is clearly broken."[64]

Unable to reconstruct the original unity of the Lomongo language,[65] Hulstaert turned to the ethnohistory. In June 1941, he started to publish in *Le Coq Chante* an account of Mongo history. He had only one goal: to prove the unity and the extent of the Mongo as an ethnic group that, once regenerated and proud, would be able to affirm themselves in concert with the other peoples of the Congo. He wrote in July 1941: "Any honest child first loves his family, his own blood.... That is certainly an order of God, that love is expressed the most strongly with regard to consanguines. For this reason everyone especially loves his village of origin. The love of origins is quite simply the 4th commandment. If somebody does not like his origins, he transgresses the fundamental law of love."[66]

In an earlier 1941 edition of *Le Coq Chante* he had written: "No people of Congo exceed the Mongo in extent."[67] He repeated and clarified this assertion in 1957, in *Bosako wa Mongo*:

A long time ago, there were many different groups of tribes and every group had its own name. They did not know that they belonged to the

---

63. This booklet from 1957 is a compilation of texts by an indigenous teacher and Edmond Boelaert, and served as a history textbook. See H. Vinck, "L'enseignement de l'histoire au Congo Belge. Deux textes contradictoires," *Annales Aequatoria* 19 (1998): 167-94.

64. Original text in Lomongo: "Wate bendele baosenjola beeko bekiso, iso Mongo tootona lumba ja bankoko Mongo; tosanola ko tootandola loko lokiso mpe bokolo wa bankoko Mongo boosenga nda limotsi lokiso ko tof'ino la losilo lonko." Quotation from *Bosako wa Mongo*, pp. 64-65.

65. In a letter from 8 February 1954 he wrote to Mccussen that he did not know what "urbantu" means (Archives Aequatoria, CH 150, MF 154-158).

66. G. Hulstaert, "Baotsi ba Mongo," *Le Coq Chante* 6 (July 1941): 4. Original text in Lomongo: "Wengi bona oa tsi alanga joso liotsi likae, ilongo ikae Mongo. . . . Ale nde bosise wa Njakomba, te lolango lolekole ele basangi la we. Ng'oko wengi bonto alanga bola kokae Mongo, alanga oleki bonanga bokae Mongo wa bankoko. Lolango jwa bonkoko lole nda bosise wa 4. Nga bonto afolange bonkoko afeja bosise wa ntsina wa lolango." Quotation from p. 4.

67. G. Hulstaert, "Mongo," *Le Coq Chante* 6 (June 1941): 3.

same people and they fought one another. But step-by-step, they began to understand that small groups did not function well, and the people began to settle together in larger units. The more people progress in terms of civilisation, the more they will be attached to the language of their *volk*, and they will desire increasingly to discover the history of their ancestors, the more they will zealously protect and defend the language and customs of their forefathers.[68]

History was the basis for the revivification of the people from lethargy and looming extinction. "We will try to dig up the history of our people. In this way ... our relatives ... will praise us for having discovered these important affairs, these wise things, these things that nurture the village, things that provide a civilisation with concern and dignity."[69]

In 1984, when all pressure had passed and Hulstaert had become aware that he had lost his ethnonationalist battle, he confessed the following in his *Histoire Mongo Ancienne:* "Several doubtful cases persist, whose solution depends on the results of more in-depth research and also, partly, the approach of the researcher, depending on the emphasis he will give to the perception of the union or the separation [of the Mongo]."[70]

The ethnohistorian Georges Van Der Kerken based his account of the original unity of the Mongo clans on doubtful genealogies and erroneous etymologies. Hulstaert, however, was no dupe, and this degree of faking was too obvious. In a 1971 lecture at the Lovanium University, he denounced openly Van Der Kerken's biased and sometimes violent practices: "A second case arrived to the inhabitants of the Boende village from the Bombwanja tribe. . . .

68. Anonyme, *Bosako wa Mongo* (1998 [1957]). French translation of two chapters in *Annales Aequatoria* 19:177-86, quotation taken from p. 178. http://www.abbol.com/commonfiles/docs_projecten/colschoolbks/sco_col_anthology.php (October 2009) and selected English excerpts on http://www.aequatoria.be/English/HomeEnglishFrameSet.html (October 2009). Original text in Lomongo: Archives Aequatoria (Bamanya RD Congo), Box 19, cote 8.2. Original text: "Kalakala, baki bont'onto baotsi l'aotsi; wengi liotsi likande lina: bateaki te baaamana lolo bayabunyaki nk'io l'io! Ikok'ikoke banto baokela wanya, baomanga okotola te baotsi ba tosisi bafoonge ko baoamanaka nd'onanga w'onene. Ko elekola banto okogoswa nda limbotsi, nk'elekol'io ofotama nda lolaka jw'onanga, elekol'io mposa ea besako bya bankoko, elekol'io jale nda mpafonga le mbiija la lolaka la bikosa bya bankoko." Quotation from p. 3.

69. G. Hulstaert, "Mongo," *Le Coq Chante* 6 (June 1941): 3-4, and Anonyme, *Bosako wa Mongo*. Original: "Tomeka l'okundola besako bya bonanga bokiso. Ngoko ... ele bankoko bakiso, ... tswifoata lokumo el'io ekiso wafongelaka baoi ba ntsina, baoi ba wanya, baoi bakemya ese, baoi bakitsa jiko la joso la limbotsi." Quotation from p. 4.

70. G. Hulstaert, *Éléments pour l'Histoire Mongo Ancienne* (Brussels, 1984), p. 11.

The elders who, notwithstanding the threats [by the commissioner], maintained their position on the rights of the female section of the clan, were imprisoned."[71]

Hulstaert and Boelaert wrote the history of the Mongo for a variety of reasons. Hulstaert's work on the history of the Mongo was motivated by his desire to produce materials for schools in the Congo. Boelaert wrote the history of the legislation of the colonial land rights to provide data in support of his calls for the restitution of the lands belonging to the natives.[72] Boelaert also elaborated the idea of a founding epic of the people, by incorporating some historical features. He called this the "Mongo *national* epic," intending that history should reveal the existence and significance of the Mongo people as a nation.

Finally, in his communications with Antoine Sohier, Hulstaert endeavored to promote the concepts and practices of indigenous law. A contentious point was the place assigned to polygamy in Mongo traditions. The issue was how to harmonize a respectful attitude for Mongo tradition with the fundamental requirements of Christian morality. He found an astute but not really very scientific solution. According to Hulstaert, Mongo customary law should evolve under the influence of new elements. One new element, introduced by evangelization, was that of monogamy, which he considered the sole, true form of marriage. Ultimately, monogamy would become the standard, and consequently the jurisprudence practiced in indigenous courts would take account of this evolution. Hulstaert's *Le mariage des Nkundo* (1938), although invaluable in many other areas, is marked by the direct influence of Western Christian concepts superimposed on a specific interpretation of local ethnological norms.[73]

Conclusion

Edmond Boelaert was a man of letters, an idealist by nature, and was inspired by Flemish cultural nationalism. He was moved by the sufferings of the peo-

---

71. G. Hulstaert, "Une lecture critique de l'ethnie mongo de G. Van der Kerken," *Etudes d'histoire africaine* 3 (1972): 35. Translated from French. "Le second fait est arrivé aux Boende de la tribu Bombwanja de l'ancien territoire de Bokatola. Les vieux qui malgré les menaces, ont maintenu leurs droits ancestraux basés sur leur position de branche féminine, ont été punis par l'emprisonnement."

72. E. Boelaert, "Législation foncière de l'Etat Indépendant et droit naturel," *Aequatoria* 16 (1954): 41-50; Boelaert, *L'Etat Indépendant et les terres indigènes*.

73. G. Hulstaert, *Le mariage des Nkundo* (Brussels, 1938).

ple subjected to colonial exploitation, and his dream was to restore the original vigor of the Mongo people. The academic work of Boelaert is important, in general quite reliable, well documented, and original. But it always remained in the service of an idea or moral goal. Gustaaf Hulstaert, his confrere, had similar sympathies, focusing also on the field of indigenous law and linguistics. He wanted to raise the ethnic linguistic form to the level of a unified, standard, literary language, written, printed, published, and studied. This he sought to do by systematic description of the vocabulary and grammar. His dream was to have Lomongo recognized as one of the official languages of the colony.

Hulstaert was challenged by, amongst others, the American linguist Edward Sapir, who wrote: "Historians and anthropologists find that races, languages, and cultures are not distributed in parallel fashion, that their areas of distribution overlap in the most bewildering fashion, and that the history of each is apt to follow his distinctive race.... Totally unrelated languages share in one culture, closely related languages — even a single language — belong to distinct culture spheres."[74]

On the other hand, we must recognize that Hulstaert was surprisingly close to the African modernity formulated by Ngugi wa Thiong'o:

> In most of my publications, principally *Decolonizing the mind*, ... I have tried to argue that the language question is so crucial.... Let me summarize the argument: Language is a product of a community in its economic, political, and cultural evolution in time and space. In their very negotiation with nature and one another humans give birth to a system of communication whose highest expression and development is the sign which we come to give the name of language. But language is also the producer of a community, for it is language after all which enables humans to negotiate effectively their way into and out of nature and indeed that which makes possible their multifaceted evolution. It is in that very negotiation that a community comes to know itself as a specific community different from others.[75]

Hulstaert drew from a variety of theories and ideologies, unaware or unafraid of contradictions. His only goal was the unity and the conservation of

---

74. Edward Sapir, *Language: An Introduction to the Study of Speech* (New York, 1921), pp. 222, 228.

75. Ngugi wa Thiong'o, *Research in African Literature: The Future of African Literature and Scholarship*. Quoted from http://www.assatashakur.org/forum/open-forum/7687-ngugi-wa-thiongo-future-african-literature.html (09 October 2009).

the Mongo people, and "the adaptation of the Christian message to the people's genius." A rationale is provided by Nancy Rose Hunt: "A Hochschild-like narrative suggests a manipulated politics of memory invested in a willed public forgetting. The microhistory that I share today suggests rather that angst and guilt were palpable among Europeans in the Congo, especially when social questions like population and fertility were raised. It also suggests that at least two Flemish missionaries — Fathers Edmond Boelaert and Gustaaf Hulstaert of the Sacred Heart Fathers — did not so easily escape from memories of death and violence."[76]

This moral endeavor impelled both scholars to exceptional efforts. But sometimes it tarnished the scientific quality and objectivity of their work. In spite of their enormous empirical knowledge, Hulstaert and Boelaert remained vulnerable because they lacked both a thorough theoretical framework and a sound methodological rigor. On the occasion of the fiftieth birthday of *Aequatoria,* Vansina offered a critical note on the ideological approach of the founders of the Aequatoria Center: "Stressing with vigour the cultural unity of the Mongo people, the importance of the differences was sometimes forgotten. However the differences among these peoples resulting from the same type of society and culture, are crucial to understanding their past. They form the substance of their being, while at the same time they constitute the trace left by the dynamics of the past."[77]

This leads to the question of whether all the Flemish missionaries were as radical and anticolonial as Boelaert and Hulstaert. Most of the Catholic missionaries in the Belgian Congo were Flemish, and the idealism that pressed them to their religious vocation had been intermingled for some time with that of the Flemish nationalist movement. Hulstaert and Boelaert were the brokers, many others followed mutely, and some did not. Clearly articulated anticolonialism in spoken or written form was certainly scarce among Flemish missionaries in the Congo. The Missionaries of the Sacred Heart did not especially stand out as anticolonial critics. It seems, rather, to be related to the individual attitude of both *Aequatoria* protagonists and their outstanding analytical and critical intellectual vigor.

Yet, scientific knowledge was never their final goal; they always remained missionaries and viewed research as a means to improve their missionary praxis. The use of the mother tongue in liturgy, catechesis, and daily contacts, and the combative Christian compassion they demonstrated in the face of colonial abuses, won the sympathy of the Mongo people. And this sympathy

---

76. Hunt, "Rewriting the Soul," p. 10.
77. J. Vansina, "Vers une histoire des sociétés mongo," *Annales Aequatoria* 8 (1987): 35.

was transferred to the Christian faith as a whole. They knew that these missionaries held their traditions in high esteem. Several letters and articles in the national and provincial newspapers on the occasion of the eightieth birthday of Gustaaf Hulstaert and at the time of his death bear witness to this. It was indeed an amazing spectacle to see: in 1990 at the closing of the mourning period, on the streets in Mbandaka, hundreds of men and women dressed in *pagnes* and shirts decorated with Hulstaert's effigy in black and yellow — the colors of the Flemish nationalist movement.

Select Bibliography

Boelaert, Edmond. "De Nkundo-maatschappij." *Kongo-Overzee* 6, no. 4-5 (1940): 148-61.
———. "De Nkundo-Mongo. Eén volk, één taal." *Aequatoria* 1, no. 8 (1937-38): 1-25.
———. "Législation foncière de l'Etat Indépendant et droit naturel." *Aequatoria* 16 (1954): 41-50.
Errington, Joseph. *Linguistics in a Colonial World: A Story of Language, Meaning, and Power.* Oxford, 2007.
Hulstaert, Gustaaf. "Le Dieu des Mongo." *Cahiers des religions africaines* 12 (1978).
———. "Le Dieu des Mongo." *Anthropos* 75 (1980).
———. *Les Mongo. Aperçu général.* Archives d'Ethnographie 5. Tervuren, 1961.
———. "Mission et langue." *Annales Aequatoria* 12 (1991).
———. *Réflexions concernant la sorcellerie.* Bandundu, CEEBA Publications II/95 (1988).
Hunt, Nancy. "Rewriting the Soul in a Flemish Congo." *Past and Present* 198 (February 2008).
Leclercq, Jacques. *De la communauté populaire.* Paris, 1938.
Meeuwis, Michael. "Flemish Nationalism in the Belgian Congo versus Zairian Anti-imperialism: Continuity and Discontinuity in Language Ideological Debates." In *Language Ideological Debates,* edited by J. Blommaert. Berlin and New York, 1999.
———. "Missions and Linguistic Choice-Making: The Case of the Capuchins in the Ubangi Mission (Belgian Congo), 1910-1945." *General Linguistics* 38 (2001).
Vansina, Jan. "Vers une histoire des sociétés Mongo." *Annales Aequatoria* 8 (1987).
Vinck, Honoré. "Influence des missionnaires sur la prise de conscience ethnique et politique Mongo." *Revue Africaine des Sciences de la Mission* 4 (1996).
———. "The Influence of Colonial Ideology on School Books in the Belgian Congo." *Paedagogica Historica* 23, no. 2 (1995).

CHAPTER 8

Christian Medical Discourse and Praxis on the Imperial Frontier: Explaining the Popularity of Missionary Medicine in Mwinilunga District, Zambia, 1906-1935

WALIMA T. KALUSA

He [Singleton Fisher, a British medical missionary] was extremely interested in Lunda herbalism and did not condemn its use. . . . He had been told [by Africans in Mwinilunga] that the cure for a scorpion bite was to eat [the offending] scorpion [with cassava meal]. When we were at Kalene Hill [in the 1920s], Elsie Burr [a missionary nurse] was bitten by a scorpion on her thumb. She was in agony, and the pain was going up to her armpit. Singleton heard her cries for help, found the scorpion, roasted it and gave her half of it to eat, while he ate the other half to encourage her. The pain was eased immediately, and soon she was left with only a slightly sore thumb. He himself was bitten by a scorpion a few days later, with no painful results, so proved, as the Africans said, that the treatment was also prophylactic.

M. K. Fisher, *Lampposts to Searchlights: Memories of M. K. Fisher of Central Africa* (Ikelenge, 1994), p. 78

European medical missionaries who used non-Western medicine to cure scorpion bites at mission hospitals on the colonial periphery in the twentieth

---

I am indebted to Dr. Henry Kaluba, Professor Megan Vaughan, and participants at the conference held at Basel University between 30 November and 1 December 2007 who commented on earlier versions of this paper.

century are seldom a subject of historical investigation. This is scarcely surprising. Throughout the imperial world, missionaries too often cast themselves as all-powerful, heroic agents who single-handedly annihilated "traditional" systems of healing and underlying religious ideologies without being soiled by the cultural transaction of the people they encountered outside Europe. This image of missionaries as agents of cultural destruction, which continues to resurface in popular and academic imaginations to this day,[1] largely derives from the assumption that mission doctors demonstrated to the subjects of empire the rationality, objectivity, and superior effectivity of Western medicine against disease. It is concluded that through practical demonstration of the power of their medicine over diseases and of its superiority to "traditional" therapeutics, missionary healers both emasculated non-Western medicine and thereby popularized their own version of biomedicine, especially in the so-called Dark Continent.[2]

The notion that Christian medics popularized Western medicine and undermined African medical knowledge and praxis through successful treatment of diseases in Africa was at first inscribed in mission writings and at best articulated in triumphalist accounts of colonial/mission medicine published in the 1950s and 1960s.[3] Like medical evangelists, writers who celebrated Western medicine in Africa projected it as an unambiguously beneficial system of healing that white practitioners introduced to grateful Africans. Scholars well versed in world systems analysis and operating within political economy paradigms did little to unmask this myth in the next two decades.[4]

---

1. See Derek Peterson and Jean Allman, "Introduction: New Directions in the History of Missions in Africa," *Journal of Religious Studies* 23, no. 1 (1999): 1-7.

2. See Megan Vaughan, *Curing Their Ills: Colonial Power and African Illness* (Stanford, 1991).

3. Examples of studies that celebrate missionary medicine include Michael Gelfand, *The Role of Medicine in the History of Southern Rhodesia* (London, 1957), and his *Northern Rhodesia in the Days of the Charter: A Medical and Social Study* (Oxford, 1961); Gelfand, *Godly Medicine in Zimbabwe* (Gwelo, 1988). See also Robert I. Rotberg, *Christian Missionaries and the Creation of Northern Rhodesia, 1880-1924* (Princeton, 1965), and Oliver Rasford, "Bid the Disease Cease": Disease in the History of Black Africa (London, 1983). A more recent study that eulogizes missionary medicine is Pauline Summerton, "'Fishers of Men': An Examination of the Influence and Missionary Methods of an Extended Family in Brethren Pioneering Work in Africa" (B.Phil. thesis, Middlesex University, 1999). For a critique of such works, see Osaak A. Olumwullah, *Dis-ease in the Colonial State: Medicine, Society, and Social Change among the AbaNyole of Western Kenya* (Westport, Conn., and London, 2002), and Gwyn Prins, "But What Was the Disease? The Present State of Health and Healing in African Studies," *Past and Present* 124 (1989): 159-79.

4. Among these authors are Randall M. Packard, *White Plague, Black Labor: Tuberculosis and Political Economy of Health and Disease in South Africa* (Berkeley and Los Angeles,

Christian Medical Discourse and Praxis on the Imperial Frontier

Preoccupied with demonstrating the deleterious impact of colonial/missionary medicine on the health of the subjects of empire, these academics portrayed allopathic medicine — the bulk of which in Africa was mission-based medicine — as little more than an ideological arm of colonialism. White dispensers of colonial/missionary medicine, according to this view, were no more than agents of cultural suppression. From this perspective, these practitioners of medicine played no minor role in legitimizing Western exploitation of natural resources and labor in colonies, in extending to those areas European cultural and medical knowledge and hegemony, and in opening them up to European settlement, investment, and hegemony.

This scholarship is undoubtedly crucial to our understanding of the centrality of biomedical power to the extension of Western domination beyond European boundaries in the twentieth century. Intriguingly, however, the scholarship in question neither demonstrates how such hegemony was actually constructed nor why Western medicine indisputably won the admiration of people in extra-European settings. This criticism may further be extended to more recent social and medical histories that place a premium on Western intellectual and cultural hegemony in colonial encounters.[5] Deeply influenced by the writings of Michel Foucault that stress the importance of medical knowledge to state power and social control, these histories have paid a great deal of attention to the myriad ways in which agents of empire deployed scientific knowledge to forge imperial culture and identity, to open colonial territories to white settlement, and to construct the colonized as the governable Other.[6] Like scholarship informed by political economy, however, what is

---

1989); Meredith Turshen, *The Political Ecology of Disease in Tanzania* (New Brunswick, N.J., 1984); Helge Kjekshus, *Ecology Control and Economic Development in East Africa: The Case of Tanganyika, 1850-1950* (Berkeley and Los Angeles, 1977); Charles van Onselen, *Chibaro: African Mine Labour in Colonial Zimbabwe, 1900-1933* (Gwelo, 1978); Shula Marks and Neil Anderson, "Industrialization, Rural Health, and the 1944 National Health Services Commission in South Africa," in *The Social Basis of Health and Healing in Africa*, ed. Steven Feierman and John Jansen (Berkeley and Los Angeles, 1992), pp. 131-74; Walima T. Kalusa, "The Impact of the Second World War on African Health at Roan Antelope Mine," *Journal of Humanities* 1, no. 1 (1997): 13-38.

5. Example of these works include Richard Waller and Kathy Homewood, "Elders and Experts: Contesting Veterinary Knowledge in a Pastoral Community," in *Western Medicine as Contested Knowledge*, ed. Andrew Cunningham and Bridie Andrews (Manchester and New York, 1997), pp. 69-93. In the same volume, see Deepak Kumar, "Unequal Contenders, Uneven Ground: Medical Encounters in British India, 1820-1920," pp. 172-90.

6. Much of this data comes from Walima T. Kalusa, "Language, Medical Auxiliaries, and the Reinterpretation of Missionary Medicine in Colonial Mwinilunga, Zambia, 1922-51," *Journal of Eastern African Studies* 1, no. 1 (2007): 57-78.

conspicuously absent from such analyses is how the architects of the Western empire practically accomplished these no mean feats in colonial settings where there was a vast social, cultural, and linguistic divide between colonial rulers and their subjects.

Most histories of Western medicine on the colonial frontier hardly explore why missionary medicine carved a niche in popular imagination beyond the metropole. Across imperial Africa, Christian doctors themselves routinely attributed the popularity of their own therapeutic system among African patients to what they saw as its objectivity, rationality, and efficacy over diseases and superiority to local medicine. However, as some scholars have more recently convincingly demonstrated, the curative power of mission-based medicine against diseases in imperial Africa was rather assumed than proved.[7] For most of the colonial era, white doctors across Africa were utterly incapable of curing a host of structural diseases, including pneumonia, yaws, tropical ulcers, and several other diseases inexorably tied to colonial underdevelopment and poverty. Indeed, as Terence Ranger correctly observes in one of his seminal papers, mission medicine reached its plateau by the 1920s, and not until the introduction of antibiotics after the Second World War did European doctors in the continent gain some measure of healing power over these and kindred afflictions.[8]

In spite of its obvious impotence against diseases, missionary medicine in Africa and beyond was ironically popular, with mission-controlled hospitals across the continent evidently attracting thousands of African patients annually.[9] How can one understand this paradox? This chapter, focusing on the medical missionaries of the Christian Missions in Many Lands (CMML; widely known as Plymouth Brethren) who evangelized at Kalene Hill hospital in Zambia's Mwinilunga district between 1906 and 1935, contributes modestly to unraveling the paradox. Drawing on current writings that emphasize the limits of imperial power[10] and that perceive biomedical knowledge and

---

7. See Walima T. Kalusa, "Disease and Remaking of Missionary Medicine in Colonial Northwestern Zambia: A Case Study of Mwinilunga District, 1902-1964" (Ph.D. diss., Johns Hopkins University, 2003).

8. Terence Ranger, "Godly Medicine: The Ambiguities of Medical Mission in Southeast Tanzania, 1900-1945," *Social Science and Medicine* 15B (1981): 261-77.

9. Kalusa, "Disease and Remaking of Missionary Medicine in Colonial Northwestern Zambia." On the popularity of Western medicine in colonial India, see David Arnold, *Colonizing the Body: State Medicine and Epidemic Disease in Nineteenth-Century India* (Berkeley, Los Angeles, and London, 1993).

10. Pier M. Larson, "'Capacities and Modes of Thinking': Intellectual Engagement and Subaltern Hegemony in the Early History of Malagasy Christianity," *American Historical Review* 102, no. 4 (1997): 969-1002; Nancy Rose Hunt, *A Colonial Lexicon of Birth Ritual,*

praxis as a socially constructed affair,[11] the essay insists that the popularity of mission medicine was less the consequence of its supposed superior effectivity than the result of the cultural accommodations CMML medics at Kalene crafted to turn their therapeutic system into a locally meaningful form of healing, and hence acceptable to Africans. For Christian medics in Mwinilunga, this entailed not only modifying the hegemonic medical discourse that portrayed African medicine as its primitive Other. It also involved crafting new medical knowledge and practices in an effort to popularize evangelical medicine. Such knowledge and practices, the paper argues, drew on local cosmologies of healing and repertoire, both of which were broadened due to their encounter with Christianity and mission medicine, and which mission doctors across the continent contemptuously dismissed as the locus of African "paganism." In reconfiguring their own discourse and inventing locally inspired medical knowledge and practices, missionaries knowingly or unknowingly fitted their therapeutic system into preexisting medical knowledge. As a sequel, they unwittingly legitimated their medicine and praxis in indigenous terms. They and their medicine thus came to be easily assimilated into local therapeutic models that European missionaries sought, in an ironic twist, to efface from the African society.[12] Consequently, mission-based medicine with its white practitioners was locally comprehended as a variation of local medicine, rather than as a superior or more effective system of confronting human affliction and suffering.

Medicalization, and Mobility in the Congo (Durham and London, 1999); and Paul Stuart Landau, *The Realm of the Word: Language, Gender, and Christianity in a Southern African Kingdom* (Portsmouth, N.H., 1995). See also Emily K. Abel and Nancy Reifel, "Interaction between Public Health Nurse and Clients on American Indian Reservations during the 1930s," *Social Science of Medicine* 9, no. 1 (1996): 89-108; Kalusa, "Language, Medical Auxiliaries, and the Reinterpretation of Missionary Medicine in Colonial Mwinilunga, Zambia, 1922-51."

11. See Vaughan, *Curing Their Ills;* Vaughan, "Syphilis in Colonial East and Central Africa: The Social Construction of an Epidemic," in *Epidemics and Ideas: Essays on the Historical Perception of Pestilence,* ed. Terence Ranger and Paul Slack (Cambridge, 1992), pp. 269-302; Vaughan, "Health and Hegemony: Representation and the Creation of the Colonial Subject in Nyasaland," in *Contesting Colonial Hegemony: State and Society in Africa and India,* ed. Dagmar Engels and Shula Marks (London and New York, 1994), pp. 173-201; A. Wright and A. Treacher, introduction to *The Problem of Medical Knowledge: Examining the Social Construction of Medicine,* ed. A. Wright and A. Treacher (Edinburgh, 1982).

12. See Uoldelul Chelati Dilar, "Curing Bodies to Rescue Souls: Health in Capuchins' Missionary Strategy in Eritrea, 1894-1935," in *Healing Bodies, Saving Souls: Medical Missions in Asia and Africa,* ed. David Hardiman (Amsterdam and New York, 2006), pp. 251-80; and Kalusa, "Reinterpretation of Missionary Medicine," pp. 60-62.

WALIMA T. KALUSA

Hegemonic Missionary Medical Discourse

To appreciate the manner in which European medics in Mwinilunga recreated their medical discourse with its praxis and to understand why they came to rely on some African therapeutics, it is first essential to underscore the nature of the missionary agency under whose umbrella Kalene-based doctors operated. Founded in Britain and Ireland in the first half of the nineteenth century by a disparate but well-educated group of people, the CMML was an atypical missionary society. Loosely structured, it possessed no central policy-making body and, other than the Bible, no book of regulations for its adherents to follow. CMML believers adhered to an extreme fundamentalist creed, fervently believed in the literal interpretation of the Bible, passionately opposed the association between the Church of England and the state, and strongly abhorred any form of institutionalized religion with centralized control of church affairs and rituals. Moreover, they believed in the priesthood of all believers.[13]

Given its loose organization and fundamentalist creed, the CMML was the hunting ground of individualistic missionaries. Its missionaries overseas enjoyed the liberty to craft their own evangelical policies and a much larger latitude than their counterparts in more hierarchically organized Protestant mission societies with respect to crafting and actualizing their own evangelical theories and praxis. They could also change their evangelical strategies as they saw fit without any direction from above. It is no surprise, then, that there was no unanimity within the movement over evangelical strategy, and many CMML Christians openly dismissed the "gospel of the syringe" as the work of the devil.[14]

But those who settled among the Lunda of Mwinilunga at the turn of the twentieth century were keen medical enthusiasts who regarded scientific medicine as the most effective means by which to convert "pagan" societies to

---

13. For a fuller discussion on the beliefs and organization of the CMML, see Robert I. Rotberg, "Plymouth Brethren and the Occupation of Katanga, 1886-1907," *Journal of African History* 5, no. 2 (1964): 285-97; F. C. Coad, *A History of the Brethren Movement: Its Origins, Its Worldwide Development, and Its Significance for the Present* (Exeter Devon, 1968); Frederick A. Tatford, *That the World May Know: Light over the Dark Continent,* vol. 6 (Bath, 1984), appendix 1; Paul D. Wilkin, "To the Bottom of the Heap: Educational Deprivation and Its Social Implications in North-Western Zambia, 1906-1945" (Ph.D. diss., Syracuse University, 1982); Kalusa, "Disease and Remaking of Missionary Medicine in Colonial Northwestern Zambia."

14. National Archives of Zambia (hereafter NAZ) HM8 F1 2/1/1, Walter Fisher to Singleton Darling, 5 June 1915.

Christianity and transform them in their own image. Heirs to the epoch-making breakthroughs in medical science toward the end of the preceding century, medical enthusiasts held that they possessed the magic bullet with which they could convincingly demonstrate the power of their medicine over disease to the local people. In this way, Christian medics in Africa hoped to annihilate their local patients' faith in "fetish" medicine with its associated cultural and religious underpinnings, which they saw as the most difficult obstacle to Christianization and to their "civilizing" crusade in Africa. Dr. Walter Fisher, the founder of the Kalene mission, thus repeatedly noted in his diaries and letters to benefactors in Europe that sweeping away African systems of healing and worship that he encountered in Mwinilunga was as essential to enhancing the receptivity of the Lunda to Christianity as it was to reclaiming their fallen souls for Christ.[15]

This hegemonic discourse therefore situated missionary medicine in stiff opposition to indigenous medicine. Without making any real effort to understand the cultural complexity that underlined the latter, the architects of the discourse subjected to virulent criticism local therapeutics that they perceived as antithetical to the spread of Christianity, modernity, and Western civilization. Walter Fisher particularly singled out Lunda healing, burial, and midwifery rites as well as the libations, songs, and prayers Africans made to their ancestors *(akishi)* in times of affliction as at best inimical to the health of the indisposed and at worst a major source of African moral and spiritual degradation. Unless these practices were done away with by persuading Africans both to reject their existing medical knowledge and to accept Euro-Christian constructions of disease, medicine, and religion, the African mental world would, the surgeon wrote in the early 1900s, continue to be crammed with irrational and other superstitious fears that were "the more real for being undefined."[16] Moreover, to undermine the ontological hold local healers held over their society, the missionary doctor repeatedly cast them as no more than tricksters who benefited from what Fisher perceived as the cultural backwardness of the African society. He therefore not infrequently instigated the British South Africa Company (BSAC) that ruled the colony from 1890 to 1924 to incarcerate "traditional" healers who contravened the antiwitchcraft legislation passed by the company-government at the start of the century.[17]

---

15. NAZ HM8 F1 2/1/1, Walter Fisher to Darling, 8 January 1907. See also NAZ HM8 F1 2/2/1, Extract from Anna and Walter Fisher's Diaries, No. 17 (undated).

16. Singleton Fisher and Julyan Hoyte, *Ndotolu: The Life and Stories of Walter and Anna Fisher of Central Africa* (Ikelenge, 1992; first published in 1948), p. 177.

17. NAZ KSE 6/2/1, Quarterly Report for July, August and September 1912; NAZ KSE 4/1,

The Inefficacy of Mission Medicine

It is obvious, then, that the discourse under review placed a handsome premium on the binary divisions between missionary and African medicine. Not only did this discourse depict the former as a more scientific, more objective, and more potent form of healing, but it also denounced the latter as irrational, ineffective, and a barrier to human health and to the Western "civilizing mission" in Africa.[18] Thus, this discourse left no room for cross-cultural commerce between the two systems of confronting disease.[19] From this standpoint, it is not surprising that some analysts construe mission-related medical discourse as a double-edged sword by which Christian doctors weakened African healing practices and related medical knowledge and, at the same time, inscribed on the colonized new ways of comprehending disease or treating it. As a result, such analysts have found it difficult to conceptualize the accommodations missionary healers made with the non-Western medical cultures in the peripheral areas of the European empire.[20] Unwittingly, academics operating in this mold have endorsed the binary divisions that colonial medical practitioners drew between "traditional" and Western medicine. They therefore have tended to explain the acceptance and popularity of Western medicine in colonial settings in ways that seldom diverge from those etched in colonial and mission-authored literature.[21]

The popularity of the medicine associated with that missionary medical discourse is predicated on the assumption that Christian doctors in colonial Africa possessed superior medical knowledge and practices and therefore

---

Mwinilunga District Notebook, 1906-1964, and Elsie Burr, *Kalene Memories: Memoirs of the Old Hill* (London, 1956).

18. For a detailed examination of how Africans responded to the Christian "civilizing mission," see Walima T. Kalusa, "Elders, Young Men, and David Livingstone's 'Civilizing Mission': Revisiting the Disintegration of the Kololo Kingdom, 1851-1864," *International Journal of African Historical Studies* 42, no. 1 (2009): 55-80.

19. Kalusa, "Language, Medical Auxiliaries, and the Reinterpretation of Missionary Medicine in Colonial Mwinilunga, Zambia, 1922-51."

20. See Cunningham and Andrews, "Introduction: Western Knowledge as Contested Knowledge," in *Western Medicine as Contested Knowledge*, pp. 1-23. For exceptions, see Heather Bell, "Midwifery Training and Female Circumcision in the Inter-War Anglo-Egyptian Sudan," *Journal of African History* 39 (1998): 293-312; Bell, *Frontiers of Medicine in Anglo-Egyptian Sudan, 1899-1940* (Oxford, 1999).

21. This insight derives from Vaughan, *Curing Their Ills*, p. x; Vaughan, "Healing and Curing: Issues in the History of Anthropology in Africa," *Social History of Medicine* 7, no. 2 (1994): 283-95; Eric Silla, *People Are Not the Same: Leprosy and Identity in Twentieth-Century Mali* (Portsmouth and London, 1998), p. 9.

more effectively combated disease than local healers and hence persuaded non-Western societies to jettison their therapeutics for allopathic medicine with its Christian ideology. Largely curative, however, missionary medicine at Kalene Hill proved impotent against a host of afflictions precipitated by the early colonial policies of the BSAC, notably taxation and labor migration.[22] A brief examination of epidemic and endemic diseases commonly treated at Kalene hospital will suffice to illustrate that despite missionary rhetoric, evangelical medicine in Mwinilunga was as often ineffective as its potency was eulogized by its European practitioners.

Most of the intractable diseases doctors and nurses at Kalene hospital had to contend with in the early twentieth century issued from Mwinilunga's rapidly deteriorating epidemiological landscape. This chiefly arose on the heels of the area's integration through labor migration into the nascent southern African capitalist economy dominated by farming and mining in South Africa and in the nearby Belgian Congo. As Lunda migrants oscillated between the district and emerging wage employment centers in those territories, they increasingly imported into the district the diseases they contracted abroad and thus exacerbated the already large cesspool of disease in the area.

Among the lethal diseases imported or easily spread in Mwinilunga through labor migration in the early days of colonial rule was pneumonia. Since the only recourse missionaries at Kalene hospital possessed against the affliction was to keep its victims warm in bed, as nurse Elsie Burr observed in the 1920s,[23] pneumonia annually left a long trail of death until well after the Second World War, when the medics could treat it successfully with antibiotics. A pneumonia epidemic reportedly introduced in the district in 1915 by Lunda migrants returning from the Belgian Congo, for example, rapidly spread to many parts of the district, killing not a small number of patients admitted to the hospital.[24] An even more virulent strain of the affliction, also believed to have been imported from the Congo, similarly ravaged the district three years later and caused "many sudden deaths" among patients and converts at the mission hospital and in surrounding villages.[25] As the victims of the epidemic included three prominent Lunda CMML converts, rumor spread throughout the African community at the hospital that the disease was caused by Dr. Fisher himself, a vivid local commentary on the limits of his healing powers.[26]

22. In "Disease and Remaking of Missionary Medicine in Colonial Northwestern Zambia," I have dealt with this topic at great length.
23. See Burr, *Kalene Memories*, p. 17.
24. NAZ KSE 6/2/1, Quarterly Report for the quarter ended September 1915.
25. CMML, *Echoes of Service*, February 1918, p. 48.
26. CMML, *Echoes of Service*, February 1918, p. 48.

If the surgeon's magic bullet failed to shoot down pneumonia, it proved equally incapable of conquering tropical ulcers. Long endemic in Mwinilunga, the disease broke out with epidemic force during the First World War. The epidemic occurred at a time of severe food shortages caused by the BSAC, which, to fight German forces in northeastern Zambia, both requisitioned food from the district for its troops and mobilized from the district thousands of war carriers, mostly able-bodied men who traditionally opened up new gardens.[27] Breaking out at a time of rising malnutrition, the disease quickly attacked 10 percent of the district's population of about 15,000 people. Described by Mwinilunga's district commissioner as "new to science," tropical ulcers ate deeply into the limbs of its victims, and missionaries' efforts to treat ulcer sores with carbonic acid mixed with glycerin met with no success.[28] Yet Dr. Walter Fisher informed his supporters in Europe that his treatment of ulcer patients enabled him to prove to them the power of biomedicine and thus to win their souls for Christ. "There is much to encourage us in the [medical] work now," he wrote enthusiastically in 1916 to his brother-in-law in England. "The natives' complete failure in treating these sores," continued the doctor, "and, through God's blessing, our success is opening the folly of their superstitions and never before have they listened so attentively to the gospel and have we had so many inquiries [about Christianity]."[29]

In retrospect, neither Dr. Walter Fisher nor medical science held a lasting solution against tropical ulcers, and whatever cures of the disease that occurred at Kalene seem to have been a matter of conjecture. The cures apparently issued from the nourishing diet his patients received at the hospital, rather than the treatment they received there. Upon returning to their impoverished villages, many former patients suffered from yet another ulcer attack. A district assistant magistrate who visited some of these villages in mid-1916 graphically described the plight of these people: "In many villages natives who are almost skeletons lie about with putrefying ulcers from which infection is so easily spread to other inhabitants who may have sustained slight abrasions and these become festering [and horribly] stinking sores."[30] Moreover, of the 600 patients treated for the disease at the mission hospital, the majority of those who escaped death became crippled for life. The surgeon himself amputated the limbs of patients de-

---

27. For a detailed discussion on this issue, see G. W. T. Hodges, "African Manpower Statistics for British Forces in East Africa, 1914-1918," *Journal of African History* 14, no. 1 (1978). See also Melvin E. Page, "The War of Thangata: Nyasaland and the East African Campaign," *Journal of African History* 19, no. 1 (1978): 87-100.

28. NAZ KSE1/4, MDN.

29. NAZ KSE F1 2/1/1, Walter Fisher to Darling, 13 January 1916.

30. NAZ KSE 6/2/1, Quarterly Report for the Quarter ended 30 June 1916.

stroyed by ulcer sores,[31] a practice that his patients must have perceived as yet another example of the limitations of biomedical power.

Following the ulcers epidemic, the scourge continued to be endemic throughout the district. It sporadically erupted with epidemic force at times of heightened social and economic stress. For example, the disease struck Mwinilunga epidemically in 1918-19 when cassava blight destroyed the area's staple crop. The resultant food shortages triggered massive movements of people across the district as famine-stricken people searched for food. This in turn facilitated the spread of the highly contagious disease. This state of affairs repeated itself during the economic slump of the early 1920s when the already poverty-stricken families in the district were reduced to living on wild fruits and roots and to wearing animal skins.[32] Tropical ulcers, moreover, continued to ravage the health of the people well into the 1940s partly because of persistent poverty and partly because of the "natives who [went] to the Congo and [returned] to their homes with ulcers in advanced stage."[33]

The ineffectiveness of missionary medicine in Mwinilunga came into even sharper relief during the Spanish influenza pandemic of 1918 and 1919. This epidemic, whose debilitating impact worldwide has spawned a veritable research industry comparable only to that existing on the rinderpest epizootic that ravaged pastoral communities in eastern and southern Africa in the late nineteenth century,[34] was first introduced in the northeast of Mwinilunga in late 1918 by Lunda migrant miners escaping from the pandemic in the mines in the Belgian Congo. Another wave of the infectious affliction hit the south of the

---

31. NAZ KSE 6/2/1, Quarterly Report for the Quarter ended 31 September 1916 and NAZ KSE 4/1, MDN.

32. NAZ KSE6/1/3, Annual Report for the Year ending 31 March 1920; NAZ KSE 6/1/4, Annual Report for the Year ending 31 March 1922.

33. NAZ KSE 4/1, MDN. A similar situation persisted elsewhere in Africa; see Rasford, "Bid the Disease Cease," pp. 160-62.

34. The literature on this topic is therefore vast. See David Patterson, "The Influenza Epidemic of 1918-1919 in Gold Coast," *Journal of African History* 24 (1983): 85-100; Terence Ranger, "The Influenza Pandemic in Southern Rhodesia: A Crisis of Comprehension," in *Imperial Medicine and Indigenous Society,* ed. David Arnold (Manchester, 1988), pp. 1/2-88; "Plagues of Beasts and Men: Prophet Responses to Epidemics in Eastern and Southern Africa," in *Epidemics and Ideas,* pp. 241-68; D. C. Ohadike, "The Influenza Pandemic of 1918-1919 and the Spread of Cassava," *Journal of African History* 22 (1981): 379-91; Mwelwa C. Musambachime, "The 1918-1919 Influenza Epidemic in Northern Rhodesia" (seminar paper presented at the University of Zambia, 15 October 1993). Works on the rinderpest pandemic include Pule Phoolo, "Epidemics and Revolutions: The Rinderpest Epidemic in the Late Nineteenth-Century Southern Africa," *Past and Present* 138 (1993): 112-43; Charles van Onselen, "Reactions to Rinderpest Epidemic in Southern Africa," *Journal of African History* 12, no. 3 (1972): 473-88.

district in the following year, as influenza- and panic-stricken war carriers fled into the district on the colony's railroad. Striking the area from these directions, Spanish influenza, whose etiology remained unknown up to the 1930s and whose cure continues to defy modern science to this day, quickly spread throughout the district, leaving behind prodigious mortality and morbidity at Kalene Hill hospital. As a missionary nurse noted, the only available remedy the hospital offered to the hundreds of influenza patients who sought treatment there was "soup and mush."[35] Nor did the pandemic spare European missionaries; a number of their children, including Dr. Walter Fisher's grandchild, quickly succumbed to the fatal disease.[36]

Apart from its failure to combat or prevent epidemics, medicine at the mission hospital proved equally ill-suited to treat a host of afflictions long endemic in the district. Among these diseases were hookworm, jiggers, whooping cough, yaws, alimentary and sexually transmitted diseases, and, after the inception of large-scale mining on the Zambian Copperbelt in the 1920s, industrial afflictions like tuberculosis and silicosis.[37] Hookworm proved particularly intractable and of great nuisance to both missionaries and their African employees because of poor sanitation at Kalene hospital itself. In the 1920s and 1930s, the disease reportedly infected 80 percent of the white and black community at Kalene Hill. At the same time, Thymol, the drug the doctors administered to the ever rising number of hookworm patients at the hospital, seems to have provided only temporary relief.[38]

It is abundantly evident, then, that mission propaganda that exhorted evangelical medicine as effective did not always square up with reality. For a long time after their settlement at Kalene, CMML healers struggled in vain to deal with most of the diseases their African patients presented for treatment. The medics could not therefore easily persuade them that mission-based medicine held the only key to good health, even though, admittedly, some of its elements such as midwifery and surgery at which Dr. Walter Fisher was skilled were undoubtedly effective.

---

35. M. K. Fisher, *Lampposts to Searchlights: Memories of M. K. Fisher of Central Africa* (Ikelenge, 1994), p. 56.

36. M. K. Fisher, *Lampposts to Searchlights*, p. 56.

37. NAZ KSE 6/1/5, Annual Report for the Year ending 31 March 1926; NAZ ZA 1/9/8/2, A. W. Bonfield to Assistant Magistrate, 8 June 1926; NAZ KSE 6/6/2, Tour Report by A. M. Alexander, 22 May 1928.

38. NAZ KSE 6/1/4, Annual Report for the Year ending 31 March 1921; NAZ SEC 2/133, Annual Report on Native Affairs for the Year ending 31 March 1937; NAZ ZA 7/6/7, H. S. de Boer, Report on Conditions in Northern Rhodesia (1933); A. E. Fulton, *From Forest Track to Tar Mac* (Bala, 1974), p. 12.

Christian Medical Discourse and Praxis on the Imperial Frontier

To the dismay of evangelists at Kalene Hill, local acceptance of their medicine yielded not a single convert to Christianity among Lunda speakers during the first six years of medical proselytization in Mwinilunga. Although some Luba refugees and slaves from the Belgian Congo who settled at Kalene Hill embraced the new faith in the early years of Dr. Fisher's medical mission, it was not until 1911 that the first Lunda convert, Nyamavunda, turned to Christianity, and only four years later did the earliest indigenous Christians receive baptism in the district.[39] Yet even the acceptance of Christianity itself heralded no wholesale rejection of indigenous knowledge of disease and practices among Lunda converts, as the CMML expected.

To the contrary, ample evidence suggests that converts in Mwinilunga were in fact propelled to Christianity not merely because of their belief in witchcraft/ancestral affliction, for example, but because they came to look upon the new faith as an alternative means to confront the malevolent powers of witches and other sources of evil, a widespread belief in other parts of colonial and postcolonial Africa.[40] "The fear of man [i.e., witches]," lamented Fisher early in 1913, "has been greater than the fear of God, and therefore the native Christians have not been our helpers in reproving and dealing with sin in their falling fellow-believers."[41] Lunda patients likewise (re)interpreted Dr. Fisher's diagnostic tools into local comprehension of divinatory apparatuses *(ngombu)*. Thus some of his patients routinely implored him and other medics to use such instruments as the microscope to detect whether their afflictions were as a result of the anger of their ancestors or witchcraft, much to the amusement and surprise of the white medics.[42]

---

39. NAZ HM8 F1 2/1/1, Walter Fisher to Darling, 16 November 1915; Lewis H. Gann, *A History of Northern Rhodesia: From Early Days to 1953* (New York, 1964), p. 49.

40. Interviews with Benwa Wiscott, pastor, Mwinilunga, 20 February 2001; Chitambala Nakalya Bayuda, church elder, Mwinilunga, 23 February 2001; Casius Tembo, pastor, and Kenneth Nkanza, pastor, Mwinilunga, 25 February 2001. See also Luise White, "Vampire Priests of Central Africa: African Debates about Labor and Religion in Colonial Northern Rhodesia," *Comparative Studies in Society and History* 35, no. 4 (1993): 746-72; Birgit Meyer, *Translating the Devil: Religion and Modernity among the Ewe in Ghana* (Trenton, N.J., and Asmara, 1999); Meyer, "'Delivered from the Power of Darkness': Confessions of Satanic Riches in Ghana," *Africa* 65 (1995); Peter Geschiere, *The Modernity of Witchcraft: Politics and the Occult in Post-Colonial Africa* (Charlottesville, Va., and London, 1997); Brian Larkin and Birgit Meyer, "Pentecostalism, Islam and Culture," in *Themes in West Africa's History*, ed. Emmanuel Kwaku Akyeampong (Athens, Ohio, Oxford, and Accra, 2006), pp. 283-312.

41. CMML, *Echoes of Service*, April 1913, pp. 155-56.

42. NAZ HM8 F 2/1/1, Walter Fisher to Darling, 5 September 1915; H. Julyan Hoyte, "The Kalene Jubilee," *Echoes Quarterly Review*, July-September 1956, p. 4.

Clearly, African patients and converts in Mwinilunga received mission-based medicine and Christianity in ways that were fundamentally at odds with the expectations of their European dispensers. Although the mission healers regarded their medicine as a scientific weapon designed to supplant local medical etiologies and associated their belief in the practices with Christian comprehension of medicine and religion, the Lunda quickly co-opted the alien system of healing with its theories of disease causation and salvation into familiar cultural and religious frameworks. They thus transformed the new medicine into an additional means of coming to terms with new and old socio-epidemiological concerns.

Within this context, the encounter between Christian and local medicine did not leave Lunda medical knowledge and praxis unscathed. Despite the shortcomings of mission-based medicine, documentary evidence indicates that African healers in Mwinilunga and beyond innovatively appropriated Christian images and symbols to reinvigorate their own healing systems and thus more effectively come to terms with their rapidly deteriorating disease landscape. When a CMML missionary visited villages south of Kalene Hill at the height of the tropical ulcers epidemic during the First World War, he witnessed a local healing procession in which the healer kept on "just jerking his fingers," repeatedly invoking "Jesus to help him" in healing those afflicted with the disease amidst animated dancing and singing. Although the evangelist dismissed these actions as the height of "the blasphemy of the heathen,"[43] the local healer's ritual actions are indicative of the "pragmatic experimentation" that the encounter between Christian and African medicine spawned.[44]

Refashioning Missionary Discourse

The inadequacy of missionary medicine against diseases combined with the refusal of Africans to broaden their own cosmologies of disease and medicine through appropriating images and symbols associated with missionary medicine and Christianity posed a major challenge to medical evangelism.

---

43. CMML, *Echoes of Service*, May 1915; Kalusa, "Reinterpretation of Missionary Medicine," p. 123.

44. I am grateful to an anonymous reviewer who emphasized the significance of this point. See also David Maxwell, "The Spirit and Scapular: Pentecostal and Catholic Interactions in Northern Nyanga District, Zimbabwe in the 1950s and Early 1960s," *Journal of Southern African Studies* 23, no. 2 (1997): 283-300, and *Christians and Chiefs in Zimbabwe: A Social History of the Hwesa People, c. 1870s-1990s* (London, 1999).

This not only added ammunition to the critics of what came to be pejoratively dubbed the "gospel of the syringe" within CMML circles.[45] It also, for the purpose of this discussion, begs the question why mission-based medicine became so popular in the face of its glaring impotence against diseases treated at Kalene Hill. As may be clear from how the Lunda received Dr. Walter Fisher's medicine and his technologies, part of the reason may be that the local people comprehended it in a manner that made cultural sense to them, rather than in the way it was articulated by missionary doctors. But this explanation alone hardly unravels the whole paradox. The missing parts of the jigsaw may be found within the context of the cultural accommodations missionaries initiated to popularize their therapies among the local people in order to more effectively draw them to the CMML version of Christianity.

Confronted with their own inability to treat a legion of diseases and frustrated by the ways Africans responded to the missionary medical discourse and religion, the CMML in central Africa made far-reaching modifications in their discourse along with its concomitant praxis. At the center stage of the reconfiguration of the discourse was Dan Crawford, an influential Scottish missionary within the CMML. Crawford, whom Fisher regarded as the most intellectually gifted academic, educator, and philosopher in the whole missionary society, first closely worked with the surgeon in Angola in the second half of the nineteenth century before he founded his own mission station among the Luba people in the southern part of the Belgian Congo. There, Crawford, who continued to maintain very close ties with the Fisher family at Kalene, became fondly known as Konga Vantu, or "Gatherer of People," due to the significant part he played in resettling refugees fleeing from the Belgian "wars of pacification" toward the end of the nineteenth century.

Like Walter Fisher, Dan Crawford was, by early in the second decade of the twentieth century, deeply disappointed with the mediocre evangelical record the CMML had scored in Angola, the Belgian Congo, and colonial Zambia, and particularly with what he perceived as skin-deep faith exhibited by African converts. To this end, the missionary-scholar published in 1912 a best seller entitled *Thinking Black*. In it Crawford maintained that the CMML's poor evangelical results issued from its "policy of make-believe" that indiscriminately assailed African medical and religious knowledge, beliefs, and practices without its missionaries making serious efforts to comprehend the

---

45. Kalusa, "Language, Medical Auxiliaries, and the Reinterpretation of Missionary Medicine in Colonial Mwinilunga, Zambia, 1922-51."

moral, social, and intellectual logic undergirding those beliefs and practices. Konga Vantu dismissed this policy as a "hollow one."[46]

A believer in the essential unity of humanity, the philosopher reasoned that Africans were not intellectually inferior to other races and that some of their social, cultural, and medical institutions and practices that European missionaries so much vilified were in fact based on solid moral and intellectual foundations. Dan Crawford thus insisted that these institutions with their underlying cultural logic were therefore not incompatible with Christian tenets. The academic argued that the successful conversion of Africans to Christianity depended not so much on emasculating their culture as on identifying which of their institutions and practices could best be pressed into the service of the gospel. In his own words, such indigenous ways of praying and healing as singing, dancing, and uttering incantations could, for example, be "consecrated to the Lord" and hence effectively utilized to draw Africans to Christ.[47]

Underlying this discourse was the assumption that by deploying African idioms and praxis in the service of Christianity, the CMML could anchor its religious ideology on what was culturally familiar and hence comprehensible to African patients and converts. In the process, Africans could on their own volition come to draw distinctions between what was "heathen" and what was acceptable in the eyes of God. Dan Crawford, who evidently admired David Livingstone's positive attitude to African medical knowledge and practices,[48] therefore saw the path to successful evangelization of the African continent as lying in selective appropriation of indigenous knowledge, idioms, and practices. Thus, he repeatedly challenged his fellow evangelists in central Africa to abandon their superiority complex and to channel their own practices into ways that were locally familiar. Most significantly, the missionary enjoined other evangelists to deeply immerse themselves in the study of local languages, proverbs, songs, riddles, and poems so that they could not merely master local modes of thought and action but also learn to "think black."

It is most unlikely that Crawford ever abandoned the widely held view that African institutions and medicine were primitive. Neither does he seem to have seriously interrogated the notion that non-Western medicine and religions and related practices were the fortress of heathenism. From this stand-

---

46. Dan Crawford, *Thinking Black: 22 Years without a Break in the Long Grass of Central Africa* (London, 1912), p. 146.
47. Crawford, *Thinking Black*, p. 55.
48. On Livingstone's attitude toward African medicine, see Vaughan, *Curing Their Ills*.

point, "thinking black" must be understood as an endeavor to create a new religious and medical discourse mutually comprehensible to missionaries and Africans. This discourse would empower the former to appropriate and deploy local knowledge, institutions, and idioms to undermine indigenous religions and medicine and so more effectively plant the seeds of Christianity, civilization, and modernity on African soil. What Dan Crawford advocated, then, was in many respects a religious replica of indirect rule in British Africa.[49] Much as the engineers of this system of governance sought to rule Africans through preexisting political institutions, the missionary envisaged attracting the subjects of empire to European ways of seeing and being through their own medico-religious knowledge, idioms, and practices — which most other missionaries vilified as the root of "paganism" in Africa.

Not all Christian evangelists, of course, agreed with Konga Vantu. As Nancy Rose Hunt remarks, some European missionaries "equated thinking black with thinking evil."[50] Nonetheless, Crawford's challenge to Christian preachers to gather information on and to steep themselves in African culture did not go unheeded among his counterparts at Kalene Hill, especially in the Fisher family. In the aftermath of Crawford's publication, the Fisher family, led by Dr. Walter Fisher's eldest son Singleton, an anesthetist and self-taught anthropologist, devoted many years to collecting data on Lunda medicine, language, folklore, religion, and culture.[51] The collection of such data inevitably required closer interaction between missionaries and the Lunda in local discourses of disease, medicine, and religion. In Mwinilunga, this growing interaction between mission doctors and the local people culminated in the publication by Singleton Fisher of ethnographic and, with his wife, valuable linguistic works between late in the second decade of the twentieth century and the 1940s.[52] As a corollary, idioms and practices allied with Lunda

---

49. For detailed studies on indirect rule in colonial Zambia, see Kusum Datta, "The Policy of Indirect Rule in Zambia (Northern Rhodesia), 1924-1953" (Ph.D. diss., University of London, 1976); Ben C. Kakoma, "Colonial Administration in Northern Rhodesia: A Case Study of Administration in the Mwinilunga District, 1900-1939" (M.A. thesis, University of Auckland, 1971).

50. Hunt, *Colonial Lexicon,* p. 135. A good example of a missionary who rejected Konga Vantu's evangelical strategy is Dr. Robert Laws of the Livingstonia Mission in colonial Malawi. See G. E. Tilsley, *Dan Crawford: Missionary and Pioneer in Central Africa* (London and Edinburgh, 1929), pp. vi-x. But many other missionaries shared Crawford's views. See Patrick Harries, *Butterflies and Barbarians: Swiss Missionaries and Systems of Knowledge in South-East Africa* (Oxford, Harare, and Athens, Ohio, 2007).

51. See Fisher and Hoyte, *Ndotolu,* p. 42.

52. See Singleton Fisher and M. K. Fisher, *Lunda Handbook* (Mutshatsha, 1919; reprint 1944); Singleton Fisher, "The Witcheries," in CMML, *A Central African Jubilee or Fifty Years*

medico-religious culture became increasingly significant in shaping mission medical and religious discourses.

The significance of the ethnographic and linguistic research carried out in Mwinilunga to shaping missionary discourse, evangelical strategies, and attitudes toward Lunda medical knowledge and praxis after Crawford published his book must not be underestimated. Henceforth, CMML missionaries who demonstrated ability to "think black" were increasingly seen as an indispensable asset in the spread of Christianity in the district and beyond.[53] More importantly, such research seems to have enabled missionaries in Mwinilunga to gain insights into the cultural complexity of local concepts of disease, medicine, and religion. A close reading of CMML memoirs reveals that by the 1920s and 1930s, some Christian evangelists at Kalene were increasingly less overtly averse to some aspects of African medicine.[54]

This view finds support in the fact that a few missionaries at Kalene were by the 1920s resorting to some Lunda therapeutics to treat their ailments against which they had no therapy, the most popular among such remedies involving killing, roasting, and eating offending scorpions to treat scorpion bites. More astonishingly, European evangelists in Mwinilunga began taking part in local burial rites, which they earlier simply stigmatized as either primitive or satanic. When Walter Fisher died in December 1935, for instance, he was interred in a reed mat in conformity with his own wish to be buried in accordance with Lunda burial rituals.[55] Many Kalene-based missionaries had by the 1940s also realized that among their African interlocutors, disease, death, funerals, medicine, and their associated rituals were arenas for harmonizing broken social relations.[56] Such missionaries regularly attended Lunda

---

with the Gospel in the Beloved Strip, 1881-1931 (London, 1932), pp. 179-81; Singleton Fisher, "Black Magic Feuds," *African Studies* 7 (1949): 20-22.

53. Singleton Fisher, for example, was sent to open a CMML mission station among the Lunda in southern Belgian Congo in the late 1920s because of his mastery of Lunda culture, customs, and language. See M. K. Fisher, *Lampposts to Searchlights*.

54. See, for example, M. K. Fisher, *Lampposts to Searchlights*.

55. Fisher and Hoyte, *Ndotolu*, p. 199; W. T. Stunt et al., *Turning the World Upside Down: A Century of Missionary Endeavor* (Eastborne, Sussex, 1972), p. 417; Monica Fisher, *Nswana, the Heir: The Life and Times of Charles Fisher of Central Africa* (Ndola, 1991), p. 114.

56. Fisher and Hoyte, *Ndotolu*, p. 177. For a fuller treatment of this topic, see Victor W. Turner, *Schism and Continuity in an African Society: A Study of Ndembu Village Life* (Manchester, 1957); Turner, *The Drums of Affliction: A Study of the Religious Process of the Ndembu of Zambia* (Oxford, 1968); Turner, *The Forest of Symbols: Aspects of Ndembu Ritual* (Ithaca, N.Y., 1967); Turner, "Chihamba, the White Spirit: A Ritual Drama of the Ndembu," *Rhodes-Livingstone Papers* 35 (Manchester, 1962).

mourning rites, even though they sometimes inveighed against the "pagan" elements of such rituals.[57]

As evangelists at Kalene Hill increasingly took part in African rituals without necessarily dwelling on them in their written accounts sent to their audience in Europe, they also increasingly channeled their medical praxis into local ways they felt could more effectively appeal to the indigenes. Thus, although the CMML as a whole abhorred religious rituals, as earlier noted, its doctors at Kalene Hill crafted rites not dissimilar from those through which the Lunda made sense of or redressed disease. By the outbreak of the First World War, it had become an established custom at Kalene for missionaries, inpatients, and their hospital escorts to meet at 8:00 A.M. daily in the hospital to sing, pray, and exhort God, the Great Healer, prior to the treatment of patients. These rituals, attended by numerous people, some of whom associated them with healing, were reenacted for outpatients at 9:30 A.M. and repeated in the evening.[58] Urged by the surgeon or missionaries assigned to the task, those in attendance closed their eyes and implored God to manifest his love by healing the sick. Whether missionaries were aware or not, these rituals reinvented the prayers and offerings the Lunda made to their ancestors in times of distress, sickness, and death.[59] Frequently, too, Dr. Walter Fisher collected and burned witchcraft paraphernalia at public gatherings that drew large crowds from across the district. In this vein, he performed functions similar to those carried out by the widely studied Muchape antiwitchcraft movements that swept across much of south-central Africa in the 1920s and 1930s.[60]

Oral evidence further strongly suggests that in the aftermath of Crawford's book, evangelists at Kalene Hill increasingly conceptually positioned Lunda epistemologies of disease and healing conceptions less and less in opposition to scientific theories of disease causation and treatment. As a missionary who had spent close to forty years evangelizing among the Lunda of Mwinilunga recalled in 2001:

57. See M. K. Fisher, *Lampposts to Searchlights*.
58. Burr, *Kalene Memories*, p. 29. These rituals were still being performed at Kalene hospital when I carried out fieldwork in Mwinilunga in 2001.
59. My insight here derives from Landau, *The Realm of the Word*.
60. There is abundant literature on this topic. See Audrey I. Richards, "A Modern Movement of Witchfinders," *Africa* 4 (1935): 448-60; Terence Ranger, "The Mwana Lesa Movement of 1925," in *Themes in the Christian History of Central Africa*, ed. Terence Ranger and John Weller (Berkeley and Los Angeles, 1975), pp. 45-75; Karen Fields, *Revival and Rebellion in Colonial Central Africa* (Princeton, 1985). The most recent work on this topic is Peter Probst, "Mchape '95, or the Sudden Fame of Billy Goodson Chisupe: Healing Social Memory and the Enigma of the Public Sphere in Post-Banda Malawi," *Africa* 69 (1999): 108-38.

> Once pioneer missionaries in [the area] realized that their attack on ancestral worship and witchcraft was fruitless, they began to preach that the *akishi* [Lunda ancestral spirit] as agents of Satan could indeed cause disease. [But they also] preached that the *akishi* were mere agents of the devil, who [had] less power than *Nzambi* [Christian God]. They taught people that those who turned to God had nothing to fear because *Nzambi* would protect them from the dark powers of their ancestors and . . . [of] witches.[61]

Conceptually and pragmatically, then, European evangelists in the district reworked their medical discourse and praxis. They integrated into their discourse idioms and other raw materials directly drawn from popular medical and religious knowledge that missionaries ironically sought to dislodge. In refashioning their discourse in this manner and crafting practices inspired by African rituals of healing, CMML medics in Mwinilunga knowingly or unknowingly indigenized their medical discourse.[62] This eroded the false dichotomies between mission therapeutics, which the evangelists eulogized as scientific and rational, and African medicine, which they fetishized as irrational, primitive, and ineffectual. As a corollary, evangelical doctors narrowed the conceptual gulf between missionary and local medicine. They thus established a *modus vivendi* through which they practiced their version of biomedicine in ways that made cultural logic to their African interlocutors, even though, unknown to the medics, this confounded their own efforts to annihilate their interlocutors' medical knowledge and culture. It is, I submit, in the reduction of the binary divisions between missionary and African medical discourse that Christian medical practitioners popularized their therapeutics on the imperial periphery.

Conclusion

Because medical missionaries are widely believed to have been linchpins in the creation of the Western empire in the nineteenth and twentieth centuries, many scholars have indicted them as no more than purveyors of Western cultural and medical imperialism. This perspective is not without reason, for missionaries throughout the imperial world repeatedly cast themselves in this mold. Indeed,

---

61. Interview with Barry Haigh, medical missionary, Nyangombe Bible School, Mwinilunga, 7 January 2001; see also Kalusa, "Disease and Remaking of Missionary Medicine in Colonial Northwestern Zambia," from which much of this data derives.

62. My inspiration here derives from Maxwell, "The Spirit and the Scapular" and *Christians and Chiefs in Zimbabwe*.

their accounts, which constitute the bulk of sources available to the student of the history of missionary medicine, depict evangelical medicine as a potent weapon by which Christian doctors rolled back and supplanted African medical beliefs and practices with Euro-Christian constructions of disease and medicine. A close reading of these accounts, however, suggests that missionary doctors and other enthusiasts of medical proselytization grossly exaggerated biomedical power. They further obscured the accommodations they made with African medical culture in order to popularize their system of healing and to turn it into a more potent tool of evangelization. This paper shows that far from being effective, medicine at the CMML-controlled hospital at Kalene Hill in modern Zambia's Mwinilunga district was often incapable of curing afflictions structurally connected to colonial impoverishment and poverty.

In Mwinilunga, missionary medicine turned out to be a blunt weapon with which to conquer African souls for Christ in the manner anticipated by missionaries. This was largely because the local people reinterpreted the Christian faith in ways that were peculiarly African. Faced with these obstacles, CMML healers at Kalene mission hospital were compelled into a relationship of dependence with Africans.[63] To convert the latter to their variety of Christianity and hence legitimate their "civilizing mission" in Africa, the medics incorporated African medical knowledge into discourse. They also, for the same reasons, crafted locally inspired rituals. Either way, mission doctors unwittingly effaced the binary divisions between their medicine and Lunda therapeutics, thereby weakening the potential of their therapeutics to act as an instrument of cultural annihilation. Thus, if missionary medical discourse together with its related praxis was a tool of imperial domination, as its critics insist, it was also a sword by which the architects of the same discourse undercut that domination.[64] In transforming their discourse and in incorporating into their repertoire locally driven rites to accommodate African ways of thinking and acting, CMML medics in Mwinilunga familiarized their therapeutic system. In this way, they rendered their medicine culturally comprehensible, acceptable, and popular to their African interlocutors. But

63. For a fuller treatment of this topic, see Jan Bart Gewald, "Flags, Funerals, and Fanfare: Herero and Missionary Contestations of the Acceptable, 1900-1930," *Journal of African Cultural Studies* 15, no. 1 (2002): 105-17.

64. Among the most ardent critics of European medicine in imperial contexts are Franz Fanon, "Medicine and Colonialism," in *The Cultural Crisis of Modern Medicine*, ed. John Ehrenreich (New York and London, 1978), pp. 229-51; James A. Paul, "Medicine and Imperialism," in *The Cultural Crisis of Modern Medicine*, pp. 271-86; John Comaroff and Jean Comaroff, *Ethnography and Historical Imagination* (Boulder, San Francisco, and Oxford, 1992), chapter 8.

such popularity was purchased at the price of the CMML's failure to annihilate local medical knowledge and culture.

SELECT BIBLIOGRAPHY

Arnold, David. *Colonizing the Body: State Medicine and Epidemic Disease in Nineteenth-Century India.* Berkeley, Los Angeles, and London, 1993.

Burr, Elsie. *Kalene Memories: Memoirs of the Old Hill.* London, 1956.

Dilar, Uoldelul Chelati. "Curing Bodies to Rescue Souls: Health in Capuchins' Missionary Strategy in Eritrea, 1884-1935." In *Healing Bodies, Saving Souls: Medical Missions in Asia and Africa,* edited by David Hardiman. Amsterdam and New York, 2006.

Fisher, M. K. *Lampposts to Searchlights: Memories of M. K. Fisher of Central Africa.* Ikelenge, 1994.

Fisher, Singleton, and Julyan Hoyte. *Ndotolu: The Life and Stories of Walter and Anna Fisher of Central Africa.* Ikelenge, 1992; first published in 1948.

Kalusa, Walima T. "Elders, Young Men, and David Livingstone's 'Civilizing Mission': Revisiting the Disintegration of the Kololo Kingdom, 1851-1864." *International Journal of African Historical Studies* 42, no. 1 (2009).

———. "The Impact of the Second World War on African Health at Roan Antelope Mine." *Journal of Humanities* 1, no. 1 (1997).

———. "Language, Medical Auxiliaries, and the Reinterpretation of Missionary Medicine in Colonial Mwinilunga, Zambia, 1922-51." *Journal of Eastern African Studies* 1, no. 1 (2007).

Marks, Shula, and Neil Anderson. "Industrialization, Rural Health, and the 1944 National Health Services Commission in South Africa." In *The Social Basis of Health and Healing in Africa,* edited by Steven Feierman and John Jansen. Berkeley and Los Angeles, 1992.

Maxwell, David. *Christians and Chiefs in Zimbabwe: A Social History of the Hwesa People, c. 1870s-1990s.* London, 1999.

———. "The Spirit and the Scapular: Pentecostal and Catholic Interactions in Northern Nyanga District, Zimbabwe in the 1950s and Early 1960s." *Journal of Southern African Studies* 23, no. 2 (1997).

Ollumwullah, Osaak A. *Dis-ease in the Colonial State: Medicine, Society, and Social Change among the AbaNyole of Western Kenya.* Westport, Conn., and London, 2002.

Packard, Randall M. *White Plague, Black Labor: Tuberculosis and Political Economy of Health and Disease in South Africa.* Berkeley and Los Angeles, 1989.

Vaughan, Megan. *Curing Their Ills: Colonial Power and African Illness.* Stanford, 1991.

Waller, Richard, and Kathy Homewood. "Elders and Experts: Contesting Veterinary Knowledge in a Pastoral Community." In *Western Medicine as Contested Knowledge,* edited by Andrew Cunningham and Bridie Andrews. Manchester and New York, 1997.

CHAPTER 9

Strange Bedfellows: The International Missionary Council, the International African Institute, and Research into African Marriage and Family

NATASHA ERLANK

In 1953 the International African Institute published a book entitled *Survey of African Marriage and Family Life,* which is exactly what its title claims it to be.[1] It consists of three volumes, *African Marriage and Social Change* (by Lucy Mair), *Marriage Laws in Africa* (by Arthur Phillips), and *Christian Marriage in African Society* (by Lyndon Harries). It was intended to be the definitive guide to these subjects, a collaborative project between missionaries and anthropologists that brought under one roof, so to speak, commentary on the above organized into distinct regions, Southern Africa, East Africa, Central Africa, and West Africa. Although *Survey* is not an ethnographic monograph, it reflects the collaboration of an eminent collection of anthropologists and its findings were culled from the eminent anthropological works of the preceding period.[2]

While *Survey* itself deserves a closer reading, my intention here is to look at the origins of its research questions, as well as the institutional and intellectual origins of the project. In particular I am interested in what it says about the intellectual agendas put forward by missionaries and anthropologists, on both sides of the Atlantic, and in the context of a decolonizing Africa.

1. Arthur Phillips, ed., *Survey of African Marriage and Family Life* (London, 1953).
2. I am very thankful to a lively and challenging African History Seminar at the University of Kwazulu-Natal for shaping and giving better form to some of the ideas in this paper. I also want to express my thanks to the workshop in Basel (organized by Patrick Harries and David Maxwell) that helped to concretize some of the "bigger" ideas in this paper.

In 1953, its foreword recorded the genesis of the volume as follows:

> Proposals for a comprehensive inquiry into African marriage customs were first brought to the attention of the International Missionary Council by the African Delegates to the World Missionary Conference at Madras in 1938. . . . Early in 1946 the suggestion that the Churches should give serious consideration to questions concerning African marriage customs and their relation to both Government and Church ordinances was made by Lord Hailey in a conversation with the research director of the International Missionary Council. Lord Hailey suggested that an inquiry into this subject would be most useful if carried out jointly by sociologists, government officers and missionaries working upon a co-ordinated plan. . . . The aim of this survey has been to present a factual account of the existing situation against the background of indigenous social organization and custom; to point out and analyse the changes in African social organization due to modern developments and contact with Western industrialized societies; and to give an account of the various ways in which administrations and missionary bodies are handling these problems.[3]

A consummately political introduction, it begins with a reference to the African origins of the project; makes reference to Lord Hailey, the author of the monumental African survey; links the work of the International Missionary Council (IMC) to that of scientists; and neatly lays out the vectors of change for a nonmodern and nonindustrialized Africa. While largely correct, the introduction truncates and neatens the different forces at work in the origins of the book. While written by the chair of the committee overseeing the book's progress, it was a faithful reflection of the initiation of the project as described by John Merle Davis, former research director of the IMC and the midwife of the funded version of the project.

On the one hand the volume can be seen as more or less reflecting the passage outlined above, where a particularly Christian and mission interest emanating in 1938 drove the issue forward. Alternately the volume can be viewed as the result of a research project undertaken by the International African Institute (IAI),[4] where the project fits into an intellectual genealogy evoking Isaac Schapera's *Married Life in an African Tribe* (IAI, 1940) and Daryll Forde

---

3. Phillips, *Survey,* pp. v-vi.
4. Until the Second World War it was known as the International Institute of African Languages and Culture. I use IAI as an abbreviation throughout for convenience.

and A. R. Radcliffe-Brown's *African Systems of Kinship and Marriage* (Oxford, 1950). The volume then fits into the history of (mainly) British colonial structural functionalism (although any examination of the mission literature of the period will show similar concerns).[5] The first impetus describes the institutional origins of the volume, emphasizing its Christian element and ecumenical drivers. The second looks to the intellectual origins of the book. In this chapter I examine both of these currents, not as dichotomous, but rather as profoundly interlinked processes in constant tension with one another.

The International Protestant Ecumenical Movement and Research on Africa

If *Survey of African Marriage and Family Life* had missionary origins, these were particular missionary origins. The volume flows directly out of the efforts of an organization known as the International Missionary Council (IMC).

In 1921 the loose ecumenical and spatially disparate movement that represented Western ecumenism was given organizational content in the formation of the IMC. The intent of the IMC was to act as a coordinating and central planning body for the efforts of its members, which included various regional mission associations in the Western world (in the United Kingdom the Conference of British Missionary Societies [CBMS] and in the United States the Foreign Missions Committee of North America [FMCNA]) and a colonial constituency in the form of Christian councils. These were national bodies that the IMC envisaged being established in countries where European missionary influence stood in contrast to the evolution of indigenous churches.[6] In addition, the success of the missionary conference in Edinburgh in 1910 (the origins of the IMC) had shown the need for similar meetings. The Edinburgh example was invoked to suggest the utility of periodic

---

5. Sally Falk Moore, *Anthropology and Africa: Changing Perspectives on a Changing Scene* (Charlottesville, Va., 1994). No one anthropologist's work ever has all the characteristics attributed to structural functionalism, but it is sometimes useful to use this categorization. Andrew Apter, "Africa, Empire, and Anthropology: A Philological Exploration of Anthropology's Heart of Darkness," *Annual Review of Anthropology* 28 (1999). Much more could be written — and has been written — about anthropology's complicity with colonialism, and not only for Africa. For one of my favorite works, see Nicholas B. Dirks, *Castes of Mind: Colonialism and the Making of Modern India* (Princeton, 2001).

6. Ruth Compton Brouwer, *Modernizing Women, Modernizing Men: The Changing Missions of Three Professional Women in Asia and Africa, 1902-1969* (Vancouver, 2002), p. 12.

international conferences designed to address international ecumenical concerns. Further, the IMC and its associates also saw themselves as advocacy bodies, there to mediate between their own national governments and the needs of those they saw as their colonial and foreign mission constituents.[7] The IMC had offices in New York, London, and Geneva, though its nerve center — especially where Africa was concerned — lay in the London offices at Edinburgh House. Here the IMC shared offices with the CBMS.

The IMC came into existence at a moment that coincided with two linked and key shifts, one sociopolitical and present in a strained colonialism, and the other theological, present in a questioning of the purpose of evangelism. Christianity in the Western world was showing signs of strain. The growth of secularism at the start of the twentieth century resulted in many adherents turning away from organized religion, turning away too their funding and support for missionary work.[8] At the same time, the shock of the First World War had brought the meaning of faith into question, the focus now falling on what has been described as "the life lived and not the message delivered."[9] This view emerged strongly at the IMC conference in Jerusalem in 1928 and took many Christian organizations into what is often referred to as the work of the social gospel, where efforts were to be expanded from mere proselytization to work that supported the economic and social needs of potential converts and their wider communities. Moreover, the Christian belief in the necessity of evangelism and its ability to produce "future" Christians meant that mission organizations had a very immanent sense of the importance of the continuance of their efforts, notwithstanding the shifting political context of their work.

Linked to this was the dislocation of African society apparent during the late colonial moment. While the First World War had affected missionary strategy, it had also started to reveal more strongly the fragility of the political project of colonialism in Africa. This fragility, the result of growing African nationalism and anticolonial protest together with a very stretched imperial presence on the ground, was cut across by the skewed impacts of industrialization and urbanization on African colonies. In many parts of Africa this resulted in the growth of migrant labor workforces, the growing marginalization of subsistence production, and growing internal social divisions

---

7. Brouwer, *Modernizing Women, Modernizing Men*, p. 12. See also chapter 1 for a more detailed history of the IMC.

8. Secularism is currently under contest in the academic literature, as to both its periodization in the West and the theoretical nature of the terms. See Talal Asad, *Formations of the Secular: Christianity, Islam, and Modernity*, Cultural Memory in the Present (Stanford, 2003); Callum G. Brown, *The Death of Christian Britain* (London, 2000).

9. Brouwer, *Modernizing Women, Modernizing Men*, p. 12.

within particular colonies. For many Europeans, the discourse used to describe these effects was one of detribalization, hiding its support for the processes under way under a call for a return to precolonial forms of social production and organization.

In this context, many Western missionary organizations active on the continent found themselves, and sought to become, more involved in the everyday lives of their converts. A focus on social gospel directed Western attention to the plight of Africans making, as many would have seen it, the slow and unconfident move out of primitive social organization into modern social mores, though many missionaries — while romantics — would not have called for a reversal of the project. Against these processes, the IMC and its members saw themselves as key intermediaries between their individual converts and congregations, and the ruling apparatus of the colonies, or newly independent states, in which they lived. On the one hand they supported a process of Westernization; on the other they held the declining colonial powers and their representatives responsible for many of the problems affecting Africans. While these issues were obviously recognized and addressed in the operations of the various societies and regional bodies, bodies like the IMC also recognized that targeted research was needed to uncover the most pressing needs of its future Christians.[10]

With this kind of attention and these kinds of concerns, it is not surprising that after Jerusalem the IMC established a research wing (based in Geneva) and fostered research through various of its own subcommittees. The early research was conducted under the auspices of John Merle Davis, who became the first director of the IMC's Economic and Social Research and Counsel wing. Bengt Sundkler later also became research secretary for the IMC, for a brief period in the 1940s. While the IMC carried out research on a number of issues, a significant bias in the research was directed toward Africa, and initially most of it was economic in scope. This research covered a variety of topics, including Davis's own work on the Copperbelt in Zambia. Through the IMC's links with Joseph Oldham, first director of the IAI, much of the early research was undertaken in conjunction with this body.[11]

---

10. Particularly through the person of Joseph Oldham. Oldham is a key figure here, his interest in mission work, ecumenism, colonialism, and anthropology, together with a number of high-placed contacts, making him ideally placed to intervene in and to structure these developments. See also George Bennett, "Paramountcy to Partnership: J. H. Oldham and Africa," *Africa: Journal of the International African Institute* 30, no. 4 (1960).

11. John Merle Davis, *Modern Industry and the African: An Enquiry into the Effect of the Copper Mines of Central Africa upon Native Society and the Work of Christian Missions* (London, 1933).

In addition, the IMC, through its European regional representatives, held regular discussion groups — an informal seminar series would be an anachronistic view — on a variety of subjects. One of the most active at Edinburgh House was the Africa Education Group (AEG), which met from the late 1920s and discussed topical issues and hosted addresses by distinguished visitors. From early on, one of the subjects to preoccupy the AEG at Edinburgh House was African marriage. This interest was the result of African intervention (see the discussion of Tambaram below) and the interest of a particular group attending the Africa Group meetings.

African Marriage at Edinburgh House

The various missionary societies in Africa had been discussing marriage for many years. Initially, much of this discussion — and there was much of it — was as a result of the Protestant missionary concern to see Christian mores, as they saw them, adopted by their charges. The literature on this is well established, and mission concern here rested on issues like polygamy, premarital sexual relations, and so on.[12]

After the First World War, the precise nature of this concern began to shift, in the light of what many mission societies perceived as the deleterious effects of modernization and urbanization on their pastoral charges. At this point, the interest of missionaries in their converts' private lives was driven (not that it really had been previously) by more than a prurient interest in Christian sexual indiscretion. The postwar period seemed to suggest new burdens for new Christians, because of issues like migrant labor, which separated men and women from their families. Previously unthought-of concerns relating to the family, to the urban family, and to single mothers, for instance, were becoming apparent in this period. Further, although missionary concern in the matter of the family was apparently gender neutral, the concern was often more about the trials faced by the educated African men who

---

12. For example, Natasha Erlank, "Missionary Views on Sexuality in Xhosaland in the 19th Century," *Le Fait Missionaire* 11 (2001); D. Jeater, *Marriage, Perversion, and Power: The Construction of Moral Discourse in Southern Rhodesia, 1894-1930* (Oxford, 1993); K. Mann, *Marrying Well: Marriage, Status, and Social Change among the Educated Elite in Colonial Lagos* (Cambridge, 1985); W. G. Mills, "Missionaries, Xhosa Clergy and the Suppression of Traditional Customs," in *Missions and Christianity in South African History*, ed. H. Bredenkamp and R. Ross (Johannesburg, 1995); C. Summers, "Mission Boys, Civilized Men, and Marriage: Educated African Men in the Missions of Southern Rhodesia, 1920-1945," *Journal of Religious History* 23, no. 1 (1999).

formed the first ministers in the Africanizing versions of the mission churches.[13] I don't really concern myself here with marriage as a gendered concern, in the sense that interventions of this nature had different aims for African men and women, but this point is of relevance for what follows in how marriage, via polygamy, becomes topical in the IMC.[14]

For missionaries, then, a thorough knowledge of matters that impacted directly on their congregants — and family life was the *sine qua non* of this — was essential. During the early twentieth century this concern was passed on to the regional organizations in Europe and America, which were asked to provide information and suggestions for dealing with such issues. On one hand these requests resulted in the proliferation of what I call moral hygiene literature,[15] some of it produced out of the IMC's International Committee on Christian Literature in Africa (ICCLA), headed by the very capable Margaret Wrong. On the other, it was a product of debates within those very structures. Before I discuss this debate, though, let me look at the way in which African marriage secured Edinburgh House interest.

By 1933, though the interest was definitely older than this, the Africa Education Group (AEG), one of the subcommittees at Edinburgh House, had begun to hold regular meetings on the subject under the auspices of the African Marriage Group. The formation of this subgroup is closely linked to the activities of a small group of women involved in the activities of the IMC at the time, of whom Betty Gibson was the linchpin.

The African Marriage Group meetings were regularly attended by Dr. Margaret Read, Dr. Monica Hunter, their friend Margaret Wrong, and Betty Gibson, longtime Britain-based administrator for the IMC. Margaret Read and Monica Hunter (herself the daughter of a South African mission family) were both Cambridge-trained anthropologists, while Margaret Wrong, Margaret Read's "personal and intellectual companion," was a Canadian who had read history at Oxford.[16] This group supplied the impetus to the discussion

---

13. See, for instance, Mann, *Marrying Well*; Summers, "Mission Boys, Civilized Men, and Marriage."

14. See also Ruth Compton Brouwer, "Books for Africans: Margaret Wrong and the Gendering of African Writing, 1929-1963," *International Journal of African Historical Studies* 31, no. 1 (1998).

15. James W. C. Dougall, ed., *Christianity and the Sex-Education of the African* (London, 1937).

16. Also see Edmund R. Leach, "Glimpses of the Unmentionable in the History of British Social Anthropology," *Annual Review of Anthropology* 13 (1984); Nancy Lutkehaus, "'She Was "Very" Cambridge': Camilla Wedgwood and the History of Women in British Social Anthropology," *American Ethnologist* 13, no. 4 (1986).

of the subject. Although the reasons for this are not so easy to pick up, all these women had a particular interest in family structures and their relationship to social stability, including the destructive effects of Christian morality on sexual mores. Margaret Read gives expression to this concern in the memorandum quoted below, in which she writes of the institution of marriage as the bedrock of society.[17] Monica Hunter's work — she was in the process of completing her doctoral dissertation on the amaMpondo of the Eastern Cape, South Africa — had similar concerns.[18]

I don't want to suggest that because these women were women they had a natural affinity with women's subjects, a highly problematic and essentialist view. Instead it is likely that their male colleagues in the IMC, conditioned by a particular understanding of male and female roles common to Western society in the early twentieth century, considered issues like marriage private issues, notwithstanding the way in which, later that decade, polygamy would seize international missionary attention as a male issue. This normative view would then make it logical that research on economics in the IMC would be conducted by men and research into private lives by women, notwithstanding the views that women themselves might have of such a division (and contemporary trends in British social anthropology). Ironically, then, although an interest in African marriage was fueled by the women attached to the AEG, it was not necessarily an interest in women's issues. A similar point is taken up by Ruth Brouwer, in her discussion of Margaret Wrong. Although Wrong had "feminist sympathies and a genuine interest in African women's education," she operated in a context that served to gender liberal mission initiatives and its results male.[19] Brouwer points to Wrong's interest in women's issues, but it was one constrained by her desire to protect African women from "destructive or inappropriate western influences."[20] While it is not clear to what extent Wrong's fellow mission activists were motivated by such a concern, it is clear that at least the mission establishment was geared toward a male gendering of

---

17. SOAS, IMC/CBMS Africa 1 Box 210, African Education Group — African Marriage, Memo from M. Read and JHO, June or July 1933.

18. Monica Hunter, *Reaction to Conquest: Effects of Contact with Europeans on the Pondo of South Africa* (Cape Town, 1961). For more on Monica Hunter and her research interests, as well as the production of her research, see Andrew Bank, "The 'Intimate Politics' of Fieldwork: Monica Hunter and Her African Assistants, Pondoland and the Eastern Cape, 1931-32," *Journal of Southern African Studies* 34, no. 3 (2008).

19. Brouwer, "Books for Africans," p. 55.

20. Brouwer, "Books for Africans," p. 56. This protectiveness, a matter more commonly seen as a concern for detribalization, and its gendering need more consideration in the literature.

its output. This may be seen below, both in the switch in impetus within the project and in Audrey Richard's comments on the inclusion of women and girls as subjects of research.

At one of its first meetings, the African Marriage Group was addressed by the Reverend James Welch on the subject of what was truly Christian about marriage, with reference to the difference that existed in African and European perceptions of the subject. Following these discussions, a version of the talk appeared in the *International Review of Missions* (the IMC journal) in early 1933. In May of the same year Monica Hunter addressed the group on the subject of illegitimacy, and perceptions of sexual purity among the amaMpondo in South Africa.[21] Margaret Read's memorandum on the gathering summarized what she and Hunter saw as the two key problems around the subject of marriage: the meaning of so-called pagan marriage and the real meaning of marriage in the West, the solution of which needed further study of these phenomena.[22]

Later that year the group issued a memorandum on the subject, for distribution to missionaries and other relevant persons in the field.

> The following memorandum has been prepared embodying some of the discussions which have taken place and indicating questions on which more light is desired.... To speak of Christian marriage in Africa does not mean that marriage is real only when it is celebrated according to Christian forms.... The important point, however, is that marriage and the family are the fundamental institutions on which our social life is based, and an understanding of them and of the sanctions attached to them might help us in our studies in Africa.... Modern anthropological opinion tends to emphasise the view that the institution of marriage, as also that of the family, is a permanent institution in society. The social organisation of native peoples may be vitally affected by contact with European culture, but so far the institution of marriage remains as the bedrock of society. This being so, it is very important that we should study marriage as an institution in African society.[23]

As the memo indicates, the object of concern in these discussions was the disjuncture that existed between African and European conceptions of mar-

---

21. SOAS, IMC/CBMS Africa 1 Box 210, Minutes 19 May 1933.
22. SOAS, IMC/CBMS Africa 1 Box 210, Read to Oldham, 22 May 1933.
23. SOAS, IMC/CBMS Africa 1 Box 210, African Education Group — African Marriage, Memo from M. Read and J. H. Oldham, June or July 1933.

riage. This concern rested on two key debates: how intrinsic to Christianity were established Protestant Christian teachings around sexual morality, including the relationship between monogamy and Christianity; and (though not so explicitly formulated) to what extent ought Christian marriage formalities be standardized across the colonies so as to bring them into line with the requirements of colonial rule. This latter, as I shall show below, was also a concern of the British Colonial Office, including its consultant on research, Lord Hailey.

Explicit also in the memorandum was the notion that research work of this nature required the input of both missionaries and anthropologists. As evidence of the importance the missionaries accorded anthropology, a number of the recipients of this memorandum were anthropologists. These included Monica Hunter, who took Oldham to task for suggesting in the memorandum that "anthropology is a type of abstract theorizing."[24]

Over the next few years, and especially around preparations for the World Missionary Conference to take place in Madras, India, in 1938, the AEG kept discussion of African marriage active within the more extended program of the group. In October 1937 Betty Gibson wrote to the members of the AEG, urging them to consider the collection of African Christian views on marriage at the upcoming conference.[25] While the foreword to *Survey of African Marriage* emphasizes the African impetus of the document, the caucusing around the subject prior to the conference should not be discounted.

Polygamy, the Younger Churches, and Tambaram

The 1938 IMC conference at Madras Christian College is important for a number of reasons, but in this paper I want to look specifically at the conference's contribution to discussion of marriage as an issue of particular importance for Africa. Discussion at the conference was grouped into a number of sections (sixteen) that met to deliberate issues of common concern, like the contemporary status of evangelism. The proceedings of the conference are published in eight volumes, which discuss the official position of the conference on the subjects under consideration.

24. SOAS, IMC/CBMS Africa 1 Box 210, African Education Group — African Marriage, Monica Hunter to Joseph Oldham, 4 July 1935. Dora Earthy was also one of the respondents to the questionnaire that went out as a result; see Deborah Gaitskell's chapter in this volume.

25. SOAS, IMC/CBMS Africa 1 Box 208, File: British Group Meetings. B. D. Gibson to Members, 8 October 1937; Address by Junod, 15 October 1937.

Apart from its central concerns, the conference also included space for the discussion of issues specific to different parts of the world. During these meetings, delegates from the East, from Latin America, and from Africa came together to discuss issues common to their regions. For the Africa Group of the conference, discussion centered on three key issues: witchcraft, Christian separatism, and polygamy. The first two are not my current concern, but I do want to look at what we know of the discussion around polygamy.

Despite the official publications that flowed from the conference, and the numerous reports included in the *International Review of Missions*, there are not many detailed reports of this discussion.[26] The issue is not a reflection of lack of debate, but lack of reportage. When it came to summarizing the African sessions, the IMC organizing committee went with the position paper prepared for it, for a number of reasons. According to Frieder Ludwig, in a very useful piece, a split occurred between the African and Asian and the Western delegates to the conference on the subject of polygamy. In a conference already rent with tension, on the position of the German churches and the Japanese invasion of China, the organizers were keen to avoid what they saw as minor issues disrupting the main proceedings.

From private sources it is apparent that many of the West African delegates had gone to the conference with the purpose of discussing the insistence on monogamy as a prerequisite for communion. Many of the other African delegates had also been prepared for such a discussion (see Edinburgh House efforts above). The origins of their concern lay in an interest in the particular character of an African Christianity, linked closely to currents driving the anticolonial nationalisms of the period. In this instance, the question devolved to a desire to establish the particular link that connected Christianity to monogamy and rendered African polygamy unchristian. Discussions of this issue are replete in the regional, African Christian literature of the period, but Tambaram was the first opportunity for an international airing (see also below). In many respects, the sub-Saharan African groundswell against noncommunion for polygamists needs to be seen against the anticolonial defense of other traditional practices. Despite this agenda, though, European missionaries dominated the conversation.[27]

The key paper on the issue was read by a Presbyterian missionary, a Dr. Turner.[28] Dr. Turner, who worked in Nyasaland, spoke openly about the bar

---

26. For the best example of this see Frieder Ludwig, "Tambaram: The West African Experience," *Journal of Religion in Africa* 31, no. 1 (2001).

27. Ludwig, "Tambaram," p. 72.

28. Ludwig, "Tambaram," p. 72, and SOAS, IMC/CBMS Africa 1 Box 210, African Education Group — African Marriage, Memorandum, Carey Francis, 3 July 1942.

polygyny placed in the face of men becoming Christians and how many Christian men carried on illicit relationships in order to overcome this prohibition. However, according to him, Christian teachings and the Bible clearly taught that monogamy was the only true path to a Christian life. This paper became the substance of the official report on the Africa Section's deliberations (and the official conference position).[29] So, while a groundswell of sentiment prior to the conference favored an open and frank discussion on this subject, and while this may indeed have happened, the official version of the discussion attributed to the black delegates a support for monogamy. Importantly, though, the issue had been raised, and in an international forum.

Edinburgh House and the International African Institute

Mission interest in African marriage and family life needs to be viewed against the development of British social anthropology in the first half of the twentieth century. Of the group of women who met to discuss African marriage at Edinburgh House, a number were also engaged in the broader discussion and practice of anthropology at two other locations in London. At least Monica Hunter and Margaret Read were regular attendees at Bronislaw Malinowski's seminar on Africa, held at the London School of Economics. In addition, both were involved with the International Institute of African Languages and Culture (the full name of the IAI). In London, in the 1920s and 1930s, the links between British social anthropology and mission endeavor were closer than many might imagine.

Sometime in 1925 a group of colonial administrators, missionaries, and anthropologists (sometimes one and the same, certainly not as distinct as this list appears) met to discuss "the need for an application of scientific method to a solution of the questions arising generally from the contact of Western civilization with African culture."[30] On 1 June 1926, the IAI opened its doors. Amongst this group, Joseph Oldham, then secretary within both the IMC and the CBMS, had key status and became its first administrative director. Oldham had managed to convince the Rockefeller Foundation, Lord Lugard, and Bronislaw Malinowski to throw their weight behind a research institute that would conduct research designed to respond to Edwin Smith's statement above. As John

---

29. Ludwig, "Tambaram," p. 73.
30. Edwin Smith, one of this group, in Daryll Forde, "Anthropology and the Development of African Studies: The Tenth Lugard Memorial Lecture," *Africa: Journal of the International African Institute* 37, no. 4 (1967): 391.

Cell has described it, the IAI "thus became a triple alliance of gifted entrepreneurs each with his own agenda: Oldham's notion of modernizing Christianity in Africa, Lugard's of promoting his own definitions of indirect rule and trusteeship, Malinowski's of obtaining support for his research students."[31]

The IAI is of interest for several reasons, principally as an undisputed and extensive source of research on Africa.[32] Although much of its research agenda, in the period under discussion, was framed by the need to examine and provide solutions to the problems of indirect rule, a tactic referred to as "applied anthropology," the monographs produced by its researchers went beyond this remit. In particular, the IAI provided researchers with fieldwork grants, a critical move for scholars interested in the continent but unable to raise alternative funding. In its first few years of operation the IAI awarded a number of grants for fieldwork, including to Audrey Richards, Monica Hunter, Isaac Schapera, and Margaret Read. The work of these scholars together with others associated with the institute, for instance, Zacchareus K. Matthews, appeared in IAI-sponsored and IAI-funded publications, like the journal *Africa*. Also to emerge from the IAI was the *African Survey*, edited by Lord Hailey, in which Joseph Oldham played a key motivating role.[33]

The IAI's role was itself the subject of investigation.[34] Daryll Forde, director of the IAI during and after the Second World War, has reflected on the history of the institute, while a critical reading of its agenda has been provided by Frank Salamone. According to Salamone, the research carried out under the auspices of the IAI was the direct result of donor-driven agendas, principally that of the Rockefeller Foundation. He links together a post–First World War Western crisis of confidence, rising anticolonial aspirations, and an increasingly self-confident United States in his explanation for the IAI's research project.[35] Although Salamone is probably overstating the case, or the

---

31. John W. Cell, "Lord Hailey and the Making of the African Survey," *African Affairs* 88, no. 353 (1989): 483.

32. Forde, "Anthropology and the Development of African Studies."

33. Frank A. Salamone, "The International African Institute: The Rockefeller Foundation and the Development of British Social Anthropology in Africa," *Transforming Anthropology* 9, no. 1 (2000); Cell, "Lord Hailey and the Making of the African Survey"; Michael Crowder, "'Us' and 'Them': The International African Institute and the Current Crisis of Identity in African Studies; A Public Lecture Delivered at the Iwalewa Haus of the University of Bayreuth on Saturday, 19 July 1986, to Mark the Diamond Jubilee of the Institute," *Africa: Journal of the International African Institute* 57, no. 1 (1987).

34. See Forde, "Anthropology and the Development of African Studies"; Cell, "Lord Hailey and the Making of the African Survey"; Salamone, "The International African Institute."

35. While Salamone's critique is overstated, it is probably largely accurate, but that is

degree to which intention translated into practice, his points about donor-driven agendas are relevant for what follows.[36]

Focusing on the IAI as a research institute, however, runs the risk of missing out on the IAI's embeddedness in other contexts. Here I am referring to the institutional support that the international ecumenical movement provided anthropologists wanting to work in Africa. Many of the IAI's researchers depended on an extensive network of mission stations in Africa to facilitate their research. The intellectual crisis within anthropology starting in the 1970s is too big a subject to cover here (and indeed the anthropologists have done this themselves), but it did include intense scrutiny of the idea of a neutrally situated ethnographic practice located in participant observation. It has, though, largely overlooked the degree to which early anthropological endeavors in Africa did not involve researchers landing in Africa and heading straight to their research sites. The intermediaries of most ethnographic work were missionaries, and missions societies, playing a rather differently conceptualized role as culture broker (not from Africa to Europe, but from Europe to Africa).

Given this situation, as well as the overlap that existed between the IMC, its supporters, and the personnel of the IAI, it is clear that British social anthropology of the 1930s was heavily indebted, indeed facilitated by, missionary endeavor.[37] In some cases the links were formalized through joint endeavors like the one mentioned in this chapter. In other respects the collaboration probably consisted of separate institutional functions being carried out by the same people wearing different hats, like Oldham himself.

Despite their deep reliance on mission networks to facilitate research, the relationship between missionaries and anthropologists was often characterized by tension. Many British anthropologists were deeply distrustful of religion, especially Christianity. They were put off by what they saw as the deleterious effects of it on indigenous societies. Christianity, according to this view, had brought about a dissolution of authentic society, and caused more problems than it had provided solutions to.[38] Secondly, anthropologists were wor-

---

not the point. Most research institutes are subject to external direction, but this direction does not always translate into the research produced.

36. See also Apter, "Africa, Empire, and Anthropology."

37. The anthropological blind spot for mission-driven research agendas is carried through in Adam Kuper's book, where there is no mention of the existence of the IMC, or even its representative in Joseph Oldham. Smith, though, does get a mention as director of the IAI, a not-entirely-correct statement. Adam Kuper, *Anthropology and Anthropologists: The Modern British School*, 3rd ed. (London and New York, 1996), p. 100.

38. Isaac Schapera was quite clear on this. See Kuper, *Anthropology and Anthropologists*, p. 71.

ried that missionary research questions, which they saw as anti-intellectual, might taint their ethnological research. That this relationship had contemporary recognition, and that anthropologists saw ways beyond it, is captured by Lucy Mair (one of the contributors to the volume on which this paper is based). In a series of interviews conducted with a range of anthropologists, one of the questions concerned "anthropologists versus missionaries." Mair answered, "As far as U.K.-based missionaries are concerned, I think it is true to say that the rapprochement between their views and ours has come about largely since the inclusion of anthropology in the preparation for mission work that arose from the collaboration of Malinowski with J. H. Oldham."[39] Here Mair neatly captures the way in which, even in the context of collaborative research with the IMC, the IAI felt a need to protect its research from an unreflexive missionary taint.

The IMC and the Professionalization of African Marriage

The year 1939 was to be decisive for the issue of African polygamy in the church, and research directed toward it. Back at Edinburgh House the Tambaram pronouncement was met with disappointment from the Africa Group members who had hoped for a more thoughtful position statement.[40] Betty Gibson's views, that Turner's statement was a political compromise and reflected input from the wrong people, was probably held by the other Africa Group participants.[41] From this point on, too, the Africa Group's concern was added to by an increasing volume of queries from Africa, from both local Christian councils and European mission societies. These queries, one of which was from the Gold Coast churches, were more properly requests for the Western churches, as represented by the IMC, to make their positions on polygamy and associated practices clear. The context of these requests was a growing (though small) support in both East and West African Christian and mission communities for the admittance of male polygamists to commu-

---

39. Claude E. Stipe et al., "Anthropologists versus Missionaries: The Influence of Presuppositions [and Comments and Reply]," *Current Anthropology* 21, no. 2 (1980).
40. SOAS IMC 26.31.31, Fiche 1, Africa Group Tambaram Follow Up Meeting. Here I am referring to the records of the IMC itself, a microfiche copy of which I consulted. My references to this archive follow the notation of the originals in Geneva, at the World Council of Churches, and the fiche number within each subseries (but not the FBN — fiche box number — used to store the microfiche copies).
41. SOAS, IMC/CBMS Africa 1 Box 210, African Education Group — African Marriage, Gibson to J. W. C Dougall, 17 November 1942.

nion.⁴² Perhaps the most vocal response to the discussion initiated at Tambaram was a paper circulated in East African and British missionary circles in 1942, by E. Carey Francis, a missionary and high school principal in Kenya.

Carey Francis's memorandum to the AEG was an explicit attack on the Tambaram position.⁴³ After quoting the Tambaram report, he wrote, "Having devoted half-a-dozen or so lines to the argument (extremely unsound) the Report goes on to a page or more of generalities about redemption and holy partnership and love of children . . . a cloud of pious words."⁴⁴ Francis's point was that the matter deserved honest discussion, that it was a burning issue, and that there was not really any scriptural defense for opposition to polygamy. However, not all the member societies of the CBMS were happy with debating marriage the way in which Edinburgh House was driving them. The Scots, for instance, were fairly adamant that polygamy was contrary to their teachings (something their offshoot in South Africa, the Bantu Presbyterian Church, had mixed views upon). Likewise the CMS in Uganda. Others, though, including some of the East African contingent, were more sanguine about the position. While this chapter does not concern itself with what became of the theological issue of polygamy, it is noteworthy that when Adrian Hastings carried out his research into African marriage in the 1970s, he uncovered similar debates. At the risk of generalizing a very complex issue, the issue of whether the (Anglican in this case) church should "admit a polygamist to the sacramental life of the Church" is still relatively current.⁴⁵

At this point there was clearly momentum within the Africa Group to take the issue of investigation into African marriage forward, now fueled from the ground up, so to speak, and expressed as a concern around polygamy. However, the turn the matter might have taken in this context is unknown, since the impetus for the project now changed shape fairly substantially, as the locus of concern for the matter moved from the Africa Group to John Merle Davis, outgoing director of the IMC's research wing. The basis of this shift probably lies in a complex combination of factors. These would probably include internal IMC power contestations, including differences in opinion between its two largest constituent bodies, the FMCNA and the CBMS (not dis-

---

42. For example, IMC 26.31.31, Fiche 1, Extract of the Minutes of the CBMS Africa Committee, 8 July 1940.

43. See also the papers of the Church of Scotland Foreign Missions Committee. National Library of Scotland (NLS), Edinburgh, Acc. 75486, Vol B: 404, African Marriage.

44. IMC 26.31.31, Fiche 1, Polygamy, E. Carey Francis, 3 July 1942.

45. See David Gitari, "The Church and Polygamy," *Transformation* 1, no. 1 (1984); Adrian Hastings, *Christian Marriage in Africa* (London, 1973).

cussed here), as well as a contestation between what Davis and his research credentials represented and the more informal atmosphere of the Africa Group and its female support base. I shall discuss this latter in what follows.

If the Edinburgh House IMC contingent continued to debate the issue of African marriage during the war, a more formal investigation into the matter was occurring on the other side of the Atlantic. In December 1939 the New York office of the IMC hosted a one-day conference on polygamy, separatism, and witchcraft. The conference was partially at the instigation of Davis, who had become interested in the subject during his time at Tambaram. At this point he assumes particular importance, because his efforts were henceforth to drive forward the research project into African marriage.

Davis, who had previously been involved in African research through his work on the Copperbelt, had become more closely interested in the subject through conversations with the South Africans (certainly James Dexter Taylor and possibly the black South African delegates) at Tambaram. By August 1939 he had flagged his interest in the project with Edinburgh House, suggesting also that the IMC's research department was best suited to such work.[46] Davis was clearly aware that the project had a special claim on the interest of Edinburgh House, especially Betty Gibson.[47] In a letter written in September, William Paton, in consultation with Gibson, indicated a reservation about Davis's ability to carry out such a study. However, he did include a suggestion for the way forward. "Miss Gibson and I . . . both feel that, in view of the strength of the British anthropological study in these matters, and the intimate connection which we here have with a number of the best people in the field, it is desirable that a very close connection be maintained with us here."[48] Paton's suggestion for coinvolvement then got down to the nitty-gritty, with a suggestion that Davis put together a research proposal for work to be carried out by the research department. The success of the project, though, would be subject to the IMC's approval (Paton meant London) and the acquisition of funding, probably from the Carnegie Corporation.

Out of this moment, then, grew the professionalization of the African marriage project. Davis's involvement, which seems to have been premised on a concern that Edinburgh House's involvement would be more pastoral and theological than intellectual, was driven by what he saw as a very scientific approach to research. In a very great measure thereafter, it was his energy and belief in the project that drove it forward, probably in a way Edinburgh

---

46. IMC 26.31.31, Fiche 1, John Merle Davis to Betty Gibson, 19 August 1939.
47. IMC 26.31.31, Fiche 1, John Merle Davis to William Paton, 1939.
48. IMC 26.31.31, Fiche 1, William Paton to John Merle Davis, 15 September 1939.

House would not have managed. Although Davis saw himself as a scientist, as his comments at the 1939 conference indicate, he was also keenly interested in the future of the Christian church. His interest in the project then reflected a kind of ecumenical Christian activism in equal measure to his intellectual curiosity. A further irony of this ecumenical/scientific tension lay in the way many who had attended the London Africa Group meetings found themselves involved in later stages of the project, though in their individual capacities as anthropologists.

The New York conference was attended by a mission who's who, including Edwin Smith, missionary and anthropologist, as well as the educationalist and liberal extraordinaire from South Africa, C. T. Loram. Davis set the tone for the conference, drawing links between the issue of marriage in Africa and "what type of Christian order we are coming to."[49] However, the conference was equally concerned with how research was to be conducted. In Smith's paper, "Polygamy and Marriage Customs," he reflected on this matter.[50] "We want an enquiry conducted on scientific lines with all the assistance that can be offered by ethnographic science." The emphasis on scientific methods is interesting, not so much because it was necessary to state that an ethnographic study would be scientific, but because missionaries found themselves needing to assert the scientific validity of their approach.

As Smith made clear, it was necessary to consider polygamy in relation to all sex customs, which by extension included marriage. Unlike the focus of Tambaram, where the missionaries rather than the anthropologists had dominated (even if they were the same person), the anthropologist within each delegate was to the fore. Smith, who had also spent much time in discussion with South Africans at Tambaram, spoke positively of practices like *ukumetsha* ("thigh"/nonpenetrative sex) and *lobola* (bride-price), which, following the only black African woman to attend Tambaram, he called the "Bantu Women's Charter of Liberty."[51] These sentiments were strongly supported by the majority of delegates at the meeting, especially Davis.

At the New York conference, he took his cue from the South Africans, as he put it, presenting the view that they should have "a belief and understanding of the facts so that we would make the bridge between the Christian heritage and the African heritage," and that the best way to effect this was to bring

49. IMC 26.31.31, Fiche 1, Conference on Marriage Customs, New York, 9 December 1939.

50. IMC 26.31.31, Fiche 1, Conference on Marriage Customs, New York, 9 December 1939.

51. IMC 26.31.31, Fiche 1, Conference on Marriage Customs, New York, 9 December 1939.

about a triangular setup (his words) between academics, missionaries, and Africans. By academics Davis meant anthropologists, since the South Africans had indicated to him that what were needed were anthropologists friendly — read "tolerant" — to the subject of African marriage practices.

The day after, at a discussion on the future of the project, Davis was given the task of drafting a research proposal. Although the final proposal (see below) differed from that discussed at this meeting (which recommended primary research at two sites in Africa: Achimtota in the Gold Coast and Fort Hare in South Africa), it was clear that henceforth the project was envisaged as an academic one.

Following the conference Davis set up an extensive correspondence, gathering information on sexual practices, polygamy, and the disjuncture that existed between marriage rites by custom, by colonial law, and under Christianity. His efforts were assisted by Edinburgh House, where the CBMS in particular began urging its members to contribute to the ongoing discussion on African marriage.[52] For very obvious reasons, though, little more occurred within the project until 1946.

Collaborative Research Agendas: The IMC and the IAI

If the preceding events had convinced Davis and the IMC of the legitimacy of the African marriage project, subsequent developments are concerned principally with the logistical and political aspects of putting together a large research project (note, I don't here deal with the actual research phase of the project). These included questions of funding, administrative location, and personnel, all cut across by the need to package the project so that it would receive the support of the Colonial Office and the Carnegie Corporation, both of which funded the final version of the proposal. While the Colonial Office, in the person of Lord Hailey, and the Carnegie Corporation, in the person of Whitney Shephardson (who was its secretary for Africa), were the principal actors, the interest of the IAI and the IMC — as well as factions within the latter — also affected the shape of the project. In addition, the unfolding of the project points to the way in which Africa and the possibility of funded research for it were of key importance to the British social anthropology profession during the 1940s.[53]

52. NLS Acc. 75486, Vol B: 404, African Marriage, Memorandum on African Marriage.
53. For more on this, see the discussion on British anthropology's connection to colonial research in Kuper, *Anthropology and Anthropologists*.

Almost as soon as the war was over, Davis began agitating for the continuance of the project. Most of his efforts in 1946 centered on concretizing interest in the project. During the year he managed to secure Lord Hailey's (see below) interest; he put a preliminary proposal in front of the Carnegie Corporation; he interested Daryll Forde at the IAI in the project; and he secured a part-time contract for after his retirement for further work on preparing a research and funding proposal. In this he was assisted by various IMC officials, particularly Charles Ranson, who was currently its London-based secretary.[54]

In all of John Merle Davis's subsequent correspondence, and in the introduction to the volume, he makes reference to a meeting held with Lord Hailey in early 1946, crediting Hailey with second authorship of a project of which the African delegates to Tambaram were the first.[55] Hailey is important for the project, both because of his status as an elder statesman of African research and also for his connection to the Colonial Social Science Research Council (CSSRC), where he acted as adviser. Hailey certainly acted as a kind of intellectual broker between the IMC and the IAI, the Colonial Office, and the Carnegie Corporation. Whether Hailey deserves or not the billing he receives in the introduction, he certainly alerted Davis to the myriad colonial administrative problems inherent in African marriage.

Through all these initial negotiations the IMC, especially Charles Ranson, retained an awareness that its support for the project had to do as much with the perceived kudos the project would bring to it as with the intellectual merits of the project. Moreover, it was very clear to the IMC that the IAI had reservations about the involvement of the organization in the research. According to Lord Hailey, to whom Forde must have expressed the sentiment, "they fear that the project may concern itself too much with the shaping of policy, & its scientific nature might thereby be weakened."[56] The subtext to Forde's policy fear, one can only assume, concerned the use of the survey to put across a set of missionary-driven ideas about morality and an agenda around African intimate social practices determined by Christian priorities. In this

---

54. See IMC 26.31.31, Fiche 2.

55. Davis was usually meticulous about keeping meeting notes, but I have not yet found a record of this one in the IMC archive. However, Hailey's interest in the matter is revealed in a letter he subsequently wrote to Davis; see below. From about this time, as the IMC engaged the IAI in its activities, it is likely there is a parallel record in the papers of the IAI (or even Forde), which are at the London School of Economics. I have unfortunately had no opportunity to consult these. They would flesh out Forde's view of the project.

56. Hailey as reported in IMC 26.31.31, Fiche 3, Charles Ranson to Merle Davis, 17 January 1947.

view, as both Hailey and various IMC personnel indicated to Forde more than once, he was mistaken.

In early 1947 Davis found himself (he was based in New York) in London with a long list of people to interview on the merits of the project. Two of the first interviews were crucial to the future of the project. In a meeting with Lord Hailey, the two of them fleshed out the idea of a project in two phases: a first phase examining the relevant literature, including mission and government documents, and a second phase of primary research concentrating on particular African sites.[57] Subsequently, the organizational component to the project emerged in a meeting with Daryll Forde.[58]

Davis was a meticulous researcher, and during this period he interviewed just about everyone of note in British anthropology and other fields of research into Africa, including Malinowski, A. R. Radcliffe-Brown, Audrey Richards (then advising the Colonial Office), Margery Perham, Meyer Fortes, and Evans-Pritchard.[59] Across these interviews Davis collected opinion as to the scope, organization, and epistemological nature of the intended research.

The project lodged with the IAI — which was its natural home. Given the links between the mission establishment and the institute, there was considerable interest in it across this establishment. Perhaps in a dig at London, Meyer Fortes told Davis that the anthropology department of a large university should coordinate the ethnological work of the project.[60]

The Colonial Office seems principally to have been interested in the content of the research, which for it rested on the collection of data, including data specifically on women and children. This latter interest came from Audrey Richards, then attached to the Colonial Office. Richards, probably in support of what I wrote above, was the only one of Davis's interviewees to mention targeting research at women and children.[61]

While the anthropologists and other academics with whom he spoke were interested in the content of the research, a common concern (as with Forde above) related to the impartiality of the work to be carried out. The context here was, of course, the involvement of missionaries. Margery Perham was

---

57. IMC 26.31.31, Fiche 3, Merle Davis, Notes of an Interview with Lord Hailey, 14 February 1947.

58. IMC 26.31.31, Fiche 3, Merle Davis, Notes of an Interview with Daryll Forde, 17 February 1947.

59. See Fiche 3.

60. IMC 26.31.31, Fiche 3, Merle Davis, Interview with Meyer Fortes and Evans-Pritchard, Oxford, 21 April 1947.

61. IMC 26.31.31, Fiche 3, Merle Davis, Interview with Audrey Richards and PA Wilson, Colonial Office, 7 March 1947.

perhaps the most explicit in this regard, citing the damage done to "native society in disintegrating their culture." This too was a concern of Radcliffe-Brown, who also wanted the inquiry to turn its attention to contemporary social contexts.

By May of that year, Davis felt he had collected enough information and support to submit a proposal to the Carnegie Corporation. The request for a grant-in-aid was submitted jointly by the IAI and IMC. It outlined the origins of the project, its organizational component, its program of research and research aims, and the funding required. These included (i) an executive committee to run the project, including representatives from the IAI, the IMC, the Colonial Office, the Royal Anthropological Institution, and the newly constituted Association of Social Anthropology; (ii) a two-phase project beginning with survey work and continuing into field studies; (iii) a budget of £4,749 for the first phase and £10,000 per case for the second phase; and (iv) a request to the Colonial Development and Welfare Fund for a contribution of £1,800 to the first phase.[62]

At this point, a number of other issues placed the future of the project in doubt. In the first place, by the end of the year Davis's participation in the project had become uncertain (he was in fact to withdraw soon after). His stipend for the preparatory phase of the project had run out, and he found himself having to contemplate other work. Allied to this, the relationship he had taken care to maintain with the Carnegie Corporation was under strain, mostly it seems, because of Forde's impatience for an answer.[63]

Although Whitney Shephardson had been firmly in favor of the project in 1946, to the extent that he had pushed Davis to contemplate a fieldwork phase for the project, by the end of 1947 he was no longer so sanguine. In April of that year Shephardson had taken issue with the project organization, over a

---

62. IMC 26.31.31, Fiche 3, Request to the Carnegie Corporation of New York for a Grant-in-Aid of an Enquiry into the Effect of Modern Contacts upon the African Family with Special Reference to Marriage Laws and Customs, 19 May 1947. By illustration, let me give two other sets of figures, against which to measure this date. According to Adam Kuper, the income of the IAI in the early 1930s was in the region of £9,000 per annum. Kuper, *Anthropology and Anthropologists*, p. 100. I would need to examine the IAI archives to gauge the worth of other projects entering its books in the 1940s. The following figures are from the Internet site Measuringworth.com (visited 5 February 2008). "In 2006, £4749 0s 0d from 1947 was worth: £127,887.61 using the retail price index, £130,796.37 using the GDP deflator, £399,374.15 using average earnings, £466,520.97 using per capita GDP, £572,933.93 using the GDP. On consultation with other historians, one of the latter figures is likely to have represented the project's worth in contemporary terms." This was not an insignificant research project.

63. IMC 26.31.31, Fiche 3, Merle Davis to Charles Ranson, 24 October 1947.

Colonial Office minute that recorded (incorrectly as it was) the near certainty of Carnegie funding for the research.[64] By the end of the year, he too was worried about Davis's potential withdrawal from the project, feeling that the other British support for the project was lackluster at best. In a meeting he held with Davis in November, he voiced a concern about the twofold nature of the project, the objectives of the research, as well as Davis's future participation in it.[65] His sympathy for the project was further tried by the announcement at the end of 1947 that the Colonial Office had approved its grant, subject to the Carnegie Corporation's participation in funding the project. Shephardson's attitude was not helped by a rather peremptory letter from Daryll Forde, requesting an immediate funding decision. Through all this, as Shephardson told Ranson in an interview in 1948, the Carnegie Corporation took umbrage at the way in which its support had been taken as a given. Part of this involved the way in which the corporation objected to the interference it saw coming from the Colonial Office. As Shephardson put it, some of this boiled down to a view that the behavior at the IAI and the IMC "seemed to assume that the Carnegie Corp had a greater obligation than the Colonial Office."[66] Clearly, this went beyond tensions between a funder and its potential projects. These issues, most of them personality-based, point to the difficulties of putting together interinstitutional, intercontinental, and interjurisdictional research projects.

By April 1948, though, after some judicious smoothing over by Charles Ranson and Lord Hailey, the Carnegie Corporation was onboard with an offer of $12,000 for the first phase of the project.[67] Ranson had just moved to the New York office of the IMC, and it seems as if his presence on the other side of the Atlantic managed to reassure Shephardson as to the British side's commitment to the project. Unfortunately the Carnegie funding came too late for Davis, who had moved on, though he continued to be involved, if only unofficially. Thereafter, the steering of the project moved over to an executive committee, which held its first meeting in June 1948. At this meeting the project researchers, Arthur Phillips, Lyndon Harries, and Lucy Mair, were appointed. The politics of the committee, which was split between representatives aligned with either the IMC or the IAI, were dominated by the IAI, whose stance was driven by the issue of missionary neutrality in research. Although the project continued — and although the IMC continued in its own

64. IMC 26.31.31, Fiche 5, Whitney Shephardson to Merle Davis, 1 April 1947.
65. IMC 26.31.31, Fiche 4, Interview Shephardson, 25 November 1947.
66. IMC 26.31.31, Fiche 5, Charles Ranson to Bengt Sundkler, 20 March 1948.
67. IMC 26.31.34, Fiche 2, Charles Ranson to Daryll Forde, 17 February 1948.

work of collecting information on marriage — the stuffing had gone out of it by 1950. I have seen no references to attempts to refloat the second phase of the project. In Forde's retrospective on the IAI, he makes no mention of it.

Subsequently, as any citation, or library catalogue search, will show, the book became a standard reference volume on marriage in Africa. Mair's contribution was reprinted in 1971, and still stands as the definitive overview of marriage and social change up until that point, much cited but seldom quoted.

Conclusion

As research projects go, the African marriage survey represented a diffuse collection of different interests under one roof. On the one hand, it was the result of a particular ecumenical initiative, begun as an IMC attempt to grapple with the new conditions in which its colonial charges found themselves. As part of this, the IMC attempted to bring modern scientific methods and research to bear on a set of very gendered concerns around marriage and the place of polygamy in modern Christianity. Through its focus on the social gospel, its connections in the third world, and the rising tide of African Christian separatism, the IMC had become alerted to the need for further research on these matters. A concern around marriage, however articulated, came from two different directions. In the first, a group at Edinburgh House, mostly women, drove forward investigation of the matter. In the second, an ostensibly more professionally oriented grouping of men took forward the concerns around polygamy they had heard expressed at Tambaram.

As part of its commitment to research, and new methods of research, the IMC found itself in partnership with British social anthropology in its pursuit of answers. The IAI, which had been partly established by mission interests, was a natural partner for that research. However, in bringing the IAI on board, the IMC found that other research agendas — not methods — affected the investigation of the issue of African marriage. These different views on the need for and methods of research around African marriage are most evident in the preparation of the research funding proposal that eventually found light as the *Survey of African Marriage and Family Life.*

For its part, the IAI conceived itself as the intellectual progenitor of the project, given its disciplinary location. Ironically of course, the very kind of research that gave the IAI its name was predicated on vast missionary-institute supply and support chains in Africa. That the IAI came together with the IMC in this research relates to the post–Second World War research climate. Prior to the war, but especially after it, the IAI had been moving in the direction of what other researchers have referred to as applied anthropology, especially in relation to the problems of British colonial rule. Much of this research capability, whatever its ultimate nature, was touted as a utilitarian intervention in the politics of colonial governance. At the same time, though, the exigencies of academic funding after the Second World War meant that funding for colonial projects was in relatively limited supply at home, necessitating a turn across the Atlantic for funding partners. Ironically for the IAI, which by the 1940s had outgrown some of its earlier missionary links, access to the Carnegie Corporation was facilitated by many of the contacts that the IMC had in the United States. Out of this rather complicated set of connections, the idea of the African marriage survey was born.

Select Bibliography

Apter, Andrew. "Africa, Empire, and Anthropology: A Philological Exploration of Anthropology's Heart of Darkness." *Annual Review of Anthropology* 28 (1999).

Asad, Talal. *Formations of the Secular: Christianity, Islam, and Modernity.* Stanford, 2003.

Bank, Andrew. "The 'Intimate Politics' of Fieldwork: Monica Hunter and Her African Assistants, Pondoland and the Eastern Cape, 1931-32." *Journal of Southern African Studies* 34, no. 3 (2008).

Bennett, George. "Paramountcy to Partnership: J. H. Oldham and Africa." *Africa: Journal of the International African Institute* 30 (1960).

Brouwer, Ruth Compton. "Books for Africans: Margaret Wrong and the Gendering of African Writing, 1929-1963." *International Journal of African Historical Studies* 31, no. 1 (1998).

———. *Modernizing Women, Modernizing Men: The Changing Missions of Three Professional Women in Asia and Africa, 1902-1969.* Vancouver, 2002.

Cell, John W. "Lord Hailey and the Making of the African Survey." *African Affairs* 88, no. 353 (1989).

Dougall, James W. C., ed. *Christianity and the Sex-Education of the African.* London, 1937.

Erlank, Natasha. "Missionary Views on Sexuality in Xhosaland in the 19th Century." *Le Fait Missionaire* 11 (2001).

Forde, Daryll. "Anthropology and the Development of African Studies: The Tenth Lugard Memorial Lecture." *Africa: Journal of the International African Institute* 37, no. 4 (1967).

Hastings, Adrian. *Christian Marriage in Africa.* London, 1973.

Hunter, Monica. *Reaction to Conquest: Effects of Contact with Europeans on the Pondo of South Africa.* Cape Town, 1961.

Jeater, D. *Marriage, Perversion, and Power: The Construction of Moral Discourse in Southern Rhodesia, 1894-1930*. Oxford, 1993.

Kuper, Adam. *Anthropology and Anthropologists: The Modern British School*. 3rd ed. London and New York, 1996.

Leach, Edmund R. "Glimpses of the Unmentionable in the History of British Social Anthropology." *Annual Review of Anthropology* 13 (1984).

Ludwig, Frieder. "Tambaram: The West African Experience." *Journal of Religion in Africa* 31, no. 1 (2001).

Lutkehaus, Nancy. "'She Was "Very" Cambridge': Camilla Wedgwood and the History of Women in British Social Anthropology." *American Ethnologist* 13, no. 4 (1986).

Mann, K. *Marrying Well: Marriage, Status, and Social Change among the Educated Elite in Colonial Lagos*. Cambridge, 1985.

Mills, W. G. "Missionaries, Xhosa Clergy and the Suppression of Traditional Customs." In *Missions and Christianity in South African History*, edited by H. Bredenkamp and R. Ross. Johannesburg, 1995.

Moore, Sally Falk. *Anthropology and Africa: Changing Perspectives on a Changing Scene*. Charlottesville, Va., 1994.

Summers, C. "Mission Boys, Civilized Men, and Marriage: Educated African Men in the Missions of Southern Rhodesia, 1920-1945." *Journal of Religious History* 23, no. 1 (1999).

CHAPTER 10

Dorothea Lehmann and John V. Taylor: Researching Church and Society in Late Colonial Africa

JOHN STUART

In 1958 two Protestant missionaries, the German linguist Dorothea Lehmann (1910-82) and the English priest John V. Taylor (1914-2001), undertook a research project in the British central African colony of Northern Rhodesia (now Zambia). Over a nine-month period they traveled widely both separately and together, visiting and staying in urban townships in the Copperbelt region and also in rural villages, in the colony's Northern Province. They relied upon the cooperation of a large number of people. European managers in the copper mines and officers of the colonial administration assisted them; so too did African chiefs, African clergy, and other missionaries, Protestant and Roman Catholic. Between them Lehmann and Taylor had many years of missionary experience in Africa, she in education and welfare work and he in the training of clergy. They both had a strong interest in African cultures and societies. Their project had a religious focus. It had been organized as part of a joint research program by two Protestant ecumenical organizations: the International Missionary Council (IMC) and the World Council of Churches (WCC). The aim of this program was to assess the present state and future potential, under indigenous leadership, of "younger churches" that had originated not in the West but in Africa and Asia. Research would have a theological aspect, and it would also take into account the effect upon churches of social and political change. The findings of the work undertaken by Lehmann and Taylor would be published in 1961 under the title *Christians of the Copperbelt*, with the two missionaries as coauthors.

Their project was indicative of Protestant missionary attempts to investigate and thereby respond to challenges facing Christianity, in Africa and in other parts of the non-Western world. The situation in Northern Rhodesia seemed particularly worthy of study. The colony was in ferment, with labor disputes in the copper mines and vocal African opposition to the Central African Federation, the British imperial entity into which Northern Rhodesia and Nyasaland (now Malawi) had in 1953 been forced, joining Southern Rhodesia (now Zimbabwe). Also in that year there had originated in the Northern Province an African independent church movement of considerable power and influence, the Lumpa Church. It was by no means a unique phenomenon, independency being a notable feature of Christianity throughout sub-Saharan Africa. To missionaries concerned with the growth and development of "younger churches," the Lumpa Church appeared of special significance, and they believed that study of its origins and also those of other African independent churches in the region, such as the African Methodist Episcopal Church (AMEC), might reveal much about the prospects for Christianity, in central Africa and beyond. The Lumpa Church, together with its founder and leader Alice Lenshina, provided notable points of focus for the research by Lehmann and Taylor.

There was by the 1950s already a long history of missionary study of Africa and its peoples. The 1920s and 1930s saw a consolidation both of resources and of research focus under the aegis of the IMC supported by philanthropic agencies usually of American origin. IMC research in Northern Rhodesia predated that carried out under the auspices of the Rhodes-Livingstone Institute, which was set up in the colony in 1937. Findings of that research, into the effects of the copper industry on African society, were published as *Modern Industry and the African* (1933) under the editorship of the American mission strategist John Merle Davis. This work proved influential in the subsequent decision to set up, in 1935, the interdenominational United Missions in the Copperbelt. The UMCB (as they were universally known) failed to prosper as expected and were disbanded in 1955. Consequently Lehmann and Taylor were also interested in how the failings of missionary cooperation in central Africa might have contributed to local growth in African Christian independency.

Christians of the Copperbelt, then, was in part a research report, notably in the sections on African independent churches authored by Lehmann. But it was also a critique, in those sections written by Taylor, of Western missions and of Western missionaries and clergy during a period of social, political, and religious upheaval. In context as well as in published conclusions, the work of Lehmann and Taylor inevitably differed from that of Davis and his colleagues, published more than a quarter-century earlier. They were aware (even self-consciously so) in ways that their predecessors had little need to be, that as Westerners and missionaries they and their work might be subjected to critical and significant African scrutiny. An IMC official cautioned Lehmann in 1957: "you are always in danger of running into the feeling that this is 'you studying us'; we have to guard very carefully against this feeling."[1] At this time missionary researchers were neither insensitive to African perceptions and opinion nor unaware of the West's harmful impact upon Africa. The work and writings of the Swedish missionary scholar Bengt Sundkler (who was IMC research secretary during 1948-49) were already influential in fostering greater self-awareness; Sundkler's *Bantu Prophets in South Africa* became required reading for missionaries on the subject of African Christian independency, almost from the moment of its publication in 1948. In 1961, in the book's second edition, Sundkler reviewed his earlier findings, finding them in certain respects "too foreign, too Western, perhaps."[2]

By that time Sundkler wished to reconsider whether syncretism, or the mixing by Africans of Christian and indigenous religious beliefs and practices, was inimical to Christianity in South Africa. As Charles Stewart and Rosalind Shaw have noted, missionary researchers working prior to the 1960s typically viewed syncretism as indicative of church fragmentation and decline. For anthropologists in the 1960s and after, this use by missionaries of the historically contingent term "syncretism" was itself revealing of missionary unease at shifts in religious authority and influence.[3] *Christians of the Copperbelt* exhibits some of that unease; African independency is seen as linked to social and political upheaval, failures of evangelism and missions' lack of political engagement. Yet independency in the individual form of people such as Alice Lenshina is seen as emblematic of the present vigor and future potential of African Christianity. In matters of church, as of state, the situation in Northern Rhodesia in 1958 appeared to Taylor and Lehmann uncertain and unpredictable yet also in some ways exciting; living there, Taylor mused at the time, was like living on a volcano.

This chapter focuses on Lehmann and Taylor, as missionary researchers. He is known as a pastor and for the many influential theological works he wrote, but hardly at all for his research with Lehmann.[4] She has largely es-

---

1. Rev. Erik W. Nielsen to Dorothea A. Lehmann, 2 July 1957, London Missionary Society (LMS) papers at School of Oriental and African Studies, London (SOAS), CWM (Council for World Mission) AF/14.

2. Bengt G. M. Sundkler, *Bantu Prophets in South Africa,* 2nd ed. (London, 1961), p. 302.

3. Charles Stewart and Rosalind Shaw, "Introduction: Problematizing Syncretism," in *Syncretism/Anti-Syncretism,* ed. Stewart and Shaw (London, 1994), pp. 1-26.

4. Recent analysis of Taylor's work includes Kevin Ward, "'A Theology of Attention':

caped the attention of historians. Their careers and research interests and the project that resulted in the publication of *Christians of the Copperbelt* are instructive about missionary attitudes to mission, to the church, and to Christian independency in late colonial Africa.

Dorothea Lehmann: African Languages and Mission in Africa

Dorothea Agnes Lehmann was born on Reformation Day (31 October) in 1910 in the central German city of Kassel, into a Lutheran family. Personal misfortune helped shape her religious faith: her father, an engineer, died when she was four years old, her fiancé when she was twenty-four. She never married. Her chosen career, as a teacher, appears to have ended due to Nazi strictures on Christian education in 1937. Lehmann then decided to become a missionary. In 1938 she signed on as a probationer with the Berlin Missionary Society (BMS), intending to work in either eastern or southern Africa. Her timing was unpropitious. German overseas mission work was already subject to official restrictions, and the onset of war in Europe brought all such activity to a halt. Through the BMS, Lehmann at this time came to the attention of Professor Diedrich Westermann, at the University of Berlin. He was seeking a research assistant.

Westermann was then sixty-four years old. Formerly a missionary in West Africa, he had become a linguist and phonetician of international renown. What distinguished Westermann from many of his compatriots was his willingness, indeed eagerness, to work with colleagues of other nationalities, including British and American. He had been an original director of the International Institute of African Languages and Cultures (IIALC), set up in London in 1926, and was on close terms with British Africanists such as Edwin Smith, Lord Lugard, and Joseph Oldham. Westermann's relationship with Nazism appears ambiguous; as Holger Stoecker has noted, for much of the Second World War he was remarkably successful in obtaining funds for research on African languages and cultures, and he attracted research students accordingly.[5] In 1939 Lehmann enrolled at the university to undertake

---

The CMS Tradition at the End of the Colonial Era in Africa; Max Warren (1904-77) and John V. Taylor (1914-2001)," in *European Traditions in the Study of Religion in Africa,* ed. Frieder Ludwig and Afe Adogame (Wiesbaden, 2004), pp. 227-36; Timothy Yates, "Reading John V. Taylor," *International Bulletin of Missionary Research* 30, no. 3 (2006): 153-56.

5. Holger Stoecker, "The Advancement of African Studies in Berlin by the Deutsche Forschungsgemeinschaft, 1920-45," in *Ordering Africa: Anthropology, European Imperialism, and the Politics of Knowledge,* ed. Helen Tilley with Robert J. Gordon (Manchester, 2007), pp. 79-83.

doctoral study under Westermann's supervision. She undertook research on phonetics in eastern Tanganyika (now Tanzania), relying on printed sources of mainly mission origin. In March 1943 she obtained the degree of doctor of philosophy (her dissertation was not published). For the remainder of the war period she worked for the university in an administrative capacity.

Because of the war only intermittent contact had been possible between Westermann and his erstwhile IIALC colleagues in Britain. Protestants in Britain and the United States meanwhile maintained contact with their counterparts in continental Europe via neutral countries, notably Switzerland. The IMC had instigated an "orphaned missions" project, whereby the overseas work of interned German missionaries was continued by colleagues of other Western nationalities. This project helped facilitate the reestablishment from 1945 of links between missionaries in Germany and those in other countries.[6] At war's end Westermann managed to contact both Oldham and the International African Institute (as the IIALC had been renamed) in London. He persuaded them to intercede with the Foreign Office and the British military authorities on his behalf.[7] By November 1945, he was back at work. Lehmann rejoined him, again as a research assistant.

Lehmann was still determined to become a missionary. This would not be possible with the BMS; its headquarters was located in the Russian occupation zone, and the Society could not rely on any assistance from the authorities either military or civil. German churches struggled to come to terms with their relationship with Nazism. In October 1945 they made the Stuttgart Declaration, ostensibly acknowledging and repenting their weaknesses.[8] So grave a matter could not be resolved so easily, however; neither could the vexed question of Christian mission to the Jews.[9] But the IMC was keen to reestablish contact and rekindle fellowship among Protestant missionaries of all nationalities. To that end it arranged for qualified Germans to take up temporary missionary posts overseas, typically in British colonial Africa. The IMC London office acted as an interlocutor between German and British missionary societies, the Colonial Office, and the authorities in colonies such as Nigeria, the Gold Coast (now Ghana), and Northern Rhodesia. Thus it was

---

6. Kenneth Scott Latourette and William Richey Hogg, *World Christian Community in Action: The Story of World War II and Orphaned Missions* (New York, 1949).

7. Betty Gibson to Beatrice Wyatt, 12 October 1945; Daryll Forde to Secretary of State for Foreign Affairs, 19 October 1945, International African Institute papers at British Library of Political and Economic Science, London, File 42/65.

8. Matthew D. Hockenos, *A Church Divided: German Protestants Confront the Nazi Past* (Bloomington, Ind., 2004), pp. 75-100.

9. Hockenos, *A Church Divided*, pp. 155-63.

that in mid-1948 Lehmann's request to serve overseas came, via the IMC, to the attention of the London Missionary Society (LMS), one of the institutions that made up the United Missions in the Copperbelt.

Nominally an interdenominational Protestant body, the LMS was essentially Congregationalist in membership and outlook. Founded in 1795 and associated most famously with David Livingstone, it had a long history of mission work in central and southern Africa and other parts of the world. Everywhere it was experiencing a serious shortage of qualified European staff. Lehmann, an experienced teacher with a working knowledge of Bemba, the lingua franca of much of the Copperbelt, was just the kind of recruit the Society wanted — and she was eager to go to Africa. "She is of course a Lutheran," the IMC reported, "but by no means a fanatical one and would be perfectly happy working in a non-Lutheran mission."[10] The Berlin Missionary Society agreed to second Lehmann to the LMS. In July 1949 she traveled to England to undergo training, in London and at Carey Hall Missionary Training College for Women, in Birmingham. Her stay in England would be a protracted one. The government of Northern Rhodesia was suspicious of immigrants from Germany and initially refused permission for Lehmann to enter the colony. The LMS, with the assistance of the IMC and the UMCB, lobbied the Colonial Office and the authorities in Lusaka, the colonial capital, and finally achieved success in February 1950. The following month Lehmann set off on the first leg of her journey to the Copperbelt, by ship to Cape Town.

Lehmann was thus an early postwar beneficiary of ecumenical networks of communication. The LMS was able to afford her travel and accommodation expenses in England only because of a grant from Christian Reconstruction in Europe, an interdenominational body set up by Protestant churches in Britain and Ireland to assist in the relief and resettlement of refugees and displaced persons. For both the LMS and the BMS the successful campaign to get Lehmann to Africa demonstrated one of the main strengths of Protestant ecumenism — its encouragement of international and interdenominational cooperation in the service of the world church.[11]

Mission and Church in the Copperbelt

UMCB affairs were coordinated locally and also through an external committee based at the IMC London office. From its beginnings, however, and not-

---

10. Gibson to Rev. Ronald K. Orchard, CWM AF41/86A.
11. Dr. Gerhard Brennecke to Orchard, 23 September 1949, CWM AF41/86A.

withstanding the efforts of several talented individuals, it was beset by difficulties.[12] Some of these related to the organization's varied denominational makeup. Apart from the LMS, the UMCB comprised Scottish Presbyterian and English Methodist and Anglo-Catholic mission institutions, among others. Also, the missions' commitment to African education and welfare necessitated uneasy relationships with government and with mining companies. Before her departure from England, LMS Africa secretary Rev. Ronald Orchard briefed Lehmann on "race relations," and on how economic and social change was subjecting African peoples and also "the emerging Church" to unprecedented strain.[13]

Lehmann was to be based in Mufulira, where the Rhodesian Selection Trust's mining operations exerted a preponderant influence on local economy and society.[14] Orchard had outlined Lehmann's objectives: to work according to the overall needs of the UMCB. But for denominational reasons the LMS wished to encourage the local African church with which it was most closely linked, the Church of Central Africa Rhodesia (CCAR).[15] This encouragement did not yet extend, however, to the granting of greater responsibilities and larger stipends to African clergy and evangelists. For her part, Lehmann was entrusted with "women's work," that of stimulating and maintaining the interest of African women and girls in the affairs of the CCAR. She would also be involved in social work, as required by the UMCB as part of agreements negotiated with the government and with the mining industry.

By 1950 the nature of women's missionary work was changing, in part because of greater British interest in "community development" and social welfare provision for Africans. Missionary societies worked with the Colonial Office to recruit qualified Christian teachers and social workers (many of them women) for the UMCB and other missions in Africa. Not all missionaries favored this arrangement. Lehmann believed that Western women recruited primarily for their skills in a nonreligious vocation (such as social

12. Sean Morrow, "'On the Side of the Robbed': R. J. B. Moore, Missionary on the Copperbelt, 1933-42," *Journal of Religion in Africa* 19, no. 3 (1989): 248-51.

13. Orchard to Lehmann, 10 March 1950, CWM AF41/86B.

14. On missionary life in Mufulira, Fergus Macpherson, *North of the Zambezi: A Modern Missionary Memoir* (Edinburgh, 1998), pp. 17-28. On the mining industry, L. J. Butler, *Copper Empire: Mining and the Colonial State in Northern Rhodesia, c. 1930-64* (Basingstoke, 2007).

15. The CCAR was formed in 1945, through union of churches of the Church of Scotland missions and of the LMS with the Union Church of the Copperbelt. On the complexities of church formation in Northern Rhodesia, see Peter Bolink, *Towards Church Union in Zambia: A Study of Missionary Co-operation and Church-Union Efforts in Central Africa* (Franeker, 1967), pp. 246-365.

work) might not be perceived by their African Christian counterparts as true "church workers."[16] She also took the view that European teachers and social workers, unlike career missionaries, tended not to stay sufficiently long in one posting to make an influential contribution to the life of the church and of African society. Indebted to the LMS, she threw herself into the work allotted her, adopting a mostly informal, unstructured approach to evangelism through sewing and knitting circles. In this way and through her linguistic abilities she encouraged local women's discussion on matters ranging from marriage (and divorce) to politics.[17]

In 1952 Lehmann, with the assistance of the LMS, successfully resisted an attempt by the Berlin Missionary Society to reclaim her, for its work in South Africa. Her political views, she protested, rendered her unsuitable.[18] Here she was being disingenuous. Her antipathy to apartheid was real enough, and was shaped by her experience of life in Germany during the Nazi era (and also by brief experience of travel in South Africa, on her initial journey to Northern Rhodesia). She acknowledged the existence of racial discrimination in the Copperbelt, but she was uncertain and ambivalent about African nationalism: "I find it very difficult to make up my mind in political matters," she would later admit.[19] She cared more for the church than for politics. The church she perceived as an agent of racial fellowship and reconciliation.[20] But she also perceived the CCAR as insufficiently encouraging of both ordained and lay African participation in church affairs. This, she believed, might render it susceptible to weakness and to undue influence by African church movements, notably the AMEC and the Watchtower Bible and Tract Society. Of American origin, the AMEC spread to the Rhodesias and Nyasaland via South Africa, its growth in the Copperbelt from the mid-1920s being strongly linked to industrialization, urbanization, and the inadequacies of the mission churches.[21] For a long time the object of government suspicion, the Watchtower movement now attracted less official attention because of its avowedly nonpolitical stance. To Lehmann, however, it was better organized, better led, and appreciably better supported than churches of mission origin. Its influence in the Copperbelt she regarded as "pervasive."[22]

16. Lehmann to Orchard, 4 December 1951, CWM AF/14.
17. Lehmann, report, November 1956, CWM AF/45.
18. Lehmann to Orchard, 28 June 1952, CWM AF/14.
19. Lehmann to Rev. A. F. Griffiths, 5 November 1956, CWM AF/14.
20. Lehmann to Orchard, 4 November 1952, CWM AF/14.
21. Adrian Hastings, "John Lester Membe," in *Themes in the Christian History of Central Africa*, ed. T. O. Ranger and John Weller (Berkeley and Los Angeles, 1975), pp. 182-85.
22. Lehmann to Orchard, 4 November 1952, CWM AF/14.

Lehmann's concern for the future of the CCAR was bound up with her missionary and welfare work. She was pleased at how the women of the church accepted her, and was surprised and gratified when the church session at Mufulira made her an elder in 1956. By then she had also become involved in matters relating to education and literacy; she served on school boards and committees on behalf of the church and the Christian Council of Northern Rhodesia. Lehmann's deep involvement in the affairs of the CCAR helped sharpen her awareness of, and interest in, African independent church movements. Discussions at a missionary conference in West Germany in mid-1952 eventually led Lehmann to resume research work. The IMC met in Willingen to discuss overseas mission and the world church, and it was decided to commit resources to the study of separatist churches.[23] Lehmann was able to take advantage of this commitment, through the UMCB and the Christian Council. With the help of local people she surveyed aspects of African society, including religious allegiance. The results confirmed for her the parlous state of the mission churches. Church affiliation was merely nominal; it appeared to be fluid and characterized by "restlessness," especially among certain men. From responses to her survey she identified nineteen religious organizations to which local people claimed allegiance. The Watchtower movement appeared most popular. Lehmann concluded that with its "multitudes of missionaries" it set an example in successful evangelism from which both LMS and CCAR might even learn.[24] Despite encouragement from LMS headquarters, Lehmann did not attempt to publicize the results of her research. It is likely that she was too busy to do so. She was also due her first furlough, and in late 1953 set off for Germany. She would spend almost twelve months there and in England. During her absence religious and political life in the Copperbelt underwent considerable upheaval.

Missionaries, Alice Lenshina, and the Lumpa Church

In September 1953 missionaries in Northern Rhodesia first became acquainted with what would become one of the most notable instances of Christian independency in colonial Africa. Rev. Fergus Macpherson was visited at the Church of Scotland's Lubwa mission, near Chinsali in the Northern Province, by a woman aged about thirty-three who claimed to have risen

---

23. International Missionary Council, *The Missionary Obligation of the Church, Willingen, Germany, July 5-17 1952* (London, 1952).
24. Lehmann to Orchard, 4 November 1952, CWM AF/14.

from the dead. This was Alice Lenshina Mulenga. Her remarkable story and that of the Lumpa Church are well documented.[25] In its origins the Lumpa Church was influenced by Christianity and also by ideas about witchcraft and its eradication. Its appeal owed much to prophecy, and to the charismatic leadership of its founder. Its gospel, Andrew Roberts has noted, "was derived as much from Lenshina's visionary experience as from study of the Bible."[26] In her study of the Lumpa Church, Lehmann wrote that its "eschatological message and the promise of redemption . . . proved far more attractive than the efforts of the mission churches to keep their flocks in orthodox ways."[27] And indeed, it represented a reaction against the mission churches and their unwillingness to accord Africans a meaningful role in church affairs. Macpherson and his mission colleagues were impressed by Lenshina, and not a little awed by her ability to attract support in numbers that the Scots, with half a century's head start, had failed to do.[28] The Lumpa Church may also have represented a reaction against imperialism; certainly the colonial authorities regarded it with some suspicion, due to its infiltration by members of the Northern Rhodesia African National Congress.[29] Lenshina's influence soon spread beyond rural Lubwa and Chinsali to the Copperbelt, following her first visit to the area in 1956.

Now back in Mufulira, Lehmann became intensely interested in the growth of the Lumpa Church and how it might affect the CCAR. It soon became clear to her that its effects would encompass politics and trade unionism as well as religion. Strike action by the African Mineworkers' Union (AMU) brought response from government in the form of a state of emergency. Open-air church services had to be curtailed. The authorities detained

---

25. The main studies are the following: Robert Rotberg, "The Lenshina Movement of Northern Rhodesia," *Rhodes-Livingstone Journal* 29 (1961): 63-78; Dorothea Lehmann, "Alice Lenshina Mulenga and the Lumpa Church," in Taylor and Lehmann, *Christians of the Copperbelt: The Growth of the Church in Northern Rhodesia* (London, 1961), pp. 248-68; Andrew D. Roberts, *The Lumpa Church of Alice Lenshina* (Lusaka, 1972); Wim M. J. van Binsbergen, *Religious Change in Zambia: Exploratory Studies* (London and Boston, 1981), pp. 266-316; Hugo Hinfelaar, "Women's Revolt: The Lumpa Church of Lenshina Mulenga in the 1950s," *Journal of Religion in Africa* 21, no. 2 (1991): 99-129; A. Ipenburg, *"All Good Men": The Development of Lubwa Mission, Chinsali, Zambia, 1905-67* (Frankfurt am Main, 1992), pp. 224-79.

26. Roberts, *Lumpa Church*, pp. 3-10, p. 14.

27. Lehmann, "Alice Lenshina Mulenga," p. 252.

28. Rev. W. Vernon Stone, "The 'Alice' Movement in Northern Rhodesia," October 1957, National Library of Scotland, Edinburgh, Accession 7548 (hereafter NLS), B315.

29. District Officer's report, "The Lenshina Movement," 3 October 1956, National Archives: Public Record Office, London, TNA: PRO CO 1015/2045.

those church members associated with the AMU and Congress. Meanwhile tensions grew within the CCAR; union and Congress officials accused it of being the church of salaried (and thus relatively better paid) mineworkers who were "blindly following the Europeans." Women of the church espoused support for what Lehmann described as "the extreme leaders" of the trade union movement, while the AMU disparaged missions and espoused the Lenshina movement as "a truly African church."[30] The situation appeared to Lehmann fraught and even perilous, for church and state alike. Religious and political upheaval seemed bound to exacerbate racial tensions. Lehmann was reminded of Germany in the 1930s. Now, however, she held out hope that the church in central Africa might act to heal discord. She advocated a greater role for African women, as lay preachers. Mothers, she suggested, might pass on their Christian faith to their children; had such a thing occurred in Nazi Germany, the "pernicious" inclinations of the state might have been curbed. Lehmann also advocated adoption by the CCAR of the Congregationalist custom that permitted (European) women in the pulpit: "I am sure that an English woman minister would be welcome at least in the Copperbelt congregations."[31]

Lehmann's thinking about the role of women in the church may have been influenced to some slight extent by the example of Alice Lenshina. But Lehmann had long perceived women (and children) as essential to the identity and future of the Free Churches in the Copperbelt. But the possibility of changes in their role was overtaken by change in the relationship between missions and local churches: the UMCB was wound up in June 1955 and its evangelistic work taken over by church organizations, its other responsibilities by a Copperbelt Christian Service Council. Further church union initiatives, in 1958, would see the creation of a new entity: the United Church of Central Africa, Rhodesia (UCCAR).

Lehmann's reports from Mufulira attracted a good deal of attention at LMS headquarters. This was far exceeded, however, by the interest aroused in Scottish mission and church circles by the Lenshina phenomenon. "Why," wondered one missionary, "has 'Alice' managed to appeal so successfully to so many hundreds of our sleeping members?"[32] A colleague attributed that success to a combination of Scottish "feebleness" and Lenshina's extraordinary ability to bring into being a "people's movement."[33] Discussion was not con-

---

30. Lehmann to Rev. Frank Griffiths, 20 September 1956, CWM AF/14; Lehmann, report for LMS, November 1956, CWM AF/45.
31. Lehmann, report, November 1956, CWM AF/45.
32. Rev. Kenneth MacKenzie to Rev. John Watt, 2 January 1956, NLS B310.
33. W. V. Stone, "The Church as the People of God," December 1957; "The 'Alice Move-

fined to missionary committees and publications; news of Lenshina and of apparent Scottish missionary failings made newspaper headlines in Edinburgh.³⁴ Representatives of Protestant ecumenical organizations such as the IMC and the WCC took note: the situation in Northern Rhodesia seemed to merit detailed study. For Lehmann this was to have unexpected consequences. In October 1956 she received a letter from a man she had never met: John V. Taylor, writing from London. He requested her assistance in a large-scale research project on the churches of central Africa. Lehmann was bemused but intrigued: He "seems to have heard from the Church of Scotland that I am an anthropologist," she noted wryly.³⁵ She was keen to take up his invitation.

John V. Taylor: From England to Uganda and Northern Rhodesia

John Vernon Taylor was born in Cambridge in 1914, the child of evangelical Anglican parents. His father would later become (as would Taylor also) a bishop. Taylor was educated at Cambridge University and also at Oxford, where he read theology. Ordained in 1939 and married a year later, Taylor served as a priest in London and later in Liverpool. During this period he got to know Canon Max Warren, general secretary of the Church Missionary Society. In 1945 Warren sent Taylor to Africa, to Bishop Tucker Theological College, Mukono, near Kampala in Uganda. There Taylor worked until 1954. His stay at Mukono exerted great influence on his thinking about Africa, its people, and the church. In 1954, with his family, Taylor returned to England. His prospects were uncertain, and he was troubled by self-doubt and financial uncertainty.³⁶ Certain British Christians with an interest in church affairs in Africa were concerned about unrest and violence in colonies such as Kenya, where a state of emergency was in force. A group of Anglicans, including Warren and the historian of Africa Roland Oliver, encouraged Taylor to write a book bringing to greater public attention the problems of church and state in the African colonies.³⁷ Two years later Taylor published *Christianity and*

---

ment' in 1958," n.d., IMC Research Department of Missionary Studies, Occasional Papers, Series 1/1, August 1958 (hereafter IMCRD papers).

34. *Scotsman*, 22 June 1956.
35. Lehmann to Griffiths, 5 November 1956, CWM AF/14.
36. David Wood, *Poet, Priest, and Prophet: Bishop John V. Taylor* (London, 2002), pp. 25-46.
37. Roland Oliver, *In the Realms of Gold: Pioneering in African History* (London, 1997), pp. 160-61.

Politics in Africa (1957), in which he argued for more sustained and effective church engagement with Africa's social and political problems.

In 1955 Taylor was appointed to the post of researcher for the IMC. This provided him with employment, much-needed income, and an opportunity to put to good use the knowledge and experience gained in Uganda. The appointment was also a sign that the IMC had now begun to act more fully upon the recommendations made at Willingen in 1952 that research be carried out on the "younger churches" of Africa and Asia. The program would be administered by the Danish clergyman Erik Nielsen, successor to Bengt Sundkler as IMC research secretary. In February 1955 Nielsen chaired a meeting at the London office of the IMC. Taylor was among those present. He suggested a study of the church in Uganda, and the meeting approved.[38] In January 1956, having made advance preparation, Taylor traveled once again to the Ugandan province of Buganda. He knew the vernacular. He lived in villages, mostly in the Lubanyi area, not far from Kampala. He did much of the fieldwork himself, but he also relied upon the expertise of local Africans and of staff at Makerere College.[39] The IMC published Taylor's findings in 1958, as *The Growth of the Church in Buganda*.

Taylor's next research assignment for the IMC would be Northern Rhodesia, now the object of considerable interest in missionary circles because of the Lenshina phenomenon. Yet the IMC was not the only ecumenical agency with a research agenda. Since its formation in 1948, the World Council of Churches had taken an active interest in an ever-increasing number of issues, including the status of religious minorities and of refugees. In 1955 it set up a research program called "On the Common Christian Responsibility towards Areas of Rapid Social Change." Its aims were both ambitious and vague: to assess "the social and economic conditions which prevail in the non-western areas of rapid social change to which Christians should give particular attention."[40] The American philanthropist John D. Rockefeller Jr., a supporter of WCC initiatives, provided $100,000 in support.[41] WCC officials decided to

---

38. Nielsen, notes on meeting at Edinburgh House, London, 22 February 1955, "Studies in the Life and Growth of Younger Churches" (hereafter "Studies") file, Conference of British Missionary Society Papers at SOAS (CBMS) 536.

39. Rev. John V. Taylor, "The Uganda Study," 11 March 1956, Conference of British Missionary Society Papers at SOAS (CBMS) 536.

40. Rev. Paul R. Abrecht, circular letter for WCC Department of Church and Society, Geneva, 15 April 1955, "The Common Christian Responsibility towards Areas of Rapid Social Change" file, CBMS 558.

41. Abrecht, "Progress Report, 1955-56," "On the Common Christian Responsibility towards Areas of Rapid Social Change" file, CBMS 558.

focus their attention on the Copperbelt as an area of "rapid social change" in consultation with the IMC research department, whose primary interest in the region related to the "younger" churches. By early 1957 ecumenical representatives, including Taylor, were ready to submit church and society in Northern Rhodesia to preliminary study, with the aim of assessing how the proposed research would be carried out. They would also consult with people on the spot, including Dorothea Lehmann.

In February 1957 Paul Abrecht, the American clergyman in charge of WCC research, arrived in Northern Rhodesia accompanied by John Karefa-Smart, a Sierra Leonean medical doctor and West Africa regional representative for the World Health Organization. In Lusaka they joined Taylor, who had traveled separately. After meeting with officials of the Christian Council, they then journeyed on to Mufulira, to discuss research with Lehmann. She found this a difficult experience. Abrecht had hoped that an African (preferably with a university degree) could be found locally to help administer the project. None proved willing or able to do so; but inspired by Karefa-Smart's presence, local people took the opportunity to openly criticize the missions, to Lehmann's dismay. Her anticipation at being involved in the project gave way to foreboding and anxiety about her capabilities, as a woman, as a missionary, and as a European. Taylor's insistence that she was the right person for the job restored her confidence.[42] The LMS agreed to second her to the project, the IMC having agreed to cover the financial cost to the mission.

For Taylor, so well acquainted with Uganda, Northern Rhodesia was a revelation. The Copperbelt, he reported to the IMC, amazed and horrified him. The effects of industrialization upon African society, he identified as "devastating." Attempts at amelioration by government and mining companies appeared inadequate and ineffectual. Racial problems were endemic. Africans, he noted, preferred "what they regard as the honesty of the Afrikaans [*sic*] to the hypocrisy of the people of British stock." And racism was something from which the churches were far from immune; they were indeed "too superficial and too complacent" on the subject, and perpetuated racial discrimination through segregated services. Fearful of controversy, the churches had meanwhile failed to side with Africans on the issue of central African federation. Taylor perceived all the Protestant churches as equally culpable, and equally susceptible to the effects of African disenchantment and disillusion. "When one looks to see how the Church is making its witness in this situation," he wrote, "one is immediately horrified by its fragmentation." He noted without naming the presence of "a number of pentecostal or parasite sects from

---

42. Lehmann to Griffiths, 24 March 1957, CWM AF/14.

America." Some independent churches appeared to be flourishing, the AMEC among them. The Watchtower movement, for its part, "subtly manages to combine an anarchic otherworldliness with strong anti-white teaching." It was unclear to Taylor what the prospects were for the Lumpa Church. Its growth had certainly been spectacular, but there were also recent signs of some falling off in support.[43]

In the United Kingdom, Taylor's reports made for disturbing reading. In later private correspondence with the general secretary of the Universities' Mission to Central Africa (UMCA), Taylor cited the situation in Northern Rhodesia as evidence of grievous Anglican missionary and church failings.[44] He would subsequently address the UMCA publicly, at its 1959 general meeting, on the danger to Christianity of its being perceived by Africans as a "white man's religion."[45] With this possibility in mind, and conscious also about the hazards to the European missionary researcher of "white blindness," Taylor made ready to study in detail with Lehmann the "younger churches" of Northern Rhodesia.

Researching and Writing *Christians of the Copperbelt*

Both Lehmann and Taylor began work more than usually conscious of the color of their skin.

The political situation, Taylor would later write, meant that an "atmosphere of suspicion" permeated Northern Rhodesia during 1958. Some people in the Copperbelt were unwilling to cooperate, fearful of being regarded as informers. Despite such difficulties, Lehmann's connection with the LMS and her facility with languages proved advantageous, especially in rural areas. There they stayed in villages, taking an active interest in everyday activities and eating with the locals, not always enjoyably: "I would draw a line at cassava mush and dried caterpillars," Lehmann admitted.[46] They strove to mini-

43. Taylor, "First Impressions of Northern Rhodesia," June 1957, "Studies" file, CBMS 536.

44. Taylor to Rev. Gerald W. Broomfield, 20 April 1959, Universities' Mission to Central Africa papers, Bodleian Library of African and Commonwealth Studies, Rhodes House, Oxford, SF 139. On the UMCA, Andrew Porter, "The Universities' Mission to Central Africa: Anglo-Catholicism and the Twentieth Century Colonial Encounter," in *Missions, Nationalism, and the End of Empire*, ed. Brian Stanley (Grand Rapids and Cambridge, 2003), pp. 79-107.

45. Rev. J. V. Taylor, "The Church in the Smelter" (address to UMCA 101st anniversary meeting, 14 May 1959), *Central Africa* 920-21 (August-September 1959): 120-27.

46. Lehmann to Griffiths, 26 July 1958, CWM AF/14.

mize the likelihood of being perceived as representative of authority. Local branch officials of the AMU and of Congress even identified for them potential interviewees. Typically, however, Taylor and Lehmann contacted local clergy, preachers, or schoolteachers to initiate contact with individuals, whom they would interview singly or in groups, transcribing the conversations as they went. They also used questionnaires. They accumulated a great deal of material, but made slow progress and were always conscious of a lack of time. At the end of the eight-month research period, they discussed their work with local colleagues and helpers and then traveled to London, to write up their findings.

The resulting book, published more than two years after the conclusion of the research, was divided into separately authored sections. In one of these, Lehmann produced sympathetic and detailed accounts of urban family life. Apart from recently conducted interviews, she also drew for this section on discussions undertaken years earlier in Mufulira with African women. She devoted a further section to some "independent" churches, describing these as "outside" groups. The term "independent," she emphasized, however, was not intended to suggest dogma, polity, or importance.[47] Attendance at Watchtower meetings reminded her of how powerful were the movement's evangelistic efforts, well supported by cheap, accessible literature.[48] As for the AMEC, Lehmann noted that it had developed a distinct identity in the Copperbelt while still retaining important links with South Africa and the United States. She emphasized its members' interest in their children's education and their apparent wariness of politics. Congress leaders, she reported one AMEC minister as saying, "try to get influence in the Lumpa church, because they say it is more African."[49] Lehmann acknowledged the attraction that the Lumpa Church might hold for Congress, but she concluded that criticism leveled against it, especially by local Europeans, was ill-informed and speculative. From her familiarity with Sundkler's *Bantu Prophets* (which she frequently cited) as well as her own experiences, she well knew that while political unrest might contribute to "a suitable climate for independent church movements," it did not follow that such movements were necessarily "political" in outlook or allegiance.[50] In any event, Lehmann's opinion on the

---

47. Lehmann, "Some Independent Churches," in Taylor and Lehmann, *Christians of the Copperbelt*, p. 213.

48. Lehmann, "The Watchtower Society or Jehovah's Witnesses," in Taylor and Lehmann, *Christians of the Copperbelt*, pp. 232-33.

49. Lehmann, "The African Methodist Episcopal Church," in Taylor and Lehmann, *Christians of the Copperbelt*, p. 226.

50. Sundkler, *Bantu Prophets*, p. 295; Lehmann, "Alice Lenshina Mulenga," p. 248.

Lumpa Church was most strongly influenced by a series of meetings, over several days, with Alice Lenshina, in the Copperbelt town of Chingola.

Lehmann found Lenshina immensely impressive, as a woman and as a Christian leader. "The prophetess, now in her early thirties," she wrote, "looks a healthy, rather plump and happily relaxed village matron, a chief in her own right, as other women in her cultural stratum of matrilineal Bantu are chiefs through heritage. She is certainly not a medium, or psychopath, used by ruthless and politically ambitious men, as some have described her. Her sense of vocation is the firm foundation upon which her work is built."[51] Lehmann described church services in detail, particularly emphasizing the importance of hymn singing that owed something to Western modes but was still "genuinely African and wholly natural in its expression." In a wedding ceremony she detected "the influence of the Church of Scotland Mission," although there were no Bible readings: "Mama Lenshina," Lehmann was informed, would provide her own Bible for her followers.[52] Near Kasomo Lehmann visited the Lumpa temple, "a great cathedral of beautiful simple lines built with real craftsmanship." The labor that went into its building was that customarily accorded a chief. It was not unusual, Lehmann concluded, to encounter a woman of high status in the region. But Lenshina's status appeared unique, having been acquired through rising from the dead and through possession and dispensation of healing powers.[53]

Lehmann concluded, as had many of the Scottish missionaries, that while the Lumpa Church may have originated in part as a reaction against missions (and against witchcraft), it was helping to fulfill a deep yearning for Christ among Africans. Lenshina's power, according to Lehmann, was furthermore "directly related to the degree of anxiety and of ill-health in which this country lives."[54] Taylor took up this theme, in his scathing analysis of the missions and their churches. He was especially critical of equivocation on political matters: "the Church," he wrote, "is called not to champion this or that side, but indubitably to champion righteousness; and righteousness is not necessarily found at that middle point between two extremes."[55] On the question of race Taylor brought both theological and sociological analysis to bear. He wrote: "the Church is *de facto* not a man-made institution but a new humanity in Jesus Christ . . . it lives by obedience not to a definitive norm but to the

51. Lehmann, "Alice Lenshina Mulenga," pp. 254-55.
52. Lehmann, "Alice Lenshina Mulenga," pp. 255, 261.
53. Lehmann, "Alice Lenshina Mulenga," pp. 264-66.
54. Lehmann, "Alice Lenshina Mulenga," p. 266.
55. Taylor, "The Reaction upon the Church," in Taylor and Lehmann, *Christians of the Copperbelt*, p. 161.

existential call of God. . . . The situation in the Copperbelt does not in fact present two separate traditional cultures existing in parallel but one emergent cosmopolitan society in which members of two races are inextricably interrelated in a variety of ways. If a whole Church is to respond to this total situation, it can only do so as a single fellowship embracing both races."[56] The churches still had much work to do, Taylor argued. Referring to the ostensibly interracial character of the recently formed UCCAR, he noted the continuing existence of separate African and European district church councils and local church sessions. He concluded ominously that "a Church which has not yet won the prior battle against discrimination is radically unfitted to tackle it."[57]

Taylor was extremely interested in the independent churches, as Lehmann was in theology. But their book has a varied focus, due to its separately authored sections. It is a kind of hybrid: part history, part sociological and anthropological analysis, and part theological exploration and critique. It proved useful to other researchers of church and society in central Africa. Taylor appears to have been dissatisfied with it; he admitted that full analysis of Northern Rhodesia's social and religious complexity would require "a series of major works." Yet his time in the colony was undoubtedly influential in shaping his view of mission and the church in Africa. As David Wood notes, for Taylor research and fieldwork were important aspects of theological activity; they facilitated "encounter" (a word Taylor used often in reference to Africa) and the asking of questions, of oneself and of others.[58] And Taylor would draw on *Christians of the Copperbelt* along with other sources for his important exploration of Christian "presence" in African religion, *The Primal Vision* (1963). For Lehmann, meanwhile, participation in the research project provided a springboard to a change of career that would eventually culminate in a research and teaching post at the African Studies Department of the University of Zambia.

Conclusion

During the 1950s the Copperbelt of Northern Rhodesia attracted the attention of sociologists, anthropologists, and government officials keen to apply

---

56. Taylor, "The Church and Race Relations," in Taylor and Lehmann, *Christians of the Copperbelt*, pp. 197-98.
57. Taylor, "Church and Race Relations," p. 208.
58. Wood, *Poet, Priest, and Prophet*, pp. 70-74; Taylor, "The Younger Church Study: A Preliminary Guide to the Asking of Questions," n.d., but circa February 1955, "Studies" file, CBMS 536.

"scientific" thinking to the problems of urban Africa.[59] In Ndola, the administrative and commercial center of the Copperbelt, the anthropologist Bill Epstein wrestled, as had Lehmann and Taylor, with the difficulties of being an "outsider" researching an urban African community.[60] However, missionary researchers brought to their work a theological dimension, and Protestant ecumenical organizations such as the IMC and the WCC accorded research considerable importance.[61] The IMC particularly intended that theologians and missionaries might benefit from the published findings of research into "younger churches." Such was the dearth of indigenous African researchers that the work was invariably carried out by Europeans.[62] Notwithstanding that work, the relationship of such churches to the wider, world church would remain a source of contention as well as of interest, in relation to matters such as syncretism. Taylor had already attempted to address that concern in parts of his work on the church in Buganda. He argued that the local church (and diocese) should accept "its own second-rate totality in the forgiveness of God" rather than insist unreasonably on uncompromising standards of belief and practice from its members.[63] Unsatisfying as he may have deemed it, in some ways his subsequent work in Northern Rhodesia at least enabled him to further develop his thoughts on the matter, in a research environment very different from that of "unashamedly rural" Buganda. Reflecting on the social, political, racial, and religious tensions of the Copperbelt, Taylor asserted that the church "should champion as something most precious to its life both the strangeness and the validity of the African contribution."[64]

That contribution might now take new and more varied form, or so it appeared to missionaries interested in the possibilities of research and keen to promote greater interaction between Christians in the West and those in Africa and Asia. In an address to the IMC in 1961, its general secretary Lesslie

---

59. On such thinking, Andrew Burton, *African Underclass: Urbanisation, Crime, and Colonial Order in Dar es Salaam* (London, 2005), pp. 238-40.

60. A. L. Epstein, *Urbanization and Kinship: The Domestic Domain on the Copperbelt of Zambia, 1950-56* (London, 1981), pp. 8-10.

61. The WCC sponsored another study of African society in the Copperbelt, by the Dutch missionary C. L. van Doorn. This resulted in a report, "The Churches and Social Change in the Copperbelt of Northern Rhodesia" (1959).

62. Other works included the following: Stone, "The Church as the People of God" and "The 'Alice Movement' in 1958"; Fergus Macpherson, "Notes on the Beginning of the Movement," April 1958, IMCRD papers; F. B. Welbourn, *East African Rebels: Some Independent African Churches* (London, 1961).

63. J. V. Taylor, *The Growth of the Church in Buganda: An Attempt at Understanding* (London, 1958), pp. 232-33.

64. Taylor, "Church and Race Relations," p. 208.

Newbigin referred to the organization's recent studies of "younger churches," and to his hope that the program might be extended "to enable representatives of the younger churches to make parallel studies in the life of the older churches." Following this, Newbigin suggested, church leaders of Asia and of Africa might be moved to send missionaries to Europe and America, "to make the Gospel credible to the pagan masses of those continents who remain unmoved by the witness of those churches in their midst."[65] Like Sundkler's reappraisal of *Bantu Prophets* and Taylor's thoughts on the "strangeness and the validity" of African Christianity, Newbigin's bold suggestion indicated that for missionaries at the beginning of the 1960s research might have helped to provide certain answers, but it was equally likely to have prompted new and difficult questions about mission and church not merely in Africa but in the West also.

Select Bibliography

Abrecht, Paul. *The Churches and Rapid Social Change*. London, 1961.
Davis, J. Merle, ed. *Modern Industry and the African*. 2nd ed. London, 1967.
Hayward, Victor E. W., ed. *African Independent Church Movements*. London, 1963.
Ipenburg, A. *"All Good Men": The Development of Lubwa Mission, Chinsali, Zambia, 1905-67*. Frankfurt am Main, 1992.
Macpherson, Fergus. *North of the Zambezi: A Modern Missionary Memoir*. Edinburgh, 1998.
Ranger, T. O., and John Weller, eds. *Themes in the Christian History of Central Africa*. Berkeley and Los Angeles, 1975.
Roberts, Andrew D. *The Lumpa Church of Alice Lenshina*. Lusaka, 1972.
Stanley, Brian, ed. *Missions, Nationalism, and the End of Empire*. Grand Rapids and Cambridge, 2003.
Stewart, Charles, and Rosalind Shaw, eds. *Syncretism/Anti-Syncretism*. London, 1994.
Sundkler, Bengt G. M. *Bantu Prophets in South Africa*. 2nd ed. London, 1961.
Taylor, John V. *The Growth of the Church in Buganda: An Attempt at Understanding*. London, 1958.
Taylor, John V., and Dorothea Lehmann. *Christians of the Copperbelt: The Growth of the Church in Northern Rhodesia*. London, 1961.
Van Binsbergen, Wim M. J. *Religious Change in Zambia: Exploratory Studies*. London and Boston, 1981.
Wood, David. *Poet, Priest, and Prophet: Bishop John V. Taylor*. London, 2002.

---

65. Lesslie Newbigin, "The Missionary Dimension of the Ecumenical Movement" (1961), in *The Ecumenical Movement: An Anthology of Key Texts and Voices*, ed. Michael Kinnamon and Brian E. Hope (Grand Rapids, 1997), pp. 344-45.

CHAPTER 11

Mission, Clinic, and Laboratory: Curing Leprosy in Nigeria, 1945-67

JOHN MANTON

Through the early decades of the twentieth century, as European colonial control and the management of unfamiliar environments and subject populations took firm hold across the African continent, a new British model of colonial administration ostensibly suited to African contexts began to take shape, guided by the principles of indirect rule formulated by Lord Lugard in northern Nigeria. Animated by a concern with minimizing the administrative cost of colonial rule in Africa, the protection of European settlers and assets exercised greatest call on the security and administrative resources of the British Empire in Africa for much of the period leading up to World War Two. However, in spite of its rural and lightly Europeanized nature, the theoretical underpinnings of colonial governance and trusteeship were tested and stretched in eastern Nigeria to a greater extent than almost anywhere else in Britain's African empire, with the crisis in rule culminating in the Women's War of 1929 (see van den Bersselaar's chapter in this volume), prompting an empire-wide reassessment of the nature of British trusteeship.[1]

In the early colonial period, the management of infectious disease most excited debates in colonial medical circles. This was often framed in terms of the regulation of contaminations ensuing from the proximity and interdependence of European and non-European. While a network of European

---

1. D. Pratten, *The Man-Leopard Murders: History and Society in Colonial Nigeria* (Edinburgh, 2007), pp. 114-29. See also M. Perham, *Native Administration in Nigeria* (Oxford, 1937), and Lord Hailey, *Native Administrations in the British African Territories: Part III; West Africa; Nigeria, Gold Coast, Sierra Leone, Gambia* (London, 1951), as exemplary of the intellectual labors surrounding questions of administrative reorganization from 1930.

hospitals had begun to emerge in colonial urban centers, urban sexual health and sanitation, and the study and containment of transcontinental epidemics such as human and animal trypanosomiasis, commanded whatever resources European colonial administrations directed at the medical problems besetting African populations. Though a certain veneer of benevolence can be attributed to the architects and administrators of these and similar policies in the field of welfare, Adrian Hastings correctly points out the "patchy and bounded" nature of colonial gestures toward development in this period.[2] Across much of Africa, what little passed for responsive social provision in health and education was coordinated by an unevenly dispersed, divisive and largely uncoordinated, heavily ideological, and poorly funded array of Christian missionary organizations.[3]

For much of the continent, the disjuncture between administrative visions of colonial health and the peculiar emphases of Christian missionaries emerges especially starkly with respect to leprosy and its control. For missionaries, leprosy came to represent a specific aspect of Christ's calling, and its biblical resonances were central in representing African leprosy as a historically contingent confection of biology, spirituality, and social meaning. Remarking on the Ghanaian case, K. David Patterson notes that leprosy, "because of the fear and revulsion it evoked in Europeans, attracted much more attention than its public health importance or the possibilities for successful therapy could justify."[4] At the same time, the call of missionaries that colonial administrations support leprosy work went largely unheeded in British Africa, and the means by which a concerted and cohesive body of expertise and policy on leprosy in Africa might emerge remained unarticulated, until conditions in eastern Nigeria prompted a massive reorganization and expansion of government-mission cooperation in leprosy control, and centralized leprosy control efforts to a degree hitherto unknown in Africa. The means that led to the emergence of this remarkably concerted exercise in colonial disease control, and the peculiarities informing and emerging from hybrid government-mission administration of leprosy control in a period of rapid development in techniques of leprosy control, are the subject of this chapter.

By the outbreak of World War Two, colonial administration across much of Africa was entrenched enough to consider the political advantages of concerted social and economic development efforts. For Britain's empire in Af-

---

2. A. Hastings, *The Church in Africa, 1450-1950* (Oxford, 1996), p. 542.
3. Hastings, *The Church in Africa*, pp. 550-58.
4. K. D. Patterson, *Health in Colonial Ghana: Disease, Medicine, and Socio-Economic Change, 1900-1955* (Waltham, Mass., 1981), p. 73.

rica, the notion of development came to center stage following the Colonial Development and Welfare Act of 1940. Over the next twenty years, the implementation and partial successes of this and subsequent acts owed much to the cooperation of nongovernmental organizations with a stake in infrastructural development, education, health, and welfare. Despite the formal insistence of colonial administrations to use the term "voluntary organizations" to describe such partners, the term referred predominantly to Christian missionaries. For leprosy control, an important subset of health provision, this was almost exclusively the case. The increasing interest and intervention of government transformed the missionary leprosy worker from charismatic carer and healer in the midst of spectacular suffering into a bureaucratic manager, technician, and scientist.

This chapter examines the entanglements of leprosy control with the reproduction of colonial control and the production of development expertise in late colonial and early independent Nigeria. It also looks at trajectories in the globalization of health care, medicine, and clinical research. Both strands in my research aim to discern linkages between the history of science and medicine and histories of welfare, community, and governance. With leprosy at their core, they bring a focus on missionaries into the heart of histories of development and decolonization, illuminating the networks and the forms of expertise that missionary involvement in these processes produced.

The chapter portrays the relations between missionary and government leprosy control and governance in late colonial Nigeria, alongside a consideration of the ad hoc evolution of a medical research capacity in eastern Nigeria's leprosy control institutions between the end of World War Two and the outbreak of the Biafran War in 1967. It also examines constructions of expertise in twentieth-century leprosy control, in relation to Christian missionary discourse and personnel, with specific reference to the production of clinical and scientific knowledge.

Leprology and the Refinement of Medical Mission

Insofar as I examine transnational medical and welfare enterprises in a variety of institutional locales, my project is anchored by the figure of the leprologist, and around leprology, characterized by the scientific and bureaucratic practice of leprosy control in all its variety. By the middle of the twentieth century, the leprologist had become at once a paramount of the medical mission, party to its noblest heritage, from Father Damien of Molokai to Albert Schweitzer, and a combination of scientist, researcher, public health planner, and colonial administrator. He or she harried district officers; badgered pharmaceutical and medical supply firms; entreated with customs officials; wrote for and to medical journals, religious papers, and the popular press; made films and took photos; and circulated among an international professional coterie. In this respect, the growing power and the changing role of the missionary leprologist follow a similar trajectory to that described by Hastings in his portrait of increasing Protestant and Catholic missionary accommodations with the welfare aims of the colonial state through the twentieth century.[5]

A would-be social engineer and welfare evangelist, the leprologist's autonomy was continually and differentially constrained by material poverty, resource shortages, administrative deficits, and community unconcern or skepticism. In significant ways, notably through the troubled legal and moral discourse on segregation of leprosy patients, the epidemiological terrain and the minutiae of social interaction in medical institutional settings produced both leprology and leprologists. This process was most intense from the late 1930s through the mid-1960s, when the classification of leprosy was subject to constant revision in dialogue with new data emerging from clinician-supervised leprosaria across the colonial and developing world.

It was, of course, the increasing bureaucracy of leprosy control that elicited this data, as leprosy control institutions sought to cleave more tightly to (i) community structures, (ii) an evolving apparatus for public health, and (iii) the contours of leprosy's prevalence. Amid the resulting fusion, a rich epidemiology emerged, sensitive to the vast array of presentations of leprosy, its mildness or severity, its epidemicity or endemicity, and its relation to conditions of housing, sanitation, and nutrition. As this process intensified, developments in chemotherapy and clinical research from the mid-1940s promised intriguing avenues of research for leprosy workers. Since testing on leprosy could not be carried out in the laboratory, and needed human subjects, the clinicians in charge of leprosy control institutions became crucial research gatekeepers, caught up in the adventure of global public health in the era of decolonization.

By 1945, segregation-based models of leprosy control had reached a high point of medical, carceral, and ideological sophistication, epitomized in the vast and isolated complexes in locations such as Molokai in Hawaii, Carville in Louisiana, USA, and Culion in the Philippines.[6] In Africa, this process was

---

5. Hastings, *The Church in Africa*, pp. 550-52, 561-62.
6. See M. Moran, *Colonizing Leprosy: Imperialism and the Politics of Public Health in the United States* (Chapel Hill, N.C., 2007), and W. Anderson, *Colonial Pathologies: American Tropical Medicine, Race, and Hygiene in the Philippines* (Durham, N.C., 2006), chapter 6, for further discussion of these institutions.

epitomized in British colonial Nigeria, where biomedical models of leprosy control had only emerged in the previous twenty years, and lacked the longer institutional roots they enjoyed elsewhere on the continent. Robert Cochrane, writing on African leprosy control in 1928, noted that the medical missionary, and by extension leprosy work in Nigeria, was not particularly advanced.[7] This was partly a result of the insecure and recent colonial "pacification" of much of Nigeria, and partly because medical workers did not want to travel beyond the coastal trading and administrative cantonments of late-nineteenth- and early-twentieth-century southern Nigeria.

In the two decades between the founding of the Itu Leper[8] Settlement by Church of Scotland missionary Andrew MacDonald in 1926 and the end of World War Two, institutions for the control of leprosy and for leprosy sufferers had been set up under biomedical supervision across Nigeria. Schemes and settlements in the Eastern Region were established on a provincial basis; in the north of the country the compact between colonial administrators and Muslim rulers determined the scope and range of many of the institutions.[9] What linked these institutions north and south was the pivotal medical and managerial role played by Christian missionaries, for whom leprosy control married tropes of concern and captivity that had distinguished evangelical strategies across early colonial Nigeria.

The construction in which the "leper" is produced as prisoner or inmate is epitomized by the leprosy colony at Itu. As late as 1946 a report could rather luridly contrast the Nigerian context of a missionary's toil with the rewards bestowed on the inmate of the model Scottish leprosy colony:

---

7. R. G. Cochrane, *Leprosy in Europe, the Middle and Near East, and Africa* (London, 1928), p. 62. He notes that of 525 missionaries in Nigeria, only 18 were doctors.

8. The use of the word "leper" to denote leprosy sufferers and patients by direct association with their illness is no longer acceptable in academic and medical discourse. The perceived issues surrounding stigmatization have always shaped the role of terminology in the description of leprosy, and increasing optimism regarding its treatment coincided with the vote to abandon use of the word "leper" in technical communication, and to encourage its abandonment in popular usage, at the Fifth International Leprosy Congress held in Havana, Cuba, in 1948. The persistence of this outmoded usage is a matter of record, and the employment of the word "leper" in this paper will always reflect an actual usage in the historical record, or a characterization of historical usage, consequently reflecting the range of social relations and meanings elicited by historical usage.

9. S. Shankar, "The Social Dimensions of Christian Leprosy Work among Muslims: American Missionaries and Young Patients in Colonial Northern Nigeria, 1920-40," in *Healing Bodies, Saving Souls: Medical Missions in Asia and Africa*, ed. D. Hardiman (Amsterdam, 2006), pp. 281-305.

"Calabar" was a heart-stirring word among the douce, hard-working folk who formed the backbone of the old U.P. Kirk in many a Scots village. . . . It called up visions of the clamorous harbour ports, Creek Town and Duke Town, where ships lay waiting for the canoes bringing palm-oil from the forbidden forest hinterland: of black kings such as Eyo Honesty (a good friend to the young mission) and Eyamba the Fifth (an ill-conditioned rascal); of crocodile-infested waters, the Calabar and Cross Rivers, flowing darkly through dim unexplored lands.

It spoke of the dreaded shrine of the Long Juju at Arochuku, on the bloodstained rock in the deep gorge — centre of the slave trade; of the wailing cry when a chief died and hundreds of his folk were massacred to provide a ghostly retinue; of the great clay crocks thrown out to the leopard-haunted bush with the tiny bodies of ill-omened twin babies . . . a perpetual call and challenge to the generous minds of Scotland's Christian youth.

For the real magic of that word "Calabar" lay in the multitudes of suffering humanity living in the pathless forests of the South, through which the river highway ran, or in the bare uplands of the North, where the salt lake at [Uburu] drew thousands to its market.[10]

From amidst this undifferentiated morass of misery, produce, gore, and commerce, the author presents us with this vision: "One of the most effective efforts to combat leprosy — that scourge of modern Nigeria — is the leper settlement at Itu. There, in a self-contained and self-maintained unit of three square miles of model township and farmlands, 3200 lepers are gaining wholeness of body and spirit."[11] I have quoted this at length as it seems to lay bare at once the missionary invention of Nigeria and the separateness of leprosy and its control from the operative conditions of ostensibly unreconstructed "Nigerian life." The rescue of leprosy sufferers, styled as "lepers," from the radical incompleteness of suffering Nigerian existence, and their sequestration in an oasis of repair and redemption, conjures an image of leprosy control that retains potency even today. Through the colonial era, countless missionary texts invoked the dark horrors of leprosy, the damaged soul, the destroyed body, and the scourged polity that bore and rejected the "leper." The mission and its colony — the leprosarium — emerged from this darkness as the promise of moral and physical salvation.

---

10. National Library of Scotland (hereafter NLS), Acc. 5204/15, "Miscellaneous Correspondence, Itu, Nigeria 1927-1937." Clipping of article by Robert Ross, "Calabar Mission: A Century of Christian Work; Inspiring Record," *Scotsman,* 10 April 1946.

11. NLS, Acc. 5204/15, "Miscellaneous Correspondence, Itu, Nigeria 1927-1937."

Indeed, much of what is unusual about leprology as a scientific discipline or discourse is bound up in the structure and the history of the leprosarium as a sociomedical space. For the purposes of this chapter, then, the term "leprology" refers to the management of medical institutions for the control of leprosy in a population. This comprises the development of epidemiological apparatus, the production and employment of medical knowledge, the iterative evolution of mechanisms to ensure complete coverage of an area, the securing of consent for medical work, the publicizing of the aims and achievements of leprosy control, and the dissemination of medical knowledge resulting from a structured encounter with leprosy. Over time, as the technology became available, the treatment and cure of leprosy and the rehabilitation of leprosy patients became a part of this complex. As a colonial science, the practice of leprology was never separated from communities or policy regarding the African community. Most starkly, the properties of *Mycobacterium leprae*, which could not be cultivated or studied outside its human host, forced patients and research scientists into an unusually intimate bind. In Nigeria, and particularly in eastern Nigeria, this structured encounter with leprosy in an area of high endemicity, and under conditions of strong operational stability, gave rise to groundbreaking research on which much of the contemporary treatment of leprosy is based. This success was predicated on the negotiation and maintenance of a heavily administered space.

Missionaries as Bureaucrats

I

Institutional capacity for leprosy control in Nigeria had developed greatly since the foundation of Itu and Uburu leprosy settlements in the late 1920s. A provincial scheme with extensive outreach facilities was developed following the 1936 visit of Ernest Muir, an India-based British leprologist, and by 1945 the leprosy-endemic areas of eastern Nigeria, constituting much of the Igbo-majority areas and their southern and eastern borders, were covered by provincial centers and schemes. All the centers had originally been set up by Christian missionaries, broadly reflecting either the catchment claimed by the mission in question or its first mover status in the area in question. Thus, the Anglican Church Missionary Society had founded the center at Oji River, as had the Methodists at Uzuakoli, both in the 1930s, later forging agreements with the government to jointly manage the schemes based at these centers.

The Church of Scotland had founded centers at Itu and Uburu close to the Cross River in the 1920s, while the interdenominational Northern Irish Qua Iboe Mission founded the hospital at Ekpene Obom in 1932. The Catholic medical expansion began somewhat later, owing to Vatican restrictions on medical practice.[12] Thus, while Catholics ran hospitals across Owerri and northwestern Calabar Provinces, in complete disregard of spheres of influence delineated among Protestant missionary groups, it was only in the missionary frontier province of Ogoja, at Abakaliki and Ogoja towns, that Catholics gained control of leprosy services, set up in 1945.

During World War Two, plans emerged for a government leprosy service, to be based in the Eastern Region and funded under the terms of the 1940 Colonial Development and Welfare Act. The original plans, submitted by J. W. P. Harkness, the director of medical services for the government of Nigeria, for the discussion of missionary bodies in London and Edinburgh, were a source of grave concern to missionaries engaged in leprosy control. Their concerns were expressed in a nutshell by J. W. C. Dougall of the Church of Scotland, who wrote to Harkness in summary:

> [I]t seems to me that you have not found the best place for the medical missionary in the plan. The contribution of the missions in leprosy-work has been notable in India and Africa for three main reasons: (1) it has attracted a number of first-rate men who gave themselves to work among lepers in the spirit of Christian vocation; (2) it has built leper-colonies into the larger life of a Christian community and stressed the positive social habits which enable the patient to recover self-respect and hope and purpose in an atmosphere of fellowship; (3) it has given the doctor-patient relationship a more personal character, enabled the missionary to practice his medicine in the name of and for the sake of His [sic] Master, and thus inspired more confidence and trust on the part of the patient.[13]

From an evangelical standpoint, the obvious appeal of leprosy colonies was the presence, at least in theory, of a captive population, subject to the healing ministries of the medical missionary. It also lent to missionary propagandists the figure of the "leper," construed with all the pejorative and pitiable resonances of this already outdated term. This figure was as central to the conduit

---

12. E. M. Hogan, *The Irish Missionary Movement: A Historical Survey, 1830-1980* (Dublin, 1990), pp. 106-8.

13. NLS, ACC 7548 — C 82 — A/132, letter from Dougall to Harkness, 11 July 1944.

of missionary-humanitarian funding as has been the figure of the starving child to emergency humanitarian aid over the last quarter-century. As an evangelical tool, however, the leprosy colony was an abject failure almost everywhere in Nigeria. Like the Christian slave-rescue and twin-rescue stations of the late nineteenth century, the evangelical work of the leprosy colony impacted little on the religious lives of the broader community, though the choral compositions of Ikoli Harcourt Whyte, a patient at Uzuakoli, and the evangelical activities of a number of former leprosy patients deserve recognition as important factors in the development of Christian cultures in Nigeria.

The reasons for this failure are complex. In part, the limited appeal of a ministry to the poor had been demonstrated by missionary entrepreneurs such as the Catholic bishop Joseph Shanahan, whose emphasis on education in English attracted those keen to maximize their economic opportunities in colonial Nigeria, where previous Catholic evangelists had seen their slave stations scorned.[14] Further, leprosy colonies were not as segregated as missionaries liked to imagine. Even in Itu, where many patients were separated from their place of birth, steady commerce existed between the colony and the town of Itu but was subject to constant complaint from Nigerians, British missionaries, and colonial administrators. The borders were never sealed, and the subjection of the leprosy patient to the ministry of the missionary was never complete.

At any rate, from 1945 the government took over joint management, with missionaries, of a number of these facilities. The new Nigeria Leprosy Service developed training and research at two eastern Nigerian facilities, Uzuakoli and Oji River, bringing leprosy control into the heart of public health and disease control through the era of decolonization. As well as evolving in tandem with the colonial apparatus for administering eastern Nigeria, leprosy control helped to shape conceptions of rural space in Nigeria. In seeking to elaborate a conception of the spatial requirements and domain of leprosy control, leprologists entered an arena of land regulation that was subject to contestation on all scales of the colonial encounter, from local, district, and provincial to regional and colony-wide. Understandings of space in precolonial eastern Nigeria, where, apart from at the coast, no one polity had territorial dominance, seem to have centered on social relations and networks, in a manner that Christopher Gray, following Edward Soja, has described as a "social definition of territory."[15] According to this model, the cir-

---

14. P. B. Clarke, "The Methods and Ideology of the Holy Ghost Fathers in Eastern Nigeria, 1885-1905," *Journal of Religion in Africa* 6, no. 2 (1974): 81-108.

15. C. J. Gray, *Colonial Rule and Crisis in Equatorial Africa: Southern Gabon, ca. 1850-1940* (Rochester, N.Y., 2002), pp. 18-22.

culation and domain of oracular experts from Arochukwu, salt panners from Afikpo, canoe makers from Ikom, and so on would have evolved in a fluid and relatively unbounded manner, determined in important ways by connection between a group and the resources to which they sought or controlled access.[16]

In colonial Gabon, Gray traces an evolution from such a "social definition of territory" to a colonial "territorial definition of society," which had markedly different effects depending in part on the resources invested in and extracted from an area by colonial agents. Land came to take on a keen significance, even as the models for land use and regulation and contestation of use were underdeveloped. In attempting to identify title, amid a crisis in mobility generated by the colonial interruption of existing trade and social networks, colonial administrators evolved a hierarchy of rule that sat uneasily with communities across eastern Nigeria based on an often ill-chosen network of local agents and allies known as warrant chiefs. The effect of this system was to make colonial rule appear capricious and irresponsible, an effect magnified by the response to an ill-judged proposal to tax market women at Aba in the late 1920s, which precipitated one of the central political events in colonial eastern Nigeria, the Women's War. This set in train a process of constitutional revision that preoccupied colonial administrators and Nigerian elites for much of the next thirty years.

II

This failure of the colonial administration to recognize and develop appropriate mechanisms for the application of indirect rule in eastern Nigeria, epitomized in the outbreak of the Women's War in 1929, has its correlative in the poor understanding of the epidemiological terrain confronting medical workers in early colonial Nigeria. Throughout the colonial period, the available epidemiological apparatus continued to be unequal to the demands of medical planning. The founding narratives of almost all the major leprosy settlements in eastern Nigeria speak of the summoning of an unending stream of suffering humanity from the bush, each and every word a telling signifier of ignorance and the potential for misconception. Again, in almost every case, the more mundane administrative records suggest difficulties in obtaining land, explaining purpose, retaining patients, making diagnoses,

---

16. John Manton, "The Roman Catholic Mission and Leprosy Control in Colonial Ogoja" (D.Phil. thesis, University of Oxford, 2004), pp. 56-80.

meeting the demands of paymasters and hosts, and determining the prevalence of the disease.

Some of the available evidence[17] suggests that eastern Nigeria was in the throes of a leprosy epidemic, and that leprosy on the scale known to observers in the 1920s and 1930s was relatively novel. Prevalence rates varying from 1 to 7 percent of the population at a divisional level, in themselves coming close to what is currently thought to be the limit of genetic susceptibility to leprosy in a population, as well as the skew in distribution toward relatively mild forms of the disease, corroborate this notion. Such figures certainly cast doubt on the notion that leprosy invoked age-old fears and strictures in Nigerian societies — indeed, contemporary evidence seems to suggest a relatively benign attitude toward leprosy in many areas of eastern Nigeria in the early colonial period. It is difficult to discern the extent to which forcible expulsion or isolation of severely impaired leprosy patients in the early years of the twentieth century was a response to colonial categorizations that for instance saw leprosy sufferers removed from prisons, or to fears occasioned by the changing distribution of leprosy in the population. It is also difficult to discern the degree of isolation experienced by sufferers. It has been suggested[18] that problems in maintaining disabled family members may have contributed to isolation as much as any active legal proscription, and that strong family links were maintained by many patients throughout periods of isolation and, later, hospitalization. The rapid growth in segregation centers in the period leading up to 1945 may in fact suggest that the emphasis on isolation and separation of leprosy was fleshed out in response to the exigencies of leprosy control.

Whatever the case, by the 1940s colonial administrators feared that the strains placed by leprosy were beginning to tell on the legal norms of Igbo society, evolved in concert with colonial customary structures. The growing urgency of the issue was signaled by the circulation of a minute from T. B. Davey, the medical superintendent of the Owerri Province leprosy settlement at Uzuakoli. This minute, circulated throughout Nigeria by the director of medical services in Lagos, concerned legal matters arising from developing leprosy control measures, and was drafted in the first instance by the resident of Owerri Province. The import of all the proposed legal measures was to

---

17. T. F. Davey, "Editorial: Common Features in Rapidly Declining Leprosy Epidemics," *Leprosy Review* 46, no. 1 (1975): 5-9.

18. Professor Edward B. Attah, UniUyo Teaching Hospital (and formerly of UniCal), at a seminar on the history of leprosy control in eastern Nigeria given by the author at UniUyo, January 2006. Prof. Attah, a leading expert on leprosy control, commented that no Nigerian society had had measures relating to the strict exclusion of leprosy sufferers prior to the advent of biomedical leprosy control.

"implement the authority of chiefs, and make that authority effective."[19] In reply, an Igbo correspondent, Mr. Okechukwu, reported that "[t]he general belief is that a leper may never recover and all things done to him are considered as waste. No law can eradicate this feeling. . . . [The leper] feels he is bound by no law to [pay taxes] for he can neither be sent to prison nor any of his infected properties be seized as a set off."[20]

In the end, though, any individual measures that were taken to control leprosy in the interwar period owed more to expediency and local developments than to any concerted colonial policy. It would seem, then, that the "leper" is a quintessentially colonial construction, whose relation to society is reencoded by means of a variety of legal, medical, and economic discourses. There was never any legal consensus behind the forcible segregation of leprosy patients, and yet an apparatus evolved in which the collaboration of the colonial administration, medical missionaries and the medical establishment, leprosy sufferers, and communities across eastern Nigeria gave rise to an extensive network of large segregation and treatment centers. In this scenario, the leprosy patient paradoxically emerges as something of a "community resource," contradicting the missionary projection of a loathsome and isolated sufferer.

In its heyday, the aforementioned Itu Leper Settlement was the largest leprosy colony in Africa, and a source of pride to the Church of Scotland. However, the model of its design and its attractiveness to patients from far and wide were a constant cause of concern to colonial administrators across eastern Nigeria. Patients came and were referred from every province of the Eastern Region, and from as far afield as Fernando Po and French Cameroun. Each patient was entitled to land and had a right to work, and many exerted demands on public coffers for maintenance. To a colonial administration bent on the principle of native authority self-sufficiency, Itu constituted a terrifying model of welfare policy, and a violation of all principles of local accountability.

In 1936, the medical secretary of British Empire Leprosy Relief Association (BELRA), and one of the leading advocates of the Propaganda-

---

19. Nigerian National Archives, Enugu (hereafter NAE), OGPROF 2/1/1789, pp. 244-48. Circular from the Director of Medical Services, Lagos, to the three Secretaries for Northern, Eastern and Western Provinces, dated 11 October 1941, with attached copy of letter and minute from T. B. Davey to the Secretary, BELRA Nigeria branch dated 4 August 1941. Endorsed to the Resident, Ogoja Province, 28 October 1941. The quoted passage is on p. 245.

20. NAE, OGPROF 2/1/1789, pp. 252-53. Response to Davey minute (NAE, OGPROF 2/1/1789, pp. 244-48) signed P. Okechukwu and date-stamped 6 November 1941. Endorsed with a comment on "educated African opinion."

Treatment-Survey (PTS) model of leprosy control, Dr. Ernest Muir, was invited to Nigeria to examine the basis on which leprosy control could be developed at a provincial level. Subsequent to this visit, and again in 1939, when he came to the Leprosy Conference in Enugu, Muir recommended that a series of clan-village schemes, one for each province, be set up along the lines already in operation at the other Church of Scotland settlement in Uburu. Here, village outreach had already begun when Dr. Harry Hastings decided to offer treatment at compounds where leprosy sufferers had previously assembled on land ostensibly owned by kin. Hastings's rationalization of what appears to have been a local arrangement for the care of leprosy sufferers was generalized into a regional template for leprosy control, and set off a series of negotiations between communities of landholders and leprosy sufferers, district officers, and newly constituted provincial leprosy superintendents.

III

This gave rise to one of the most striking processes in which leprosy control institutions became embroiled — over the control of land. The terms and extent of leaseholdings, the negotiations surrounding these, comprising justifications, assurances, obstructions, mappings, and border walking, were complex, long-lasting, and recurrent. Typically, the district officer — the European official most closely associated with British indirect rule across eastern Nigeria — would guide the leprosy superintendent (either an independent medical missionary or a missionary seconded to government service) through the clan or ethnic composition of the province, the amenability of local leaders, and a notional prevalence of leprosy. The superintendent would then approach local leaders and attempt to ascertain a suitable plot for the founding of a leprosy segregation or settlement village. This would need to be extensive enough to allow for the expansion of numbers and services, and for farm plots. Secure access to water was important from the outset, and the policing of access to local food, cultural, and marketing resources often arose at a later stage. The sites were chosen after much consultation, and often amid strong resistance by landholders. In a number of cases, the land chosen was in dispute among local groups — the founding of a leprosy village at once resolved the dispute on an immediate level and preserved it for when the land was no longer needed.

The district officer played an important role in bringing the negotiations to a successful conclusion. Reminding local leaders that they had to discharge fiscal responsibilities for leprosy sufferers among their kin, and that the mission (almost invariably) in charge of leprosy control was kindly offering to assist them in this responsibility, the district officer mediated this reinterpretation of the rights and duties of rule, predicated on the insertion of a large expatriate-run medical apparatus into local life. In underlining the colonial association between ethnicity and territory, continually subject to contestation in the early twentieth century as colonial aggression interrupted military, migratory, and trade networks all across eastern Nigeria, leprosy control narrowed the sphere for contest over land and helped to legitimize state intervention in land issues, in the guise of an enterprise for development.

The existence of a developmental agenda behind leprosy control is confirmed in the plans put forward under the Colonial Development and Welfare Act of 1940. Leprosy control was one of the largest headings for spending in eastern Nigeria, amounting to 13 percent of the estimated expenditure on development between 1951 and 1956.[21] This amount was greater than that set aside for roads, agriculture, water, and sanitation; indeed, only education and nonleprosy medical and health care warranted higher proportions of spending. When it is further taken into account that most of this money was spent on government schemes in Onitsha and Owerri Provinces, the huge scale of concern with and mobilization around leprosy becomes apparent.

One result that does seem to hold across rural eastern Nigeria, but which needs to be subjected to further analysis, is that an accommodating local response to the development of leprosy control, which was often among the first large-scale welfare interventions in a given rural area, acted as a spearhead for further infrastructural development. In this we begin to see how leprosy, for all the problematic aspects of its portrayal and stigmatization in the colonial period, might have a strategic relevance for local resource politics. The language of resource politics and intercommunity disputes in contemporary Nigeria reminds us of the important spatial dimension to the reproduction of inequality and the perception of inequality to which leprosy control, as a capital-extensive and ideology-intensive enterprise, may prove to be a surprising contributor.

Its relation to the mobilization of community and political resources aside, one of the most significant changes to occur in the development of leprosy in colonial Nigeria was that leprosy became curable. Itu was set up and became successful on the basis of a perceived cure for mild forms of the disease known as chaulmoogra oil, derived in India from a local remedy for skin conditions. However, many of the cures attributed to chaulmoogra seem to

---

21. T. Falola, *Development Planning and Decolonization in Nigeria* (Gainesville, Fla., 1996), p. 108.

have owed more to improved conditions of nutrition at the colony, which could lead to natural attrition of the disease.²² By the 1940s, a new group of drugs known as sulphones were becoming available for the treatment of tuberculosis in experimental conditions, and when tried in leprosy, had remarkable anti-mycobacterial activity. With the rapid spread of institutional leprosy control from 1936, and the development of the government Nigeria Leprosy Service from 1945, Nigerian leprologists were able to mobilize an apparatus for clinical research in leprosy.

Missionaries as Experts

I

The most significant development in post-1945 leprosy control was that leprosy was recognized as curable, using a family of sulphone drugs of which the most notable was dapsone. At the Leprosy Research Unit in Uzuakoli, a formerly Methodist-run leprosy settlement under control of the government Nigeria Leprosy Service, Nigeria-based researchers were able to standardize the dosage of dapsone, the cheapest of the sulphone drugs, whose toxic side effects needed management if cost-effective leprosy control were to be a success. They also continued to investigate other compounds developed in European labs, resulting in a striking success with clofazimine, a powerful anti-inflammatory with enhanced activity in the treatment of leprosy, in the early 1960s. Alongside the research apparatus, the epidemiological capacity of the Nigeria Leprosy Service was enhanced by the growing influence of WHO and UNICEF. The large-scale UNICEF Yaws surveys from 1953, carried out alongside government and missionary leprosy services, were crucial in identifying areas and cases that had not been subject to leprosy control measures in the previous two decades.

Paradoxically, one of the impacts of developments in the treatment of leprosy was that the rationale for large-scale segregation-based leprosy control diminished. In the case of Itu, the 1950s saw a progressive undermining of the agricultural and industrial bases of the settlement's survival. Able-bodied and mildly disabled patients were discharged after successful treatment with dapsone, and Itu was forced to integrate itself into growing mechanisms for outpatient treatment, leaving the settlement with a population of incapacitated long-term residents and a rolling population of new and often young

---

22. John Iliffe, *The African Poor: A History* (Cambridge, 1987), p. 225.

patients. The growing ambitions of a number of other schemes, notably the one in Ogoja where the prevalence of leprosy continued to rise into the early 1960s, were also undermined by the falling numbers in residence — a number of rehabilitation schemes based on weaving, shoemaking, and farming had to be scaled back considerably.

In the late 1940s, however, continued problems in supervising the administration of dapsone in the following years ran alongside an increasingly active search for alternative drugs. It was not until 1948 that the Nigeria Leprosy Service Research Unit at Uzuakoli came into operation, and much later in the 1950s before it came into its own. Research continued to be decentralized and disarticulated through to the mid-1950s, with each provincial service, the wholly missionary as well as those run in cooperation with government, participating in the refinement of clinical knowledge and research practice. This can be shown with reference to one group of compounds with evident potential for the treatment of leprosy, developed at the laboratories of Vincent Barry of the Medical Research Council of Ireland (MRCI) through the 1940s and 1950s, leading to the synthesis of clofazimine.[23] This compound, trialed in Nigeria in the early 1960s, is still an effective component of the multidrug regimen used to treat leprosy today.

The first of this group of compounds to be trialed in leprosy, known as B.283, was introduced in 1949 by Drs. Joe Barnes and Elizabeth Allday at the Roman Catholic Mission Ogoja Leprosy Scheme, which Barnes had set up in 1945. Barnes and Allday were concerned about the use of new chemotherapeutic agents in Nigerian leprosy settlements. Barnes, especially, was unconvinced by the use of dapsone in treating leprosy, as he objected to what he saw as its excess toxicity in the doses administered in the late 1940s. They compared the toxicity of sulphetrone, dapsone, and thiosemicarbazone — the most significant drugs in terms of worldwide research in leprosy chemotherapy at the time — and the results produced at Ogoja contributed to attempts to refine and standardize the administration of these drugs.

For B.283, however, the experimental work carried out in Ogoja was both novel and somewhat exotic. The initial trial begun in January 1951 was with ten patients diagnosed with lepromatous leprosy.[24] No reports were yet avail-

---

23. I routinely use the standard name clofazimine to refer to the drug synthesized by the MRCI as B.663 (Dublin), produced by Geigy as G 30 320 (Basle), and marketed as Lamprene. In the main set of clinical trials to which I refer, the compound was known as B.663, and I will adopt this usage in reference to these trials and to its original synthesis in Dublin.

24. E. J. Allday and J. Barnes, "Treatment of Leprosy with B.283," *Irish Journal of Medical Science*, 6th ser., no. 322 (1952): 422.

able on the success of the drug in treatment of tuberculosis in Ireland, where the compound had been developed, although concurrent human trials were in progress. Alongside the trial in lepromatous leprosy, a report on which was published in the *Irish Journal of Medical Science,* ten patients with tuberculoid leprosy were also treated with B.283 under the supervision of Dr. Denis Freeman, Barnes's replacement at Ogoja from mid-1951.[25]

The trial was subject to diagnostic difficulties reflecting the uncertain state of knowledge on leprosy in Nigeria at the time, and a series of technical issues obviated the validity of some of the trial's eventual conclusions. The nearest pathology laboratory was in Lagos, and at the time of the jointly conducted trial on B.283 Barnes and Freeman relied on black-and-white photography to document their diagnoses. Neither doctor was confident in his documentary abilities with a camera, and the results, some of which have entered the published record, satisfied none of the investigators.

Unusually, the patient notes and published report on the trial were not anonymized; Barnes inquired about the physical and material progress of a number of patients in his correspondence with Freeman,[26] and his notes contain remarks such as "Wona's physique is, like his character, tough and lean" and "Dick presents a most striking picture in his red jersey, cast-off battle dress and navy shorts." Indeed, for Barnes the distinction between trial and treatment, key to the specifications outlined in Havana, was at best distracting, and possibly spurious, as evidenced by his report that "we have been unable to employ an untreated control group as our patients would not remain isolated without the inducement of treatment."[27] The trial was seen as a limited success; the emergence of cheaper and better alternatives to B.283 and its analogues meant that the trial seemed destined to remain a curious footnote in the history of leprosy control.

II

The synthesis, evaluation, and production of B.663 (G 30 320, clofazimine) were the result of a growing collaboration between the Dublin laboratory that had synthesized B.283 and the Swiss drug company Geigy. The com-

---

25. Medical Missionaries of Mary Ogoja Convent Files (hereafter MMM Ogoja), Ogoja, Nigeria. Letter dated 29 September 1951 from J. Barnes (Dublin) to D. Freeman (Ogoja) mentions the two sets of cases.

26. MMM Ogoja. Letters from Barnes to Freeman, dated "last Sunday in Sept." (1951) and 2 April 1952.

27. Allday and Barnes, "B.283," p. 422.

pound, first of a family named rimino-compounds, or rimino-phenazines, was originally synthesized in Dublin in 1954[28] by means of a fortuitous catalytic reduction of a glyoxalino-phenazine.[29] While less active in vitro than the family of compounds from which B.283 had emerged, it proved prodigiously active in vivo. The exceptional difficulties of synthesizing many of the compounds developed by Barry's team on site in Dublin, B.663 among them, lent great importance to the collaboration with Geigy, who could provide facilities for production, toxicology, and coordination of animal and human trials on a scale to which the MRCI could never aspire.

From Geigy's perspective, preliminary investigations on clofazimine in human tuberculosis had not been encouraging. Further assessment was almost abandoned,[30] but interim results in murine leprosy[31] trials conducted by Y. T. Chang, a previous collaborator of Barry's at the National Institutes of Health, USA,[32] evidently persuaded Geigy to reconsider, and at a 1960 London meeting between Barry, Wolfgang Vischer of Geigy, and R. G. Cochrane, by that time director of the Leprosy Research Unit in London, it was suggested that Stanley Browne trial B.663 in leprosy at Uzuakoli, Nigeria.[33]

Having been appointed director of the Leprosy Research Unit at Uzuakoli in 1959, Browne returned there to begin the trial in September 1960[34] in collaboration with Lykle Hogerzeil. By the time of his arrival in Nigeria, Browne had earned a notable reputation as a leprologist as a result of work carried out in the Belgian Congo, where he had begun as a missionary and a surgeon in 1936.[35] His structured way of working, and of organizing, reporting, and publicizing his investigations,[36] underlined the contrast between his trials in

28. S. J. Yawalkar, *Leprosy for Medical Practitioners and Paramedical Workers*, 7th ed. (Basle, 2002), p. 121.

29. V. C. Barry, "Boyle Medal Lecture: Synthetic Phenazine Derivatives and Mycobacterial Disease; A Twenty Year Investigation," *Scientific Proceedings of the Royal Dublin Society*, ser. A, 3, no. 16 (1969): 157-58. Barry notes here that it was later discovered that the rimino-compounds could be derived from the anilinoaposafranines, of which B.283 was one.

30. Yawalkar, *Leprosy*, p. 121.

31. References to murine leprosy in the medical literature acknowledge the development by the 1960s of an experimental model for assaying toxicity in chemotherapeutic agents for leprosy on the mouse footpad successfully inoculated with *Mycobacterium leprae*.

32. Barry, "Boyle Medal Lecture," p. 159.

33. Yawalkar, *Leprosy*, p. 121.

34. Wellcome Library Archives, London. WTI/SGB/C.1/4/1 — B.663 in leprosy. This date is given in a handwritten note dated August 1960.

35. N. R. Hunt, *A Colonial Lexicon of Birth Ritual, Medicalization, and Mobility in the Congo* (Durham, N.C., 1999), pp. 209, 228.

36. Wellcome Library Archives. WTI/SGB/C.1/4/1 — B.663 in leprosy. Browne's notes

Mission, Clinic, and Laboratory

B.663 and the earlier trials of B.283 carried out in Ogoja. Already at the time of Barnes's trials, the unit at Uzuakoli was at the forefront of systematic evaluation of chemotherapy in leprosy, with the scale and facilities to carry out complex series of investigations such as those needed to standardize the dosage of dapsone in the treatment of leprosy, research carried out at Uzuakoli in the early 1950s. By the time of Nigerian independence in October 1960, it had a worldwide reputation for the quality of its research. Together with the leprosy training facility at Oji River, Uzuakoli had spearheaded the standardization of leprosy control structures in Nigeria, focusing increasingly on outpatient treatment of leprosy. The theoretical distinction between treatment and research, unworkable for Barnes, seemed acceptable, if not routine, to Browne.

However, the pilot trial of B.663 was very small in scale, three patients receiving B.663 in combination with dapsone, and three receiving B.663 alone.[37] All had lepromatous leprosy, of comparable severity. There seem to have been four other patients receiving B.663, in an exercise not recorded in the published results of the trial.[38] Further, Browne sought to observe the effects of clofazimine in selected patients as consultant at other leprosy schemes in eastern Nigeria, a process that does not seem to have been closely documented.[39] The trial determined that B.663 improved the clinical state of the patient with lepromatous leprosy, leading to a fall in the bacterial index, an effect that was enhanced in combination with dapsone. A supplementary report noted a form of drug resistance, and discounted B.663 as a serious rival to dapsone, due to its high cost.[40] The definitive terms in which this trial was reported contrasts with the potentially tendentious nature of the data and the manner in which it was elicited. However, the presentation of striking effects by noted researchers based at a high-profile institution, together with further studies, by Browne, and by F. Imkamp at Liteta Leprosarium, Zambia, which

---

for F. Imkamp's trial of B. 663 in corticosteroid-dependent patients give some idea of the rigor of his observations regarding patient history, type and degree of side effects observed, degree of neuritis and lepra reaction observed, psychological effects of treatment, method of drug administration, and toxic effects observed.

37. Wellcome Library Archives. WTI/SGB/C.1/4/1 — B.663 in leprosy. Note headed "B 663 — Uzuakoli patients," detailing the timing and labeling of biopsies taken from the patients in the trial subject group.

38. S. G. Browne and L. M. Hogerzeil, "B.663 in the Treatment of Leprosy," *Leprosy Review* 33 (1962): 6-10.

39. Conversation with Dr. Esther Davis, formerly of Ekpene Obom Leprosy Scheme, 23 June 2006.

40. S. G. Browne and L. M. Hogerzeil, "B.663 in the Treatment of Leprosy — Supplementary Report," *Leprosy Review* 33 (1962): 182-84.

demonstrated anti-inflammatory properties of B.663, and lessened the dependence of an important cohort of leprosy patients on corticosteroids, proved a crucial boost to the reputation of the drug, which was introduced under the trademark Lamprene in 1969.

III

Stanley Browne derived significant acclamation from his role as director of the Leprosy Research Unit, first at Uzuakoli, and later in London, and from his early success with B.663. This acclamation enabled him to act as arbiter with respect to later trials of the compound, and signaled a sea change in the relation of the research institute to the treatment of leprosy. Much of this change was due to the existence of successful chemotherapeutic agents, starting with dapsone in the late 1940s, but developments in the conduct, reporting, and reception of clinical trials in the postwar decades are clearly discernible in the contrast between the trials of B.283 in Ogoja and B.663 in Uzuakoli.

Whatever the validity of Barnes's methods and diagnoses, their publication in the *Irish Journal of Medical Science* gave them currency, and gave the relation of Vincent Barry's Dublin-based work on tuberculosis chemotherapy to leprosy a continuing identity, which emerged as vital in the development of clofazimine, from Barry's work, and in the Nigerian research center at Uzuakoli, in the 1960s. More to the point, at a time when the balance in medical research was shifting ever more decisively from the clinical to the laboratory-based, and the clinical trial took its place, as an ancillary of healing, among the range of technical operations performed in expanding colonial health-care institutions, the trial of B.283 at Ogoja provided an especially eloquent index of the plans, aspirations, and capacities of even the most remote of medical enterprises. Indeed, the less than ideal physical and geographical circumstances of most leprosy research, the impossibility of cultivating leprosy outside a living human host, and the persistent privileging of local clinical knowledge — at times promoted in the most willful terms — all help us understand the experimental clinical setting of Ogoja as characteristic rather than anomalous.

The technical capacity to sustain a successful clinical trial and to firmly ground the results of a clinical research intervention did not exist in Ogoja in the early 1950s: Barnes's counterarguments to objections to the conduct of the trial of B.283 in lepromatous leprosy, based in notions of personal practice and individual clinical expertise, expose a moment of transition in clinical research in leprosy. Over the next decade, leprosy work in Nigeria contributed to an enriching of the classificatory and diagnostic contexts elaborated in Havana, enabling a more robust circulation between the local instance and the global phenomenon of leprosy and its control, and providing a more systematic grounding for the appreciation of research results in clinical leprosy trials. Much of this work was carried out by missionaries or former missionaries such as T. F. Davey, and Stanley Browne, incorporating the limited and site-specific scientific investigations of a generation of Christian missionary doctors in Nigeria while enhancing the prestige of scientific research as an enterprise of government in Nigeria.

Conclusion

Late colonial Nigeria saw missionaries become increasingly entangled in the bureaucratic aims of the developmental state. If viewed in terms of continuities with pre-1939 patterns of missionary work, the evangelical character of mission seems to have become diluted amid the instrumental nature of mission-government relations. Measured in terms of contribution to statecraft, the forms of knowledge generated and the status of science practiced by missionaries certainly increased in utility as missionary welfare provision approximated to the policy needs of the developmental state, both before and after African independence. However, the ambiguous relation of leprosy control to evangelism needs to be kept in mind. "Leprosy" served the relations between missionary and donor community far more than it informed evangelical strategies in Africa, while "leprosy control" gave missionaries key leverage in activities of state, alongside an important status in the practice of science in the developing world. I have examined leprosy and its control here primarily as a "creative endeavor": commentary on leprosy as a repository of critical perspectives on state, society, and community elucidates more of the missionary content of leprosy control, while critical perspectives on leprosy control itself offer insights into African and nationalist commentary on relations between the missionary and the colonial state. It remains the case, though, that the significance of instrumental forms of knowledge, both bureaucratic and scientific, cannot be underestimated in assessing the contribution of Christian missionaries to the discourse and practice of development in late colonial and postcolonial Africa, as clearly illuminated by the heyday of leprosy control in eastern Nigeria from 1945 to 1967.

Select Bibliography

Allday, E. J., and J. Barnes. "Treatment of Leprosy with B.283." *Irish Journal of Medical Science*, 6th ser., no. 322 (1952).

Anderson, W. *Colonial Pathologies: American Tropical Medicine, Race, and Hygiene in the Philippines.* Durham, N.C., 2006.

Barry, V. "Boyle Medal Lecture: Synthetic Phenazine Derivatives and Mycobacterial Disease; A Twenty Year Investigation." *Scientific Proceedings of the Royal Dublin Society*, ser. A, 3, no. 16 (1969).

Browne, S. G., and L. M. Hogerzeil. "B.663 in the Treatment of Leprosy." *Leprosy Review* 33 (1962).

Buchanan, A. *Visitation: The Film Story of the Medical Missionaries of Mary.* Drogheda, Ireland, 1948.

Chukwu, J. N., and U. M. Ekekezie. *The Leprosy Centre Uzuakoli (1932-1992).* Owerri, 1992.

Davey, T. F. "Editorial: Common Features in Rapidly Declining Leprosy Epidemics." *Leprosy Review* 46, no. 1 (1975).

Falola, T. *Development Planning and Decolonization in Nigeria.* Gainesville, Fla., 1996.

Hogan, E. M. *The Irish Missionary Movement: A Historical Survey, 1830-1980.* Dublin, 1990.

Hunt, N. R. *A Colonial Lexicon of Birth Ritual, Medicalization, and Mobility in the Congo.* Durham, N.C., 1999.

MacDonald, A. *No More "Afar Off."* London, [1964?].

Manton, J. "Administering Leprosy Control in Ogoja Province, Nigeria, 1945-67: A Case Study in Government-Mission Relations." In *Healing Bodies, Saving Souls: Medical Missions in Asia and Africa,* edited by D. Hardiman. Amsterdam, 2006.

Medical Missionaries of Mary. *The First Decade: Ten Years' Work of the Medical Missionaries of Mary, 1937-1947.* Dublin, 1948.

Muir, E. "Leprosy in Nigeria: A Report on Anti-leprosy Work in Nigeria with Suggestions for Its Development." *Leprosy Review* 7, no. 4 (1936).

Pratten, D., *The Man-Leopard Murders: History and Society in Colonial Nigeria.* Edinburgh, 2007.

Index

Abolition, 46, 48, 49
Abrecht, Paul R., 305
Aequatoria Center, 221, 243; philosophy of, 225-26, 227-28, 229-34
African Christian independency, 26-27, 164, 293-96, 301, 307, 308, 310
African Methodist Episcopal Church (AMEC), 164, 294, 300, 307, 308
Afzelius, Adam, 45, 51
Akan, 79, 80, 97
Akuapem: language choice in, 79-82; region of, 73, 74, 77, 86, 91, 93, 94, 95, 96
Akyem: language group, 79-80, 95; region of, 73, 87, 96
Allen, Roland, 159, 168, 169-70
Ancestors, 216, 217, 237, 239, 240, 257; and fetishism, 114, 117; and totemism, 121, 122, 123, 125, 126, 128, 129; worship of, 186, 207, 238, 251, 263, 264
Angola, 35, 36, 56, 259
Animism, 14, 128, 130
Anthropology: Africanist, 103-4, 131-32; Anglo-Saxon, 101-2, 106, 131, 151, 176, 187-88, 274, 278-81, 285, 290-91; Belgian, 160-63, 221-44; Catholic, 14-15, 64-65, 110, 125, 233-34; development of field of, 63-64, 66, 68-70, 135-36, 185; French, 108-10; missionaries' relations with professional anthropologists, 103-5, 119, 129, 135, 146, 153, 157, 176-77, 183, 188, 197-206, 212, 215-16, 219, 222, 243, 276, 280-81, 284-85, 287-88, 289; missionary contribution to, 64-67; and totemism, 101, 103, 120-24, 128-29, 130; women in, 202-3, 206-8, 210, 211, 213, 218-19
Anticolonialism, 10, 229, 243, 270, 277, 279; and indigeneity, 232-34
Asante, David, 25, 87, 90, 91-93, 95-97

B.283, 328-29, 330, 331, 332
Balfour, John Hutton, 54, 59-60
Bantu language, 223, 226, 228, 236
Barnes, Joseph, 328-29, 331, 332
Barry, Vincent, 328, 330, 332
Basden, George Thomas, 7, 9, 11, 16-17, 19, 22, 24, 67; *Among the Ibos of Nigeria*, 136-37, 140-42, 143, 145; career and ethnographic work of, 137-47; themes in writing of, 147-53
Basel Mission, 62, 72, 73, 94; missionaries of, 17, 25, 52, 83, 86, 89, 91, 97; and missionary language acquisition, 74, 75-81, 82, 91, 98
Belgian Congo. *See* Congo
Berlin Missionary Society, 10, 296, 297, 298, 300

335

Bezoars, 34, 36, 39, 40
Boelaert, Edmund, 10, 18, 25, 162, 221, 223, 224-25, 229; goals of research, 222, 241-42, 243-44; ideological influences of, 229-34; and linguistics, 234-38
Botany, 4, 43, 48-49, 55, 161; missionary practice of, 31, 33, 45, 47, 54, 56, 57, 67, 162, 168, 207, 208; missionary use of botanical knowledge, 59-62; professionalization of, 32, 63-64, 67-68, 69
British South Africa Company (BSAC), 251, 253, 254
Browne, Stanley, 330-32, 333
Bryant, Alfred, 59, 65, 67
Burton, William Frederick Padwick, 9, 11, 16, 17, 18, 24; academic work of, 170, 171-73, 174, 176-77; attitudes toward Luba, 157, 169, 170, 175-76, 181-82, 183-85; biographic sketch of, 158-59; ethnographic research of, 156, 169-71, 173-77, 179-81, 185

Cape of Good Hope, 40-42, 44-45, 47, 54, 56, 67, 274
Capuchins, 36-38, 108
Carnegie Corporation, 283, 285, 286, 288, 289, 291
Catholic Church: and medical missions, 14, 320, 321, 328; missionaries and knowledge production, 8, 9-10, 31, 35-40, 55-59, 160-61, 162, 163-64; relations with Protestants, 166-68. *See also* Capuchins; Holy Ghost Fathers (Spiritans); Jesuits; Missionaries of the Sacred Heart; White Fathers
Cavazzi, Antonio, 36-37, 50
Christaller, Johannes Gottlieb, 25, 72, 73, 74, 79, 80, 85, 98; and language work, 86-97
Christian Missions in Many Lands (CMML), 248, 253, 256, 257, 258, 259, 265; and cultural accommodation, 249, 259-64, 266; history of, 250-51
Church Missionary Society (CMS), 48-49, 141, 282; missionaries of, 51, 67, 142, 143, 144, 145, 146, 150, 304; in Nigeria, 137-38, 139, 319
Church of Central Africa Rhodesia (CCAR), 299, 300-301, 302-3
Clan, 103, 120, 130, 240-41, 325; and totem, 121, 122, 123-24, 125-26, 127, 128, 129, 131
Clofazimine (B.663), 327, 329-32
Colenso, John, 6, 55
Colonial Development and Welfare Act (1940), 315, 320, 326
Colonial/missionary medicine, 313-14; African acceptance of, 248-49, 252-53, 257-58; effectiveness of, 253-56, 265; as evangelization tool, 257, 258, 261, 320-21, 333; and traditional medicine, 35, 118, 245, 246-49, 250-51, 252, 257, 258-59, 262, 264, 265-66
Colonial science, 160-63, 167-71, 179, 180, 319
Congo, 33; Belgian, 155, 156, 157, 160-71, 181, 184, 185, 221-44, 253, 255, 257, 330; and fetishes, 113-15, 119; missionaries in, 11, 37, 56, 162-67, 171, 185, 225, 226, 228-29, 243-44, 259; natural history of, 36-38, 57
Congo Evangelistic Mission (CEM), 155, 165-67, 172, 174, 176, 178; and colonial science, 167-71, 179
Conversion, 6, 158, 159, 172, 175, 180, 211; and linguistics, 78, 81, 98; missionary methods of, 17, 145, 149, 260; and witchcraft, 170-71
Coquilhatville. *See* Mbandaka
Crawford, Daniel, 159, 180, 259-61; *Thinking Black*, 17, 170, 259, 262, 263
Customary law, 16, 24, 200, 223, 226-27, 234, 241, 242

Davis, John Merle, 18, 23, 268, 271, 282-89, 294
Degeneration theory, 19-20, 112, 116-17, 120
Democratic Republic of the Congo. *See* Congo

Index

Denationalization, 141-42, 147, 150-51, 165
Duparquet, Charles, 56, 65, 66
Durkheim, Emile, 5, 14, 15, 103, 120, 121, 122-23, 124, 125, 130
Dutch East India Company (VOC), 40-42, 44

Earthy, E. Dora, 9, 18, 19; academic work of, 198-205; anthropological research of, 196-98, 203-6; mission setting of, 190-96; theology and anthropology, 212-17; *Valenge Women*, 187, 206-10, 211
Ecumenism, ecumenical movement, 179, 293, 298, 304, 305, 306, 311; and development of anthropology, 7, 12, 269-72, 280-81, 284, 290-91
Education, 12, 159; African, 11, 207, 209, 225, 233, 274, 299, 301, 308, 314, 315, 321; schooling, in Belgian Congo, 168, 184; schooling, in Gold Coast, 77, 80, 92, 98; schooling, in Mozambique, 194
Empire, 4, 8, 35, 41, 44, 56, 69, 246-48, 252, 261, 264-65; British, 6, 17, 47, 211, 212, 313, 314
Entomology, 43, 161; missionary practice of, 11, 31, 45, 54, 57, 67, 230; professionalization of, 32, 67-70
Ethnicity, 161, 164, 325, 326; Igbo, 24, 151; Luba, 24, 182; Mongo, 10, 231, 234, 238-41, 242
Ethnography, 103, 104, 229, 280, 284; in Belgian Congo, 161-63; missionary contribution to, 100, 101, 118-19, 129, 130, 132, 135-36, 144-45, 153, 162-63, 173-81, 223, 228, 261; purpose of missionary, 156-57, 159, 169, 171, 179, 182, 185, 216-17
Ethnology, 63-64, 110, 131, 281, 287; missionary contributions to, 101, 107, 124-28, 130, 144-45, 198-99, 203-6, 223, 241
Evolution, evolutionary theory, 5, 13, 19, 56, 62-63, 102, 112, 120-24, 130

Fante language, 79-80, 93, 94, 95
Fetish, 101, 104, 112, 121, 131-32, 157, 170, 251, 264; history of concept, 110-11, 113-15; Nassau's definition of, 117
Fetishism, 101, 103, 104, 105, 120, 127-28, 130, 131; development of term, 111-13; Nassau's study of, 116-20, 150
First World War, 101, 120, 172, 211, 254, 258, 263, 270, 272, 279
Fisher, Singleton, 245, 261
Fisher, Walter, 251, 253, 254, 256, 257, 259, 261, 262-63
Flemish cultural nationalism, 222, 224, 229-32, 241, 243, 244
Frazer, James, 103, 120, 121-22, 123, 124, 126, 130
Functionalism, 5, 6, 20, 22, 26, 28, 174, 177; structural, 135, 136, 145, 269

Gabon, 322; Catholic missions in, 108-10; missionary science in, 53, 57, 61, 100-132
Geigy, 329-30
Gender relations, 193, 211, 212, 218, 272-73, 274-75, 290
Geographical societies, 16, 65; British (Royal), 12, 49, 50, 172, 174; Paris, 56, 57
Ghana, 281, 285, 314; and missionary linguistics, 72-99; missionary scientists in, 42, 48, 52-53, 62
Gibson, Elizabeth, 273, 276, 281, 283
Gold Coast. *See* Ghana

Haddon, Alfred Cort, 187-88, 189, 191, 199
Hailey, Lord William Malcolm, 268, 276, 279, 285, 286-87, 289
Hamitic Hypothesis, 140, 144-45, 147-49, 178
Heurnius, Justus, 40-41
High Leigh, 7, 22, 26
History of science, 30-31, 69-70, 315
Hoernlé, Winifred, 211, 212, 218; and Dora Earthy, 187, 198, 202-3; and W. F. P. Burton, 170-71, 176-77, 180
Holy Ghost Fathers (Spiritans), 56-58, 60-61, 64, 167; in Gabon, 100, 108-9
Hooker, William, 47, 48, 50-51, 55

337

Hookworm, 256
Hulstaert, Gustaf, 162, 221, 223, 225, 226, 227; goals of research, 222, 238-41, 242, 243-44; ideological influences on, 229-34, 242-43; and linguistics, 234-38
Hunter, Monica. *See* Wilson, Monica Hunter

Idolatry, 111, 114, 116, 120-21, 183, 214
Igbo, 24, 138, 144, 319; culture and society, 136, 139-41, 143, 145, 149, 153, 323-24; and Hamitic Hypothesis, 140, 147-50; impact of colonialism and Christianity on, 137, 139, 141-42, 145-46, 150-53
Indigeneity, indigenist, 222, 226, 229, 230-32, 237; and anticolonialism, 232-34
Indigenous: knowledge, 31-32, 40, 59, 67, 69-70; medicine and missionary medicine, 249, 251, 257-58, 260-64; religion and Christianity, 64, 149-50, 170, 215-17, 295; society/custom, 62, 170, 227, 241, 268, 280
Indirect rule, 261, 279; in Belgian Congo, 161, 171; in Nigeria, 151-53, 313, 322, 325
International African Institute (IAI), 18-19, 146, 179, 206, 209, 219, 271, 297; African research support of, 267, 268, 278-81; and International Missionary Council, 280, 285-91
International Institute of African Languages and Cultures (IIALC), 183, 187, 296, 297
International Missionary Council (IMC), 179, 183, 215, 219, 297, 298; and African marriage, 268, 273-76, 281, 283, 290; African research support of, 271-72, 282, 293, 294-95, 301, 304, 305-6, 311; ecumenical origins of, 269-71; and International African Institute, 278-81, 285-90
Itu Leper Settlement, 317-18, 319, 320, 321, 324, 326, 327-28

Jesuits, 33, 40, 162, 226; as missionary naturalists, 38-39, 41, 45, 46, 58, 59

Junod, Henri-Alexandre, 62, 201, 208, 211; missionary anthropologist, 142, 153, 209; missionary naturalist, 54, 58-59, 63, 65, 67, 68

Kalene Hill Mission, 245, 248, 250, 251, 257, 258, 261, 265; medical practice at, 253, 254, 256, 259, 262, 263
Kenyatta, Jomo, 26, 145
Kew Gardens, 45, 48, 49, 50-51, 55, 68
Knowledge production, 25, 52, 67-69, 100, 101, 105-7, 129; in Belgian Congo, 160-61; missionary role in, 8, 26, 32-46, 55-59, 135-36, 137
Kongo. *See* Congo
Krapf, Johann, 51

Language: acquisition, 72, 73, 75, 77, 78, 80-83, 98, 138, 195-96; local/vernacular, 73-74, 85, 181-85; work/linguistics, 72, 77-78, 84-85, 86-88, 90-91, 98, 225, 229, 230, 234-38, 242, 261, 297
Lehmann, Dorothea A., 293, 294, 295, 306, 311; background of, 296-301; and *Christians in the Copperbelt*, 294, 295, 307-10; and Lumpa Church, 302-4, 309
Leprosy, 323; control in Nigeria, 314-21, 323-27, 331, 332, 333; Leprosy Research Unit, 327, 328, 332; Nigeria Leprosy Service, 321, 327; treatment of, 327-33
Le Roy, Alexandre, 15, 58, 61, 64, 65, 108-9
Le Zoute, 7, 22, 26, 215-16
Linnaeus, Carl, 44-45, 46, 230
Linschoten, Jan Huygen van, 33-34
Livingstone, David, 18, 63, 159, 260, 298; science and missions, 11-12, 16, 49-51, 52, 60
Lobo, Jerónimo, 38-39
Lobola, 194, 205, 207, 217, 284
Lomongo language, 221, 225, 227, 235-37, 239, 242
London Missionary Society (LMS), 298, 299, 301, 303; missionaries of, 47, 48, 300, 306, 307
Luba, 24, 159, 162, 168, 177, 257, 259; be-

liefs of, 169, 178, 181-82, 184; material culture of, 156, 170-71, 173, 175, 176; society and culture, 157, 169, 170, 172, 173, 174-75, 179-80
Lumpa Church, 294, 301-4, 307, 308, 309
Lunda, 250, 251, 253, 255, 257, 259; medicine of, 245, 258, 261-63, 265

Magic, 32, 39, 66; African/traditional, 169, 170, 174, 176-77, 182, 195, 207; and fetishes, 111, 113, 117, 119, 120, 128
Marriage, 191-92, 208, 217, 241; customs in Africa, 122, 194, 205, 285, 286; missionary research about, 268, 272-76, 278, 281-85, 289-90, 300
Mbandaka, 221, 222, 224, 226, 228-29, 244
Medicine. *See* Colonial/missionary medicine
Meek, C. K., 146, 151
Mermaid, 35, 36, 37, 40
Missionaries: amateurs, 32, 44, 67, 68-70, 119, 188; as ethnographers, 100, 101, 106, 135-53, 170-71, 173-81, 280; fieldworkers, 31, 52-59, 105-8, 142, 171-73, 203-4, 295-96, 305, 307-8, 310; informants, 33, 34-42, 44-46, 47-52; professionals, 153, 178-79, 183, 185, 209, 284-85, 296-97; relations with colonial governments, 136, 138, 144, 150-53, 160, 163-68, 179-80, 185, 231-34, 299-300, 314, 315, 316, 319-20, 325, 333
Missionaries of the Sacred Heart (MSC), 162, 222, 225, 228-29, 243
Missionary societies. *See* Basel Mission; Berlin Missionary Society; Catholic Church; Christian Missions in Many Lands; Church Missionary Society; Congo Evangelical Mission; London Missionary Society; United Missions in the Copperbelt
Modernity, 37-38, 39, 104, 184, 242, 251, 261; effects on indigenous cultures, 139, 141-42, 145-46, 150-51, 174, 268, 271, 272-73; and science, 50-51, 64-65, 69-70
Mongo, 221, 225, 227, 228-29, 230, 237,

242, 243; ethnic and linguistic unity of, 231-32, 236, 238-41; language and literature of, 223, 224
Monotheism, 116, 149-50, 238
Mozambique, 33, 40, 62; anthropological research in, 188, 195, 198, 203-6, 210, 211, 214; missionaries in, 190, 191, 192, 193, 194, 213; natural history of, 34-35, 38-39, 54, 58-59
Mulenga, Alice Lenshina, 294, 295, 301-4, 305, 309
Museums: Basel, 52-53; British, 42, 49, 53; Central African Museum, Tervuren (MRAC), 18, 156, 161, 171-74, 175, 176, 177, 223, 227, 238; and knowledge formation, 16, 18, 43, 49, 64-65, 66, 157, 199; Neuchâtel, 54; Paris, 53, 56, 57, 58, 60
Mwinilunga, 245, 248, 249, 265; and CMML medical missionaries, 250-51, 253-58, 261-64

Nassau, Robert Hamill, 100, 101-3, 112, 113, 129; *Fetichism in West Africa*, 112, 116, 119, 127, 149-50; and fetishism, 116-20; sources and methods, 105-8, 116
Natural theology, 43-44, 62-63, 229-30
Newbigin, Lesslie, 311-12
Nigeria, 54; *Among the Ibos of Nigeria*, 140-43, 145; leprosy work in, 313-34; mission work in, 136, 137-38, 139, 144
Northern Rhodesia, 165, 293, 298, 301, 307, 310, 311; selected as research site, 294, 303-4, 305-6

Ogoja, 320, 328-29, 332
Oji River, 319, 321, 331
Oldham, Joseph H., 146, 157, 185, 276, 296, 297; director of IAI, 278-79, 280, 281; ecumenical role of, 19, 183, 215, 271

Paludanus, Bernardus, 34
Pentecostal, Pentecostalism, 155, 156-57, 158-59, 165-66, 167, 306
Pharmacopoeia, 59-60, 66

339

Plymouth Brethren, 158, 159, 165, 248. *See also* Christian Missions in Many Lands (CMML)
Polygamy, 118, 272, 273, 274, 283, 285; in African tradition, 141, 241, 284; and the church, 276-78, 281-82, 290

Racism, racial discrimination: in Belgian Congo, 148, 173, 206, 232; in Northern Rhodesia, 299, 300, 303, 306, 309-10, 311
Radcliffe-Brown, Alfred, 103, 135, 187, 238, 287, 288; and South African anthropology, 68-69, 198-99, 200, 201
Read, Margaret, 273, 274, 275, 278, 279
Religious studies, 157, 176, 182-83
Riis, Andreas, 52, 75, 76, 77, 78
Riis, Hans Nicolai, 17, 72-73, 78, 98; and linguistic work on Twi, 83-86, 87
Rockefeller Foundation, 278, 279-80
Royal Navy, 47-48, 49

Santos, João dos, 34-35
Saunders, Agnes, 193-95, 198, 214, 217
Savage, Thomas, 53
Schapera, Isaac, 18, 176-77, 179, 211, 212, 268, 279
Scripture, 147-49, 178, 250, 309; and nature/science, 39, 43, 102; translation of, 78, 80, 83, 86-87, 92-93, 94
Secret societies, 116, 120, 126, 127, 169, 176, 179-80
Segregation, 306-7; of leprosy patients, 316-18, 321, 323-25, 327
Sex, sexuality, 112, 114, 121, 123, 126, 284-85
Sexual morality, 217, 272, 274, 275, 276, 278, 286
Slaves, 34, 60, 61, 76, 149, 172, 257
Slave trade, 33, 42, 46, 48, 49, 50, 51, 52, 160, 177, 180, 228
Smith, Andrew, 48, 50
Smith, Edwin, 28, 67, 153, 183, 278, 296; anthropological work of, 157, 177-78, 185, 209, 284-85; and IMC, 18-19
Social Gospel, 23, 270-71, 290
Society for the Propagation of the Gospel (SPG), 190, 193, 212-13; missionaries of, 187, 189, 194-95
Sorcery, 127; and fetishism, 113, 114-15, 118
Spanish influenza, 172, 255-56
Sundkler, Bengt G. M., 22, 27-28, 271, 295, 305, 308, 312
Survey of African Marriage and Family Life, 267, 290, 291; missionary origins of, 269-76
Syncretism, 27-28, 167, 170, 185, 295, 311

Tambaram, 268, 272; and marriage in Africa, 276-78, 281-82, 283, 284-85, 286, 290
Taylor, John V., 28, 293, 294, 311, 312; background of, 304-7; and *Christians in the Copperbelt*, 294, 295, 307-10
Theology, 184; African, 117, 157, 183; missionary, 104-5, 119-20, 159, 195, 196, 201-2, 212-17, 218, 219, 270, 310, 311
Totem, totemism: and anthropology, 101, 105, 110, 120-24, 126, 130, 131, 132; and the Fang, 103, 124-29
Tribes, 24, 69, 127, 215; description of tribal life, 65-66, 162; and social change, 19-20, 23, 176-77, 207
Trilles, Henri, 57, 65, 100, 101, 103, 105, 113, 116, 124; missionary career of, 108-10; work on Fang totemism, 124-29, 130-31
Tropical ulcers, 248, 254-55, 258
Twi, 73, 74, 91; and Bible translation, 92, 93; dictionaries/grammars, 78, 84-85, 88, 90, 97; language work in, 72, 75, 77, 81-83, 86-88; spread of, 96-97; variations of, 79-80, 87, 94, 95

Uburu, 318, 319, 320, 325
Uganda, 61, 282, 304, 305, 306, 311
Unicorn, 34, 38, 39, 43, 50
United Church of Central Africa Rhodesia (UCCAR), 303, 310
United Missions in the Copperbelt (UMCB), 294, 298-301, 303
University of Witwatersrand, 18, 59, 156; and Dora Earthy, 198, 203, 204, 219;

Index

and William Burton, 170-71, 174, 176, 177, 181, 183
Uzuakoli, 319, 321, 323; and Leprosy Research Unit, 327, 328, 330-31, 332

Watchtower Bible and Tract Society, 164, 300, 301, 307, 308
Welch, James, 146, 275
Wesleyan Missionary Society, 80, 93, 94
Westermann, Diedrich, 157, 183, 185, 238; and Dorothea Lehmann, 296-97; and William Burton, 170, 176, 179
White Fathers, 58, 162, 164
Widmann, Georg, 53, 62, 77, 78, 81-82

Wilson, Monica Hunter, 206-7, 211, 273-74, 275, 276, 278, 279
Witchcraft, 55, 180, 186, 251, 257, 277, 283, 309; eradication of, 170, 263-64, 302; and fetishes, 110-11, 113, 114, 116, 118-19, 120
Women's War, 138, 143, 151, 313, 322
World Council of Churches (WCC), 293, 304, 305-6, 311
World Missionary Conference at Madras. *See* Tambaram
Wrong, Margaret, 273, 274

Zulu, 59, 67

www.ingramcontent.com/pod-product-compliance
Lightning Source LLC
Chambersburg PA
CBHW030105010526
44116CB00005B/106